KEY AND MANUAL TO THE NORMAL UNION ARITHMETIC

KEY AND MANUAL TO THE NORMAL UNION ARITHMETIC

AND ALSO METHODS OF TEACHING ARITHMETIC

EDWARD BROOKS

GYAN

Published by

Gyan Publishing House
5, Ansari Road
Daryaganj, New Delhi-110002
Phone: 011-47034999, 9811692060
E-mail: books@gyanbooks.com

Distribution Network
gyanbooks.com
India, USA, Canada, UK, Australia

ISBN: 978-93-7447-649-9 (PB)

First Published, 1878

2nd Impression 2026

Printed at: Gyan Press, Delhi.

KEY AND MANUAL TO THE NORMAL UNION ARITHMETIC

Author: EDWARD BROOKS

KEY AND MANUAL

TO THE

NORMAL UNION ARITHMETIC

AND ALSO

METHODS OF TEACHING ARITHMETIC.

BY

EDWARD BROOKS, A. M., PH. D.,

SUPERINTENDENT OF PUBLIC SCHOOLS OF PHILADELPHIA,
PRINCIPAL AND PROFESSOR OF MATHEMATICS IN PENNSYLVANIA STATE NORMAL SCHOOL, AND AUTHOR OF "THE NORMAL SERIES OF ARITHMETICS," "NORMAL ELEMENTARY ALGEBRA," "NORMAL GEOMETRY AND TRIGONOMETRY," "PHILOSOPHY OF ARITHMETIC," ETC.

"Analysis and Synthesis;—the magic wand whose touch unfolds the mysterious and beautiful relation of numbers."

PHILADELPHIA:
CHRISTOPHER SOWER COMPANY,
614 ARCH STREET.

PREFACE.

THIS work consists of four parts:—*First,*—a short treatise upon the Didactics of Arithmetic, consisting of remarks upon the characteristics of a good work on Arithmetic and the Methods of teaching the same.

Second,—a Key to the *Normal Union Arithmetic,* in which the principles and methods therein presented are more fully developed by remarks, suggestions, and the solution of many of the problems.

Third,—a complete set of answers to all the problems.

Fourth,—a Manual containing additional problems under the heads of *Arithmetical Analysis* and *Miscellaneous Problems;* and also other subjects not treated in the Arithmetic.

The object of the first part is to give young teachers some general suggestions in regard to teaching Mental and Written Arithmetic with special reference to aiding those who are using the Normal Union Arithmetic. The suggestions, though brief, will, it is believed, be found interesting and instructive.

The object of the Key is two-fold:—*First,* to aid those who are pursuing the study of Arithmetic without an instructor. To such the Key stands in the place of the teacher. When a subject is too difficult they can resort to the Key as the pupil does to the instructor. I advise such, however, to depend upon the Key as little as possible, since whatever one overcomes himself is a triumph that gives strength for new difficulties. *Mental strength is the result of mental labor.*

Second, to assist young and inexperienced teachers. There are many young teachers in the common schools who often feel the need of some such work of reference. Even when they can solve the problem, they like to compare their solution with some other, to see whether they are teaching their pupils the best methods. To such also it is hoped this work will prove acceptable.

The object of giving a full set of answers to the problems is the convenience of such teachers as may prefer to use an edition of the Arithmetic without answers.

The object of the Manual is to supply additional problems on the subjects presented in the book, and also to give a knowledge of the elements of a few subjects sometimes required by common school pupils.

EDWARD BROOKS.

NORMAL SCHOOL, 1878.

PART I.

CHAPTER I.

NATURE OF A COURSE IN ARITHMETIC.

ARITHMETIC is the science of numbers, and the art of calculation. For the purpose of instruction it may be divided into two parts: MENTAL ARITHMETIC and WRITTEN ARITHMETIC. In *Mental Arithmetic* the problems are solved without the aid of written characters, the numbers and conditions being retained in the mind and the operation being *purely a mental one.* In *Written Arithmetic* the operations are performed partly by the aid of *written characters.*

It will be noticed that we use the *terms Mental* and *Written,* instead of the more frequently used terms, "Intellectual" and "Practical." The reason is that the former terms are much more appropriate, as a very little thought will show. The term *"Practical,"* as applied to Arithmetic, is a misnomer—all Arithmetic should be practical. In one case we solve questions *mentally,* and in the other case we employ *written* characters to aid the mind in the computation; hence the propriety of the division of Arithmetic into *Mental* and *Written.*

Many authors and teachers distinguish these two methods by the terms *oral* and *written,* but this is also a mistake. Neither Mental nor Written Arithmetic is *oral* unless it is *recited,* and when recited Written Arithmetic is *as much oral* as Mental Arithmetic. We may solve a problem in Mental Arithmetic without speaking a single word, and surely such a solution could not be called an oral one. The simple ditinction is that in one case the solution is *purely mental*, and in the other case the mind is aided by written characters; and it is natural and convenient to distinguish the two methods by this distinguishing characteristic of *purely mental* and *partly written*, calling the former *Mental Arithmetic* and the latter *Written Arithmetic.*

A common school course of Arithmetic may be completed in two or in three books, according as the *Mental* and *Written* exercises are separated or combined in the second book of the series. If these exercises are combined in the second book, the entire course will consist of two books, which may be called the *Primary Arithmetic* and the *Union Arithmetic.* These should be preceded by *oral exercises* in the art of computation, which may be called *Oral Arithmetic.*

ORAL ARITHMETIC.—Oral Arithmetic consists of such instructions in the science and art of numbers as should precede the use of a text-book by the student. The learner needs such instructions for several reasons. First, pupils can learn Arithmetic before they can *read*, and hence, of course, before they can use a book. Secondly, even with pupils who can read, such exercises are a very valuable preparation to the study of the subject from the text-book.

The chief instrument to be employed in these oral exercises is the "Arithmometer," or Numeral Frame, although *books, pens, pencils, grains of corn*, etc., form a valuable introduction to it.

In the "Normal Primary Arithmetic" we have given many suggestions for exercises of this kind, which we trust will be found valuable. The teacher can vary and modify them to suit the capacity and advancement of the class.

These oral exercises should be continued throughout the entire course in arithmetic. Every subject, even in the Written Arithmetic, should be *introduced* by such exercises. This is regarded as very important, and is a distinguishing characteristic of the author's arithmetical series.

PRIMARY ARITHMETIC.—The author believes that the *Primary Arithmetic* should be based upon the following principles, some of which have not previously been recognized in the preparation of such books:

1st. It should consist of both Mental and Written exercises, and not of either alone.

2d. Every subject should be introduced by suitable oral exercises, leading the pupil to the idea before he begins the subject in the text-book.

3d. The process should be *from the concrete to the abstract.* The *pictures* of objects, *marks*, *stars*, etc., are not necessary, since the objects themselves are better than their pictures or the marks, etc., and also, since the pupils should not leave the *Oral Exercises* until they can operate without the aid of objects or pictures.

4th. Addition and Subtraction should be so presented in the Mental Exercises that they may be taught simultaneously, or that an additive process should be immediately reversed, thus giving rise to a subtractive one.

5th. In the Mental exercises Multiplication and Division should be taught simultaneously, Division being made to depend upon Multiplication, as it logically does, by reversing the multiplicative process.

6th. The pupils should derive their own "Multiplication Table," so that they may understand its meaning and use, being required to commit it to memory after they have obtained it.

7th. The method should be thoroughly *Inductive*, proceeding *from the idea to the expression* of it, from the *method of operation to the reason for it*, or as it is sometimes expressed,—*first the how, then the why.* Principles and definitions should be taught *Inductively*, and the *methods* in every part should be derived by inductive inferences from analytic processes.

It is upon these principles that the author's *Primary Arithmetic*, first published in 1859, is based,—principles which are now beginning to be more or less fully recognized by authors and teachers all over the country.

CHAPTER II.

THE MENTAL EXERCISES OF THE SECOND BOOK ON ARITHMETIC.

AFTER completing the Primary Arithmetic the pupil may take a complete course of *Mental Arithmetic* in one book and a complete course of *Written Arithmetic* in another book; or these two courses may be combined in one book. Such a combination we have made under the head of *The Union Arithmetic*

Whether these two subjects should be combined in one book or be treated in separate works is a question upon which there is considerable diversity of opinion. In favor of two separate books, one treating of *Mental* and the other of *Written Arithmetic*, it is urged,—1st, The object of the two subjects is not the same, the object of Mental Arithmetic being discipline in analysis, and the object of Written Arithmetic being skill in practical calculation; 2d, The spirit of the two subjects is diverse, one being analytical and the other synthetic and demonstrative in its character; 3d, The two subjects cannot be properly coördinated, since there are many subjects, like Decimals, Proportion, Equation of Payments, etc., which cannot be treated mentally; 4th, Therefore, to attempt to combine the two in one book would result in subordinating Mental Arithmetic to such an extent as to practically ignore it.

On the other hand, the advocates of the combination plan make the following claims: 1st, To combine will economize time by having only one recitation in arithmetic, and thus give time for other studies; 2d, It will be an economy in the purchase of books, as the entire subject can be presented in one book no larger than the ordinary common school Written Arithmetic; 3d, The two being thus taught together, the one will aid the pupil to understand the other; whereas, if taught separately, the pupil will study different subjects at the same time and thus obtain a confused idea of each; 4th, The only use of Mental Arithmetic is to aid the pupil in acquiring a knowledge of Written Arithmetic, which would be most readily accomplished by having the two in one book.

What will be the final adjustment of this matter, it is difficult to decide. The present tendency for combination is an example of history repeating itself. Soon after the method of arithmetical analysis, now taught in Mental Arithmetic, was presented, several authors published text-books combining mental and written exercises, among whom may be mentioned Emerson and Roswell C. Smith. These books were very popular for awhile; but the public taste changed, and the two subjects became separated, and Mental Arithmetic took its place alongside of Written Arithmetic, and has maintained it for many years. At present there is a demand for the combination of the two in one book. Whether this demand will be permanent, or like a new fashion, will change again in a few years, time alone can decide.

To meet this demand, however, the author of the Normal Series has made a complete and harmonious combination of the two subjects, introducing many of those forms of analysis that have given such popularity to his Mental Arithmetic. It is this combination that gives the work its name, *The Union Arithmetic;* and this union will be found to be not a mere nominal thing, as in many authors, but a reality.

In this chapter I shall speak of the *nature* of the *mental exercises* and *how to teach* them, prefacing the same with a few thoughts on the importance of the study.

The greatest improvement in modern education is due to the introduction of the subject of *Mental Arithmetic.* The science of Arithmetic, before this introduction, was much less useful as an educational agency than it should have been. Consisting mainly of rules and methods of operations, without presenting the reasons for them, it failed to give that high degree of mental discipline which, when properly taught, it is so well calculated to afford. But a great change has been wrought in this respect; a new era has dawned upon the science of numbers; a "royal road" to mathematics has been discovered, so graded and strewn with the flowers of reason and philosophy that the youthful learner can follow it with interest and pleasure; and one of the most influential agents in this work has been the system of mental arithmetic.

The importance of this change can hardly be overestimated. The study of mental arithmetic, introduced by Warren Colburn, to whom teachers and pupils owe a debt of gratitude which can never be paid, affords the finest mental discipline of any study in the public schools. When properly taught, it gives quickness of perception, keenness of insight, toughness of mental fibre, and an intellectual power and grasp, that can be acquired by no other elementary branch of study. An old writer on arithmetic quaintly called his work "The Whetstone of Wit;" mental arithmetic is, in my opinion, truly *a whetstone of wit.* It is a *mental grindstone;* it sharpens the mind and gives it the power of concentration and penetration. To omit a thorough course of mental arithmetic in the common school is to deprive the pupil of one of the principal sources of mental power.

The principles upon which this part of arithmetic should be based may be briefly stated:

1st. A system of mental arithmetic should be based upon the principles of *Analysis* and *Induction.* Results should be derived by *analytic processes,* and *methods* inferred from these processes; and this is the philosophy upon which the author's treatise is founded. Analysis and Induction are the golden keys which unlock the various complex combinations of numbers—the magic wand by which the intricate and abstruse are unfolded in logical simplicity.

The great element of Analysis is *comparison,* and the *equation* is the Archimedean lever of comparison. It enters into every operation, from the simplest combination of Arithmetic to the most complicated problem of the transcendental Analysis. In Geometry the axioms and definitions are the standards of comparison; in Algebra we compare the unknown with the known to determine its value; and in Arithmetic we compare all numbers, and the effects produced by a number of equal causes, with the unit, or effect of the single cause. And thus the science of Mathematics is evolved, comprising a vast series of dependent truths derived from successive comparisons of the unknown with the known, the theoretic with the axiomatic, the complex with the simple.

In the science of numbers, this relation of the collection to the unit is so evident that it is intuitively apprehended, and hence the simplicity of this elementary process of Analysis. But as the pupil progresses in the science, it will be perceived that different collections bear certain relations to each other, and he should be taught to discover and apply these new relations. To develop this theory fully and completely should be the object of an author.

The principle of analysis consists in making the *unit* the basis of the reasoning process. In analysis we regard the unit as the starting-point of numbers, and reason *to the unit* and *from the unit*. The unit thus becomes the *central point* around which the reasoning process revolves, like planets around the central sun. The whole work in Mental Arithmetic should be a complete embodiment of the spirit of analysis, which, when fully acquired by a pupil, gives him power to work independently of memory or method, and enables him to originate his own methods and form his own rules.

2d. Fractions should be treated by Analysis and Synthesis and Induction, or more briefly by Comparison and Induction. In the treatment of fractions it is necessary to obtain methods for operating upon them, such as reducing to lowest terms, to common denominator, etc. These methods may be derived by Induction from the results obtained by the analytic process. This feature, which has not previously been introduced into Arithmetic, we deem a very valuable one, viewed either from the standpoint of science or teaching.

3d. The problems should be so varied that pupils will be forced to think for themselves. If all the problems under any class of problems are like the one which is solved in the text-book, the pupils can take the solution given and apply it directly to them all, and thus no more thought is required than by the old method of working by Rule. To prevent this mechanical way of operating, we have taken much pains to give great variety to the problems.

METHODS OF RECITATION.

The attention of teachers is respectfully solicited to the following Methods of Recitation. Some of them are preferable to others, but all may occasionally be used with advantage.

COMMON METHOD.—By this method the problems are read by the teacher and assigned promiscuously, the pupils not being permitted to use the book during recitation, nor retain the conditions of the problems by means of pencil and paper, as is sometimes done. The pupil selected by the teacher arises, repeats the problem, and gives the solution, at the close of which the mistakes that may have been made should be corrected by the class or teacher.

SILENT METHOD.—By this method the teacher reads a problem to the class, and then the pupils silently solve it, indicating the completion of the solution by the upraised hand. After the whole class, or nearly the whole class, have finished the solution, the teacher calls upon some member, who arises, repeats the problem, and gives the solution, as in the former method.

By this method the whole class must be exercised upon every problem, thus securing more discipline than by the preceding method. It, however, requires more time than the former method; hence, not so many problems can be solved at a recitation. We prefer the first method for advanced pupils, and the second, at least a portion of the time, with younger pupils.

CHANCE ASSIGNMENT.—This method differs from the first only in the assignment of the problems. The teacher marks tne number of the lesson and the number of the problem upon small pieces of paper, which the pupils may take out of a box passed around by the teacher or some member of the class. The teacher, then, after reading a problem, instead of calling upon a pupil, merely gives the number of the problem, the person having the number arising, repeating, and solving it. By this method the teacher is relieved of all responsibility with reference to the hard and easy problems, and it is also believed that better attention is secured with it. It is particularly adapted to reviews and public examinations.

Double Assignment.—By this method the pupil who receives the problem from the teacher arises, repeats it, and then assigns it to some one else to solve. It may be combined with either the first or second methods. The objects of this method are variety and interest.

Method by Parts.—By this method different parts of the same problem are solved by different pupils. The teacher reads the problem and assigns it to a pupil; and after he has given a portion of the solution, another is called upon, who takes up the solution at the point where the first stops; the second is succeeded in like manner by a third; and so on until the solution is completed. The object of this method is to secure the attention of the whole class, which it does very effectually. It is particularly suited to a large class consisting of young pupils.

Unnamed Method.—By this method the teacher reads and assigns several problems to different members of the class before requiring any solutions, after which those who have received problems are called upon in the order of assignment for their solutions. The advantages of this method are—first, the pupil having some time to think of the problem, is enabled to give the solution with more promptness and accuracy; and secondly, the necessity of retaining the numbers and their relations in the mind for several minutes affords a good discipline to the memory.

Choosing Sides.—This is a modification of the old spelling-class method, and is one calculated to elicit a very great degree of interest. By it two pupils, appointed by the teacher, select the others, thus forming two parties for a trial of skill, as in a game of cricket or base-ball. The problems may be assigned alternately to the sides by the teacher, by chance by the leaders of the sides, or in any other way that may be agreed upon by the teacher and class.

In regard to these methods, the first, second, and third are probably the best for the usual recitations, but the other methods can very profitably be employed with younger classes, or, in fact, with any class, to relieve monotony and awaken interest. With advanced pupils we prefer the first method, or the first combined with the third.

ERRORS TO BE AVOIDED.

There is a large number of errors to which pupils in every section of the country are liable, a few of which we will mention. We classify them as errors of Position and errors of Expression.

ERRORS OF POSITION.—Pupils are exceedingly liable to assume improper positions and awkward attitudes during recitation, such as leaning on the desk or against the wall, putting the foot upon a seat, jamming the hands in the pockets, particularly when the problem is hard, playing with a button, watch-chain, etc. All of these faults should be carefully guarded against, for reasons so obvious that they need not be mentioned. An erect and graceful carriage, aside from its relation to health, is of advantage to every lady and gentleman.

ERRORS OF EXPRESSION.—Under this head we include errors of Articulation, Pronunciation, Grammar, &c. There is quite a large number of words which pupils in their haste mispronounce, and also quite a large number of combinations, which by a careless enunciation make ridiculous sense, or nonsense. We will call the attention to a few of them, suggesting to the teacher to correct these and others he may notice.

"*And*" is often called "*an;*" "*for*" is called "*fur;*" "*of*" is pronounced as if the *o* was omitted; words commencing with *wh*, as when, which, where, etc., are pronounced as if spelled "*wen,*" "*wich,*" "*were,*" etc.

"*Gave him*" is called "*gavim;*" "*did he*" is called "*diddy;*" "*had he*" is called "*haddy;*" "*give him*" is called "*givim;*" "*give her*" is called "*giver;*" "*which is*" is often changed into "*witches;*" and "*how many*" is frequently transformed into "*hominy.*" "How many did each earn" is often rendered "hominy did *e churn.*"

A very common error, and one exceedingly difficult to correct, is involved in the following solution: "If 2 apples cost 6 cents, one apple will cost *the* ½ of 6 cents, which *are* 3 cents." Here "*the*" is superfluous, and "*are*" is ungrammatical.

The following is a frequent error: "*If one apple cost* 3 *cents, for* 12 *cents you can buy as many apples as* 3 *is contained in* 12, *which are* 4 *times.*" The objections are, first, 3 is not contained any *apples* in 12; secondly, the result obtained is *times*, when it should be *apples*, or a *number* which applies to both times and apples. The solution should be, "*You can buy as many apples for* 12 *cents as* 3 *is contained times in* 12, *which are* 4.

With regard to *is* and *are*, it is not easy to determine which should be used in some cases in Arithmetic. I am rather inclined to think that it would be better to use the singular form always when the subject is either an abstract or a concrete number; thus, 8 is 2 times 4, or 8 apples is 2 times 4 apples. But since custom sanctions the use of "*are*" with a concrete number as a subject, we have adhered to that form. There is some authority for using "*is*" in the "Multiplication Table," and I think it would be better if the singular form was universally adopted. We have adopted the following rule in determining the form of the verb when it has a *numerical* subject: If the idea is plural use "*are;*" if the idea is that of a whole—singular—use "*is.*"

Pupils have some difficulty in knowing how to read suc expressions as $\$\frac{4}{3}$. They object to saying "$\frac{4}{3}$ *dollars*" sinc there are not enough to make *dollars*, and they also objec to saying "$\frac{4}{3}$ *of a dollar*," since there are only 3 thirds in dollar. The correct reading is undoubtedly the second remembering that $\frac{4}{3}$ is an *improper* fraction.

The following error is almost universal: $2\frac{3}{4}$ apples is rea "2 *and* 3 *fourth apples*," instead of "2 *and* 3 *fourth apples*." The expression "$\frac{3}{4}$ *times*" is sanctioned b custom, although it is not in accordance with grammatic principles. It is rather more convenient than the expressio $\frac{3}{4}$ *of a time*, although evidently a violation of the rules o language.

But it is unnecessary for us to swell this list larger. little care on the part of the teacher will detect a larg number of errors, similar to those we have noticed, and w suggest that the attention given in this direction will b time profitably employed.

CHAPTER III.

CHARACTERISTICS OF A WRITTEN ARITHMETIC.

IN this chapter I shall speak of some of the principal characteristics of the *Written Exercises* of the *Union Arithmetic.* These exercises, constituting necessarily the body of the book, it being impossible to treat a large number of subjects mentally—the work may be spoken of as a text-book on *Written Arithmetic.* I shall thus speak of the characteristics of a work on *Written Arithmetic.*

METHOD OF TREATMENT.—The method of treatment should be both Inductive and Deductive, the solutions and demonstrations involving analysis and synthesis. The definitions, etc., in the Primary and Mental Arithmetic should be presented Inductively, but in the Written Arithmetic they should be given in the Deductive form. In these former works the solutions should be analytical and the Processes and Rules derived Inductively; in the Written Arithmetic the Deductive method may also be employed, and sometimes to great advantage. In Written Arithmetic many things are to be demonstrated, and the method of demonstration is Deductive. It will thus be seen that the two methods, Induction and Deduction, should be united in the Written Arithmetic. In the Normal Written Arithmetic both of these methods are frequently combined in the development of the same subject, as in Fractions, Proportion, Percentage, Involution, Evolution, etc.

ARRANGEMENT.—The arrangement should be both scientific and practical. By a scientific arrangement I mean such an arrangement as the logical development of the subject suggests. By a practical arrangement I mean a practical adaptation to the wants of pupils in pursuing the study. A merely scientific arrangement, however satisfactory to the accomplished arithmetician, would not be sufficiently progressive to meet the purpose of instruction. A merely practical adaptation of the easy and difficult subjects to suit the young learner, might completely ignore the logical relations of the science, and thus fail to give that mental discipline which the logical evolution of truth imparts. It is therefore clear that these two methods should run together; the work should be practically adapted to instruction, and, at the same time, the philosophical spirit of the science should be preserved as far as possible. This principle has determined the arrangement of the present work.

ADAPTATION TO PUPILS OF VARIOUS GRADES.—One of the most important and difficult things in the preparation of a text-book of this kind, is its adaptation to the many different classes of pupils who are to study it. A work of this character and scope is to be the first and last book on the subject of Written Arithmetic, to the pupils of our common schools, etc., excepting, of course, the written exercises found in the Primary Arithmetic. It must, therefore, be simple enough for young pupils, and yet sufficiently advanced for those of more mature minds. This adaptation may be accomplished in two or three different ways.

First, by making the first part of the book very simple, gradually increasing the difficulties as the pupil acquires strength and culture. Secondly, the teacher may omit certain subjects with elementary classes until review, or until the pupil is prepared for them. Thus the more difficult matter will be left for the pupil until he shall have become somewhat familiar with the easier principles and rules, and shall have gained mental strength to cope with the greater difficulties.

The same thing may also be done with problems; the easier ones are to be solved the first time, and the more difficult ones omitted until review. Another object gained by this plan, not of secondary importance either, is the interest that new matter gives to a review. Many pupils and even teachers tire and become listless on the review, the subject having lost its novelty; but by having new principles and problems, new difficulties to test their strength, new interest will be awakened and greater progress made.

Thus the work, which, if prepared for elementary classes alone, would be too easy for more advanced pupils, and if prepared alone for the advanced pupils would be entirely too difficult for beginners, is adapted to both elementary and advanced pupils. The younger pupils may omit a few of the harder principles and problems until review, as suggested, while the older pupils will have matter equal to their mental strength and culture. The intelligent teacher will exercise his judgment in this matter.

METHOD OF REASONING.—All reasoning is *comparison*. A comparison requires a standard, and this standard is the *fixed*, the *axiomatic*, the *known*. The law of correct reasoning, therefore, is to compare the *complex* with the *simple*, the *theoretic* with the *axiomatic*, the *unknown* with the *known*. By this comparison we pass from the *simple* to the *complex*, from the *old* to the *new*, from the *known* to the *unknown*.

Much of the reasoning of arithmetic is known by the term *Analysis*. Numbers are formed by synthesis, hence in the solution of problems, this synthetic process must often be reversed by the process of analysis. In the comparison of numbers, we find it necessary to determine their relation by the intermediate relation which they bear to the unit. Thus, if *three* cows cost $60, *one* cow costs $20, and *five* cows cost $100; here we compare the *three* and *five* by the relation they bear to the unit.

This simple process of analysis runs through the whole science of arithmetic. It is its key-note, its basis principle. The *unit* is the basis, the fundamental idea to which and from which we reason. It is a sort of arithmetical centre around which reasoning revolves, as the planets around their solar centre. The process, it is said, is called *analysis*; it should be remembered, however, that it is synthetic as well as *analytic*. When we pass from a collection to the single thing, that is, from a *number* to *one*, the process is analytic; but when we pass from *one* to a *number*, the process is essentially synthetic. Both processes are included under the more general one of *Comparison*. Comparison is properly the *thought* process; Analysis and Synthesis the mechanical processes.

In Written Arithmetic, however, the methods of reasoning are more synthetic and demonstrative than in Mental Arithmetic. Thus, many subjects which in Mental Arithmetic we would treat analytically, in Written Arithmetic we should treat by demonstration, as may be seen in Fractions, Percentage, etc. Besides this, there are many subjects in Written Arithmetic which are purely deductive and demonstrative in their nature, as Proportion, Progressions, Evolution, etc. Hence, the pupil will be required to learn demonstrative reasoning as well as arithmetical analysis; and this part of the subject should be clearly and logically developed.

PRINCIPLES.—Arithmetic as a science involves, and as an art is based upon, certain principles; and the most important of these should be distinctly stated and clearly demonstrated. The form of statement should be deductive, and, when not too difficult, the method of demonstration should be deductive also. In other cases the truth may be shown inductively, suggesting to the pupil, however, that it is susceptible of rigid deductive demonstration.

Where the principles are essential to the development of a subject, they should be given at the beginning of the treatment of it; in other cases they may be stated at the close of the subject. Thus, in Least Common Multiple, Greatest Common Divisor, Fractions by the Deductive treatment, Proportion, etc., the principles are given first, and the development based upon them; in the Fundamental Rules, etc., a knowledge of some of the principles not being essential to the development of the subjects themselves, they are given after them.

The importance of principles in a work of this character

should not be overlooked. Until within a few years, American text-books and American instruction almost completely ignored the principles of the science, making Arithmetic to consist entirely in the solution of problems. This is a great error, and one most pernicious to mental discipline. In nothing have I labored more diligently than in my efforts to reform this taste, and in nothing have I met with more opposition and more gratifying success. Especially is attention to principles important in Normal Instruction, where the pupil expects to teach others. No matter how hard a problem he can solve, if he cannot give neat and clear explanations, he is unfit to be an instructor of learners. It should also be remembered that a clear knowledge of the principle makes a problem, otherwise difficult, comparatively easy.

PROBLEMS.—Problems are of two kinds, *abstract* and *concrete*. Abstract problems are generally simple, being merely designed to illustrate the principle, or fix the rule in the mind. They also serve to make pupils ready and accurate in the mechanical operations. Such problems should be suited to the rule they illustrate and the capacity of the pupil, being simple at first and gradually increasing in difficulty.

Concrete problems are the application of the abstract principles to something that either does or may exist in actual life. These problems should also be adapted to the subject and the capacity of the learner. Simple at first, they should be gradually complicated until the pupil needs to think closely to unravel the complication and attain the result.

Number of Problems.—In an elementary text-book, there should be a large number of problems. Principles and methods are fixed in the mind by their application, and problems are intended for such application. In this respect there is a great difference between the French and English works. The French have many principles and few problems, the English fewer principles but more problems.

The true method is principles and problems, enough of the former, the more the better of the latter. Especially should there be a large collection of problems under the fundamental rules, as the first grand object in the study of Arithmetic is to acquire skill in the mechanical processes of adding, multiplying, etc. One excellence of the Normal Union Arithmetic consists in the number of its problems.

Variety of Problems.—The object of concrete problems is to give exercise to the reasoning faculties, to call out original thought. They should, therefore, be so varied that the solution of one cannot be directly and mechanically applied to all the others of the same class. Here is an important point. Many teachers who condemn the faults of the old schoolmasters in working everything by rule, fall into a similar error by requiring pupils to solve everything by "*model solutions.*" To give a pupil a solution of one of a class of problems, and then have him apply it to a dozen others of the same class, without any variation or new complication of the conditions so as to require original thought on the part of the pupil, is not much better than to solve by the old method of "*the rule says so.*"

Problems should, therefore, be varied so as to give the pupil opportunity for original thought and investigation, that he may become an independent reasoner and not a mental parrot. The object should be to develop mind as well as the power of computation,—to make thinkers rather than *arithmetical machines.*

Practical Character.—The practical character of the problems should be a prominent feature of them. They should represent the *actual business of the day*, and not the scholar's idea of what business might be. The problems and processes should be derived from actual business transactions. The author has endeavored to make this one of the leading characteristics of his works.

SOLUTIONS AND DEMONSTRATIONS.—The solutions and demonstrations should be simple and clear that they may be readily understood, but they should also be expressed in language concise and logically accurate, and *in the form which the pupil should be required to use at recitation.* A solution may be too concise to be readily understood, and it may also be too prolix, the idea being smothered or concealed in a multiplicity of words. Both of these errors should be avoided. There is a language of arithmetical science, simple, clear, and concise, as appropriate to the science as the language of geometry to the science of geometry. This language is the natural expression of the logical analytical evolution of the subject, and should be employed in the most elementary processes; for it is an indubitable truth, that *the highest science is the greatest simplicity.*

RULES.—The rules, or methods of operation, should be expressed in brief and simple language, and in a form easily understood by the learner. The statement should not be too comprehensive, but should indicate each step in its natural order. In most cases the rule should be derived from the solution of a problem, that the pupil may see the reason for it, and be able to derive it himself, as an inference from the solution. In a few cases it is more convenient to state the rule first and then demonstrate it, and this has occasionally been done in the present work.

DEFINITIONS.—The definitions should be clear, concise, and accurate. There are two methods of giving definitions, which are distinguished as the Inductive and Deductive methods. By the Inductive method we pass from the idea to the word; by the Deductive method we pass from the word to the idea. Thus, by the Inductive method we would say, "The process of finding the sum of two or more numnumbers is Addition;" by the Deductive method we would say, "Addition is the process of finding the sum of two or more numbers." In the Primary and Mental Arithmetics, the Inductive method is preferred; in the Written Arithmetic, the Deductive is used. Special attention is invited to the definitions of *Number, Fraction, Ratio, Percentage,* etc

ANSWERS.—The question is often raised whether a textbook on Written Arithmetic should contain the answers to the problems. My own opinion is, that the majority of the problems should have no answers given in the text-book. In case of any peculiarity in a problem by which pupils would be liable to obtain an incorrect result, the correct answer should be given; in other cases it would be better omitted. In practical life, our problems are without answers; we must determine the correct results for ourselves. Education should be disciplinary for life, hence the pupil should learn to rely upon himself in studying his text-book. We have no answers in our Mental Arithmetic, and get along well without them. Could we not do as well without them in Written Arithmetic?

These views, however, conflict with the popular view and practice. Nearly all teachers prefer having answers to the problems in the text-book. I can see that with elementary classes they may be of some practical advantage, to both pupil and teacher. There will be two editions of this work published, one with and the other without answers; it will thus meet the wants of all in this respect.

CHAPTER IV.

METHODS OF TEACHING WRITTEN ARITHMETIC.

AS conditions for thorough instruction in Written Arithmetic, each pupil should be provided with an arithmetic, slate, and pencil. The school-room should also be furnished with a blackboard of suitable size and quality. The necessity of a blackboard in the school-room is imperative. No good teaching can be done without it, especially in Mathematics.

Blackboards may be prepared in a variety of ways. The best are slate-boards or composition surfaces; these, however, are not always possible in a common school. Colored surfaces may be made of boards evenly planed; or the wall of the school-room, to the height of about six feet, may be painted black. If the wall is laid on brick, it is sufficient to stain it; but if upon lath, it should first be covered with thick, firm wall-paper, and then colored. There are several fluid preparations for giving a colored surface, which are highly recommended. "Pierce's Patent Slate Surface" is the best and cheapest with which I am acquainted.

ASSIGNMENT OF THE LESSON.—The lesson should be assigned at the close of each recitation, that the pupil may have time to prepare it for the next recitation. In this matter the teacher should be definite as to *place* and *extent*, stating just where a lesson commences and where it ends, so that there can be no doubt about it by the pupil. The extent of the lesson should be adapted to the ability of the class, care being taken that neither too much nor too little be assigned. This point is important, for if too little be given, the pupils become lazy; if too much, they will become discouraged and disgusted with the study. Attention should also be called to prominent points or unusual difficulties, that they may receive special attention in the preparation of the lesson.

PREPARATION OF THE LESSON.—The lesson having been assigned, the pupil should be required to give it careful study as a preparation for recitation. In this preparation, the pupil should be thrown, as far as possible, upon his own resources. The teacher should give him no assistance, or at least very little, and he should prevent, as far as possible, his obtaining any from any other members of the class or the more advanced pupils. The habit of running to the teacher with every little difficulty is a most pernicious one, and destructive of invigorating mental discipline. Independence of thought and bold self-reliance are indispensable traits of manhood, and should be cultivated in the studies of youth, and especially in the study of mathematics, which is particularly adapted to give such training.

This point cannot be too strongly urged; its neglect has been productive of much mischief. I have known pupils who, for a whole session, scarcely ever solved a problem for themselves, but prepared their lessons with the aid of other pupils. At other times they have obtained notes from those who had previously passed over the same subject, and have used these notes to the utter neglect of self-thought. It is needless to say that much time was thrown away, and that such study is worse than useless.

Let the pupil, then, in the preparation of his lesson, depend mainly upon himself, and what he fails to get out in this way, the teacher can explain to him at the recitation.

THE RECITATION.—The Recitation is the great instrument of instruction. In it the teacher comes in contact with the mind of the pupil, calls out its energies and moulds it to his will. Mind meets mind here—the pupil's mind and the teacher's mind—thought is evolved, and mental activity stimulated. It is here that the teacher shows his power as a teacher, rousing up dormant faculties, directing mental activity, and creating interest and enthusiasm in that which was before dry and repulsive. The method of recitation must be determined by the ends of the recitation; hence, we will state some of the principal objects of the recitation.

1. *To see what the pupil knows of the subject.* The lesson having been assigned, the pupils are expected to prepare it, and the recitation serves the purpose of ascertaining the extent of the preparation. If they have studied well, the recitation will enable the teacher to credit them for their industry and the knowledge of the subject; if they have neglected study, the recitation will detect it and show their indolence and negligence. The first object of the recitation is therefore to ascertain how much the pupils know of the subject.

2. *To fix the subject clearly in the mind.* Another object of the recitation is to fix the subject clearly in the mind. This perhaps does not apply to mathematics with precisely the same force that it does to some other branches which depend more upon the memory. Mathematics is logic, or reasoning, the activity of the thinking faculty rather than the storing of the memory, yet even in mathematics repetition is important. The definitions, principles and mechanical methods, are to be remembered, and repetition also serves to fix the form of reasoning in the memory. The effort to explain a subject which we do not fully understand, often gives us a clearer conception of it; during the explanation sometimes light suddenly bursts upon the mind, and darkness and uncertainty vanish from the subject as clouds before the sunlight of morning.

3. *To cultivate expression.* A third object of the recitation is the cultivation of the power of expression. The importance of correct and elegant expression cannot be questioned. The power to tell a thing is almost as important as to know it. Our forms of expression exercise an influence upon our habits of thought. Thought and expression affect each other reciprocally. Accuracy of thought begets accuracy of expression, and accuracy of expression leads to accuracy of thought. Pupils should, therefore, be required to tell what they know in a clear, concise, and logical manner and the recitation affords the opportunity for such exercise

4. *To impart instruction.* A fourth object of the recitation is to impart instruction No matter how well the pupils may have studied the subject, there will always be some points which they do not fully understand, or at least, upon which they have not the clearest views. Though they may solve all the problems, they do not always have the best or shortest method of solution. The recitation presents the opportunity for the teacher to give these better and clearer views, and these shorter and easier solutions. When a principle has been explained or a problem solved, either incorrectly or in a manner that will admit of improvement, the teacher should pass to the board and, securing the attention of the whole class, point out the errors or indicate the improvements. Much instruction can also be given by judicious questions, and by raising points for the discussion of the class, and such indirect teaching is generally to be preferred to direct explanation.

ADAPTATION TO DIFFERENT GRADES.—The recitation in Written Arithmetic should be adapted to the advancement of the pupils. In the Primary class the teacher should give more explanation than in the advanced class. The exercises should be less theoretical and more practical. The main object with beginners is that they may become familiar with the practical part of Arithmetic, that they may acquire facility in the mechanical operations. Advanced pupils should always understand the reason for every operation ; Primary classes often learn the practical working of a rule before understanding the reason for it. Advanced pupils should always be required to explain the reason for each process ; Primary classes need not be required to give such explanation even though they have some idea of it.

In the assignment of Problems, each pupil of the advanced class should receive a different problem ; with the primary class, all may receive the same problem, and then go to work to see who can have it done first and without mistakes. With young pupils, the definitions, when required, should generally be given in the exact language of the author ;

older pupils should be encouraged to describe the process in their own language. Older pupils should be required to enunciate and explain the principles of the science; with younger pupils these may, to a great extent, be omitted. In a word, the method of recitation with younger pupils should be more Inductive; with advanced pupils more Deductive.

METHOD OF RECITATION.—The lesson being prepared and the hour of recitation having arrived, the class take their seats in the recitation-room for the purpose of reciting. The teacher calls the roll to see if all are present, and then proceeds with the recitation, the most important points of which will be briefly specified.

Preparation of the Blackboard.—The first step is the preparation of the blackboard. The teacher says "prepare the board," and the pupils arise and pass orderly to the board, erase what work there may be on it, and then divide it into equal spaces by vertical lines, each pupil drawing a line to his right. This done, as quietly as possible, the pupils turn and stand with their backs to the board, and face towards the teacher.

Assignment of Problems.—The next step is the assignment of problems. As before suggested, with young classes the same problem should be assigned to all the pupils, or at least one problem to four or five pupils; with advanced classes each pupil should receive a different problem. If the class is not too large, the problem should be read by the teacher, and the pupil be required to copy the conditions as he reads. When the class is large, the pupils, or at least a part of them, may be permitted to copy the problem assigned from the book. They should be required, however, to close their books as soon as the conditions are written.

Writing the Problem.—The next step, or one co-ordinate with the above, is the writing of the problem upon the board. When the problem is abstract, merely requiring an operation upon abstract numbers, the pupil will copy such numbers as the teacher reads. If the problem is concrete, involving several conditions, the pupils should be required to mark the conditions by a sort of short-hand or abbreviated process which he can write rapidly, and which will be readily understood. He should also write his name, the page, and number of the problem, at the upper part of his space, so that the teacher may readily refer to the problem in the text-book.

Working the Problem.—The next step is the working of the problem upon the board. In this the pupils should practise neatness and exactness. The figures should be plainly and neatly made. The lines drawn beneath any part of the work should be straight and horizontal. The work for explanation should be written in an analytical form, the operations and general form of solution being indicated by the form of writing. The pupil should be exact in such expressions, and not write one thing and mean another. Every point, symbol, etc., should be written in its proper place, the teacher not being satisfied by the pupil's saying he meant so and so, when he had written something else, or neglected writing some essential part. Having completed the solution of the problem, the pupil should take his seat and retain it until called upon by the teacher for his explanation.

PUPIL'S EXPLANATION.—The next step is the explanation of the problem. This is a very important part of the recitation, and should be conducted with great care. There are several points to which attention is called.

Position at the Board.—The pupil should stand in an erect and easy attitude, with the pointer in one hand and the other hanging down by the side. His side, and not his face, should be turned towards the board, so that he can see both the solution and the teacher. The teacher should be particular upon these points, allowing no awkwardness or clownishness of attitude, but endeavoring to cultivate an easy and graceful carriage. At West Point, one of the best mathematical schools in the country, they *are very particular* upon such points as these, and the effect of it is seen in the progress and attainments of the pupils.

Explanation.—The explanation of the problem should be given in a full and natural tone of voice, with great care to clearness of thought, accuracy of expression and distinctness of enunciation. Those who speak too low should be encouraged to speak louder; and those who speak in a loud and declamatory style should be taught to speak in an easier and more natural tone. If the form of solution is analytical, each point should be clearly stated as it follows a preceding one, care being taken that the whole chain of analysis be kept complete. If the solution is deductive, the different steps being based upon principles previously explained, these principles should be referred to in their proper order and connection. The explanation should be clear and full in all its parts, and complete as a logical whole.

CRITICISMS.—The pupils who are not engaged at the board should be required to observe closely each explanation, noticing carefully all mistakes in solution, expression, etc. At the close of the solution, the class should be called upon for correction of errors, suggestions of improvements, etc. The character of the solution, whether incorrect, too long, or not sufficiently clear, the form of statement upon the board, position at the board, style of expression, etc., are all legitimate subjects of criticism. After the pupils have given their criticisms, the teacher should present any other suggestions or corrections which may be required. At the close of such criticisms, the pupil who explained will erase his work upon the board, and receive another problem, or take his seat and the next pupil proceed to explain

TEACHER'S EXPLANATION.—It is often necessary for the teacher to explain some principle or problem to the class; the proper time of doing this will be suggested by circumstances A principle that several members of the class do not understand, and which is essential to the lesson to be recited, should be explained at the beginning of the recitation. A difficult problem should not be explained by the teacher until the class have tested their strength with it. It had better be left over a week or two, even, for the class to see if they cannot solve it without assistance. A spirit of this kind can be cultivated so that pupils will not be willing to have the teacher explain a problem until they have assured themselves, by severe labor, that it is beyond their powers. Assistance of this kind is often better given by suggestion than by full explanation. This leaves the victory partly theirs, and affords at least a partial satisfaction of a triumph.

The question is sometimes asked,—Should a teacher give an explanation of a subject before the pupils have studied it? This, of course, depends upon circumstances. Every teacher of experience can determine beforehand just what difficulty a class will have with any subject. When these difficulties are so great that classes generally fail in the preparation of the lessons without assistance, the teacher should occupy the latter part of the previous recitation period in giving such explanations as the subject requires, thus enabling them to surmount the difficulties, and come to the next recitation prepared to recite.

New Matter.—For the purpose of exciting a deeper interest in the subject, the teacher should occasionally introduce new matter adapted to the comprehension of the class. This may be done at the latter part of the recitation hour, or he may occasionally occupy the whole period in a lecture upon the subject. This will give enlarged views of the subject, and awaken the desire of going beyond the limits of the present text-book. With classes sufficiently advanced, a philosophical discussion of the subject, showing its logical evolution from a few fundamental ideas, the relation of the different parts to each other, natural transition from Arithmetic to Algebra, etc., will be instructive and interesting.

Reviews.—I recommend regular reviews. With the younger classes, where they are learning merely the mechanical part, they need not be so frequent; but with other classes I suggest a review at the close of each week. In this review, less attention may be given to the problems, and more to definitions and principles. I would have pupils write analytical outlines of the week's work, embracing the definitions, principles, different cases under each subject, etc., in their logical order. This will give a comprehensive idea of the subject as a whole, and exhibit the logical relation of the parts to each other. With these suggestions, which I hope may not be without interest or instruction, I pass to the second part of the work, the KEY.

PART II.

A KEY

TO THE NORMAL UNION ARITHMETIC.

IN this Key will be found the solutions of the more difficult problems. It is designed to aid the pupil studying alone, or the teacher wishing to compare his own work with the method of the author. The subject is indicated sometimes by the Article, and sometimes by the Page, as is thought to be most convenient. The answers to all the problems will be found in Part III.

ARITHMETICAL LANGUAGE.

Art. 33. EXERCISES IN NUMERATION.

2. Three thousand, 8 hundred and seventy-six.

13. One million, 234 thousand, 567.

23. 80 billion, 735 million, 468 thousand, 579.

25. 798 quadrillion, 653 trillion, 13 billion, 285 million, 678 thousand, 521.

NOTE.—In reading numbers it is customary not to pluralize the denominations; thus we say, 5 million, 6 thousand, etc., instead of 5 millions, 6 thousands, etc.

Art. 34. EXERCISES IN NOTATION.

23. 2000006.	**30.** 1230456.	**34.** 47038208.
27. 8002067.	**31.** 4307409.	**35.** 200004928.
28. 5296000.	**32.** 15408084.	**36.** 6705035006
29. 70001045.	**33.** 28594709.	**37.** 49000000058798.

Art. 36. Page 16.

1. 24. 2. 460. 3. 903. 4. 30607. 5. 500480.

Art. 45. Page 18.

1. 14.5. 3. 203.67. 5. $60.07. 7. $450.50.
2. 84.25. 4. 796.875. 6. $87.25. 8. $864.375.

Art. 48. Page 18.

1. 1000000. 3. 1000000000000000000.
2. 1000000000000. 4. 1000000000000000000000000.

ROMAN NOTATION.

Page 20.

1. XXVII. 2. LXXVII. 3. CCI. 4. DCLVI. 5. MDCCLXXVI. 6. MMMMDCCLVII or $\overline{\text{IV}}$DCCLVII. 7. $\overline{\text{XXV}}$VII. 8. $\overline{\text{CCVI}}$CCCCLXXXIV.

1. 77. 2. 1090. 3. 1876. 4. 3333. 5. 15744. 6. 188. 7. 49. 8. 99.

REMARK.—I cannot impress upon the teacher's mind too strongly, the importance of thorough drill in Numeration and Notation. Time spent here will pay a large interest in the future.

SECTION II.

FUNDAMENTAL RULES.

The problems under Addition and Subtraction are so simple as to require no solutions in the Key.

MULTIPLICATION.

Page 52. WRITTEN EXERCISES.

1. $1.50×3=$4.50; $1.25×5=$6.25; $.75×4=$3; $4.50+$6.25+$3=$13.75.
2. 3+1=4; $975×4=$3900; $5875−$3900=$1975.
3. 246×4=984; 984+145=1129; 246+1129+1687=3062; 24500−3062=21438 men.
4. Difference per minute=81−76=5; 5×25=125
5. 18×15=270; 353−270=83 miles.

6. 192500×86400×365×7=42494760000000.

7. $7.20×500=$3600; $4.75×375=$1781.25; $2.70×240=$648; $.29×200=$58; $3600+$1781.25+$648+$58=$6087.25.

8. $5×52=$260; $4×12=$48; $2×365=$730; $260+$48+$730=$1038; $1500−$1038=$462.

9. $55×2=$110; $3.50×12=$42; $4.25×3=$12.75; $150+$110+$42+$12.75=$314.75.

10. $.16×150=$24; $.17×450=$76.50; $.13×260=$33.80; $.11×850=$93.50; $24+$76.50+$33.80+$93.50=$227.80.

11. $.07×125=$8.75; $.08×147=$11.76; $.08×156=$12.48; $.07×122=$8.54; $1.15×125=$143.75; $8.75+$11.76+$12.48+$8.54+$143.75=$185.28.

12. $.38×450=$171; $.43×375=$161.25; $1.45×240=$348; $171+$161.25+$348=$680.25; $.91×460=$418.60; $1.10×175=$192.50; $1.25×720=$900; $418.60+$192.50+$900=$1511.10; $1511.10−$680.25=$830.85.

DIVISION.

Page 62. WRITTEN EXERCISES.

13. $2575×15=$38625; $38625−$7300=$31325; $31325÷$25=1253.

14. $75×125=$9375; $9375−$675=$8700; $8700÷$150=58 acres.

Page 64. WRITTEN EXERCISES.

24. $75×150=$11250; $20000−$11250=$8750; $8750÷$125=70 acres.

Art. 97. TO FIND THE TRUE REMAINDER.

(2)	(3)	(4)	(5)
5)582	4)503	5)2497	7)4507
3)116+2	3)125+3	4)499+2	2)643+6
38+2	41+2	124+3	32+1
5×2+2=12	4×2+3=11	5×3+2=17	7×1+6=13

(6)	(7)	(8)
2)3717	3)13853	4)41837
3)1858+1	5)4617+2	5)10459+1
5)619+1	7)923+2	9)2091+4
123+4	131+6	232+3
6×4+1×2+1=27	15×6+3×2+2=98	20×3+4×4+1=77

(9)	(10)	(11)	
4)47117	2)96711	2)87831	120×5=600
7)11779+1	5)48355+1	3)43915+1	24×4= 96
11)1682+5	31)9671+0	4)14638+1	6×2= 12
152+10	311+30	5)3659+2	2×1= 2
28×10+4×5+1=301	10×30+1=301	6)731+4	1
		121+5	711

Page 69.

21. 325−124=201; \$804÷201=\$4; \$28+\$4=\$32.

22. \$75×110=\$8250; \$8250−\$2200=\$6050; \$6050÷5=\$1210.

23. 765−65=700; \$442.00÷\$0.85=520; 700−520=180; 180÷60=3 horses.

24. \$6500×2=\$13000; \$5000×3=\$15000; \$13000+\$1000+\$15000+\$25000=\$54000; \$54000÷6=\$9000.

25. \$13×12=\$156; \$14×6=\$84; \$17×18=\$306; \$930+\$156+\$84+\$306=\$1476; \$1476÷36=\$41.

SECTION III.

SECONDARY OPERATIONS.

GREATEST COMMON DIVISOR.

Art. 123. Case II.

(5)

697	820	1
	697	
615	123	5
82	82	1
82	41	2
0		

(8)

1220	2013	1
	1220	
793	793	1
427	427	1
366	366	1
61	366	6

(9)

730	1241	1
	730	
511	511	1
219	438	2
219	73	3

1460÷73=20.

(10)

72491	103121	1
	72491	
61260	30630	2
11231	22462	2
8168	8168	1
3063	6126	2
2042	2042	1
1021	2042	2

(11)

347387	561851	1
	347387	
214464	214464	1
132923	132923	1
81541	81541	1
51382	51382	1
30159	30159	1
21223	21223	1
17872	8936	2
3351	6702	2
2234	2234	1
1117	2234	2

6. Find the G. C. D of 364 and 585, which is 13.

7. G. C. D.=6; \$678÷\$6=113; \$906÷\$6=151; \$1146÷\$6=191.

12. G. C. D.=41; 533÷41=13; 574÷41=14; 861÷41=21; 13+14+21=48.

LEAST COMMON MULTIPLE.

Art. 130. Page 85.

This method is important, as without it it would be almost impossible to solve many problems which arise. Take the 6th problem for illustration: by the ordinary method it would require a pupil many hours to solve it, and most pupils would fail entirely. By the method here given the solution is quite easy.

(3)

G. C. D.=113

$$\text{L. C. M.}=\frac{4859}{113}\times 3503$$

=150629, *Ans.*

(4)

G. C. D.=107

$$\text{L. C. M.}=\frac{7597}{107}\times 6527$$

463417, *Ans.*

(8)

G. C. D.=131

$$\text{L. C. M.}=\frac{9432}{131}\times 7205$$

=518760, *Ans.*

(9)

G. C. D.=211

$$\text{L. C. M.}=\frac{15403}{211}\times 11183$$

=816359, *Ans.*

(10)

L. C. M. of 357 and 612=4284

L. C. M. of 4284 and 663=55692.

(11)

L. C. M. of 6161 and 7171=437431.

L. C. M. of 437431 and 4141=17934671.

The problems following are designed to be solved by the easiest methods. Since the numbers are small and easily factored, they may be solved by CASE I.

6. Find the L. C. M. of the numbers, which is \$560.

7. Find the L. C. M. of the numbers, which is 5544 rods.

8. Find the L. C. M. of the numbers, which is 1680 bushels.

12. Find the L. C. M. of the number of minutes, which is 180 minutes.

13. L. C. M.=2520; 2520÷18=140; 2520÷24=105; 2520÷30=84; 2520÷35=72.

CANCELLATION.

Page 87. WRITTEN EXERCISES.

2. No. of bu.$=\frac{\overset{25}{\cancel{125}}\times\overset{2}{\cancel{18}}}{\underset{9}{\cancel{45}}}=50$, *Ans.*

3. No. of bu.$=\frac{\overset{13}{\cancel{78}}\times\overset{7}{\cancel{98}}}{\underset{6}{\cancel{84}}}=91$, *Ans.*

4. No. of bu.$=\frac{\cancel{7}\times 40\times\overset{6}{\cancel{36}}}{\underset{\cancel{6}}{\cancel{42}}}=240$, *Ans.*

5. No. of bu.$=\frac{\overset{\cancel{3}}{\cancel{27}}\times\overset{7}{\cancel{56}}\times\overset{2}{\cancel{20}}}{\underset{\cancel{3}}{\cancel{24}}\times\underset{\cancel{10}}{\cancel{90}}}=14$, *Ans.*

6. Cost$=\frac{\cancel{9}\times\overset{\cancel{3}}{\cancel{18}}\times\cancel{2}\times\overset{7}{\cancel{35}}}{\underset{\cancel{2}}{\cancel{12}}\times\underset{\underset{\cancel{3}}{\cancel{27}}}{\cancel{135}}}=7$ cts., *Ans.*

SECTION IV.

COMMON FRACTIONS.

REDUCTION.

Art. 165. WRITTEN EXERCISES.

6. $\frac{72}{288}=\frac{6}{24}=\frac{1}{4}$; divide by 12 and then by 6. $\frac{288}{864}=\frac{24}{72}=\frac{2}{6}=\frac{1}{3}$; divide by 12, then by 12, then by 2.

7. $\frac{120}{168}=\frac{30}{42}=\frac{5}{7}$; we divide first by 4 and then by 6. $\frac{648}{720}=\frac{108}{120}=\frac{9}{10}$; divide by 6, and then by 12.

8. $\frac{792}{864}=\frac{66}{72}=\frac{11}{12}$; divide by 12 and then by 6. $\frac{192}{216}=\frac{24}{27}=\frac{8}{9}$; divide by 8 and then by 3.

9. $\frac{840}{4312}=\frac{105}{539}=\frac{15}{77}$; we divide first by 8 and then by 7. $\frac{1176}{1512}=\frac{98}{126}=\frac{14}{18}=\frac{7}{9}$; we divide by 12, 7, and 2.

SUG.—With these larger problems it is better to find the greatest common divisor of both terms, and divide by it.

10. $66)\frac{726}{792}=\frac{11}{12}$; $1908)\frac{9540}{13356}=\frac{5}{7}$.

11. $101)\frac{6161}{7171}=\frac{61}{71}$; $421)\frac{42521}{118301}=\frac{101}{281}$.

Art. 166. WRITTEN EXERCISES.

(11)

$$\frac{2}{\cancel{3}}\times\frac{\cancel{4}}{5}\times\frac{\overset{2}{\cancel{6}}}{\cancel{7}}\times\frac{\overset{3}{\cancel{21}}}{\underset{7}{\cancel{28}}}=\frac{12}{35}.$$

(12)

$$\frac{\cancel{4}}{\underset{3}{\cancel{9}}}\times\frac{\overset{4}{\cancel{12}}}{\underset{5}{\cancel{15}}}\times\frac{\cancel{25}}{\underset{\cancel{4}}{\cancel{64}}}\times\frac{\overset{\overset{2}{\cancel{6}}}{\cancel{96}}}{\underset{3}{\cancel{75}}}=\frac{8}{45}.$$

(13)

$$\frac{\overset{2}{\cancel{18}}}{\underset{5}{\cancel{25}}}\times\frac{\overset{7}{\cancel{35}}}{\underset{\cancel{3}}{\cancel{27}}}\times\frac{\cancel{77}}{88}\times\frac{\overset{39}{\cancel{117}}}{\underset{\cancel{2}}{\cancel{154}}}=\frac{273}{440}.$$

Page 98. MENTAL EXERCISES.

4. I gave her $\frac{2}{3}$ of $\frac{3}{4}$ of a bushel, or $\frac{1}{2}$ of a bushel.

5. I found $\frac{1}{2}$ of $\frac{1}{4}$, or $\frac{1}{8}$, hence my final loss was $\frac{1}{8}$; $\frac{8}{8}-\frac{1}{8}=\frac{7}{8}$; since $140 is $\frac{7}{8}$ of my money, $\frac{1}{8}$ of my money equals $\frac{1}{7}$ of $140, or $20, and $\frac{8}{8}$ equals 8 times $20, or $160.

6. Since 1 gallon costs $\frac{3}{4}$ of a dollar, $\frac{5}{6}$ of a gallon will cost $\frac{5}{6}$ of $\frac{3}{4}$ of a dollar, or $\frac{5}{8}$ of a dollar.

Page 98. WRITTEN EXERCISES.

6. $\frac{3}{4}$ of $\frac{4}{7}=\frac{3}{7}$; since $\frac{3}{7}$ of the stock$=3\frac{3}{7}$ B's, $\frac{1}{7}$ of the stock$=1\frac{1}{7}$ B's, and $\frac{7}{7}$, or the whole stock$=8$ times B's; hence B owns $\frac{1}{8}$ of the stock.
7. If she *shared* with 8 companions, $\frac{18}{19}$ of a bushel was divided into 9 parts, and each received $\frac{2}{19}$.
8. Since \$580 was $\frac{5}{6}$ of what remained, $\frac{6}{6}$ of what remained equals 6 times $\frac{1}{5}$ of \$580, or \$696; the deposit=\$696+\$580=\$1276.
9. $\frac{2}{3}$ of $\frac{5}{6}=\frac{5}{9}$, hence he had $\frac{4}{9}$ remaining; $\frac{3}{4}$ of $\frac{8}{9}$ of $\frac{11}{12}$ of $\frac{4}{9}=$ \$132; $\frac{22}{81}$ of his money=\$132; hence his money was \$486.

COMMON DENOMINATOR.

Art. 169. WRITTEN EXERCISES.

2. $\frac{3}{4}=\frac{3\times6\times8}{4\times6\times8}=\frac{144}{192}$.

$\frac{5}{6}=\frac{5\times4\times8}{6\times4\times8}=\frac{160}{192}$.

$\frac{7}{8}=\frac{7\times4\times6}{8\times4\times6}=\frac{168}{192}$.

$4\times6\times8=192$.

3. $\frac{2}{5}=\frac{2\times7\times6}{5\times7\times6}=\frac{84}{210}$.

$\frac{4}{7}=\frac{4\times5\times6}{7\times5\times6}=\frac{120}{210}$.

$\frac{5}{6}=\frac{5\times7\times5}{6\times7\times5}=\frac{175}{210}$.

$5\times7\times6=210$.

The remaining examples in this case are solved in a similar manner.

LEAST COMMON DENOMINATOR.

Art. 170.

2. L. C. M.=36; then $\frac{5}{6}=\frac{5\times6}{6\times6}=\frac{30}{36}$; $\frac{4}{9}=\frac{4\times4}{9\times4}=\frac{16}{36}$; $\frac{7}{12}=\frac{7\times3}{12\times3}=\frac{21}{36}$.

3. L. C. M.=60; then $\frac{3}{4}=\frac{3\times15}{4\times15}=\frac{45}{60}$; $\frac{7}{10}=\frac{7\times6}{10\times6}=\frac{42}{60}$; $\frac{5}{6}=\frac{5\times10}{6\times10}=\frac{50}{60}$.

4. L. C. M.$=60$; then $\frac{1}{4}=\frac{1\times 15}{4\times 15}=\frac{15}{60}$; $\frac{11}{12}=\frac{11\times 5}{12\times 5}=\frac{55}{60}$; $\frac{13}{20}=\frac{13\times 3}{20\times 3}=\frac{39}{60}$.

The remaining examples are solved in a similar manner.

ADDITION OF FRACTIONS.

Art. 171. WRITTEN EXERCISES.

2. $\frac{4}{5}+\frac{3}{4}+\frac{3}{4}=\frac{16}{20}+\frac{15}{20}+\frac{15}{20}=\frac{46}{20}=\frac{23}{10}=2\frac{3}{10}$, *Ans.*
3. $\frac{4}{6}+\frac{7}{9}+\frac{5}{8}=\frac{48}{72}+\frac{56}{72}+\frac{45}{72}=\frac{149}{72}=2\frac{5}{72}$, *Ans.*
4. $\frac{5}{6}+\frac{11}{12}+\frac{13}{18}=\frac{30}{36}+\frac{33}{36}+\frac{26}{36}=\frac{89}{36}=2\frac{17}{36}$, *Ans.*
5. $\frac{4}{7}+\frac{3}{4}+\frac{11}{14}=\frac{16}{28}+\frac{21}{28}+\frac{22}{28}=\frac{59}{28}=2\frac{3}{28}$, *Ans.*
6. $2+4=6$; $\frac{1}{2}+\frac{3}{4}+\frac{11}{12}=2\frac{1}{6}$; $6+2\frac{1}{6}=8\frac{1}{6}$.
7. $\frac{18}{24}+\frac{20}{24}+\frac{21}{24}+\frac{22}{24}=\frac{81}{24}=3\frac{3}{8}$.
8. $\frac{2}{3}+\frac{4}{5}+\frac{5}{6}+\frac{7}{8}=\frac{80}{120}+\frac{96}{120}+\frac{100}{120}+\frac{105}{120}=\frac{381}{120}=3\frac{7}{40}$.
9. $\frac{5}{6}+\frac{7}{8}+\frac{9}{10}+\frac{11}{12}=\frac{100}{120}+\frac{105}{120}+\frac{108}{120}+\frac{110}{120}=\frac{423}{120}=3\frac{21}{40}$.
10. $2+4+3+1=10$; $\frac{1}{2}+\frac{2}{3}+\frac{1}{4}+\frac{9}{10}=2\frac{19}{60}$; $10+2\frac{19}{60}=12\frac{19}{60}$.
11. $4+7+9+7=27$; $\frac{3}{4}+\frac{1}{8}+\frac{1}{16}+\frac{1}{50}=\frac{383}{400}$; $27+\frac{383}{400}=27\frac{383}{400}$.
12. $21+35+22+4=82$; $\frac{4}{7}+\frac{1}{11}+\frac{3}{21}+\frac{1}{2}=1\frac{47}{154}$; $82+1\frac{47}{154}=83\frac{47}{154}$.
13. $17+49+24+18=108$; $\frac{7}{8}+\frac{8}{55}+\frac{6}{11}+\frac{1}{88}=1\frac{438}{440}$; $108+1\frac{438}{440}=109\frac{438}{440}$.
14. $\frac{3}{4}\times\frac{5}{6}=\frac{5}{8}$; $\frac{4}{5}\times\frac{6}{7}=\frac{24}{35}$; $\frac{5}{6}\times\frac{7}{8}=\frac{35}{48}$.
    $\frac{5}{8}+\frac{24}{35}+\frac{35}{48}=\frac{1050}{1680}+\frac{1152}{1680}+\frac{1225}{1680}=\frac{3427}{1680}=2\frac{67}{1680}$, *Ans.*
15. $\frac{1260}{2520}+\frac{840}{2520}+\frac{630}{2520}+\frac{504}{2520}+\frac{420}{2520}+\frac{360}{2520}+\frac{315}{2520}+\frac{280}{2520}+\frac{252}{2520}=\frac{4861}{2520}=1\frac{2341}{2520}$.

SUBTRACTION OF FRACTIONS.

Art. 172. WRITTEN EXERCISES.

10. $\frac{28}{36}-\frac{14}{26}=\frac{7}{9}-\frac{7}{13}=\frac{91}{117}-\frac{63}{117}=\frac{28}{117}$, *Ans.*
11. $\frac{3}{4}\times\frac{9}{10}=\frac{27}{40}$; $\frac{27}{40}-\frac{7}{12}=\frac{81}{120}-\frac{70}{120}=\frac{11}{120}$, *Ans.*
12. $\frac{4}{7}\div\frac{10}{3}=\frac{40}{21}$; $1\frac{1}{2}=\frac{3}{2}$; $\frac{40}{21}-\frac{3}{2}=\frac{80}{42}-\frac{63}{42}=\frac{17}{42}$, *Ans.*
13. $\frac{8}{9}$ of $\frac{18}{36}=\frac{4}{9}$; $\frac{4}{9}-\frac{3}{7}=\frac{28}{63}-\frac{27}{63}=\frac{1}{63}$, *Ans.*
14. $\frac{2}{5}\times\frac{15}{18}=\frac{1}{3}$; $\frac{7}{8}\times\frac{24}{28}=\frac{3}{4}$; $\frac{3}{4}-\frac{1}{3}=\frac{9}{12}-\frac{4}{12}=\frac{5}{12}$, *Ans.*
15. $\frac{3}{4}\times\frac{7}{8}=\frac{21}{32}$; $\frac{4}{5}$ of $\frac{15}{16}=\frac{3}{4}$; $\frac{3}{4}-\frac{21}{32}=\frac{24}{32}-\frac{21}{32}=\frac{3}{32}$, *Ans.*
17. $\frac{7}{6}-\frac{5}{6}=\frac{2}{6}=\frac{1}{3}$; $11-8=3$; $3\frac{1}{3}$, *Ans.*

18. $\frac{11}{8}-\frac{7}{8}=\frac{4}{8}=\frac{1}{2}$; $9-5=4$; $4\frac{1}{2}$, *Ans.*
19. $20\frac{7}{9}=19\frac{16}{9}$; $19\frac{16}{9}-10\frac{8}{9}=9\frac{8}{9}$, *Ans.*
20. $24\frac{3}{11}=23\frac{14}{11}$; $23\frac{14}{11}-12\frac{7}{11}=11\frac{7}{11}$, *Ans.*
21. $\frac{3}{4}=\frac{9}{12}$; $\frac{21}{12}-\frac{11}{12}=\frac{10}{12}=\frac{5}{6}$; $29-20=9$; $9\frac{5}{6}$, *Ans.*
22. $\frac{5}{12}=\frac{15}{36}$; $\frac{7}{9}=\frac{28}{36}$; $\frac{51}{36}-\frac{28}{36}=\frac{23}{36}$; $59-40=19$; $19\frac{23}{36}$, *Ans*

Page 103. WRITTEN PROBLEMS.

1. $5+4+6=15$; $\frac{1}{2}+\frac{1}{4}+\frac{3}{4}=1\frac{1}{2}$; $\$15+\$1\frac{1}{2}=\$16\frac{1}{2}$, *Ans.*
2. $7+9+10=26$; $\frac{1}{3}+\frac{3}{4}+\frac{1}{5}=1\frac{17}{60}$; $26+1\frac{17}{60}=27\frac{17}{60}$ bu.
3. $1\frac{11}{40}+\frac{9}{40}=1\frac{1}{2}$; $\$5-\$1\frac{1}{2}=\$3\frac{1}{2}$.
4. $\$12\frac{1}{2}+\$32\frac{3}{4}+\$52\frac{5}{8}=\$97\frac{7}{8}$; $\$100-\$97\frac{7}{8}=\$2\frac{1}{8}$.
5. $12+18+37+62=129$; $\frac{1}{2}+\frac{3}{4}+\frac{1}{2}+\frac{1}{2}=2\frac{1}{4}$; $129+2\frac{1}{4}=131\frac{1}{4}$¢ $=\$1.31\frac{1}{4}$.
6. $41\frac{5}{8}+41\frac{5}{8}=83\frac{1}{4}$; $83\frac{1}{4}-57\frac{3}{4}=25\frac{1}{2}$ yd.
7. $1+2+2+1=6$; $\frac{1}{2}+\frac{5}{8}+\frac{3}{16}+\frac{3}{8}=1\frac{11}{16}$; $6+1\frac{11}{16}=7\frac{11}{16}$.
8. $49\frac{7}{25}-15\frac{7}{25}=34$; $43\frac{4}{25}-15\frac{7}{25}=27\frac{22}{25}$; $39\frac{1}{20}-15\frac{7}{25}=23\frac{77}{100}$; $45\frac{9}{100}-15\frac{7}{25}=29\frac{81}{100}$; $34+27\frac{22}{25}+23\frac{77}{100}+29\frac{81}{100}=115\frac{23}{50}$.

MULTIPLICATION OF FRACTIONS.

Art. 175. WRITTEN EXERCISES.

12. $28\frac{15}{20}\times 5=140\frac{15}{4}=143\frac{3}{4}$.
13. $17\frac{18}{21}\times 7=119\frac{18}{3}=125$.
14. $24\frac{19}{24}\times 12=288\frac{19}{2}=297\frac{1}{2}$.
15. $46\frac{15}{26}\times 13=598\frac{15}{2}=605\frac{1}{2}$.
16. $128\frac{19}{54}\times 18=2304\frac{19}{3}=2310\frac{1}{3}$.
17. $428\frac{18}{121}\times 11=4708\frac{18}{11}=4709\frac{7}{11}$.

Art. 176. WRITTEN EXERCISES.

(8)

5)180
$15\frac{4}{5}$
36
4
144
900
180
2844

(9)

$$144\times\frac{17}{24}=\frac{\overset{6}{\cancel{144}}\times 17}{\cancel{24}}=102$$

(10)

$$284\times\frac{35}{36}=\frac{\overset{71}{\cancel{284}}\times 35}{\underset{9}{\cancel{36}}}=276\frac{1}{9}$$

(11)

16)256
$7\frac{15}{16}$
16
15
80
16
240
1792
2032

12. $180\times\frac{17}{24}=\frac{\overset{15}{\cancel{180}}\times 17}{\underset{2}{\cancel{24}}}=127\frac{1}{2}$; $180\times 25=4500$; $4500+127\frac{1}{2}=4627\frac{1}{2}$.

13. $\overset{49}{\cancel{196}}\times\frac{9}{\cancel{15}}\times\frac{\overset{3}{\cancel{45}}}{\underset{\underset{4}{\cancel{12}}}{\cancel{48}}}=\frac{441}{4}=110\frac{1}{4}$.

14. $\overset{54}{\cancel{648}}\times\frac{\overset{8}{\cancel{40}}}{\underset{5}{\cancel{65}}}\times\frac{\overset{6}{\cancel{78}}}{\underset{7}{\cancel{84}}}=370\frac{2}{7}$.

Art. 177. WRITTEN EXERCISES.

8. $\frac{\overset{2}{\cancel{18}}}{\underset{6}{\cancel{24}}}\times\frac{\overset{7}{\cancel{28}}}{\underset{\cancel{5}}{\cancel{45}}}\times\frac{\overset{23}{\cancel{115}}}{\underset{58}{\cancel{116}}}=\frac{161}{348}$.

9. $\frac{45}{49}\times\frac{56}{65}\times\frac{91}{72}=1$.

10. $12\frac{1}{2}=\frac{25}{2}$; $8\frac{1}{3}=\frac{25}{3}$; $\frac{25}{2}\times\frac{25}{3}=104\frac{1}{6}$.

11. $17\frac{2}{5}=\frac{87}{5}$; $16\frac{2}{3}=\frac{50}{3}$; $\frac{\overset{29}{\cancel{87}}}{\cancel{5}}\times\frac{\overset{10}{\cancel{50}}}{\cancel{3}}=290$.

12. $27\frac{3}{11}=\frac{300}{11}$; $21\frac{5}{6}=\frac{131}{6}$; $\frac{\overset{50}{\cancel{300}}}{11}\times\frac{131}{\cancel{6}}=595\frac{5}{11}$.

13. $39\frac{3}{5}=\frac{198}{5}$; $33\frac{1}{3}=\frac{100}{3}$; $\frac{\overset{66}{\cancel{198}}}{\cancel{5}}\times\frac{\overset{20}{\cancel{100}}}{\cancel{3}}=1320$.

14. $\frac{\overset{\cancel{3}}{\cancel{9}}}{\underset{5}{\cancel{10}}}\times\frac{\overset{2}{\cancel{18}}}{\underset{5}{\cancel{85}}}\times\frac{\cancel{7}}{\underset{\cancel{3}}{\cancel{24}}}\times\frac{\overset{2}{\cancel{16}}}{\underset{\cancel{3}}{\cancel{27}}}=\frac{2}{25}$.

15. $\frac{\overset{2}{\cancel{16}}}{\cancel{23}}\times\frac{\overset{2}{\cancel{18}}}{\underset{3}{\cancel{24}}}\times\frac{\overset{7}{\cancel{28}}}{\underset{\cancel{5}}{\cancel{45}}}\times\frac{\overset{\cancel{5}}{\cancel{115}}}{\underset{29}{\cancel{116}}}=\frac{28}{87}$.

16. $\frac{\cancel{19}}{27}\times\frac{\overset{17}{\cancel{102}}}{\underset{5}{\cancel{95}}}\times\frac{\cancel{144}}{\underset{9}{\cancel{189}}}\times\frac{\overset{13}{\cancel{273}}}{\underset{\underset{2}{\cancel{12}}}{\cancel{1728}}}=\frac{221}{2430}$.

Page 107. MENTAL EXERCISES.

4. One inkstand will cost $\$\frac{2}{5}$, and 15 will cost \$6.
5. 12 is 4 times 3, hence 12 Letter-writers will cost 4 times $\$\frac{9}{10}$, or $\$3\frac{3}{5}$.
6. $4\frac{1}{2}$, or $\frac{9}{2}$ times $\frac{7}{8}$ rods, or $3\frac{15}{16}$ rods.
7. It is the same as taking $\frac{1}{4}$ of a number.

8. $\frac{1}{4}$ of 1 is $\frac{1}{4}$, and $\frac{1}{4}$ of 12 is 12 times as great, or 12 times $\frac{1}{4}$, and this may be shown with any fraction and integer.

9. $2\frac{1}{2}$ times $\$3\frac{1}{4}$, or $\frac{5}{2} \times \$\frac{13}{4}$, which equals $\$8\frac{1}{8}$.

10. 7 times $25\frac{1}{2}$ cents equals $\$1.78\frac{1}{2}$, and $\frac{1}{4}$ of $25\frac{1}{2}$ cents equals $6\frac{3}{8}$ cents; $\$1.78\frac{1}{2} + \$.06\frac{3}{8} = \$1.84\frac{7}{8}$.

11. 4 times $\$6\frac{3}{5}$ equals $\$26\frac{2}{5}$; $\frac{3}{4}$ of $\$6\frac{3}{5}$ equals $\$4\frac{19}{20}$; $\$26\frac{2}{5} + \$4\frac{19}{20} = \$31\frac{7}{20}$.

12. 8 times $\$7\frac{1}{2} = \$60$; $\frac{4}{5}$ of $\$7\frac{1}{2} = \$6$; $\$60 + \$6 = \$66$.

Pages 107-108. WRITTEN EXERCISES.

1. $2\frac{5}{6}¢ \times 96 = 272¢ = \$2.72$.

2. $\$.06\frac{3}{4} \times 475 = \$32.06\frac{1}{4}$.

5. $\$10.62\frac{1}{2} \times 180 = \$1912.50$.

10. $\$.87\frac{1}{2} \times 24 = \$21$.

15. $\dfrac{\overset{8}{\cancel{24}}}{\cancel{25}} \times \dfrac{\overset{\cancel{3}}{\cancel{75}}}{\underset{\underset{\cancel{3}}{\cancel{9}}}{\cancel{81}}} \times \dfrac{\cancel{9}}{\cancel{64}} \times \dfrac{\overset{4}{\cancel{256}}}{289} = \frac{32}{289}$.

16. $\dfrac{\cancel{49}}{\underset{4}{\cancel{64}}} \times \dfrac{\cancel{27}}{\underset{8}{\cancel{128}}} \times \dfrac{\overset{\cancel{16}}{\cancel{144}}}{\underset{\underset{\cancel{3}}{\cancel{27}}}{\cancel{729}}} \times \dfrac{\overset{\cancel{16}}{\cancel{48}}}{\underset{7}{\cancel{343}}} = \frac{1}{224}$.

17. $\dfrac{\overset{243}{\cancel{729}}}{\underset{\cancel{31}}{\cancel{961}}} \times \dfrac{\overset{\cancel{32}}{\cancel{992}}}{\underset{\underset{121}{\cancel{363}}}{\cancel{1089}}} \times \dfrac{\overset{\cancel{3}}{\cancel{231}}}{\underset{\underset{8}{\cancel{32}}}{\cancel{1024}}} \times \dfrac{\overset{\cancel{31}}{\cancel{124}}}{\underset{13}{\cancel{1001}}} = \frac{243}{12584}$.

18. $\dfrac{\overset{\cancel{17}}{\cancel{289}}}{\underset{\underset{\cancel{7}}{\cancel{21}}}{\cancel{441}}} \times \dfrac{\overset{\cancel{11}}{\cancel{231}}}{\underset{\underset{\cancel{10}}{\cancel{20}}}{\cancel{340}}} \times \dfrac{\overset{\overset{20}{\cancel{100}}}{\cancel{700}}}{\underset{29}{\cancel{841}}} \times \dfrac{\overset{\overset{\cancel{3}}{\cancel{30}}}{\cancel{870}}}{\cancel{999}} \times \dfrac{\overset{2}{\cancel{1998}}}{\underset{\underset{\cancel{5}}{\cancel{55}}}{\cancel{935}}} = \frac{40}{29}$.

19. $\frac{1}{3} + \frac{8}{15} = \frac{13}{15}$; $\frac{13}{15} \times \frac{3}{11} = \frac{13}{55}$; $\frac{4}{17} + \frac{5}{6} = \frac{109}{102}$; $\frac{109}{102} \times 3 = 3\frac{7}{34}$; $\frac{13}{55} + 3\frac{7}{34} = 3\frac{827}{1870}$.

20. $\frac{5}{6} + \frac{10}{11} = \frac{115}{66}$; $\frac{3}{4} + \frac{7}{15} = \frac{73}{60}$; $\dfrac{\cancel{115}}{\underset{\cancel{11}}{\cancel{66}}} \times \dfrac{\cancel{73}}{\underset{5}{\cancel{60}}} \times \dfrac{\overset{\cancel{6}}{\cancel{72}}}{\cancel{73}} \times \dfrac{\overset{33}{\cancel{363}}}{\underset{2}{\cancel{230}}} = 3\frac{3}{10}$.

21. $7\frac{7}{10} = \frac{77}{10}$; $4\frac{6}{11} = \frac{50}{11}$; $4\frac{1}{2} - 3\frac{4}{5} = \frac{7}{10}$; $5\frac{6}{7} + 6\frac{3}{11} = 12\frac{10}{77}$;

$\dfrac{\overset{7}{\cancel{77}}}{\cancel{10}} \times \dfrac{\overset{5}{\cancel{50}}}{\cancel{11}} = 35$; $35 + \frac{7}{10} - 12\frac{10}{77} = 23\frac{439}{770}$.

22. $33\frac{1}{3} + 37\frac{1}{2} = 70\frac{5}{6}$; $6\frac{1}{4} + 6\frac{7}{12} = 12\frac{5}{6}$; $12\frac{5}{6} \times 49\frac{15}{16} = 640\frac{83}{96}$; $732\frac{1}{11} - 70\frac{5}{6} - 640\frac{83}{96} = 20\frac{415}{1056}$.

23. $\$42\frac{3}{4}\times 12\times 3\frac{1}{4}=\$1667\frac{1}{4}$.

24. $\frac{3}{8}-\frac{1}{8}=\frac{2}{8}$; $\frac{50}{50}-\frac{3}{50}=\frac{47}{50}$; $\frac{47}{50}$ of $\frac{2}{8}$ of $\$376\frac{3}{8}=\$235\frac{517}{600}$.

25. $62\frac{1}{2}$¢ $\times 52\frac{1}{2}=\$32.81\frac{1}{4}$; $\frac{1}{3}\times 52\frac{1}{2}=17\frac{1}{2}$; $69\frac{1}{2}$¢ $\times 17\frac{1}{2}=\$12.16\frac{1}{4}$; $71\frac{2}{3}$¢ $\times 35=\$25.08\frac{1}{3}$; $\$12.16\frac{1}{4}+\$25.08\frac{1}{3}=\$37.24\frac{7}{12}$; $\$37.24\frac{7}{12}-\$32.81\frac{1}{4}=\$4.43\frac{1}{3}$.

DIVISION OF FRACTIONS.

Art. 180. WRITTEN EXERCISES.

In several of the problems it is most convenient to express the operation in a fractional form and then cancel.

(5) $\frac{18}{25}\times\frac{1}{36}=\frac{1}{50}$.

(6) $\frac{3}{4}\times\frac{14}{9}\times\frac{1}{7}=\frac{1}{6}$.

(7) $\frac{5}{6}\times\frac{72}{125}\times\frac{1}{9}=\frac{4}{75}$.

(8) $\frac{7}{8}\times\frac{72}{91}\times\frac{1}{18}=\frac{1}{26}$.

(9) $2\frac{4}{21}=\frac{46}{21}$; $3\frac{3}{7}=\frac{24}{7}$; $\frac{46}{21}\times\frac{8}{7}\times\frac{7}{24}=\frac{46}{63}$.

10. $785\div 7=112$ and 1 remaining; $1+\frac{3}{5}=\frac{8}{5}$; $\frac{8}{5}\div 7=\frac{8}{35}$; $112\frac{8}{35}$, *Ans.* It may also be solved by reducing $785\frac{3}{5}$ to 5ths and dividing by 7.

11. $287\div 12=23$ and 11 remaining; $11+\frac{5}{8}=\frac{93}{8}$; $\frac{93}{8}\div 12=\frac{31}{32}$; $23\frac{31}{32}$, *Ans.*

The remaining problems may be solved in a similar manner.

Art. 181. WRITTEN EXERCISES.

9. $256\div 3\frac{7}{35}=256\times\frac{35}{112}=80$.

10. $552\div 2\frac{11}{29}=552\times\frac{29}{69}=232$.

11. $558\div 8\frac{6}{7}=558\times\frac{7}{62}=63$.

12. $638\div 19\frac{1}{3}=638\times\frac{3}{58}=33$.

13. $729\div 22\frac{1}{2}=729\times\frac{2}{45}=32\frac{2}{5}$.

Art. 182. WRITTEN EXERCISES.

11. $7\frac{5}{24}\div 12\frac{8}{15}=\frac{173}{24}\times\frac{15}{188}=\frac{865}{1504}$.

12. $15\frac{15}{16}\div 8\frac{5}{11}=\frac{255}{16}\times\frac{11}{93}=\frac{935}{496}=1\frac{439}{496}$.

13. $17\frac{7}{19}\div 10\frac{4}{9}=\frac{330}{19}\times\frac{9}{94}=\frac{1485}{893}=1\frac{592}{893}$.

14. $21\frac{3}{7}\div 12\frac{8}{21}=\frac{150}{7}\times\frac{21}{260}=\frac{45}{26}=1\frac{19}{26}$.

15. $25\frac{4}{9}\div 15\frac{4}{11}=\frac{229}{9}\times\frac{11}{169}=\frac{2519}{1521}=1\frac{998}{1521}$.

16. $33\frac{1}{3}\div 12\frac{1}{25}=\frac{100}{3}\times\frac{25}{301}=\frac{2500}{903}=2\frac{694}{903}$.

18. $\frac{28}{42}\times\frac{79}{10}\times\frac{84}{72}=\frac{553}{90}=6\frac{13}{90}$.

19. $\frac{45}{80}\times\frac{112}{90}\times\frac{40}{27}\times\frac{135}{112}=\frac{5}{4}=1\frac{1}{4}$.

Page 111. MENTAL EXERCISES.

7. The ribbon cost 6 times $5\frac{1}{3}$ cents, or 32 cents, and she could buy as many apples for 32 cents as $1\frac{1}{3}$ cents is contained times in 32 cents, or 24 apples.

8. The butter cost 20 times 15 cents, or \$3, and she could buy with it as many yards of calico as $12\frac{1}{2}$ cents is contained times in \$3, which is 24.

9 As many persons received apples as $3\frac{1}{2}$ is contained times in 14, or 4; 4 persons, minus the schoolboy, leaves 3 companions.

10. The potatoes cost \$5, and he received $12\frac{1}{2}$ dozen eggs.

Page 112. WRITTEN EXERCISES.

3. $\$5\frac{37}{50} \div 7 \times 5 = \frac{287}{50} \times \frac{1}{7} \times 5 = \$4\frac{1}{10} = \$4.10.$

8. $\frac{\overset{2}{\cancel{4}}}{5} \times \frac{\cancel{7}}{\underset{2}{\cancel{12}}} \times \frac{\overset{3}{\cancel{9}}}{\cancel{10}} \times \frac{\cancel{6}}{5} \times \frac{\overset{4}{\cancel{64}}}{\underset{5}{\cancel{15}}} \times \frac{\overset{2}{\cancel{20}}}{\underset{3}{\cancel{21}}} \times \frac{3}{\cancel{16}} = \frac{48}{125}.$

9. $\frac{\cancel{39}}{\underset{36}{\cancel{72}}} \times \frac{\overset{2}{\cancel{218}}}{\underset{25}{\cancel{425}}} \times \frac{\overset{17}{\cancel{289}}}{\underset{3}{\cancel{327}}} \times \frac{\overset{3}{\cancel{75}}}{\underset{3}{\cancel{117}}} = \frac{17}{108}.$

10. $\frac{210}{924} \times \frac{156}{165} \times \frac{255}{234} \times \frac{264}{238} = \frac{2.3.5.7}{2.2.3.7.11} \times \frac{2.2.3.13}{3.5.11} \times \frac{3.5.17}{2.3.3.13} \times \frac{2.2.2.3.11}{2.7.17} = \frac{20}{77}.$

11. $1\frac{1}{2} \times 3\frac{1}{5} + \frac{5}{11}$ of $\frac{3}{7} = \frac{1923}{385}$; $6\frac{2}{3} - 4\frac{3}{4} = \frac{23}{12}$; $\frac{\overset{641}{\cancel{1923}}}{\underset{5}{\cancel{385}}} \times \frac{\cancel{77}}{\underset{\underset{9}{\cancel{27}}}{\cancel{81}}} \times \frac{\overset{4}{\cancel{12}}}{23} = \frac{2564}{1035} = 2\frac{494}{1035}.$

12. $\frac{54}{63} + 3\frac{4}{7} = \frac{31}{7}$; $6\frac{2}{3} - 4\frac{1}{4} = \frac{29}{12}$; $\frac{31}{7} \times \frac{12}{29} \times \frac{88}{9} = \frac{10912}{609} = 17\frac{559}{609}$; $17\frac{559}{609} + 76\frac{1}{10} = 94\frac{109}{6090}.$

13. $77\frac{20}{21} - 44\frac{3}{7} = \frac{704}{21}$; $5\frac{5}{11} + 6\frac{2}{7} - 7\frac{21}{77} = \frac{344}{77}$; $42\frac{3}{4} + 16\frac{3}{8} = \frac{473}{8}$;

$\frac{\overset{64}{\cancel{704}}}{21} \times \frac{\overset{8}{\cancel{344}}}{77} \times \frac{8}{\underset{\cancel{11}}{\cancel{473}}} = \frac{4096}{1617} = 2\frac{862}{1617}.$

15. $28\frac{7}{8} = \frac{231}{8}$; $231 \times \frac{8}{231} = 8$ persons.

17. $1+5=6$; $\$9600 \div 6 = \$1600.$

18. $127\frac{2}{3} + 112\frac{3}{4} = 240\frac{5}{12}$; $240\frac{5}{12} \div 15 = 16\frac{1}{36}.$

19. $102 \div 6\frac{3}{8} = 102 \times \frac{8}{51} = 16$; $16 - 1 = 15$, number of companions.

21. $\$85.50 - \$40 = \$45.50$; $\$45.50 \div 7 = \$6.50.$

22. $\$3\frac{4}{5}-\$1\frac{7}{8}=\$1\frac{37}{40}=\$\frac{77}{40}$; $\$46\frac{1}{5}=\frac{231}{5}$; $\frac{231}{5}\times\frac{40}{77}=24$ days.
23. $\$382-\$228=\$154$; $\$154\div6\frac{7}{8}=\$154\times\frac{8}{55}=\$22.40$.

REDUCTION OF COMPLEX FRACTIONS.

Art. 183. WRITTEN EXERCISES.

5. $\frac{9}{10}\times\frac{25}{27}\times\frac{16}{15}\times\frac{18}{17}=\frac{16}{17}$.

6. $\dfrac{\frac{10}{13}\times\frac{54}{45}}{\frac{16}{25}\times\frac{45}{64}}=\dfrac{\frac{2}{3}}{\frac{9}{20}}=\frac{2}{3}\times\frac{20}{9}=\frac{40}{27}=1\frac{13}{27}$.

7. $\frac{17}{35}\times\frac{95}{85}\times\frac{28}{19}\times\frac{152}{105}=\frac{608}{525}=1\frac{83}{525}$.

10. $10\frac{10}{13}\div12\frac{1}{4}=\frac{140}{13}\times\frac{4}{49}=\frac{80}{91}$.

11. $\frac{1}{5}+\frac{3}{7}=\frac{22}{35}$; $\frac{4}{9}+\frac{2}{5}=\frac{38}{45}$; $\frac{22}{35}\times\frac{45}{38}=\frac{99}{133}$.

12. $3\frac{1}{2}-2\frac{1}{3}=\frac{7}{6}$; $4\frac{1}{4}-2\frac{1}{5}=\frac{41}{20}$; $\frac{7}{6}\times\frac{20}{41}=\frac{70}{123}$.

13. $(12\frac{1}{2}\div41\frac{2}{3})\times(3\frac{7}{8}\div6\frac{1}{5})=\frac{25}{2}\times\frac{3}{125}\times\frac{31}{8}\times\frac{5}{31}=\frac{3}{16}$.

RELATION OF NUMBERS.

Art. 185. MENTAL EXERCISES.

4. 20 yards will cost 4 times \$21, or \$84.
5. 30 tons will cost 5 times $\$19\frac{1}{2}$, or $\$97\frac{1}{2}$.
6. $\frac{3}{5}$ of \$20 = \$12; \$12 + \$3 = \$15; \$15 is $\frac{3}{4}$ of \$20.

Art. 185. WRITTEN EXERCISES.

14. $\frac{225}{105}\times77=\frac{15}{7}\times77=165¢=\$1.65$.

15. $\frac{4}{5}$ B's = 20, B's = 25; A obtains $\frac{3}{5}$ of 25 = 15; A then has 20 + 15 = 35, and B has 25 − 15 = 10; 10 is $\frac{10}{35}$ of 35, or $\frac{2}{7}$, *Ans.*

Art. 186. MENTAL EXERCISES.

4. $\$\frac{3}{4}$ is $\frac{3}{8}$ of \$2.
5. $5-3\frac{1}{3}=1\frac{2}{3}$; $1\frac{2}{3}$ is $\frac{1}{3}$ of 5.
6. B paid $\frac{2}{3}$ of 26 cents, or $17\frac{1}{3}$ cents.

Art. 186. WRITTEN EXERCISES.

8. $\frac{3}{7}\div12=\dfrac{3}{7\times12}=\frac{1}{28}$.

9. $\frac{21}{16}\times\frac{1}{35}=\frac{3}{80}$.

10. After giving B 5 he had 20; he gave $\frac{1}{4}$ of 20 to C, and had remaining $\frac{3}{4}$ of 20, or 15; 15 is $\frac{15}{25}$, or $\frac{3}{5}$, *Ans.*

Art. 187. MENTAL EXERCISES.

3. \$9 will buy as many yards as $\$\frac{3}{4}$ is contained times in \$9, or 12.
4. As many times as $2\frac{1}{2}$ is contained times in 6, or $2\frac{2}{5}$.
5. As many times as $\frac{3}{4}$ is contained times in 4, or $5\frac{1}{3}$.

Art. 187. WRITTEN EXERCISES.

6. $588 \div 3\frac{9}{11} = 588 \times \frac{11}{42} = 154$.
7. $63504 \div 50\frac{2}{5} = 63504 \times \frac{5}{252} = 1260$.
8. Sarah had $\frac{4}{5}$ of $12 = \frac{48}{5}$; $\frac{48}{5} - \frac{3}{4} = \frac{177}{20}$; $12 \div \frac{177}{20} = \frac{240}{177} = \frac{80}{59} = 1\frac{21}{59}$.

Art. 188. MENTAL EXERCISES.

4. $7\frac{1}{2}$ is 3 times $2\frac{1}{2}$, hence $7\frac{1}{2}$ yards will cost 3 times $\$7\frac{1}{2}$, or $\$22\frac{1}{2}$.
5. He sold $\frac{3}{4}$ of $\frac{5}{6}$, or $\frac{5}{8}$ of the cargo.
6. Edwin had $\frac{3}{4}$ of \$2, or $\$1\frac{1}{2}$ remaining, and Emma had $\frac{4}{5}$ of \$2, or $\$1\frac{3}{5}$: $\$1\frac{1}{2}$ is $\frac{15}{16}$ of $\$1\frac{3}{5}$.

Art. 188. WRITTEN EXERCISES.

11. $\frac{3}{7}$ of $\frac{7}{9} = \frac{3}{9}$; $\frac{9}{9} - \frac{3}{9} = \frac{6}{9}$; $\frac{6}{9} = \frac{6}{7}$ of $\frac{7}{9}$.
12. First sold $\frac{2}{3}$ of $\frac{9}{10} = \frac{6}{10}$ to the second; hence the first had $\frac{9}{10} - \frac{6}{10} = \frac{3}{10}$, and the second had $\frac{9}{10} + \frac{6}{10} = \frac{15}{10}$; and $\frac{3}{10}$ equals $\frac{3}{15}$ or $\frac{1}{5}$ of $\frac{15}{10}$; hence the result is $\frac{1}{5}$.
13. $\frac{4}{5}$ of $\frac{4}{9} = \frac{3\frac{1}{5}}{9}$; $\frac{3}{4}$ of $\frac{5}{9} = \frac{3\frac{3}{4}}{9}$; $\frac{3\frac{1}{5}}{9} + \frac{3\frac{3}{4}}{9} = \frac{6\frac{19}{20}}{9}$.

ARITHMETICAL ANALYSIS.

Art. 190. MENTAL EXERCISES.

3. He can plow 1 furrow in $\frac{1}{5}$ of $13\frac{3}{4}$ minutes, or $2\frac{3}{4}$ minutes, and 8 furrows in 8 times $2\frac{3}{4}$, or 22 minutes.

Art. 190. WRITTEN EXERCISES.

4. $\$\frac{19}{20} \div 5 \times 22 = \$4.18$. | 5. $\$15\frac{3}{7} \div 9 \times 21 = \$36$.
8. $\$17.50 \div 3 \times 21 = \$122.50$.
9. $\$43.50 \div \$7.25 = 6$; $3 \times 6 = 18$.
10. $\$54 \div \$6 = 9$; $4\frac{1}{3} \times 9 = 39$ bushels.

Art. 191. MENTAL EXERCISES.

4. 1 apple cost $\frac{9}{8}$ of a cent, and 9 apples cost $10\frac{1}{8}$ cents.
5. 1 peach cost $\frac{16}{15}$ of a cent, and 25 peaches cost $26\frac{2}{3}$ cents.
6. The cost of the cow was \$40, and of the horse \$200.

Art. 191. WRITTEN EXERCISES.

7. $\frac{16}{5}$ of $\$46\frac{7}{8} \times 8 = \$1200$.
8. $60 \div 10\frac{2}{3} \times 10 \times 6 = 337\frac{1}{2}$ pages. | 9. $\$4 \div 2\frac{2}{11} \times 25 = \$45\frac{5}{6}$.

Art. 192. MENTAL EXERCISES.

4. He will walk $3\frac{1}{5}$ miles in 1 hour, and in $3\frac{1}{2}$ hours he will walk $11\frac{1}{5}$ miles.

5. One pound will cost 8 cents, and $4\frac{1}{2}$ pounds cost 36 cents.

6. It sailed 5 miles in 1 hour, and in $4\frac{3}{5}$ hours it sailed 23 miles

7. She earns $\$\frac{2}{3}$ in a day, and in $10\frac{1}{2}$ days she will earn $7.

Art. 192. WRITTEN EXERCISES.

8. $\frac{1}{9}\times\$100\frac{4}{5}\times14\frac{13}{14}=\frac{1}{9}\times\frac{504}{5}\times\frac{209}{14}=\$167\frac{1}{5}$.

9. $\frac{1}{12}\times\$11\frac{1}{4}\times15\frac{14}{15}=\frac{1}{12}\times\frac{45}{4}\times\frac{239}{15}=\$14\frac{15}{16}$.

10. $\frac{1}{17}\times\$33\frac{3}{4}\times18\frac{16}{18}=\frac{1}{17}\times\frac{135}{4}\times\frac{340}{18}=\$37\frac{1}{2}$.

11. Find the cost of 1 acre, add $4, and take $\frac{18}{19}$ of the sum; which gives $\$92\frac{4}{7}$.

12. Find the cost of 1 ton, subtract $\$2\frac{1}{2}$, and take $\frac{18}{25}$ of the difference; which gives $15.20.

Art. 193. MENTAL EXERCISES.

8. 1 yard will cost $\$1\frac{3}{7}$, and $8\frac{3}{4}$ yards will cost $\$12\frac{1}{2}$.

9. 1 apple is worth $2\frac{2}{3}$ cents, and for $53\frac{1}{3}$ cents you can get as many apples as $2\frac{2}{3}$ is contained times in $53\frac{1}{3}$, or 20 apples.

10. 1 barrel costs $\frac{16}{3}$ of $\$1\frac{1}{2}$, or $8, and $7\frac{1}{2}$ barrels cost $60.

Art. 193. WRITTEN EXERCISES.

7. $12\frac{3}{8}=\frac{99}{8}$; $115\frac{1}{2}=\frac{231}{2}$; the number of pigs equals $\frac{231}{2}\times\frac{8}{99}\times9=84$.

9. $6\frac{3}{5}=\frac{33}{5}$; $.44\frac{4}{9}=\frac{4.00}{9}$; $2\frac{2}{7}=\frac{16}{7}$; then the cost is $\$\frac{4.00}{9}\times\frac{7}{16}\times\frac{33}{5}$ which equals $\$1.28\frac{1}{3}$.

11. $19\frac{3}{5}=\frac{98}{5}$; $42\frac{6}{7}=\frac{300}{7}$; $357\frac{1}{7}=\frac{2500}{7}$; $\frac{2500}{7}\times\frac{7}{300}\times\frac{98}{5}=163\frac{1}{3}$ tons.

NOTE.—In practice we can readily form the compound fraction without going through the analysis. We write the term like the answer, invert the one associated with it, and place the other term before the one inverted.

18. $24\frac{3}{4}=\frac{99}{4}$; $25\frac{2}{3}=\frac{77}{3}$; $50\frac{5}{9}=\frac{455}{9}$; $\$\frac{99}{4}\times\frac{455}{9}\times\frac{3}{77}=\$48\frac{3}{4}$.

19. $582\frac{6}{7}=\frac{4080}{7}$; $13\frac{5}{7}=\frac{96}{7}$; $1416\frac{2}{3}=\frac{4250}{3}$; $\frac{96}{7}\times\frac{4250}{3}\times\frac{7}{4080}=33\frac{1}{3}$.

20. $26\frac{8}{11}=\frac{294}{11}$; $6\frac{8}{15}=\frac{98}{15}$; $46\frac{1}{5}=\frac{231}{5}$; $\frac{294}{11}\times\frac{231}{5}\times\frac{15}{98}=189$.

21. $7\frac{2}{9}=\frac{65}{9}$; $12\frac{2}{15}=\frac{182}{15}$; $19\frac{1}{21}=\frac{400}{21}$; $\frac{182}{15}\times\frac{400}{21}\times\frac{9}{65}=32$.

Art. 194. MENTAL EXERCISES.

4. $16 is $\frac{2}{3}$ of $\frac{3}{5}$ or $\frac{2}{5}$; hence he had at first $40.

5 $\frac{2}{5}+\frac{2}{6}=\frac{11}{15}$, hence 800 men were $\frac{4}{15}$ of the army, and the army consisted of 3000 men.

6. A number plus $\frac{1}{2}$ of the number, minus $\frac{2}{3}$ of the number, equals $\frac{5}{6}$ of the number, which equals 50, hence the number is 60.

7. $\frac{2}{3}$ of 27=18, which is 4 years more than $\frac{2}{3}$ of his wife's age, hence $\frac{2}{3}$ of his wife's age is 14 years, and her age was 21 years.

8 $\frac{1}{4}+\frac{1}{6}=\frac{5}{12}$; $\frac{12}{12}-\frac{5}{12}=\frac{7}{12}$; 20 cents equals $\frac{2}{7}$ of $\frac{7}{12}$, or $\frac{1}{6}$ of his money, hence his money was $1.20.

9 The remainder was $20 less than he stole, hence $20 was what he spent ; but he spent $\frac{2}{3}$ of $\frac{3}{5}$, or $\frac{2}{5}$ of Harry's money, hence $20 was $\frac{2}{5}$ of Harry's money, and his money was $50.

Art. 194. WRITTEN EXERCISES.

5. There first remained $\frac{1}{4}$; he paid $\frac{3}{5}$ of this, then there remained $\frac{2}{5}$ of $\frac{1}{4}=\frac{1}{10}=4671$, hence $\frac{10}{10}=46710$.

6. $\frac{1}{4}+\frac{1}{3}=\frac{7}{12}$, hence the son received $\frac{5}{12}$, which equals $6720; $\frac{1}{12}$=$1344 ; $\frac{3}{12}$, daughter's share=$4032 ; $\frac{4}{12}$, widow's =$5376.

7. $\frac{1}{3}+\frac{1}{4}=\frac{7}{12}$; then $\frac{12}{12}-\frac{7}{12}$, or $\frac{5}{12}=100$, $\frac{1}{12}=20$, $\frac{12}{12}=240$.

8. He had $\frac{1}{3}$ of the string remaining, $\frac{3}{4}-\frac{1}{3}=\frac{5}{12}$, which equals $53\frac{3}{4}$ ft.; $\frac{1}{12}=\frac{1}{5}$ of $53\frac{3}{4}=10\frac{3}{4}$; $\frac{12}{12}=129$ ft.

Pages 125-6. MENTAL EXERCISES.

2. $$6\frac{2}{3}\div4=\$1\frac{2}{3}$.

11. $\frac{1}{2}+\frac{1}{3}=\frac{5}{6}$; $\frac{6}{6}-\frac{5}{6}=\frac{1}{6}$.

15. The butter cost 150 cents, and she received 24 yards of calico.

20. Since 60 cents is $\frac{5}{8}$ of what he then had, he had 96 cents, and he had at first 96—60 cents, or 36 cents.

21. 20 cents equals $\frac{4}{5}$ of what Henry had at first, hence he had at first 25 cents ; 20 cents is $\frac{1}{2}$ of what his sister now has, hence she had at first 20 cents.

22. She had remaining $\frac{1}{5}$ of 50, or 10 pins, and she found $\frac{2}{5}$ of 10 or 4 ; hence she then had 10+4, or 14 pins.

23. $\frac{5}{6}$ of 48=40, which is 4 times what he had left; he had 10 left, and 48+10, or 58 at first.

24. If 4 horses eat the hay in 8 weeks, one horse would require 32 weeks, and 5 horses would require $\frac{1}{5}$ of 32, or $6\frac{2}{5}$ weeks.

25. The number+$\frac{1}{2}$ of the number+$\frac{1}{3}$ of the number=$\frac{11}{6}$ of the number; since 55 is $\frac{11}{6}$ of her number, she has 30 roses.

26. $\frac{1}{2}+\frac{2}{3}=\frac{7}{6}$; $\frac{7}{6}$ of $24=$28, which is 4 times the cost of the chain, hence the chain cost $7.

27. He had remaining $\frac{1}{4}$ of 36, or 9 marbles ; $\frac{5}{6}$ of 36 is 30, hence he had 30+9, or 39 marbles.

28. The cost of the horse was \$100; \$100+\$60=\$160, which is 5 times the cost of the sleigh; hence the sleigh cost \$32.

29. $\frac{4}{10}$ of 40=16, number of apple-trees; 40—16=24; $\frac{1}{2}$ of 24=12, number of pear and peach trees.

30. $\frac{1}{4}+\frac{1}{5}=\frac{9}{20}$, hence $\frac{11}{20}$ of his age equals 22 years, his age is 40 years and his uncle's 50 years.

31. There were 5 schoolmates; hence the candies were to be divided into 5+1 or 6 equal parts; $\frac{1}{6}$ of $\frac{2}{5}=\frac{1}{15}$.

32. $\frac{1}{5}+\frac{1}{2}=\frac{7}{10}$, which equals 14 marbles, hence he had at first 20 marbles.

33. $14 \div 3\frac{1}{2}=4$, the number of companions.

34. The potatoes were worth \$5, and it required $12\frac{1}{2}$ dozen eggs to pay for them.

35. 10 boxes will cost 3 times as much as $3\frac{1}{3}$ boxes, or \$$15\frac{3}{4}$.

36. $\frac{4}{5}$ of \$50=\$40, which is 4 times the cost of her bonnet, and $\frac{2}{3}$ of the cost of her cloak, hence the bonnet cost \$10, and the cloak \$60.

37. She had remaining $\frac{1}{4}$ of her money, and found $\frac{2}{3}$ of $\frac{3}{4}$, or $\frac{1}{2}$, of her money, hence she then had $\frac{3}{4}$, which was \$30; therefore at first she had \$40.

38. He returned $\frac{1}{4}$ of $\frac{2}{3}$, or $\frac{1}{6}$, which was \$20; hence she had \$120.

39. It arose $\frac{1}{3}$ of $\frac{1}{2}$, or $\frac{1}{6}$; since it fell $\frac{1}{4}$, the distance it did not fall was $\frac{3}{4}$ of $\frac{1}{6}$, or $\frac{1}{8}$; $\frac{1}{2}+\frac{1}{8}=\frac{5}{8}$ of the distance.

Pages 127-9. WRITTEN EXERCISES.

These problems, from the 1st to the 25th, are simple applications of the rules of fractions, and are readily solved. In the 25th, 26th, 27th, and 28th, we take the product of the two numbers given. When both terms are mixed numbers, we may multiply as they are given or reduce both to improper fractions, and then multiply.

14. $\frac{7}{8}$ of $3\frac{3}{7}=3$; $\frac{3}{4}$ of $\frac{16}{21}$ of $9\frac{3}{4}=5\frac{4}{7}$; $5\frac{4}{7}-3=2\frac{4}{7}$.

15. $3\frac{3}{7}=\frac{24}{7}$; $\frac{3}{4}$ of $\frac{24}{7}\times\frac{3}{4}\times\frac{7}{8}\times\frac{16}{21}\times\frac{16}{27}=\frac{16}{21}$.

16. $\frac{8}{9}\times\frac{27}{40}\times\frac{29}{5}\times\frac{4}{3}\times\frac{9}{2}\times\frac{12}{16}=15\frac{33}{50}$.

17. $8\frac{4}{9}\div16\frac{8}{9}=\frac{76}{9}\times\frac{9}{152}=\frac{1}{2}$; $\frac{1}{2}$ of $\frac{4}{5}=\frac{2}{5}$; $\frac{1}{2}+\frac{2}{5}=\frac{9}{10}$.

18. $\frac{3\frac{1}{2}}{7}=\frac{1}{2}$; $\frac{4\frac{1}{3}}{17\frac{1}{3}}=\frac{1}{4}$; $\frac{10}{26\frac{1}{4}}=10\times\frac{4}{105}=\frac{8}{21}$; $\frac{1}{2}+\frac{1}{4}+\frac{8}{21}=\frac{42}{84}+\frac{21}{84}+\frac{32}{84}=1\frac{11}{84}$.

19. $\frac{45}{270}=\frac{1}{6}$; $\frac{8\frac{1}{3}}{25}=\frac{1}{3}$; $\frac{1}{3}-\frac{1}{6}=\frac{1}{6}$.

21. $15\frac{\frac{4}{5}}{16}=15\frac{1}{20}=\frac{301}{20}$; $\frac{2}{7}$ of $\frac{21}{38}\times\frac{5}{8}$ of $\frac{301}{20}=1\frac{295}{608}$.

22. $\frac{1}{4}-\frac{1}{9}=\frac{5}{36}$; $\frac{1}{2}+\frac{1}{3}=\frac{5}{6}$; $\frac{5}{36}\times\frac{6}{5}=\frac{1}{6}$; $\frac{1}{6}+\frac{1}{2}=\frac{2}{3}$; $\frac{2}{3}\times12\frac{1}{7}=8\frac{2}{21}$.

23. $3\frac{2}{3}=\frac{11}{3}$; $\frac{1}{2}$ of $9\frac{1}{2}\times\frac{1}{4}=\frac{19}{16}$; $\frac{11}{3}\times\frac{16}{19}=3\frac{5}{57}$.

24. $\frac{\cancel{3}}{\cancel{4}}$ of $\frac{\overset{2}{\cancel{8}}}{\cancel{9}}$ of $\frac{37}{\underset{4}{\cancel{12}}}\times\frac{\cancel{7}}{1}$ of $\frac{\overset{3}{\cancel{15}}}{\underset{2}{\cancel{14}}}$ of $\frac{\overset{3}{\cancel{27}}}{\underset{2}{\cancel{10}}}=41\frac{5}{8}$.

25. $45\frac{3}{4}=\frac{183}{4}$; $12\frac{1}{2}=\frac{25}{2}$; $\frac{183}{4}\times\$.\frac{25}{2}=\$5.71\frac{7}{8}$.

33. $2\frac{1}{2}=\frac{5}{2}$; $57\frac{3}{4}=\frac{231}{4}$; $\$30\times\frac{2}{5}\times\frac{231}{4}=\$693$.

36. $725\times\frac{13}{5}=145\times13$; $\frac{26}{7}$ C's$=145\times13$, $\frac{1}{7}$ C's$=\frac{145\times13}{26}$ $=\frac{145}{2}$, and C's$=\frac{145}{2}\times7=\frac{1015}{2}=507\frac{1}{2}$, *Ans.*

37. Add 4 to both terms and we have $\frac{5+4}{6+4}=\frac{9}{10}$, and $\frac{9}{10}$ is more than $\frac{5}{6}$; hence the fraction will be increased.

38. Subtract 4 from both terms and we have $\frac{5-4}{6-4}=\frac{1}{2}$, and $\frac{1}{2}$ is less than $\frac{5}{6}$; hence the fraction will be diminished.

39. Add 4 to both terms and we have $\frac{10}{9}$, which is less than $\frac{6}{5}$; subtract 4 from both terms, and we have $\frac{2}{1}$, which is greater than $\frac{6}{5}$.

40. He sold $\frac{3}{5}$; hence there will remain $\frac{2}{5}$, which is worth $\frac{2}{5}$ of $6500=$2600. Selling $\frac{5}{7}$ of the remainder there will remain $\frac{2}{7}$, which is worth $\frac{2}{7}$ of $2600=$742$\frac{6}{7}$.

41. $12.36=$\frac{3}{5}$ of his earnings; hence his earnings equal $20.60; and his daily earnings equal $20.60÷25$\frac{3}{4}$= 80 cts.

42. $12\frac{3}{4}=\frac{51}{4}$; $18\frac{3}{4}=\frac{75}{4}$; $30\times\frac{51}{4}\div\frac{75}{4}=30\times\frac{51}{4}\times\frac{4}{75}=20\frac{2}{5}$.

43. The gain $=\frac{1}{19}$ of $10260=$540; $540÷$3=180.

44. After selling $\frac{1}{4}$ there remained $\frac{3}{4}$ of 100=75; selling $\frac{2}{5}$ of this there remained $\frac{3}{5}$ of 75=45; 45×25$\frac{3}{4}$=11.58\frac{3}{4}$.

45. $36\frac{3}{4}=\frac{147}{4}$; $33\frac{3}{5}=\frac{168}{5}$; $63\times\frac{4}{147}\times\frac{168}{5}=57\frac{3}{5}$.

46. $25\frac{1}{3}-5\frac{1}{7}=20\frac{4}{21}=\frac{424}{21}$; $289\frac{1}{11}=\frac{3180}{11}$; $\frac{3180}{11}\times\frac{21}{424}=\frac{315}{22}$ $=14\frac{7}{22}$ hours.

47. $\frac{1}{3}+\frac{1}{4}+\frac{1}{12}=\frac{8}{12}=\frac{2}{3}$; hence he has $\frac{1}{3}$ remaining, which equals $540, and the whole amount equals 3 times *$540, or* $1620.

48. $\frac{4}{7}$ of $\frac{3}{8}=\frac{3}{14}$; $5\frac{1}{14}-4\frac{51}{56}=\frac{9}{56}$; $\frac{3}{14}\times\frac{56}{9}=\frac{4}{3}$; $\frac{5}{11}$ of $\frac{18}{15}=\frac{18}{33}$; $7\frac{15}{22}-6\frac{1}{2}=1\frac{2}{11}$; $\frac{18}{33}\times\frac{11}{18}=\frac{1}{3}$; $\frac{4}{3}-\frac{1}{3}=\frac{3}{3}=1$.

49. $1+\frac{1}{5}=\frac{6}{5}$; $1-\frac{1}{5}=\frac{4}{5}$; $1\times\frac{1}{5}=\frac{1}{5}$; $1\div\frac{1}{5}=5$; $\frac{6}{5}\times\frac{5}{4}\times5\times5=37\frac{1}{2}$.

50. $6\frac{1}{4}+5\frac{1}{2}=11\frac{3}{4}$; $6\frac{1}{4}-5\frac{1}{2}=\frac{3}{4}$; $\frac{47}{4}\times\frac{4}{3}=15\frac{2}{3}$; $\frac{6\frac{1}{4}\times5\frac{1}{2}}{6\frac{1}{4}\div5\frac{1}{2}}=\frac{25}{4}\times\frac{11}{2}\times\frac{4}{25}\times\frac{11}{2}=30\frac{1}{4}$; $\frac{7\frac{1}{2}}{3}=2\frac{1}{2}$; $15\frac{2}{3}+30\frac{1}{4}-2\frac{1}{2}=43\frac{5}{12}$.

51. $\frac{1}{3}+\frac{3}{10}=\frac{19}{30}$; $6\frac{1}{3}=\frac{19}{3}$; $\frac{19}{30}\times\frac{3}{19}=\frac{1}{10}$; $\frac{40}{7}\times\frac{9}{40}=\frac{9}{7}$; $\frac{1}{10}+\frac{9}{7}=\frac{97}{70}$; $\frac{97}{70}\times\frac{1}{11}\times\frac{77}{5}\times\frac{12}{97}=\frac{6}{25}$.

52. $\frac{1-\frac{1}{5}}{2}=\frac{2}{5}$; $\frac{2-\frac{1}{5}}{3}=\frac{3}{5}$; $\frac{3-\frac{1}{5}}{4}=\frac{7}{10}$; $\frac{4-\frac{1}{5}}{5}=\frac{19}{25}$; $\frac{2}{5}\times\frac{3}{5}\times\frac{7}{10}\times\frac{25}{19}=\frac{21}{95}$.

DECIMAL FRACTIONS.

Much of the difficulty which pupils experience in decimals, arises from their not being familiar with the Decimal Notation and Numeration; hence they should be carefully drilled upon the preliminary exercises until the teacher is certain that they are fully understood.

Page 132. EXERCISES IN NUMERATION.

NOTE.—These are easily read by either rule. Another way of reading is by *numerical periods*. Thus, .25678304 may be read as 25 hundredths, 678 hundred thousandths, 304 hundred millionths; also, .035400006 may be read 3 hundredths, 54 ten thousandths, 6 billionths. Pupils may *point off*, if they wish, as in whole numbers. Thus, .25,678,304 and .035,400,006.

Page 133. EXERCISES IN NOTATION.

8.	500.025.	13.	.04076.	17.	35000.000008.
10.	.0709.	14.	.00969.	18.	.0009307.
11.	300.0078.	15.	.200003.	19.	.00018001.
12.	.56007.	16.	.056008.	20.	2000000.00006009.

REDUCTION OF DECIMALS.

Art. 205. Page 135.

18. $\frac{8\frac{1}{3}}{10}=\frac{25}{30}=\frac{5}{6}$.

17. $\$.16\frac{2}{3}=\frac{16\frac{2}{3}}{100}=\frac{50}{300}=\$\frac{1}{6}$.

19. $12.18\frac{3}{4} = 12\frac{18\frac{3}{4}}{100} = 12\frac{75}{400} = 12\frac{3}{16}$.

20. $\$6.66\frac{2}{3} = 6\frac{66\frac{2}{3}}{100} = 6\frac{200}{300} = \$6\frac{2}{3}$.

ADDITION OF DECIMALS.

Art. 207. WRITTEN EXERCISES.

6.	8.	9.	10.
\$25.75	187.005	798.0009	.3
37.20	49.00009	.000017	.065
28.37½	1876.000245	.0180098	.00425
50.06¼	.0187	.0006795	.0003125
15.37½	.0000999	798.0196063	.000062
57.37½	2112.0241349		.3696245
15.87½			
23.87½			
\$253.88¾			

SUBTRACTION OF DECIMALS.

Art. 208. WRITTEN EXERCISES.

When there are not as many places in the minuend as in the subtrahend, let them be supplied with ciphers.

6.	7.	8.	9.
2.070000	.30000000	1.001	2.5000000000
1.432765	.00000003	.010001	.0025000025
.637235	.29999997	.990999	2.4974999975

MULTIPLICATION OF DECIMALS.

Art. 209. WRITTEN EXERCISES.

Pupils should be careful in pointing off the decimal places in the product; bearing in mind that ciphers must be prefixed when needed to make as many places in the product as there are in both multiplier and multiplicand.

12. $9.5 \times .0875 \times 10 = 8.3125$. | **13.** $.5 \times \frac{7}{\not{1}\not{1}} \times \overset{.005}{.\not{0}\not{5}\not{5}} = .0175$.

14. $\overset{.01}{.\not{0}\not{7}} \times \frac{5}{\not{6}} \times 300 \times \frac{\overset{.11}{.\not{6}\not{6}}}{\not{7}} = 1.65$.

15. $\$25.6875 \times .\frac{16}{3} = \$1.37$; $\$15 \times 6.0325 = \$90.4875$; $\$1.37$ $\$90.4875 = \$91.8575$.

16. $200+.02-\frac{1}{2}=199.52$; $199.52\times.8\frac{1}{4}=164.604$; $.127\times\frac{3}{4}$ of $7.2=.6858$; $.825-.6858=.1392$; $164.604+.1392=164.7432$.

17. $.01\times.001=.00001$; $.00001+.1=.10001$.

18. $.1\times.1=.01$; $100\times.01=1$; $1000000\times.000001=1$.

DIVISION OF DECIMALS.

The pupil should always see that the dividend contains at least as many decimal places as the divisor, before beginning the division. When there is a deficiency, ciphers should be annexed to the dividend. Let the pupils be careful in placing the decimal point properly.

Art. 210. WRITTEN EXERCISES.

10.

```
32.185)195.388698(6.0708
       193110
         227869
         225295
           257480
           257480
```

11.

```
185.79321)1678.54300(9.03446+
          167213889
              64041100
              55737963
               83031370
               74317284
                87140860
                74317284
                12823576
```

12.

```
.026).065(2.5
      52
      130
      130
```

13.

```
.025).375(15
      25
      125
      125
```

14.

```
04).008
      .2
```

15.

```
.06).012
      .2
```

16.

```
2.5).0040(.0016
      25
      150
      150
```

17.

```
125)1.000(8
    1000
```

18.

```
015).510(34
      45
      60
      60
```

20.

```
25).00625(.00025
     50
     125
     125
```

21.

```
.00625)25.00000(4000
       25.00
          000
```

22. $2.04 \div 17 = .12$; $47 \div 200 = .235$; $.235 \times 5000 = 1175$; $1175 + .12 - \frac{7}{8} = 1174.245$.

23. $789 - .789 = 788.211$; $.75 - .075 = .675$; $.675 \times .75$ of $8 = 4.05$; $788.211 \div 4.05 = 194.62$.

24. $45 \times .181 = 8.145$; $3.5 - \dfrac{3.43}{7} = 3.01$; $3.6 \times .3\frac{1}{3} \times \dfrac{1}{3.01} = .3986\frac{214}{301}$; $8.145 + .3986\frac{214}{301} = 8.5436\frac{214}{301}$.

25. $\$347.84 \div \$10.87 = 32$; $.0025 + .0175 = .02$; $32 \times .02 \times 50 = 32$.

26. $\$1080 \times 3.27 \times \dfrac{1}{\$10.90} = 324$; $\$790 \div \$3.95 = 200$; $324 - 200 = 124$.

MISCELLANEOUS EXAMPLES.

Pages 141-143.

2. $\dfrac{.2}{2.7} = \frac{2}{10} \times \frac{10}{27} = \frac{2}{27}$; $\dfrac{\frac{1}{2}}{5.4} = \frac{1}{2} \times \frac{10}{54} = \frac{5}{54}$; $11\dfrac{\frac{1}{2}}{5.4} = 11\frac{5}{54}$; $\frac{2}{27} + 11\frac{5}{54} + 2\frac{7}{45} + \frac{1}{10} = 13\frac{19}{45}$.

3. $\dfrac{.4}{5} = \frac{4}{10} \times \frac{1}{5} = \frac{2}{25}$; $2\frac{5}{6} \div 5\frac{2}{3} = \frac{17}{6} \times \frac{3}{17} = \frac{1}{2}$; $2\frac{4}{9} \div 1\frac{7}{18} = \frac{22}{9} \times \frac{18}{25} = \frac{44}{25} = 1\frac{19}{25}$; $\frac{21}{48} = \frac{7}{16}$; $\frac{2}{25} + \frac{1}{2} + \frac{7}{16} + 1\frac{19}{25} = 2\frac{311}{400}$.

5. $28\dfrac{\frac{1}{5}}{.7} = \frac{1}{5} \times \frac{10}{7} = \frac{2}{7}$; $28\frac{2}{7} = \frac{198}{7}$; $13\frac{22}{35} = \frac{477}{35}$; $\frac{477}{35} \div \frac{198}{7} = \frac{477}{35} \times \frac{7}{198} = \frac{53}{110}$.

6. $\frac{7}{8} \times \frac{10}{2} = \frac{35}{8}$; $1.25 \times .875 \times \frac{321}{35} \times .8 \times \frac{35}{8} \times 8.75 = 307\frac{53}{256}$.

7. $118\frac{1}{4} \div .04\frac{1}{2} = \frac{473}{4} \times \frac{200}{9} = 2627\frac{7}{9}$; $2.4001\frac{3}{5} = 2.40016$; $1.25 \times \frac{4}{25} = .2$; $2.40016 \div 1.562 = 1.53\frac{515}{781}$.

8. $\frac{2}{3} \times \frac{1}{27} = \frac{2}{81}$; $14\frac{2}{81} = \frac{1136}{81}$; $\frac{7}{4} \times \frac{2}{27} = \frac{7}{54}$; $11\frac{7}{54} = \frac{601}{54}$; $\frac{1136}{81} \times \frac{54}{601} = 1\frac{469}{1803}$.

9. $240\frac{3}{4} = \frac{963}{4}$; $24\frac{1}{2} \times \frac{1}{28} = \frac{7}{8}$; £$\frac{963}{4} \times \frac{4}{3} \times \frac{8}{7} \times \frac{7}{5} \times \frac{5}{9} =$ £$285\frac{1}{3}$.

12. $8\frac{1}{2} \times \frac{1}{36} = \frac{17}{72}$; $\frac{1}{4} + \frac{17}{72} + \frac{3}{8} + \frac{1}{2} = \frac{49}{36}$; $6.2\frac{1}{2} = 6\frac{1}{4} = \frac{25}{4}$; $\frac{49}{36} \times \frac{25}{4} = 8\frac{73}{144}$.

13. $8\frac{3}{4} \div \frac{2}{5} = \frac{35}{4} \times \frac{5}{2} = \frac{175}{8}$; $\frac{5}{8}$ of $\frac{175}{8} = \frac{875}{64}$; $\frac{3}{7}$ of $\$12 = \frac{36}{7}$; $\frac{875}{64} - \frac{36}{7} = \frac{3821}{448}$; $\frac{3821}{448} \times \frac{7}{5} = 11\frac{301}{320}$.

14. $\dfrac{3\frac{1}{2}}{14} = \frac{1}{4}$; $.5 = \frac{1}{2}$; $\frac{1}{2} + \frac{1}{4} = \frac{3}{4}$; $\dfrac{8\frac{1}{2}}{17} = \frac{1}{2}$; $\dfrac{10}{26\frac{2}{3}} = 10 \times \frac{3}{80} = \frac{3}{8}$; $\frac{1}{2} - \frac{3}{8} = \frac{1}{8}$; $\frac{3}{4} \times \frac{1}{8} = \frac{3}{32}$.

15. $\frac{62\frac{1}{2}}{1000}=\frac{1}{16}$; $\frac{1}{16}\times.000025\times\frac{1}{.00125}=.00125.$

16. $\frac{3}{8}$ of $\frac{5}{9}$ of $2=\frac{5}{12}$; $\frac{4}{9}\times\frac{12}{5}=\frac{16}{15}=1\frac{1}{15}$.

18. The number equals $\frac{2}{3}$ of $\frac{9}{11}$ of $27\frac{1}{2}$, divided by $\frac{4}{9}$ of $\frac{18}{17}$ of $5\frac{1}{2}$, which, inverting the divisor, becomes $\frac{2}{3}\times\frac{9}{11}\times\frac{55}{2}\times\frac{9}{4}\times\frac{17}{18}\times\frac{2}{11}=8\frac{7}{286}$.

19. $.006+.000006=.006006$; $.006-.000006=.005994$; $.006006\div.005994=1.002002+$.

20. $\frac{2}{11}+\frac{9}{5}+\frac{1}{8}=2\frac{47}{440}$; $\frac{4}{13}$ of $\frac{65}{8}$ of $\frac{1}{7}=\frac{5}{14}$; $\frac{5}{14}-\frac{7}{35}=\frac{11}{70}$; $2\frac{47}{440}-\frac{11}{70}=1\frac{585}{616}$.

21. The number equals the product of the two given numbers; $5\frac{1}{2}\div1\frac{3}{8}=\frac{11}{2}\times\frac{8}{11}=4$; $\frac{3}{8}$ of $\frac{8}{3}$ of $4=4$; $1\frac{1}{2}\div10=\frac{3}{2}\times\frac{1}{10}=\frac{3}{20}$; $\frac{20}{3}$ of $\frac{3}{20}$ of $6=6$; $4\times6=24$.

22. $\frac{1}{5}$ of $\frac{10}{9}$ of \$$\frac{265}{8}$=\$$58\frac{8}{9}$; \$$225\frac{5}{8}$+\$$58\frac{8}{9}$—\$$186\frac{5}{8}$=\$$97\frac{8}{9}$.

26. $41.25\times31.5=1299.375$; $1500-1299.375=200.625$ gal.

28. $1086\div20.25=53$ bins and 12.75 bushels remaining.

29. $.37\frac{1}{2}=\frac{3}{8}$; $.61\frac{1}{2}=\frac{5}{8}$; $\frac{3}{8}$ of 4320 acres=1620 acres; $\frac{5}{8}$ of 4320 acres=2700 acres.

31. \$76.25 × 27.25 = \$2077.8125; \$4000 — \$2077.8125 = \$1922.1875; \$1922.1875÷85.75=$22.41\frac{212}{343}$; 27.25+$22.41\frac{212}{343}=49.66\frac{212}{343}$ acres.

32. $\frac{1}{3}$ of 345.75=115.25; \$17.75—\$16.25=\$1.50; \$1.50×115.25=\$$172.87\frac{1}{2}$.

33. He sold .15+.25=.40, and kept $\frac{100}{100}-\frac{40}{100}=\frac{60}{100}=\frac{3}{5}$, which equals 572.85; then $\frac{5}{5}=954.75$.

34. He spends .12+.25+.45=.82; there remains .18, which equals \$284.76; his income was \$284.76÷.18=\$1582.

35. 91.25 bu., at \$1.40, cost \$127.75; 85 bu., at \$1.25, cost \$106.25; both are worth \$234; hence he must give $234\div5.12\frac{1}{2}=45.66$ cords, nearly.

36. Number of revolutions of fore wheel equals 5280÷12.75=414.117+; number of revolutions of hind wheel equals 5280÷14.25=370.526+; 414.117—370.526=43.591.

37. He would lose $.25\times.45\frac{1}{2}\times$\$25000=\$2843.75.

38. $\frac{1}{3}$ of \$6210=\$2070; 2070÷1.25=1656 bu. of wheat; $\frac{1}{4}$ of \$6210=\$1552.50; \$1552.50÷\$0.75=2070 bu. of

corn; $\$2070+\$1552.50=\$3622.50$; $\$6210-\$3622.50=\$2587.50$; $\$2587.50\div\$1.12\frac{1}{2}=2300$ bu. of rye.

UNITED STATES MONEY.

FUNDAMENTAL OPERATIONS.

Art. 220. Pages 146-8.

1. $\$62\frac{1}{2}=\$62.50$; $62\frac{1}{2}$ cents$=\$0.625$; the sum of these is $\$63.12\frac{1}{2}$.
2. 25 cents and 5 mills$=\$.255$; $\$25.000-\$.255=\$24.745$.
3. $\$18\frac{3}{4}=\$18.75$; $18\frac{3}{4}$ dimes$=\$1.875$; $18\frac{1}{2}$ cts.$=\$0.185$; 18 mills$=\$0.018$; and the sum of these is $\$20.828$.
4. $\$1.000-\$.001=\$.999$; 505 cents$=\$5.05$; $\$505-\$5.05=\$499.95$.
5. $\$6\frac{1}{2}=\$6.50$; $6\frac{1}{2}$ cents$=\$.065$; $6\frac{1}{2}$ dimes$=\$.65$; $\$6.50-\$.065+\$.65=\$7.085$.
9. $\$36.25\div5=\$7.25$; $\$7.25\times17=\$123.25$.
13. $\$16.75\div\$.12=139\frac{7}{12}$; $\$48.00\div\$.60=80$; $18\frac{3}{4}$ dimes$=\$1.875$; $\$1.875\div\$.015=125$.
15. Find the sum of the cost of all and subtract it from $15, and we have $\$0.37\frac{1}{2}$.
16. $63\times12=756$; $50-42\frac{1}{2}=7\frac{1}{2}$; $756\times.07\frac{1}{2}=\$56.70$, *Ans.*
17. $\$.06\frac{1}{4}\times3=\$.18\frac{3}{4}$; $\$.87\times7=\$6.09$; $\$6.09+\$.18\frac{3}{4}=\$6.27\frac{3}{4}$; $\$10-\$6.27\frac{3}{4}=\$3.72\frac{1}{4}$; but she would not receive the fraction; hence her change would be $3.72.
19. $\$7.25\times3=\$21.75$; $\$5.25\times2=\$10.50$; $\$4.65\times3=\$13.95$; $\$1.75\times45=\$78.75$; $\$21.75+\$10.50+\$13.95+78.75=\$124.95$.
20. Gain on 1 gallon$=\$1.37\frac{1}{2}-\$1.12\frac{1}{2}=\$.25$; whole gain$=\$.25\times31.5\times8=\$63$.
21. $\$250+\$37.50=\$287.50$; $\$287.50\div\$5.75=50$ tons.
22. $24-10=14$; $\$.05\times14=\$.70$; $\$.70+\$.40=\$1.10$.
23. $60¢\times420=\$252$; $43¢\times120=\$51.60$; $\$252-\$51.60=\$200.40$; $\$200.40\div\$1.67=120$.

COMMERCIAL TRANSACTIONS.

Art. 226. Case I.

4. $33\frac{1}{3}¢=\$\frac{1}{3}$; $\$\frac{1}{3}\times40=\$13.33\frac{1}{3}$; $12\frac{1}{2}¢=\$\frac{1}{8}$; $\$\frac{1}{8}\times10=\$1.25$; $\$13.33\frac{1}{3}+\$1.25=\$14.58\frac{1}{3}$.

5. $\$1.37\frac{1}{2}=\$1\frac{1}{2}-\$\frac{1}{8}$; $\$1\frac{1}{2}\times 20=\$30$; $\$\frac{1}{8}\times 20=\$2\frac{1}{2}$; $\$30-\$2.50=\$27.50$; $10¢=\$\frac{1}{10}$; $\$\frac{1}{10}\times 20=\$2$; $25¢=\$\frac{1}{4}$; $\$\frac{1}{4}\times 3=\$\frac{3}{4}=\$.75$; $\$27.50+\$2+\$.75=\$30.25$.

Art. 227.. Case II.

6. $\$4.50\times 62,560=\$281.52$.

7. $560\times 1120=627200$; $627200\times \$.45=\$282.24$.

8. Profit ₩ M. = $\$7.50-\$5.75=\$1.75$; $\$1.75\times 43,780=\$76.61\frac{1}{2}$.

Art. 228. Case III.

4. $320\times 850=272,000$; $\$340\div 272=\$1.25$.

5. $\$.12-\$.03=\$.09$; $\$.09\div 24\times 1000=\$3.75$.

Art. 229. Case IV.

5. $\$93.215\div 7240=\$.012875$; $\$.012875\times 2000=\$25.75$.

6. $\$20.88\div 5760=\$.003625$; $\$.003625\times 2000=\$7.25$.

7. $\$3.75\div 2=\$1.875$; $\$1.875\times 34,761=\$65.176875$; $\$2.50\div 2=\$1.25$; $\$1.25\times 97,486=\$121.8575$; $\$65.176875+\$121.8575=\$187.034375$.

8. $\$3.60\div 2=\$1.80$; $\$1.80\times 36,850=\$66.33$; $\$.22\frac{1}{2}\times 36,850=\$82.9125$; $\$82.9125-\$66.33=\$16.5825$.

BILLS AND ACCOUNTS.

Art. 235. Page 153.

BALTIMORE, *July* 15, 1876.

JOHN B. WYLIE & Co.,

Bought of MACNEIL, WALCOTT & CO.

Qty.		Article	Price	$	¢
24	Prs.	Men's French Calf Boots, @	$10.	240	
65	"	Women's Enameled "	1.87½	121	87½
75	"	" Fox'd Gaiters,	1.50	112	50
88	"	Boys' Kip Boots,	2.50	220	00
110	"	" Brogans,	1.25	137	50
90	"	Misses' Rubber Shoes,	75	67	50
60	"	Women's Arctics,	2.25	135	00
				1034	37½
		Less ⅕,		206	87½
				827	50

Rec'd payment,

MACNEIL, WALCOTT & CO.

WILMINGTON, DEL., *April* 27, 1876.

MR. JAMES LANE,

To A. B. HAYES, DR.

To Setting Boiler and Excavating,		100	00
" 13½ Days' Work of Bricklayer,	@$4	54	00
" 5½ " " " Laborer,	1.12½	6	18¾
" 1 Load Sand,		2	50
" 15 Bushels Lime,	.38	5	70
" 500 Dark Stretchers,	@$14 ⅌ M	7	00
" 500 Salmon Bricks,	" 8 " "	4	00
		179	38¾

PROVIDENCE, R. I., *June* 1, 1876.

MR. JAMES HEDGE,

Bought of GLADDING & BRO.

1876							
Apl.	3	1 Webster Unabridged,	$\frac{3}{10}$	12		8	40
	7	4 Leisure Day Rhymes,	$\frac{1}{4}$	2	00	6	00
May	2	3 Eight Cousins,	$\frac{1}{4}$	1	50	3	37½
	6	2 Ticknor's Life and Letters,	$\frac{1}{4}$	3	50	5	25
	"	4 Mysterious Island,	$\frac{1}{3}$	3	00	8	00
	29	3 Farm Legends,	$\frac{3}{10}$	2	50	5	25
	"	2 Three Brides,	$\frac{1}{3}$	1	75	2	33⅓
						38	60⅚

Rec'd payment,
JOHN B. TIBBETTS,
for GLADDING & BRO.

PHILADELPHIA, *Oct.* 1, 1876.

MRS. GEORGE GORDON,

Bought of WALKER & BROUGHER,

Terms: 30 days.

2	Pr. W. G. Ewers and Basins,	1.40	2	80		
2	" Cov'd Soaps,	50	1			
2	" Brush Trays,	50	1			
½	Doz. " Bowls,	1.75		87½		
1	" " Mugs,		1	50		
2	" Stem Wines,	1.00	2	00		
2	" Glass Peppers,	1.25	2	50		
2	" Individual Salts,	50	1	00		
3	" Oval Glass Dishes, $\frac{\text{1-3 in.}}{100}$, $\frac{\text{1-6 in.}}{150}$, $\frac{\text{1-7 in.}}{200}$,		4	50		
	Crate and Porterage,		1	25	18	42½

STATEMENT OF ACCOUNT.

NEW YORK, *April* 7, 1876.

MR. HENRY CADY,

To BADEAU & LOCKWOOD.

1875		DR.					
Oct.	9	To 15 Drums of Figs,	2 25	33	75		
"	30	" 9 boxes Oranges,	4 75	42	75		
Dec.	3	" 12 " Lemons,	5 25	63	00		
1876							
Jan.	29	" 4 barrels Dried Apples,	6 75	27	00		
Feb.	"	" 10 " Peaches,	5 25	52	50		
Mar.	18	" 30 lb. Leghorn Citron,	25	7	50	226	50
		CR.					
1876							
Jan.	11	By 2 bbl. Superfine State Flour	6 00	12	00		
"	"	" 200 lb. Buckwheat "	.03½	7	00		
Feb.	1	" 1 firkin Butter, 56 lb.,	28	15	68		
"	29	" 100 lb. Corn Meal, ℔ C.,		1	35		
Mar.	1	" Cash,		108	00	144	08
		Balance due Badeau & Lockwood,				82	47

CINCINNATI, O., *Sept.* 25*th*, 1874.

MR. JOHN WALLER,

Bought of TIERNEY & GARDEN,

Terms: 30 days.

½	Dozen Gents' Blk. Fur Hats,	16	50	8	25
½	" " " " "	19	50	9	75
1	" " " " "			18	00
½	" Boys' " Sax "	9	00	4	50
½	" " " " "	12	00	6	00
½	" Children's Fancy "	6	00	3	00
½	" Ladies' Trimmed "	15	00	7	50
½	" " Untrimmed "	7	50	3	75
				60	75
	Less 6%,			3	64½
				57	10½

Received payment,

TIERNEY & GARDEN,

Per J. W. M.

PITTSBURGH, *Nov.* 1, 1876.

Messrs. WILEY & MORTON,

Bought of J. G. HERR & CO.

Qty.	Article	Price $	¢	Amount $	¢
2	Doz. Rubber Long Combs,	4	50	9	00
$\frac{1}{4}$	Gro. Horn " $\frac{3.50}{\#8}$, $\frac{4.50}{10}$, $\frac{6.00}{12}$			3	50
$\frac{10}{12}$	Doz. Tooth Brushes,	1	75	1	45$\frac{10}{12}$
$\frac{7}{12}$	" Jet Sets,	7	25	4	22$\frac{11}{12}$
1	Gro. Rubber Coat and Vest Buttons ea. 1.00 & .75			1	75
$\frac{1}{2}$	Gt. Gro. Black Suspender "	1	62		81
40	yd. Jaconet,		20	8	00
14	" Irish Linen,		67	9	38
3	Pcs. Silk Velvet Ribbon $\frac{65}{1\frac{3}{4}}$, $\frac{72^2}{2\frac{1}{2}}$, $\frac{1.35}{4}$, $\frac{2.00}{6}$			14	17$\frac{1}{2}$
				52	30$\frac{1}{4}$
	Less $\frac{1}{10}$,			5	23
				47	07$\frac{1}{4}$

Rec'd payment,

J. G. HERR & Co.

J. T. WAY & Co.

In %/ with WOOD, MARSH & HEYWARD,

DR. CR.

Date		Items	$	¢	Date		Items	$	¢
1875 Sept.	25	To 1 pc. Blue Anchor Cloth 38^1 yd.@\$5.62^2,	215	15$\frac{5}{8}$	1875 Oct.	2	By 1 pc. Irish Linen 17^1 yd @57^2¢,	9	91$\frac{7}{8}$
"	30	" 2 pcs. Blk Cloth 42 yd.@\$7.65.	321	30	"	20	" 3 pcs. Plaid Jaconet 60 yd.@ 37^2¢,	22	50
Oct.	8	" 1 pc. Doeskin Cassimere 24 yd @1.87^2.	45	00	Nov.	30	" 1 pc. Swiss Mull 20 yd.@32^2¢,	6	50
Nov.	9	" 2 pcs. Blk Rib'd Cassimere 63 yd.@\$1.63,	102	69	Jan.	2	" Note for Balance @30 days,	739	82$\frac{1}{8}$
Dec.	14	" 2 pcs. Fisher's Tweed 64^1 yd. @75¢,	48	18$\frac{3}{4}$					
"	30	" 2 pcs. Brown Corduroy 41^1 yd.@\$1.12^2,	46	40$\frac{5}{8}$					
			778	74				778	74

Art. 236. Page 156.

1. PHILADELPHIA, *Oct.* 10, 1876.

LAFAYETTE RESTAURANT,

Bought of THOMAS BRADLEY.

Item	Rate	$	¢	$	¢
67 lb. Ribs of Beef,	@ .20	13	40		
2 Kidneys,	.15		30		
3 Lambs,	5.00	15	00		
3 Calves' Heads,	.75	2	25		
8 Sweetbreads,	.30	2	40		
2 Calves' Livers,	.70	1	40		
37 lb. Veal,	.17	6	29	41	04

2. PHILADELPHIA, *June* 12, 1876.

CONTINENTAL HOTEL,

To EUGENE G. BLACKFORD, DR.

Item	Rate	$	¢	$	¢
To 15 Salmon,	.30	4	50		
" 37 Lobsters,	.10	3	70		
" 5 Fresh Mackerel,	.12		60		
" 7 Spanish "	.20	1	40		
" 2 Shad,	.40		80		
" 12 Soles,	.10	1	20		
" 9 Sea-Bass,	.10		90		
" 15 Sheep heads,	.12	1	80		
" 3 doz. Soft Crabs,	.50	1	50		
" 1½ " Frogs,	1.75	2	62½	19	02½

3. PITTSBURGH, *Jan.* 20, 1873.

MR. JAMES THOMSON,

Bought of WM. WILSON.

Item	Date	$	¢	$	¢
1 lb. Citric Acid,				1	55
5 " Chlor. Lime,	Jar 20.		08		60
10 " Epsom Salts,			05		50
3 " Gum Shellac,			60	1	80
1 Doz. Wilson's Cod Liver Oil,				7	00
½ " Mishler's Herb Bitters,		8	00	4	00
2 lb. Carbolic Acid Crys.,		1	75	3	50
				$18	95

4. PHILADELPHIA, *Dec.* 31, 1874.

MRS. JOHN SMITH,

Bought of TYNDALE & CO.

Qty	Item	Price	$	¢	$	¢
1	Soup Tureen,		3	50		
2	Sauce "	$1.25	2	50		
1	Doz. Tulip Goblets,		1	40		
1	" Individual Salts,			50		
2	Glass Pitchers,	.62½	1	25		
3	Oval Glass Dishes,	.50	1	50		
1	Glass Nappy,			75		
4	Cov. Dishes,	1.25	5	00		
3	Doz. Stoneware Plates $\frac{1\text{–}6\text{ in.}}{125}$, $\frac{1\text{–}7\text{ in.}}{140}$, $\frac{1\text{–}8\text{ in.}}{160}$		4	25	20	65

Rec'd payment,

TYNDALE & Co.

---

5. NEWARK, N. J., *March* 1, 1875.

MR. JAMES HAVEN,

To MRS. AMELIA WATSON. DR.

Item	Rate	$	¢
To Board 4 Weeks,	@$9.00	36	
" Fuel & Light 4 Weeks,	1.50	6	
" Washing, 5½ dozen,	1.00	5	50
		47	50
CR.			
By Mdse. as per Bill,		46	50½
Balance,			99½

Rec'd payment,

AMELIA WATSON.

MRS. AMELIA WATSON,

To JAMES HAVEN, DR.

1875					
Feb.	5	To 15 lb. Tea,	.75	11	25
"	"	" 10 " Coffee,	.35	3	50
"	9	" 25 " Granulated Sugar,	.12½	3	12½
"	"	" 5 " Brown "	.10		50
"	"	" 1 Barrel No. 1 Mackerel,		25	
"	26	" 5 lb. Butter,	.50	2	50
"	"	" 1½ dozen Eggs,	.42		63
				46	50½

Rec'd payment,

JAMES HAVEN.

6. PHILADELPHIA, *Aug.* 25th, 1875.

MR. FRANKLIN S. FULLER, *Memphis, Tenn.*

Bought of KUHN & FURST.

25	Boxes Raisins, $\frac{10}{325}$, $\frac{15}{255}$,		70	75		
350	lb. Currants, $\frac{100}{7\frac{1}{2}}$, $\frac{250}{7}$,		25			
150	" Dates,	$5\frac{1}{4}$	7	$87\frac{1}{2}$		
100	" Turkish Prunes,	$8\frac{1}{2}$	8	50		
125	" French " $\frac{50}{15}$, $\frac{75}{12\frac{1}{2}}$,		16	$87\frac{1}{2}$		
12	Bunches Baracoa Bananas,	1.75	21	00	150	00

Rec'd payment by due bill,

KUHN & FURST.

---

7. PHILADELPHIA, *Oct.* 14, 1876.

MR. THOMAS WALKER, *Aiken, S. C.*

Bought of HESS, ROGERS & CHAMBERS.

3	Doz. Ladies' Berlin Gloves,	2	25	6	75
1	" " White Silk Gloves,			5	50
1	" " Berlin ½ Gauntlets,			3	75
1	" " Colored Buck Gauntlets,			15	
1	" " Black Jouvin Kid Gloves,			16	
½	" " White " " "	15		7	50
2	" Gents' Buck Driving Gauntlets,	16	50	33	
2	" " White Kid Gloves,	11		22	
1	" Child's White Cotton Hose, $\frac{80}{3}$, $\frac{90}{3^2}$, $\frac{95}{4}$, $\frac{100}{4^2}$, $\frac{110}{5}$			4	75
				114	25
	Less 20%,			22	85
				91	40

Rec'd payment,

HESS, ROGERS & CHAMBERS.

SECTION VI.

DENOMINATE NUMBERS.

Art. 251. WRITTEN EXERCISES.

NOTE.—In the Arithmetic we have given one method of explanation; in solving the 3d problem, we present another which many prefer to the former.

```
3.  s.  d.  far.
    9   8   3
   12
  ---
  116
    4
  ---
  467
```

SOL.—In 1 s. there are 12 pence, hence 12 times the number of shillings equals the number of pence; 12 times 9 equals 108, and 108 d.+8 d.=116 pence. In 1 penny there are 4 farthings, hence 4 times the number of pence equals the number of farthings; 4 times 116=464, and 464 far. plus 3 far. equals 467 farthings.

```
5.   4)7859                 6.   4)58763
    12)1964 - 3 far.            12)14690 - 3 far.
        163 s. - 8 d.          2|0) 122|4 - 2d.
                                    £61 - 4 s.
```

FRENCH AND GERMAN MONEY.

Art. 257. WRITTEN EXERCISES.

1. $.193 × 25.50 = $4.9215.
2. $256 ÷ $.193 = 1326.42+.
3. $.2385 × 753.15 = $179.626275.
4. $456.25 ÷ $.2385 = 1912.99+.
5. $.193 × 20 = $3.86.

TROY WEIGHT.

Art. 260. WRITTEN EXERCISES.

```
4.  24)6275                       lb.  oz.  pwt.  gr.
   2|0) 26|1 - 11 gr.         5.   19   11   17    19
        13 oz. 1 pwt.               12
                                   ---
                                   239
6.  24)18759                        20
   2|0)  78|1 - 15 gr.             ----
    12)  39 - 1 pwt.               4797
          3 lb. - 3 oz.              24
                                 ------
                                 115147 gr.
```

APOTHECARIES' WEIGHT.

Art. 261. WRITTEN EXERCISES.

```
        (5)                      (6)
   2|0)9237|5                   ʒ   ℈
       3)4618 - 15 gr.          3   2
       8)1539 - 1℈              3
      12) 192 - 3ʒ             ---
           16 lb.               11
                                20
                             4)220
                                55 gr.
```

AVOIRDUPOIS WEIGHT.

Art. 262. WRITTEN EXERCISES.

6. A pound of lead weighs 7000 gr., and a pound of gold 5760 gr., hence the lead is really heavier than the gold.

7. An ounce of feathers weighs $\frac{1}{16}$ of 7000 gr., or $437\frac{1}{2}$ gr., and an ounce of silver weighs $\frac{1}{12}$ of 5760 gr., or 480 gr.; hence an ounce of silver is heavier than an ounce of feathers.

LONG MEASURE.

Art. 268. WRITTEN EXERCISES.

2.
```
  rd. yd. ft.
   3   4   2
  5½
  ---
  19
  1½
  ---
  20½
   3
  ---
  63½ feet.
```

8.
```
  12)567
   3)47 - 3 in.
  5½)15 - 2 ft.
   2  2
  11 )30
       2 rd. - 8/2 = 4 yd.
```
Ans. 2 rd. 4 yd. 2 ft. 3 in.

NOTE.—In dividing by $5\frac{1}{2}$ we reduce the divisor and dividend to halves, and then divide by 11; the remainder is, of course, halves, and hence we must divide by 2 to obtain the true remainder.

9. 3000 mi. = 15840000 ft.; 15840000 ÷ 3 = 5280000.

SQUARE MEASURE.

Art. 274. WRITTEN EXERCISES.

NOTE.—In dividing by $30\frac{1}{4}$, reduce both divisor and dividend to *4ths*, and then divide; the remainder will be a number of *4ths*, hence we must divide by 2 to obtain the true remainder.

(5)
```
  272¼)238975
     4      4
  ----  ------
  1089) 955900
  16|0)   87|7 = 211¾ sq. ft.
        5 A. 77 P.
```
¾ sq. ft. = 108 sq. in.

Ans. 5 A 77 P. 211 sq. ft. 108 sq. in.

(6)
```
   144)9876543
  272¼)68587 - 15 sq. in.
     4     4
  ----  ------
  1089)274348
  16|0)   25|1 = 252¼ sq. ft.
        1 A. 91 P.
```
¼ sq. ft. = 36 sq. in.

36 sq. in. + 15 sq. in. = 51 sq. in.

Ans. 1 A. 91 P. 252 sq. ft. 51 sq. in.

CUBIC MEASURE.

Art. 279. WRITTEN EXERCISES.

5. 78 cords=9984 cu. ft.=17252352 cu. in.

6. 5876543 cu. in.=3400 cu. ft. 1343 cu. in.=26 cd. 72 cu. ft 1343 cu. in.

MEASURES OF CAPACITY.

Art. 286. WRITTEN EXERCISES.

7. 5 gal. 3 qt. 1 pt.=47 pt.; $.03×47=$1.41.

8. 217 bu. 3 pk. 5 qt.=6973 qt.; $.18¾×6973=$1307.43¾.

CIRCULAR MEASURE.

Art. 291. WRITTEN EXERCISES.

4. 195600″=3260′=54° 20′=1 S. 24° 20′.

5. 3 quadrants = 3 × 90° = 270°; 270°+15° = 285° = 1026000″.

TIME.

Art. 296. WRITTEN EXERCISES.

6. By the table, from May 8th to October 8th is 153 days, and from Oct. 8th to Oct. 19th is 11 days; hence the whole time is 153+11, or 164 days.

7. From March 28th to December 28th is 275 days, but to December 16th is 12 days less, or 263 days.

8. By the table, to Sept. 21st it is 212 days, and since 1860 is a leap year, it is 213 days; hence to Sept. 10th, which is 11 days less, the time is 202 days.

Art. 298. MENTAL EXERCISES.

1. 18 whole centuries; since the 19th century is not finished.

2. 18th century ended with the year 1800; 19th began with 1801.

3 In any century not including a centennial year which is a leap year, there will be 24 leap years and 76 common years; in the centuries including a centennial year which is a leap year, there will be 25 leap years and 75 common years.

4. 1760; 1776; 1876; 1880; 2000.

5. There are 86400 seconds in a day, therefore it ticks 4×86400= 345600 times.

MISCELLANEOUS TABLES.

Art. 301. MENTAL EXERCISES.

6. As many as 360÷24=15; as many as 480÷24=20.

7. As many as 320÷16=20; as many as 400÷16=25.

8. As many as 16÷8, which is 2.

Art. 301. WRITTEN EXERCISES.

1. 1 gross=144; 144×42=6048.

2. 3×63=189 dozen=15 gross 9 dozen.

3. No. of quires=3240÷24=135; 36¢×135=$48.60.

4. 12¢×795.5=$95.46.

5. 5 quires and 19 sheets=139 sheets=$\frac{139}{480}$ of a ream. The waste being 1 quire in a ream, in $3\frac{139}{480}$ reams there will be $3\frac{139}{480}$ quires wasted, which equals 3 quires 7 sheets nearly; 3 quires 7 sheets deducted from 3 reams 5 quires 19 sheets, leaves 3 reams 2 quires 12 sheets, or 1500 sheets, the amount actually used, but the posters being printed on half sheets, there were 2 times 1500, or 3000 posters.

6. This book is a 12mo., hence there are 24 pages on each sheet, and as there are 424 pages, it requires $17\frac{2}{3}$ sheets, but as only whole sheets are used, 18 sheets will be required for 1 copy, and in 5000 copies, it will require 5000×18=90000 sheets; but 1 quire in a ream, or $\frac{1}{20}$, is wasted by being badly printed, etc., hence the amount actually used is $\frac{19}{20}$ of the whole amount required, hence 90000 sheets=$\frac{19}{20}$ of the amount, and $\frac{20}{20}$=197 reams, 7 quires, $8\frac{16}{19}$ sheets.

REDUCTION OF COMPOUND NUMBERS.

Art. 304. REDUCTION DESCENDING.

11. 6 Cong.=48 O.; 48 O.+7 O.=55 O.=880 f℥; 880 f℥+15 f℥=895 f℥=7160 fʒ; 7160 fʒ+4 fʒ=7164 fʒ=429840♏; 429840♏+30♏=429870♏.

12. 98 gallons=392 qt.=784pt.=3136 gi.

13. 3S.=90°; 90°+25°=115°=6900′=414000″; 414000″+40″=414040″.

14. If we wish to be very exact we reduce 365da. 5h. 48min. 49.7sec. to seconds, and multiply by 930, which gives 29347944621sec.

15. 1 week=7da.=168h.=10080min.; 75×10080=756000.

16. 68 miles$=$21760 rd.$=$119680 yd.$=$359040 ft.$=$4308480 in.

Art. 305. REDUCTION ASCENDING.

10. 144)67437842351

9) 468318349 - 95 sq. in.

$30\frac{1}{4}$) 52035372 - 1 sq. ft.

4) 4

121)208141488

160) 1720177 - $17\frac{3}{4}$ sq. yd.

640) 10751 - 17 P.

16 sq. mi. 511 A.

$\frac{3}{4}$ sq. yd.$=$6 sq. ft. 108 sq. in.

Ans. 16 sq. mi., 511 A., 17 P., 17 sq. yd., 8 sq. ft. 59 sq. in.

15. 1 geographical mile$=1'$ (Art. 268, III.); $721'=12^\circ\ 1'$.

16. $6476\div56=$115 firkins 36 lb.

17. If $72=\frac{1}{10}$, $\frac{10}{10}$, or the whole quantity$=$720 lb.; if for every 3 lb. of flour there were 4 lb. of grain, there will be $720\times\frac{1}{3}\times4=960$ lb.; $960\div48=20$ bu.

Page 185. MENTAL EXERCISES.

16. Half a gallon equals 16 gills, hence 16 vials will contain half a gallon.

17. 2 gallons equal 32 half pints.

18. There are 32 quarts in a bushel, hence a quart costs $.05.

19. 2 gross equal 288 buttons, and these will trim $288\div6$, or 48 shirts.

20. 1 pace equals 3.3 feet, or $\frac{1}{5}$ of a rod, hence 132 paces equal $26\frac{2}{5}$ rods.

21. $\frac{15}{100}$ of $4 equals $.60.

22. Since there are 32 quarts in a bushel, he sold them for $3.84; hence he gained $1.44.

23. One pound of flour cost $.05, hence a hundred-weight cost $5.

24. 5 feet equals 60 inches, and since there are 4 inches in a hand, it is 15 hands high.

25. It sails 4 leagues, or 12 miles an hour, hence it will take 10 hours to sail 120 miles.

Pages 186-7. MISCELLANEOUS EXAMPLES.

2. £47 5 s.$=$945 s.$\div21=$45 guineas.

6. Divide by 7000, since 7000 Troy gr. equal a lb. Av., and we have 15 lb.

7. 1℥ 2ʒ 2℈ 11 gr.=651 gr.; 651÷7=93.

8. 1 T.=32000 oz.; 41 lb. $10\frac{2}{3}$ oz.=$666\frac{2}{3}$ oz.; 32000÷$666\frac{2}{3}$ =48.

10. 6 dozen dozen=6×12×12=864; half a dozen dozen =6×12=72; 864−72=792.

11. One tun=2016 pt.; 5 gal. 2 qt. 1 pt.=45 pt.; 2016÷45 =$44\frac{4}{5}$.

12. 66 A. 24 P.=10584 P.; 5 A. 82 P.=882 P.; 10584÷882 =12.

14. The problem is solved without regard to leap years. There may be either 12 or 13 leap years, which would increase the time 12 or 13 days. 50×365=18250 h. =$760\frac{5}{12}$ da.=2 yr. $30\frac{5}{12}$ da.

15. 7° 5′=425′; 270°=16200′; 16200′÷425=$38\frac{2}{17}$ da.

16. Jan. 31 da., Feb. 29 da.; hence 24×60×2=2880 min.

17. 5℥ 7ʒ 1℈ 4 gr.=2844 gr.; 2844×29=82476 gr.=14 lb. 3℥ 6ʒ 1℈ 16 gr.

18. 80×60×12=57600; 1000000÷57600=$17\frac{13}{36}$ da.

19. 6 gal.=48 pt.=96 half pints.

20. 1876 being a leap year, contained 31622400 seconds; a solar year contains 31556929.7 seconds; 31622400—31556929.7=65470.3 sec.

21. (50+27)×2=154 rd., distance round the field; 154 rd.= 2541 ft.; 2541÷12=$211\frac{3}{4}$; $211\frac{3}{4}$×3=$635\frac{1}{4}$.

22. 5×980=4900 gr.; 4900 gr.=10℥ 1ʒ 2℈.

23. If it has 5600 subscribers, it requires 5600 sheets each week, and in a year it will require 5600×52=291200 sheets=606 reams 13 quires 8 sheets.

24. In the spring months there are 31+30+31 =92 days; in the autumn, 30+31+30=91 da.; 92 da.—91 da.= 1 da.=1440 min.

25. There are 16 pages in 1 sheet; 16×20=320 pages.

26. 30 da.+31 da.+31 da.=92 da.=132480 min.; $.04× 132480=$5299.20.

27. 32400×31=1004400=6975 gross.

28. $116 \times 2 = 232$ lb.; $\frac{1}{4}$ oz. $= \frac{1}{64}$ lb.; hence the false weight is $\frac{63}{64}$ lb., and he will sell as many false pounds as $\frac{63}{64}$ lb. is contained times in 232 lb., or $235\frac{43}{63}$ lb.; $235\frac{43}{63}$ lb. $-$ 232 lb. $= 3\frac{43}{63}$ lb.; $\$.18\frac{3}{4} \times 3\frac{43}{63} = \$.69\frac{1}{21}$.

29. 5 T. 14 cwt. $=$ 11400 lb.; 1 T. 3 cwt. 56 lb. $=$ 2356 lb.; 11400 lb. $-$ 2356 lb. $=$ 9044 lb.; if I only received 9044 lb. I should pay $\frac{9044}{11400}$ of \$88.35 $=$ \$70.091.

30. 15 bu. 3 pk. 1 qt. $=$ 505 qt.; 11¢ $\times$ 505 $=$ \$55.55; cost of 1 barrel of flour $= \$.03\frac{1}{2} \times 196 = \$6.86$; \$55.55 $\div$ \$6.86 $=$ 8 barrels and 67¢ remaining.

ADDITION OF COMPOUND NUMBERS.

Art. 306.

The attention of pupils should be called to the analogy existing between addition of compound numbers and addition of simple numbers. In simple numbers we "*carry*" one for every 10, the scale being uniform; in compound numbers we "*carry*" one for the number of units in each lower denomination which makes one in the next higher. The difference between them, which is no less important, and which is sometimes unappreciated, should also be shown, compound numbers requiring the decimal scale to express them; as, 16 oz. $=$ 1 lb., etc.

NOTE.—These problems are so easy they need not be solved in the Key. We will only make a suggestion for the 11th.

11. Sum $=$ 63 mi. 272 rd. 5 yd. 2 ft. 6 in.; but 5 yd. 2 ft. 6 in. $= 5\frac{1}{2}$ yd. 1 ft., and $5\frac{1}{2}$ yd. $=$ 1 rd., hence the answer becomes 63 mi. 273 rd. 1 ft.

SUBTRACTION OF COMPOUND NUMBERS.

Art. 307.

Pupils should be led to see the analogy between subtraction of compound numbers and simple numbers. In simple numbers the scale is regular, in compound numbers it is irregular. They should also be shown the distinction between them: that compound numbers are expressed in the decimal scale, and that, therefore the two processes are not identical.

13. He sold to both 28 bu. 2 pk. 5 qt. 1 pt.+28 bu. 2 pk. 5 qt. 1 pt.=57 bu. 1 pk. 3 qt., which subtracted from 200 bu., leaves 142 bu. 2 pk. 5 qt.

14. He sent his father 17 lb. 10 oz. 15 pwt. 20 gr.—3 lb. 16 pwt., or 14 lb. 9 oz. 19 pwt. 20 gr., and to both 32 lb. 8 oz. 15 pwt. 16 gr., and had remaining 79 lb. 3 oz. 4 pwt. 8 gr.

16. \$25.207$\frac{1}{8}$—\$16.575$\frac{1}{2}$=\$8.631$\frac{5}{8}$; 2 eagles and 25$\frac{3}{4}$ dimes equal \$22.575; \$8.631$\frac{5}{8}$+\$22 575=\$31.206$\frac{5}{8}$.

17. 240 A. 85 P. 16 sq. yd. 96 sq. in.—125 A. 37 P. 29 sq. yd. 4 sq. ft. 140 sq. in.=115 A. 47 P. 16$\frac{1}{4}$ sq. yd. 4 sq. ft. 100 sq. in.=115 A. 47 P. 16 sq. yd. 6 sq. ft. 136 sq. in.

18. 11 gal. 3 qt. 1 pt. subtracted from 12 gal. equals 1 pint; then 16 gal. 1 pt. plus 1 pint, equals 16 gal. 1 qt., which subtracted from 63 gal. equals 46 gal. 3 qt.

MULTIPLICATION OF COMPOUND NUMBERS.

Art. 308.

15. He sold both 5 times 96 A. 150 P., or 484 A. 110 P.; 1000 A.—484 A. 110 P.=515 A. 50 P.

16. Find what he sold each, take their sum and subtract from 4000 bu.; or, multiply 50 bu. 3 pk. 7 qt. by 56, and subtract the product from 4000 bu., which leaves 1145 bu. 3 pk.

DIVISION OF COMPOUND NUMBERS.

Art. 312. Case II.

5. 71 gal. 3 qt. 1 pt.=575 pt; 2 gal. 3 qt. 1 pt.=23 pt.; 575 ÷23=25.

6. 33 T. 19 cwt. 35 lb.=67935 lb.; 6 T. 15 cwt. 87 lb.= 13587 lb.; 67935÷13587=5.

DIFFERENCE BETWEEN DATES.

Art. 313. Case I.

5. From Dec. 30, 1862, to Dec. 30, 1863, is 1 year, and from Dec. 30, 1863, to Jan. 16, 1864, is 17 days.

9. He was born on the 29th of February, and since he was 36 years old he saw 10 leap years, and dying after the 28th of February, he saw 10 birthdays.

10. The one born in 1756 saw 10 leap years, the other saw 9 leap years; hence one was one day older than the other.

11. From May 20, 1874, to July 4, 1876, the time is 2 yr. 45 da., or 2 yr. 1 mo. 15 da.; as the day is reckoned to begin at midnight, 4 o'clock P. M. is 16 hours after midnight, hence the exact time is 2 yr. 1 mo. 15 da. 3 h. 39 min. 11 sec.

NOTE.—It will be noticed that the two years include a leap year, but as the extra day is included in the whole years we take no account of it, considering the expression 2 years to include the exact number of years, whether common or leap years.

Art. 314. Case II.

2. From January 1 to July 4, 1776, the time is 185 days, which equals 26 weeks and 3 days; hence July 4 fell 3 days after Monday, or on Thursday.

3. From July 4, 1776, to Oct. 17, 1777, the time is 470 days, or 67 weeks and 1 day, but by the previous problem we found that July 4, 1776, fell on Thursday; hence Oct. 17, 1777, fell on Friday.

4. From Oct. 17, 1777, to Jan. 18, 1782, the time is 1554 days, or 222 weeks; hence Jan. 18, 1782, fell on the same day of the week as Oct. 17, 1777, or Friday.

5. From Jan. 18, 1782, to June 18, 1815, the time is 12203 days, or 1743 weeks and 2 days; hence the battle of Waterloo was fought two days after Friday, or on Sunday.

6. From June 18, 1815, to April 14, 1865, the time is 18198 days, or 2599 weeks and 5 days; hence April 14, 1865, fell 5 days after Sunday, or on Friday.

7. From April 14, 1865, to March 4, 1869, the time is 1420 days, or 202 weeks and 6 days; hence March 4, 1869, fell 6 days after Friday, or on Thursday.

8. In the century from May 10, 1876, to May 10, 1976, there are 24 leap years; hence there are 36524 days

or 5217 weeks and 5 days; hence it will open on Monday.

9. From Jan. 8, 1815, to June 18, 1815 (Ex. 5), the time is 161 days, or 23 weeks, hence Jan. 8 falls on the same day as June 18, or Sunday, and a letter dated Wednesday, Jan. 8, 1815, would show that the writer did not know on what day of the week the date fell, and hence could not have written the letter at that date.

LONGITUDE AND TIME.

Art. 320. Page 200.

5. The difference of time we find to be 37 min. $21\frac{1}{15}$ sec., and since Cincinnati is west of Philadelphia, the time is 37 min. $21\frac{1}{15}$ sec. *earlier*; hence it is 10 h. minus 37 min. $21\frac{1}{15}$ sec., or 9 o'clock 22 min. $38\frac{4}{15}$ sec.

6. Difference of longitude$=75° \; 9' \; 5''+16° \; 23'=91° \; 32' \; 5''$; hence the difference of time is 6 h. 6 min. $8\frac{1}{3}$ sec., and it is so much later, or 6 min. $8\frac{1}{3}$ sec. past 3 o'clock P. M.

7. Difference of longitude $=76° \; 56'$, therefore difference of time equal 5 h. 7 min. 44 sec.; and since Washington is west of London, the time is earlier, and the watch must be set back 5 h. 7 min. 44 sec.

8. The longitude of New York is 74° 3′ west, hence the difference of longitude is 74° 3′ plus $2° \; 20'=76° \; 23'$, which divided by 15 gives the difference of time, 5 h. 5 min. 32 sec.; and since Paris is east, the time is later, etc.

9. Difference of longitude$=12° \; 27'+122° \; 26' \; 15''=134° \; 53' \; 15''$; difference of time$=$8 h. 59 min. 33 sec.; time$=(4+12)-$8 h. 59 min. 33 sec.$=$7 h. 27 sec.

Art. 321. Page 201.

6. 3 h. 9 min. $8\frac{2}{3}$ sec.$\times 15=47° \; 17' \; 10''=$diff. of longitude; $75° \; 9' \; 5''+47° \; 17' \; 10''=122° \; 26' \; 15''$.

7. 4 h. 44 min. $50\frac{4}{5}$ sec. multiplied by 15 gives the difference of longitude, 71° 12′ 42″, and since Cambridge, *Eng., is 5′ 21″* east, the longitude of Cambridge

Mass., is the difference between them, which is 71° 7′ 21″.

8. 74° 3′+35° 32′=109° 35′; 109° 35′÷15=7 h. 18 min. 20 sec. diff. of time; since Jerusalem is east of New York, the time is later; 4 h. 30 min.+7 h. 18 min. 20 sec.=11 h. 48 min. 20 sec.

REDUCTION OF DENOMINATE FRACTIONS.

REDUCTION DESCENDING.

Art. 326. Case I.

2. $\frac{1}{160}\times\frac{4}{1}\times\frac{8}{1}\times\frac{2}{1}=\frac{2}{5}$, *Ans.*
3. $\frac{1}{1440}\times\frac{20}{1}\times\frac{24}{1}=\frac{1}{3}$, *Ans.*
4. $\frac{3}{1920}\times\frac{24}{1}\times\frac{60}{1}=\frac{9}{4}=2\frac{1}{4}$, *Ans.*
5. $\frac{7}{288}\times\frac{4}{1}\times\frac{2}{1}\times\frac{4}{1}=\frac{7}{9}$, *Ans.*
6. $\frac{5}{1386}\times\frac{11}{2}\times\frac{3}{1}\times\frac{12}{1}=\frac{5}{7}$, *Ans.*
7. $\frac{3}{22400}\times\frac{20}{1}\times\frac{100}{1}\times\frac{16}{1}=\frac{30}{7}=4\frac{2}{7}$, *Ans.*
8. $\frac{5}{64152}\times\frac{121}{4}\times\frac{9}{1}\times\frac{144}{1}=3\frac{1}{18}$, *Ans.*
9. $\frac{1}{18720}\times\frac{320}{1}\times\frac{11}{2}\times\frac{3}{1}\times\frac{12}{1}=3\frac{5}{13}$, *Ans.*

Art. 327. Case II.

2. $\frac{5}{6}\times20=16\frac{2}{3}$ pwt.; $\frac{2}{3}\times24=16$ gr.
3. $\frac{4}{5}\times4=3\frac{1}{5}$ pk.; $\frac{1}{5}\times8=1\frac{3}{5}$ qt.; $\frac{3}{5}\times2=1\frac{1}{5}$ pt.
4. $\frac{2}{3}\times320=213\frac{1}{3}$ rd.; $\frac{1}{3}\times5\frac{1}{2}=1\frac{5}{6}$ yd.; $\frac{5}{6}\times3=2\frac{1}{2}$ ft.
5. $\frac{7}{8}\times5\frac{1}{2}=4\frac{13}{16}$ yd.; $\frac{13}{16}\times3=2\frac{7}{16}$ ft.; $\frac{7}{16}\times12=5\frac{1}{4}$ in.
6. $\frac{9}{10}\times320=288$ rd.
7. $\frac{7}{8}\times30=26\frac{1}{4}°$; $\frac{1}{4}\times60=15′$.
8. $\frac{5}{7}\times160=114\frac{2}{7}$ P.; $\frac{2}{7}\times30\frac{1}{4}=8\frac{9}{14}$ yd.; $\frac{9}{14}\times9=5\frac{11}{14}$ ft.; $\frac{11}{14}\times144=113\frac{1}{7}$ in.

Art. 328. Case III.

(2)	(3)	(4)	(5)
.825	.675	.364	.3275
12	$5\frac{1}{2}$	160	63
9.900	3.7125	58.240	20.6325
20	3	$30\frac{1}{4}$	4
18.000	2.1375	7.260	2.5300
	12		2
	1.6500		1.06

(6)	(7)	(8)
.9735	.3218	.1365
4	20	4
3.8940	6.4360	.5460
8	100	63
7.1520	43.6000	34.3980
	16	4
	9.6000	1.5920
		2
		1.1840

REDUCTION ASCENDING.

Art. 329. Case I.

2. $\frac{3}{4}\times\frac{1}{24}\times\frac{1}{20}=\frac{1}{640}$, *Ans.*
3. $\frac{9}{10}\times\frac{1}{3}\times\frac{2}{11}\times\frac{1}{320}=\frac{3}{17600}$, *Ans.*
4. $\frac{8}{9}\times\frac{1}{4}\times\frac{1}{2}\times\frac{1}{4}=\frac{1}{36}$, *Ans.*
5. $\frac{5}{7}\times\frac{1}{12}\times\frac{1}{3}\times\frac{2}{11}=\frac{5}{1386}$, *Ans.*
6. $\frac{7}{8}\times\frac{1}{100}\times\frac{1}{20}=\frac{7}{16000}$, *Ans.*
7. $\frac{30}{7}\times\frac{1}{16}\times\frac{1}{100}\times\frac{1}{20}=\frac{3}{22400}$, *Ans.*
8. A cord=128 cu. ft.; 48 is $\frac{48}{128}$ of 128, or $\frac{3}{8}$, *Ans.*

Art. 330. Case II.

2. 3 oz. 8 pwt. 12 gr.=1644 gr.; 1 lb.=5760 gr.; $\frac{1644}{5760}=\frac{137}{480}$
3. 2 bu.=64 qt.; 1 bu. 4 qt.=36 qt.; 36 is $\frac{36}{64}$ of 64, or $\frac{9}{16}$.
4. A barrel of beer=36 gal.; 22 gal. 2 qt.=$22\frac{1}{2}$ gal.; hence $\frac{45}{72}=\frac{5}{8}$, *Ans.*
5. A barrel of wine=$31\frac{1}{2}$ gal.=252 pt.; 4 gal. 3 qt. 1 pt.= 39 pt.; hence $\frac{39}{252}=\frac{13}{84}$, *Ans.*
6. 5℥=2400 gr.; 2ʒ 1℈ 10 gr.=150 gr.; $\frac{150}{2400}=\frac{1}{16}$.
7. 3 yr.=26280 h.; 3 wk. 6 da. 20 h.=668 h.; $\frac{668}{26280}=\frac{167}{6570}$.
8. 4 in. square=16 sq. in.; 4 sq. in. is $\frac{4}{16}$ of 16 sq. in., or $\frac{1}{4}$.
   A $2\frac{1}{2}$ inch cube=$\frac{125}{8}$ cu. in.; $2\frac{1}{2}=\frac{5}{2}$; $\frac{5}{2}\div\frac{125}{8}=\frac{4}{25}$.

Art. 331. Case III.

(4)

20	8.0
3	2.4
8	1.8
12	9.225
	.76875

(5)

12	3.6
3	0.3
$5\frac{1}{2}$	1.1
320	286.2
	0.894375

(6)

5 gal.=160 gills.

1 qt. $3\frac{3}{5}$ gi.=$11\frac{3}{5}$ or $\frac{58}{5}$ gills

hence, $\frac{58}{5\times160}=\frac{29}{400}=.0725$.

(7)

12	8
3	2.6666+
$5\frac{1}{2}$	3.88888+
320	295.707070+
	.9240845959+

(8)

16	12.875
100	91.8046875
20	.918046875
	.04590234375

MENTAL EXERCISES.

Page 206-7. MISCELLANEOUS EXAMPLES.

1. $360 \times 60 \times 60 = 1296000''$.
2. 50 quarts$=6\frac{1}{4}$ pecks.
3. $4\frac{1}{2}$ signs $= 135° = 8100' = 486000''$.
4. On 1 sheet there are 16 pages, and in 3 quires, or 72 sheets, there are 1152 pages.
11. If they cost $9.60 a dozen, they cost $.80 apiece, and to gain 20 cents apiece they must be retailed at $1 apiece.
12. If I gain 2 cents a dozen by selling at 5 cents a dozen, I bought them at 3 cents a dozen, or 36 cents a gross.
15. 24 or 25; January 1, 1801.
17. He gains 4 cents a quart; he paid 20 cents a quart, hence he must sell them at 24 cents a quart.
18. 1 bushel $=128$ half pints; 5 cents$\times 128 = \$6.40$.
19. 4 vases, 18 chairs, 12 knives and 12 forks$=46$.
20. $90 \times 60 = 5400$.
21. $40 \div 12 = 3\frac{1}{3}$; 5 cents $- 3\frac{1}{3}$ cents $= 1\frac{2}{3}$ cents.

WRITTEN EXERCISES.

Pages 207-9. MISCELLANEOUS PROBLEMS.

In practice, where we have to divide by one number and multiply by another, it is often less work to multiply first, and then divide.

1. Divide by 8 and multiply by 12; or divide by 2 and multiply by 3, and we have £36 19 s.
2. Divide by 7 and multiply by 56; or multiply by 8, and we have 166 cwt.
3. £11 5 d.$=2645$ d.; $2645 \div 5\frac{3}{4} \times 8\frac{2}{3} = 2645 \times \frac{4}{23} \times \frac{26}{3} =$ $3986\frac{2}{3}$ d $=$£16 12 s. $2\frac{2}{3}$ d.
5. $8\frac{1}{2}$ d.$\times 6.33\frac{1}{3} = 53\frac{5}{6}$ d.$=4$ s. $5\frac{5}{6}$ d.; 4 s. $5\frac{5}{6}$ d.-2 s. 6 d.$=$ 1 s. $11\frac{5}{6}$ d.
6. $.00\frac{7}{8}$ sq. yd.$=.00\frac{7}{8} \times 9 \times 144 = 11.34$ sq. in.; $.04\frac{3}{4}$ sq. ft.$=$

$.04\frac{3}{4} \times 144 = 6.84$ sq. in.; 11.34 sq. in. + 6.84 sq. in. + .0008 sq. in. = 18.1808 sq. in.

7.

4	1.0384
12	11.2596
21	1.9383
	.0923

9. $2000 \times .0016 = 3.2$ lb.

10. $\$6.50 \times 24.87 = \$161.655$.

13. 16 lb. $10\frac{1}{2}$ oz. $= 16\frac{21}{32}$ lb.; $\$12.25 \times 16\frac{21}{32} = \$204.039\frac{1}{16}$.

14. $4° \; 23' \; 24'' \div 15 = 17$ min. $33\frac{3}{5}$ sec.; 9 h. + 17 min. $33\frac{3}{5}$ sec. = 9 h. 17 min. $33\frac{3}{5}$ sec.

16. One gold dollar weighs 25.8 gr.; hence \$1000000 in gold weighs 25800000 gr. = 4479 lb. 2 oz.; a silver half dollar weighs 192.9 gr.; hence 2000000 half dollars weigh 385800000 gr. = 66979 lb. 2 oz.

17. $1800 \div 69.16 = 26° \; 1' \; 35''+$; $38° \; 37' \; 28'' + 26° \; 1' \; 35'' = 64° \; 39' \; 3''$.

18. Since the first is 5 times the second, multiply \$31.40 by 5, and we have \$157.

20. £2 10s. 6d. = 606d.; $606 \div 5.55 \times 10.81 = 1180$d.+ = £4 18s. 4d.+

21. £124 16s. 6d. = 29958d.; £136 10s. 6d. = 32766d.; $\$599.16 \times \frac{32766}{29958} = \$655.32$.

22. 120 mi. 160 rd. equals 10 times 12 mi. 16 rd.; hence it will take 10 times 3 h. 20 min., or 33 h. 20 min.

23. 6 h. 30 min. $= \frac{13}{2}$ h.; 9 h. 45 min. $= \frac{39}{4}$ h.; $\frac{39}{4}$ is $\frac{3}{2}$ of $\frac{13}{2}$; hence $\frac{3}{2}$ of the distance = 36 mi. 298 rd. 1 ft. 6 in.

24. 1200 bu. $= 1200 \times 60$ lb. = 72000 lb.; 72000 lb. = 720 centals; 150 bar. = 196 lb. $\times 150 = 29400$ lb. = 294 centals.

25. By table, Art. 286, 520 bu. buckwheat in Illinois = 40 lb. $\times 520 = 20800$ lb.; $20800 \div 52 = 400$; 650 bu. in Penna. = 48 lb. $\times 650 = 31200$ lb.; $31200 \div 52 = 600$.

26. 32 bu. oats in Conn. = 896 lb.; 2¢ $\times 896 = \$17.92$; 896 lb. = 28 bu. in N. Y.; 80¢ $\times 28 = \$22.40$; $\$22.40 - \$17.92 = \$4.48$.

27. 363 rd. 7 yd. = 2003.5 yd.; 35 wk. 5 da. = 215 da.; 910 rd. $3\frac{3}{4}$ yd. = 5008.75 yd.; then $5008.75 \div 2003.5 = 2.5$; $215 \times 2.5 = 537.5$; dividing by 6, and then by 4, we have 22 mo. 1 wk. $3\frac{1}{2}$ da.

28. 4 mi. 265 rd.=1545 rd.; 309 mi.=98880 rd.: 98880+1545=64; 64 h.=2 da. 16h.

29. 15 bu. 3 pk. 4 qt.=$15\frac{7}{8}$ bu.; \$2.75×$15\frac{7}{8}$=\$43.65$\frac{5}{8}$; cost of 1 barrel of flour=$3\frac{1}{2}$¢×196=\$6 86; \$43.65$\frac{5}{8}$÷\$6.86 =6 barrels, and \$2.49$\frac{5}{8}$ rem.; \$2.49$\frac{5}{8}$÷12¢=$20\frac{77}{96}$ lb.

30. Difference of time of starting points=45 min.+1 hr. 15 min.=2 h.; 2 h. are equivalent to 30°; 30°=2074.8 miles; the first went east, and the second west.

31. From tavern to school-house=$3\frac{4}{11}$ miles+$45\frac{10}{33}$ rods=3 mi. $161\frac{2}{3}$ rd.; to the middle of the creek is half the distance between tavern and school-house, or 1 mile $240\frac{5}{6}$ rd.; subtracting distance between school-house and toll-gate, we have 1 mi. $240\frac{5}{6}$ rd.—$45\frac{10}{33}$ rd.=1 mi. 195 rd. 2 yd. 2 ft. 9 in.; to the further side of the creek is fifty yards more, or 1 mi. 204 rd. 3 yd 1 ft. 3 in.

32. 119 mi. $266\frac{2}{3}$ rd.=$38346\frac{2}{3}$ rd.; $38346\frac{2}{3}$ rd.×$1\frac{1}{5}$=46016 rd.; 51 mi. 80 rd.=16400 rd.; 46016÷16400=2 h. 48 min. $21\frac{3}{41}$ sec.; 4 h.+2 h. 48 min. $21\frac{3}{41}$ sec.=6 h. 48 min. $21\frac{3}{41}$ sec. A. M.

SECTION VII.

PRACTICAL MEASUREMENTS.

MEASURES OF SURFACE.

Art. 337. THE RECTANGLE.

2. 27×4=108 sq. ft.=12 sq. yd.

3. 215×109=23435 sq. ft.=$2603\frac{8}{9}$ sq. yd.

4. 500÷25=20 ft.

5. $466\frac{1}{3}$+$16\frac{1}{2}$=$28\frac{1}{4}$ ft.=28 ft. 3 in.

6. Area of 2 sides=18×$9\frac{1}{2}$×2=342 sq. ft.; area of 2 ends =$14\frac{1}{2}$×$9\frac{1}{2}$×2=$275\frac{1}{2}$ sq. ft.; 342+$275\frac{1}{2}$=$617\frac{1}{2}$ sq. ft.

7. $3\frac{1}{2}$×$2\frac{1}{4}$×2=$15\frac{3}{4}$ sq. ft.; $3\frac{1}{2}$×$1\frac{1}{3}$×2=$9\frac{1}{3}$ sq. ft.; $2\frac{1}{4}$×$1\frac{1}{3}$×2=6 sq. ft.; $15\frac{3}{4}$+$9\frac{1}{3}$+6=$31\frac{1}{12}$ sq. ft.= 31 sq. ft. 12 sq. in.

8. Area of one side=$1\frac{1}{2}$×$1\frac{1}{2}$=$2\frac{1}{4}$ sq. ft.; area of the 6 sides =$2\frac{1}{4}$×6=$13\frac{1}{2}$ sq. ft.

Art. 340. THE TRIANGLE.

2. $\frac{1}{2}$ of 9 ft. 9 in.$=4\frac{7}{8}$ ft.; $18\frac{1}{2}\times4\frac{7}{8}=90\frac{3}{16}$ sq. ft.$=90$ sq. ft. 27 sq. in.
3. Altitude is 12 ft.; $\frac{1}{2}$ of $12=6$; $29\times6=174$ sq. ft.
4. $\frac{1}{2}$ the base is 5 ft.; $25\div5=5$ ft.
5. 250 sq. yd.$=2250$ sq. ft.; 250 ft.$\div2=125$ ft.; $2250\div125=18$ ft.
6. 14 yd.$=42$ ft.; $\frac{1}{2}$ of $42=21$; $378\div21=18$ ft.

Art. 343. THE CIRCLE.

2. $7800\times3.1416=24504.48$ miles.
3. Circumference$=500$ ft.; 500 ft.$\times.3183=159.15$ ft.
4. 10 miles$=52800$ ft.; in one revolution it passes over a distance equal to its circumference; hence it will revolve $52800\div4\frac{1}{2}$, or $11733\frac{1}{3}$ times.
5. Diameter $=.3183\times50=15.915$; area$=\frac{1}{4}$ of $15.915\times50=198$ sq. ft. 135 sq. in.
6. 16 ft.$=$radius of circle; area$=256\times3.1416=804.2496+$ sq. ft.$=89.361+$sq. yd.
7. Circumference $=7925.75\times3.1416=24899.5362$ miles; length of a degree$=24899.5362\div360=69.16+$mi.
8. Since it is divided into four equal parts by lines drawn from the centre, the outer edge must be $\frac{1}{4}$ of the circumference; hence the circumference is 28 ft., and the diameter $28\times.3183=8.9124$ ft. The area of $\frac{1}{4}$ of the bed equals $\frac{1}{4}$ of $(28\times\frac{1}{4}$ of $8.9124)=7\times2.2281=15.5967$ sq. ft.

MEASUREMENT OF LAND.

Art. 344. Page 214.

2. $725\times400=290000$ P.$=1812$ A. 80 P.
3. $208.7\times120=25044$ P.$=156\frac{21}{40}$ acres; $\$81\frac{3}{4}\times156\frac{21}{40}=\$12795.91\frac{7}{8}$.
4. 64 A. 116 P.$=10356$ P.; the gain on 1 perch is $\$3.75-\$3.50=\$.25$; $10356\times\$.25=2589$.
5. 200 rd. 17 yd.$=1117$ yd.; 150 rd. 15 yd.$=840$ yd.; then $1117\times840=938280$ sq. yd.; and reducing this we have 193 A. 137 P. $15\frac{3}{4}$ sq. yd.

6. $16.5 \times 9.75 = 160.875$ sq. ch. $= 16$ A. 14 P.

7. 163 A. 3 ch. $= 1633$ sq. ch.; breadth $= 1633 \div 71 = 23$ ch.; $(71+23) \times 2 = 188$ ch. $= 752$ rd.

8. 1 Township $= (640 \times 36)$A.; $\frac{640 \times 36}{480} = 48$ A.; 48 A. $= \frac{48}{640}$, or $\frac{3}{40}$ of a section.

9. A quarter-quarter-section $= 40$ acres $= 6400$ P.; one side $=$ the square root of $6400 = 80$ rd.; $80 \times 4 = 320$ rd. $= 5280$ ft.; $5280 \div 8 = 660$; No. of rails $= 660 \times 5 = 3300$; $\$35 \times 3.300 = \$115.50$

10. 15 A. $= 2400$ P.; $2400 \div 80 = 30$ rd.; 9 A. $= 1440$ P.; $1440 \div 30 = 48$ rd.

11. $72 \times 4 = 288$ rd.; $288 \times \$2.50 = \$720$; $72 \times 3 = 216$; $\frac{1}{3}$ of $72 = 24$; $(216+24) \times 2 = 480$ rd.; $480 \times \$2.50 = \$1200$; $\$1200 - \$720 = \$480$.

12. $50 \times 50 = 2500$ P.; 3 acres $= 480$ P.; $15 \times 15 = 225$ P.; $480 + 200 + 225 = 905$ P.; 2500 P. $-$ 905 P. $= 1595$ P. $= 9$ A 155 P.

COST OF ARTIFICERS' WORK.

Art. 347. Page 215.

2. Area of 2 sides $= 40 \times 10 \times 2 = 800$ sq. ft.; area of 2 ends $= 20 \times 10 \times 2 = 400$ sq. ft.; area of ceiling $= 40 \times 20 = 800$ sq. ft.; $800 + 400 + 800 = 2000$; 2000 sq. ft. $\div 9 = 222\frac{2}{9}$ sq. yd.; $36¢ \times 222\frac{2}{9} = \$80$.

3. (28 ft. $+$ 15 ft. 4 in.) $\times 2 = 86$ ft. 8 in.; $86\frac{2}{3} \times 4\frac{1}{4} = 368\frac{1}{3}$ sq. ft. $= 40\frac{25}{27}$ sq. yd.; $\$.45 \times 40\frac{25}{27} = \$18.41\frac{2}{3}$.

4. $52\frac{5}{6} \times 20 \times 2 = 2113\frac{1}{3}$ sq. ft $= 21.13\frac{1}{3}$ squares; $\$1525 \times 21.13\frac{1}{3} = \$322.28\frac{1}{3}$.

5. $(50+28) \times 2 \times 35 = 5460$ sq. ft. $= 54.60$ squares; $\$12.25 \times 54.60 = \$668.85$.

6. $64 \times 32 \times 2 = 4096$ sq. ft.; $40.96 \times 1000 = 40960$; 64 ft. $= 768$ in.; $768 \times 2 = 1536$ in.; $1536 \div 4 = 384$, No. shingles extra in double course; whole number of shingles $= 40960 + 384 = 41344$; $\$14.87\frac{1}{2} \times 41.344 = \$614.992$.

7. $(40 + 32\frac{1}{3}) \times 2 \times 15\frac{1}{2} = 2242\frac{1}{3}$ sq. ft.; $2242\frac{1}{3}$ sq. ft. $-$ 815 sq. ft. $= 1427\frac{1}{3}$ sq. ft.; $1427\frac{1}{3} \times 25¢ = \$356.83\frac{1}{3}$.

8. Area of 2 sides $=7\frac{5}{12}\times 6\frac{1}{4}\times 2=92\frac{17}{24}$ sq. ft.; area of ends $=4\frac{1}{2}\times 6\frac{1}{4}\times 2=56\frac{1}{4}$ sq. ft.; area of bottom $=7\frac{5}{12}\times 4\frac{1}{2}$ $=33\frac{3}{8}$ sq. ft.; $92\frac{17}{24}+56\frac{1}{4}+33\frac{3}{8}=182\frac{1}{3}$ sq. ft.; No of lb. $=182\frac{1}{3}\times 5=911\frac{2}{3}$; 12¢ $\times 911\frac{2}{3}=$ \$109.40.

CARPETING, PAPERING, ETC.

Art. 348. Page 216.

2. Running lengthwise, it will require $15\div 2\frac{1}{2}=6$ breadths or strips; hence in all it will require $31\times 6=186$ ft. or 62yd. $31\div 2\frac{1}{2}=12\frac{2}{5}$; hence it will take 13 strips running crosswise; and in all $15\times 13\div 3=65$ yd.

3. 15 ft. = 5 yd.; dividing 5 by $\frac{3}{4}$ we find it will take 7 strips. The first strip will be 26 ft. long; the other strips will be $26\frac{1}{2}$ ft. long; hence it will take $26+26\frac{1}{2}\times 6=185$ ft., or $61\frac{2}{3}$ yd.

4. $(14\frac{1}{2}\div 3)\div\frac{5}{8}=7\frac{11}{15}$; hence it will take 8 strips. 8×18ft. $=144$ ft. $=48$ yd.; 48yd. + 2 yd. = 50 yd.; $50\times$ \$1.25 = \$62.50.

5. Area of walls $=(30+22\frac{1}{2})\times 2\times 10\frac{2}{3}=1120$ sq. ft.; area of ceiling $=30\times 22\frac{1}{2}=675$ sq. ft.; $1120+675=1795$ sq. ft.; $1795-142=1653$; contents of 1 roll $=8\times\frac{5}{9}=\frac{40}{9}$ sq. yd. $=40$ sq. ft.; $1653\div 40=41\frac{13}{40}$.

6. $41\frac{13}{40}\times$ \$2.40 = \$99.18; $(30+22\frac{1}{2})\times 2=105$ ft.; 12¢ $\times 105=$ \$12.60; \$99.18 + \$12.60 = \$111.78.

7. $10\times 3=30$ yd.; \$1.50 $\times 30=$ \$45; $30\times\frac{1}{2}=15$ sq. yd.; $15\div\frac{5}{8}=24$ yd.; \$.87$\frac{1}{2}\times 24=$ \$21; \$45 + \$21 = \$66.

MEASURES OF VOLUME.

Art. 352. Page 218.

2. 1 yd. 1 ft. $=1\frac{1}{3}$ yd.; $1\frac{1}{3}\times 1\frac{1}{3}\times 1\frac{1}{3}=2$ cu. yd. 10 cu. ft.

3. $9\times 9=81$; $405\div 81=5$.

4. $6\times 4\times 2\frac{1}{2}=60$ cu. ft. $=103680$ cu. in.

5. $25\times 12\frac{1}{2}\times 9\frac{1}{2}=2968\frac{3}{4}$ cu. ft. $=109\frac{103}{108}$ cu. yd.

6. $13\frac{1}{3}\times 8\frac{1}{3}=112\frac{1}{2}$ sq. ft.; 125 cu. yd. $=3375$ cu. ft.; $3375\div 112\frac{1}{2}=30$.

7. $72\times 48\times 7\frac{1}{4}=25056$ cu. ft. $=928$ cu. yd.

Art. 355. THE CYLINDER.

2. 20 ft. $=\frac{20}{12}$ inches; $\frac{20}{12}\times 3.1416=5.236$ ft.; $5.236\times 18=$ *94.248 sq. ft.*

3. $\frac{3}{2}\times\frac{3}{2}\times 3.1416\times 10=70.686$ cu. ft.

4. Diam. $=9\times .3183$; area$=9\times .3183\times\frac{9}{4}$; contents$=9\times .3183\times\frac{9}{4}\times 15=96.6836\frac{1}{4}$ cu. ft.$=3.5808\frac{3}{4}$ cu. yd.; $\$.62\frac{1}{2}\times 3.5808\frac{3}{4}=\$2.238046\frac{7}{8}$.

5. Convex surface $=8\times 3.1416\times 8\frac{1}{4}=207.3456$ sq. ft.$=23.0384$ sq. yd.

6. Contents$=5\times 5\times 3.1416=78.54$; $78.54\times 4\frac{1}{2}=353.43$ cu. ft.

WOOD MEASURE.

Art. 358. Page 220.

2. $96\times 12\times 8=9216$ cu. ft.; $9216\div 128=72$ cords.

3. $5\frac{1}{3}\times 3\frac{3}{4}=20$ sq. ft.; $128\div 20=6\frac{2}{5}$ ft.

4. $75\times 10=750$ sq. ft.; $128\times 27\frac{3}{4}=3552$ sq. ft.; $3552\div 750=4.736$ ft.

5. $20\times 10\times 8=1600$ sq. ft.; $1600\div 128=12\frac{1}{2}$ cords; $\$4.75\times 12\frac{1}{2}=\$59.37\frac{1}{2}$.

BOARDS AND TIMBER.

Art. 360. Page 221.

2. $16\times 1\frac{1}{2}=24$ sq. ft.

3. $\frac{1}{2}\times(18+14)\times 20=320$; $320\div 12=26\frac{2}{3}$ sq. ft.

4. $16\times 18\times 4\times 14=16128$; $16128\div 12=1344$ sq. ft.

5. $14\times 9\times 40=5040$; $5040\div 12=420$ sq. ft.

6. $9\frac{1}{2}\div 6\frac{1}{3}=1\frac{1}{2}$ ft.$=18$ inches.

7. It will be seen on examining such a box that *twice* the thickness of the board must be deducted from the height of the sides and ends, and also from the length of the ends; hence the area of the two sides is *twice* 3 ft. $\times$ 16 in.$=8$ sq. feet.; area of two ends equals *twice* 2 ft. 4 in. $\times$ 16 in.$=6\frac{2}{9}$ sq. ft.; area of top and bottom $=$ *twice* 3 ft. $\times 2\frac{1}{2}$ ft.$=15$ sq. ft.; $8+6\frac{2}{9}+15=29\frac{2}{9}$ sq. ft.

8. $12\times 15\times 40=7200$; $7200\div 12=600$ sq. ft.; $\$2.75\times 6.00=\$16.50$.

9. $4\times 5\times 10\times 9=1800$; $1800\div 12=150$ sq. ft.; $\$8.75\times .150=\$1.3125$.

10. $56\times 32\times 1\frac{1}{2}\times 3=8064$ sq. ft.; $8.064\times\$33=\$266.112$.

11. $(36+18)\times 2=108$ rd. $=1782$ ft.; number of posts $=1782 \div 9=198$; number of sq. ft. of boards $=1782\times 11\times 3\div 12=4900\frac{1}{2}$ sq. ft.; cost of posts $=\$30\times 1.98=\$59.40$; cost of lumber $=\$15.50\times 4.900\frac{1}{2}=\$75.95775$; cost of labor $=\$3.50\times 2\times 3=\$21$; whole cost $=\$59.40+\$75.957+\$21=\$156.357$.

MASONRY, BRICKWORK, ETC.

Art. 364. Page 223.

2. Contents $=42\times 28\times 6\frac{1}{2}=7644$ cu. ft. $=283\frac{1}{9}$ cu. yd.; $\$.42\times 283\frac{1}{9}=\$118.90\frac{2}{3}$.

3. To find the true length of the wall, we deduct the length of the 4 corners from the distance round the wall; length of corner equals thickness of wall; 20 rd. $=330$ ft.; 18 rd. $=297$ ft.; length of wall $=2\times(330+297)-4\times 2\frac{1}{2}=1244$ ft.; $1244\times 5\times 2\frac{1}{2}\div 24\frac{3}{4}=628\frac{28}{99}$ perches.

NOTE.—The actual length of the wall may also be found by subtracting twice the thickness of the wall from each end, and then finding the sum of the four sides; thus, the length of each end is $297-2\frac{1}{2}\times 2=292$ ft.; the length of wall $=330+330+292+292$, or $(330+292)\times 2=1244$ ft., as found in the previous solution.

4. $600\times 65\times 4\frac{1}{2}=175500$ cu. ft. $=6500$ cu. yd.; $\$.52\times 6500=\$3380$.

5. The whole distance around the building $=2\times(48+25)=146$ ft.; length of corners $=4\times\frac{13}{12}=4\frac{1}{3}$ ft.; length of wall $=146-4\frac{1}{3}=141\frac{2}{3}$ ft.; surface of wall $=141\frac{2}{3}\times 21-240=2735$ sq. ft.; since the wall is 13 in. thick, there will be 24 bricks in a square foot, hence $2735\times 21=57435$ bricks.

6. Thickness of wall 3 bricks thick, 13 in.; distance around building $=40\times 4=160$ ft.; length of corner $=4\times\frac{13}{12}=4\frac{1}{3}$ ft.; length of wall $=160-4\frac{1}{3}=155\frac{2}{3}$ ft.; surface of wall $=155\frac{2}{3}\times 22=3424\frac{2}{3}$ sq. ft.; surface of one brick and mortar $=8\frac{1}{2}\times 2\frac{5}{8}=22\frac{5}{16}$ sq. in.; No. of bricks in square foot $=144\div 22\frac{5}{16}=6\frac{54}{119}$; whole number of bricks $=6\frac{54}{119}\times 3\times 3424\frac{2}{3}=66306\frac{18}{119}$; $\$15\frac{1}{2}\times 66.306\frac{18}{119}=\$1027.745\frac{41}{119}$.

NOTE.—In the first edition the answer is given as \$1026.93; this was obtained by reckoning the thickness of the wall at $13\frac{3}{4}$ inches, on account of the greater thickness of the bricks; but it is thought to be more convenient and accurate in practice to consider the wall as having the same thickness, whatever the width of the brick.

7. Contents $=3^2\times3.1416\times15\frac{3}{4}=445.3218$ cu. ft. $=16.4934$ loads; $50¢\times16.4934=\$8.2467$.

8. Contents of cellar $=45\times24\times6=6480$ cu. ft. $=240$ loads; $45¢\times240=\$108$; contents of wall $=2\times(45+24)\times7\frac{1}{2}\times1\frac{1}{2}=1552\frac{1}{2}$ cu. ft. $=62\frac{8}{11}$ perches; as we are calculating the value of the labor and material together, we make no deduction for corners; $\$4.25\times62\frac{8}{11}=\$266.59\frac{1}{11}$; whole cost $=\$108+\$266.59\frac{1}{11}=\$374.59\frac{1}{11}$.

MEASURES OF CAPACITY.

Art. 369. CAPACITY OF CISTERNS.

2. Contents $=15\times3\times3\frac{1}{2}=157\frac{1}{2}$ cu. ft.; reducing to inches, and dividing by 231, we have $157\frac{1}{2}\times1728\div231=1178\frac{2}{11}$ gal.

3. Reducing the contents to cubic inches and dividing by 277.274, we have $157\frac{1}{2}\times1728\div277.274=981.55+$.

4. Reduce 45 hhd. to gallons, and then to cubic inches; 45 hhd. $=45\times63\times231\div1728=378\frac{63}{64}$ cu. ft.

5. 54 hhd. $=54\times63\times231\div1728=454\frac{25}{32}$ cu. ft.; surface $=8^2=64$; depth $=454\frac{25}{32}\div64=7.10595625$.

6. Contents $=7\times7\times4=196$ cu. ft.; $196\times1728\div231=1466\frac{2}{11}$ gal $=46\frac{6}{11}$ bar.

7. Contents $=(2\frac{1}{4})^2\times3.1416\times12=190.8522$ cu. ft.; $190.8522\times1728\div231=1427.6736$ gal. $=22.6614+$ hhd.

8. $16\frac{1}{2}$ hhd. $=16\frac{1}{2}\times63\times231\div1728=138\frac{123}{128}$ cu. ft.; $138\frac{123}{128}\div(1.75^2\times3.1416)=14.44+$ ft.

9. 4 yd. $=12$ ft.; 2 yd. $=6$ ft.; contents $=12\times6\times6=432$ cu. ft.; $\frac{1}{2}$ full $=\frac{1}{2}$ of $432=216$ cu. ft.; weight of water $=1000$ oz. $\times216=216000$ oz. $=13500$ lb.

10. Contents $=7\times5\times3=105$ cu. ft.; $105\times1728\div231=785\frac{5}{11}$ gal.; 2 h. $=120$ min.; $785\frac{5}{11}\div120=6\frac{6}{11}$ gal.

11. Contents $=8\frac{1}{2}\times4\frac{1}{4}\times2\frac{1}{2}=90\frac{5}{16}$ cu. ft.; $90\frac{5}{16}$ cu. ft. $=90\frac{5}{16}\times1728\div(231\times63)=10.72+$ hhd.; 1000 oz. $\times90\frac{5}{16}\div16=5644\frac{17}{32}$ lb.

12. Contents$=32\times27\times10=8640$ cu. ft.; $\frac{3}{4}$ of 8640 cu. ft.$=$ 6480 cu. ft.; 6480 cu. ft.$=769.42+$hhd.; 10¢$\times769.42$ \$76.94$+$.

Art. 371. CAPACITY OF BINS.

2. Contents$=16\times7\times2\frac{1}{2}=280$ cu. ft.; $280\times1728\div2150.42$ $=224.99+$bu.

3. 640 bushels$=640\times2150.42\div1728=796.45$ cu. ft.; $24\times3\frac{1}{3}=80$ sq. ft; $796.45\div80=9.955+$ft.

4. 2000 bushels$=2000\times2150.42\div1728=2488.91+$ cu. ft.; $25\times15=375$ sq. ft.; $2488.91\div375=6.63+$ ft.

5. Contents$=10\frac{5}{12}\times7\times3\frac{1}{2}=255\frac{5}{24}$ cu. ft.; shelled corn is sold by stricken measure, and carrots by heaped measure; $\frac{4}{5}$ of the number of cubic feet equals the number of stricken bushels (see Note), hence $\frac{4}{5}$ of $255\frac{5}{24}=204\frac{1}{6}$ bu.

9. Contents$=4\times3\times2\frac{1}{3}=28$ cu. ft.; $\frac{4}{5}$ of $28=22\frac{2}{5}$ bu. cranberries; $\frac{4}{5}$ of $22\frac{2}{5}=17\frac{23}{25}$ bu. apples.

10. Contents$=8\times6\times3=144$ cu. ft.; $\frac{3}{4}$ of 144 cu. ft.$=108$ cu. ft.; $\frac{4}{5}$ of $108=86\frac{2}{5}$ bu.; \$1.25$\times86\frac{2}{5}=$\$108.

11. $12\times7\frac{1}{2}\times4=360$ cu. ft.$=288$ bu.; No. of barrels$=48\times288\div196=70\frac{26}{49}$.

6. $5\times4\frac{1}{2}\times3=67\frac{1}{2}$ cu. ft.; No. of tons $=67\frac{1}{2}\div35=1\frac{13}{14}$; \$6.50$\times1\frac{13}{14}=$\$12.53$\frac{4}{7}$.

7. 6 yd.$=18$ ft.; $4\frac{1}{2}$ yd.$=13\frac{1}{2}$ ft.; $18\times13\frac{1}{2}\times8=1944$ cu. ft.; $\frac{1}{2}$ of 1944 cu. ft.$=972$ cu. ft.; No. of tons$=972\div34\frac{1}{2}$ $=28\frac{4}{23}$; \$7.50$\times28\frac{4}{23}=$\$211.304$+$.

8. $40\times25\times15=15000$ cu. ft.; $58\frac{1}{8}\times15000=871875$ lb.$=435\frac{15}{16}$ tons.

12. $24\times18\times16=6912$ cu. ft.; No. of tons$=6912\div400=17\frac{7}{25}$; \$12$\times17\frac{7}{25}=$\$207.36.

13. $8\times7\times6=336$ cu. ft.$=12\frac{4}{9}$ cu. yd.; No. of tons$=12\frac{4}{9}\div10=1\frac{11}{45}$; \$15$\times1\frac{11}{45}=$\$18.66$\frac{2}{3}$.

14. $20\times12\times7=1680$ cu. ft.; corn in the ear is measured by heaped measure, hence $\frac{4}{5}$ of $\frac{4}{5}$ of $1680=1075\frac{1}{5}$ bu.; No. of bu. of shelled corn $=\frac{1}{2}$ of $1075\frac{1}{5}=537\frac{3}{5}$; \$1.05$\times537\frac{3}{5}=$\$564.48.

Page 227. MISCELLANEOUS PROBLEMS.

1. 1 mile 16 rd.=5544 ft.; the planks are laid across the walk, and as each plank is 1 ft. wide, there will be 5544 planks.
2. 122 gal.$=122\times231=28182$ cu. in.; $28182\div2150.42=$ 13.1+ bu.
3. 1 step requires $10+7\frac{1}{2}=17\frac{1}{2}$ in.; whole quantity$=17\frac{1}{2}\times18=315$ in.$=8\frac{3}{4}$ yd.
4. $1\frac{1}{2}$ miles=2640 yd.; No. of cu. yd$=2640\times\frac{5}{3}\times\frac{8}{3}=11733\frac{1}{3}$; $\$3716\div11733\frac{1}{3}=\$.31\frac{59}{88}$.
5. Contents$=20\times12\times10=2400$ cu. ft.; 2400 cu. ft.$\div$400 cu. ft.=6 tons.
6. The weight$=\frac{7564}{12875}$ of 1 ton=12 cwt. $22\frac{46}{99}$ lb.
7. Area of square$=32\times32=1024$ P.=30976 sq. yd.; $30976\times4=123904$.
8. Area of walls$=2\times(18+14)\times10=640$ sq. ft.; area of ceiling$=18\times14=252$ sq. ft.; whole area=640 sq. ft.+252 sq. ft.=892 sq. ft.$=99\frac{1}{9}$ sq. yd.; $99\frac{1}{9}\div5=19\frac{37}{45}$ bunches.
9. Dividing 17 ft. by 26 in., we find it will take 8 strips; 25 ft.$\times$8 ft.=200 ft.$=66\frac{2}{3}$ yd.; $66\frac{2}{3}$ yd.$+3\frac{1}{3}$ yd.=70 yd.; $\$1.87\frac{1}{2}\times70=\$131.25$.
10. 32 rd.=528 ft.; area of square$=528\times36=19008$ sq. ft.= 2112 sq. yd.; $\$3.25\times2112=\$6864$.
11. $\frac{1}{8}$ of a mile=660 ft.; contents$=660\times24\times20=316800$ cu. ft.$=11733\frac{1}{3}$ cu. yd.; $\$1.50\times11733\frac{1}{3}=\$17600$.
12. At 60 lb. a bushel, 12000 bushels=720000 lb.; $720000\div24000=30$ cars.
13. 1 ton of Schuylkill red ash coal=36 cu. ft.; $7\frac{1}{2}\times4\frac{1}{2}=33\frac{3}{4}$ sq. ft.; $36\div33\frac{3}{4}=1\frac{1}{15}$ ft.$=12\frac{4}{5}$ in.
14. $30\times21=630$ sq. ft; $28\times18=504$ sq. ft.; $24\times16=384$ sq. ft.; $32\times24=768$ sq. ft.; $630+504+384+768=2286$ sq. ft.; $2286\times5=11430$ cu. ft.$=423\frac{1}{3}$ loads.
15. $30\times25\times5\frac{1}{2}=4125$ cu. ft.; as the L rests against the main building, there would be but three walls; $16\times1\frac{1}{2}\times2\times3=144$ cu. ft.; the 2 corners to be deducted $=(1\frac{1}{2})^2\times2\times2=9$ cu. ft.; whole excavation=4125 cu.

ft.+144 cu. ft.—9 cu. ft.=4260 cu. ft.=$157\frac{7}{9}$ cu. yd.; 50¢×$157\frac{7}{9}$=\$$78.88\frac{8}{9}$.

16. Surface of rooms on 1st story=(2×(14+15)×10+14×15)×4=3160 sq. ft.; hall=2×(30+8)×10+30×8=1000 sq. ft.; whole surface of first story=4160 sq. ft; rooms on 2d story=(2×(14+15)×$9\frac{1}{2}$+14×15)×4=3044 sq. ft.; hall=2×(30+8)×$9\frac{1}{2}$+30×8=962 sq. ft.; whole surface of 2d story=4006 sq. ft; rooms on 3d story=(2×(14+15)×$8\frac{1}{2}$+14×15)×4=2812 sq. ft.; hall=2×(30+8)×$8\frac{1}{2}$+30×8=886 sq. ft.; whole surface of 3d story=3698 sq. ft.; doors =7×$3\frac{1}{2}$×24=588 sq. ft.; windows=6×3×30=540 sq. ft.; whole surface to be plastered=4160+4006+3698—588—540=10736 sq. ft.=$1192\frac{8}{9}$ sq. yd.; 30¢×$1192\frac{8}{9}$=\$$357.86\frac{2}{3}$.

2d Solution. Whole height of 3 stories=10+$9\frac{1}{2}$+$8\frac{1}{2}$=28 ft.; surface of walls=$(2\times\overline{14+15}\times4+2\times\overline{30+8})\times28$ =8624 sq. ft.; surface of ceilings=(14×15×4+30×8)×3=3240 sq. ft.; surface to be plastered=8624+3240—588—540=10736, etc., as before.

17. Amount dug from cellar=40×30×4=4800 cu. ft =$177\frac{7}{9}$ cu. yd.; 50¢×$177\frac{7}{9}$=\$$88.88\frac{8}{9}$; lower part of wall=2×(40+30)×$1\frac{1}{2}$×4=840 cu. ft.=$33\frac{31}{33}$ perches; \$3.15×$33\frac{31}{33}$=\$$106.90\frac{10}{11}$; upper part of wall=2×(40+30)×3=420 sq. ft.; 16¢ × 420 = \$67.20; \$$88.88\frac{8}{9}$ + \$$106.90\frac{10}{11}$+\$67.20=\$$262.99\frac{79}{99}$, or \$263—.

18. Surface of wall = 2×(40+30)×35 = 4900 sq. ft.; the gable is a triangle, hence surface of the 2 gables= 2×(30×$\frac{10}{2}$)= 300 sq. ft.; 4900+300 = 5200 sq. ft.; No. of bricks reckoned to find cost of labor=5200×21=109200; cost of labor=\$3×109.200=\$327.60; corners=$1\frac{1}{12}$×35×4=$151\frac{2}{3}$ sq. ft.; doors=7×$3\frac{1}{2}$×3 =$73\frac{1}{2}$ sq. ft.; windows=6×3×30=540 sq. ft.; $151\frac{2}{3}$+$73\frac{1}{2}$+540=$765\frac{1}{6}$ sq. ft.; 5200=$765\frac{1}{6}$=$4434\frac{5}{6}$ sq. ft.; No. of bricks reckoned for cost of material=$4434\frac{5}{6}$×21 = $93131\frac{1}{2}$; \$10 × $93.131\frac{1}{2}$ = \$$931.31\frac{1}{2}$; \$327.60 + \$$931.31\frac{1}{2}$=\$1258.915.

SUPPLEMENT TO DENOMINATE NUMBERS.

COMPARISON OF MEASURES OF CAPACITY.

Art. 372. Page 228.

1. Difference between 1 dry gallon and 1 liquid gallon equals $268.8 - 231 = 37.8$ cu. in.; $37.8 \times 495.3 = 18722.34$ cu. in.
2. 5 gal. 2 qt. $=5\frac{1}{2} \times 282 = 1551$ cu. in.; 3 gal. 2 qt. 1 pt. $=3\frac{5}{8} \times 231 = 837\frac{3}{8}$ cu. in.; $837\frac{3}{8} \div 1551 = .53989+$.
3. 1 gallon of water $=231$ cu. in.; 1 bushel contains 2150.42 cu. in.; $4550 \times 231 = 1051050$ cu. in.; No. of bushels $=1051050 \div 2150.42 = 488.765-$.
4. $2150.42 \div 231 = 9.309+$ gal.
5. 1 quart of water $=\frac{1}{4}$ of 231 cu. in. $=57\frac{3}{4}$ cu. in; 1 quart of strawberries $=\frac{1}{4}$ of 268.8 cu. in. $=67.2$ cu. in.; $67.2 - 57\frac{3}{4} = 9.45$ cu. in.; $9.45 \times 32 = 302.4$ cu. in.
6. 25 gal $=100$ qt.; molasses was sold for $100 \times \$.15 = \$15$; 25 gal. dry measure $=268.8 \times 25 = 6720$ cu. in.; 6720 cu. in. $=(6720 \div 231)$gal. or $6720 \div 231 \times 4 = 116\frac{4}{11}$ qt.; $\$15 \div 116\frac{4}{11} = \$.12\frac{57}{64}$.

COMPARISON OF WEIGHTS.

Art. 373. Page 229.

1. $2\frac{7}{8}$ pwt. $=69$ gr.; 1 lb. Av. $=7000$; $7000 \div 69 = 101$ rings, 31 gr. remaining.
2. 2 lb. 10 oz. Av. $=18375$ gr.; $18375 \div 480 = 38\frac{9}{32}$ oz. Troy; $\$2.25 \times 38\frac{9}{32} = \$86.13\frac{9}{32}$.
3. A pound of lead is weighed by Avoirdupois weight, and therefore weighs 7000 gr.; a pound of silver is weighed by Troy weight, and therefore weighs 5760 gr.; hence $52\frac{5}{8}$ lb. of lead weigh more than $52\frac{5}{8}$ lb. of silver.
4. 10 lb. iron. $=70000$ gr.; $70000 \div 5760 = 12\frac{11}{72}$ lb. of gold.
5. 5 lb. 12 oz. Av. $=40250$ gr.; 3 lb. 10 oz. Troy $=22080$ gr.; $40250 \div 22080 = 1.8229+$.

6. 120 lb. Av. $=120\times7000\div5760=145\frac{5}{6}$ lb.

7. $\$8\frac{1}{3}\times25=\$208\frac{1}{3}$; 25 lb. Av. $=175000$ gr. $=364\frac{7}{12}$ ℥; 75¢ $\times364\frac{7}{12}=\$273.43\frac{3}{4}$; $\$273.43\frac{3}{4}-\$208.33\frac{1}{3}=\$65.10\frac{5}{12}$.

COMPARISON OF MONEY.

Art. 375. Page 230.

1. £25 $=\$4.8665\times25=\$121.66\frac{1}{4}$.
2. £14 12 s. $=$ £14.6 $=\$4.8665\times14.6=\$71.0509$.
3. $\$256.16\div\$4.8665=$ £52 12 s. 9 d.—
4. 240 G. $=$ £252 $=\$4.8665\times252=\$1226.358$.
5. £42 $=\$4.8665\times42=\$204.393$; $\$204.393\div\$.193=$ 1059.03+ fr.
6. 875 fr. $=\$.193\times875=\$168.875$; $\$168.875\div\$4.8665=$ £34 14.03+ s.
7. £340 $=\$4.8665\times340=\$1654.61$; $\$1654.61\div\$.2385=$ 6937.568+ marks.
8. 4375 marks $=\$.2385\times4375=\$1043.4375$; $\$1043.4375\div$ $\$4.8665=$ £214 8 s. 3d.—
9. Weight of 1000 sovereigns $=123.274$ gr. $\times1000=123274$ gr.; $123274\div7000=17.610\frac{2}{7}$ lb. Av.
10. 15 lb. 8 oz. $=188$ oz. $=90240$ gr.; since $\frac{1}{10}$ of the coin is alloy, the gold in 1 dollar $=\frac{9}{10}$ of 25.8 gr., or 23.22 gr.; No. of dollars $=90240\div23.22=3886$ and 7.08 gr. remaining.

NOTE.—In the 1st edition the second answer was inadvertently given 7.8⅗ gr. which is the number of grains remaining of the mixed metal used for coining.

SECTION VIII.

PERCENTAGE.

Art. 385. MENTAL EXERCISES.

10. 20% is $\frac{1}{5}$; hence there were $\frac{4}{5}$ of 120, or 96, which were good.

11. $33\frac{1}{3}$% is $\frac{1}{3}$; hence $\frac{2}{3}$ of 108, or 72 gallons remained.

12. 15% is $\frac{3}{20}$; hence the speed was $\frac{23}{20}$ of 20, or 23 miles.

13. $11\frac{1}{9}$% is $\frac{1}{9}$; hence he received $\frac{10}{9}$ of \$45, or \$50.

14. $\frac{1}{4}$% is $\frac{1}{400}$; hence he paid $\frac{1}{400}$ of \$3000, or \$7.50.

15. 120 is base, 20% the rate, and 24 the percentage.

Art. 385. WRITTEN EXERCISES.

11. $\frac{15}{16}$ lb.=15 oz.; 15 oz.×.00$\frac{4}{5}$=.12 oz.

12. 46 lb. $12\frac{3}{4}$ oz.×.25=11 lb. $11\frac{3}{16}$ oz.

13. 6 lb. 8 oz. 12 pwt.=1612 pwt.; 1612 pwt.×.$42\frac{1}{2}$=685.1 pwt.=2 lb. 10 oz. 5.1 pwt.

14. He sold 600×.$16\frac{2}{3}$=100 bar.; there remained 600—100, or 500 bar. Or, there remained 100%—$16\frac{2}{3}$%=$83\frac{1}{3}$%; 600×.$83\frac{1}{3}$=500 bar.

16. A barrel of flour weighs 196 lb.; 196×1.$33\frac{1}{3}$=$261\frac{1}{3}$ lb.

17. 100%—$33\frac{1}{3}$%=$66\frac{2}{3}$%; 360 acres×.$66\frac{2}{3}$=240 acres.

18. 100%—10%=90%; $16\frac{2}{3}$ oz.×.90=15 oz.

19. He sold .$12\frac{1}{2}$×1016, or 127 acres to Mr. Chase, and had remaining 889 acres; he then sold .$37\frac{1}{2}$×889, or $333\frac{3}{8}$ acres to Mr. Dunn, and had remaining $555\frac{5}{8}$ acres. Or, he had remaining $62\frac{1}{2}$% of $87\frac{1}{2}$%, or $54\frac{11}{16}$%; 1016 ×.$54\frac{11}{16}$=$555\frac{5}{8}$.

20. 1 cwt. 27 lb.=127 lb.; 127×.11=13.97 lb.; 13.97÷$\frac{3}{4}$= $18.62\frac{2}{3}$ pt.=2 gal. $1.31\frac{1}{3}$ qt.

21. He spends 10%+15%+6%+4%=35%; hence there remains 100%—35%, or 65% of \$2000=\$1300.

22. He spends in all 30%+$12\frac{1}{2}$%+10%=$52\frac{1}{2}$%; hence there remains 100%—$52\frac{1}{2}$%, or $47\frac{1}{2}$% of \$2500= \$1187.50.

23. 100%—$16\frac{2}{3}$%=$83\frac{1}{3}$%; $83\frac{1}{3}$ of $\frac{3}{4}$=$\frac{5}{8}$; $\frac{5}{8}$ of \$10000=\$6250.

Art. 386. MENTAL EXERCISES.

10. If 30 is 25%, or $\frac{1}{4}$ more than some number, it is $\frac{5}{4}$ of the number; *hence the* number is 24. The other results are 20 and 15.

11. If 60 is 25%, or $\frac{1}{4}$ less than some number, it is $\frac{3}{4}$ of the number, hence the number is 80; since any number minus 100% of itself is zero, 60 cannot be 100% less than any number.

12. It has gained $12\frac{1}{2}$%, or $\frac{1}{8}$, hence 2700 is $\frac{9}{8}$, and $\frac{1}{8}$, the gain, is 300; the yearly gain is $\frac{1}{5}$ of 300, or 60.

13. $\frac{2}{5}$% equals $\frac{1}{250}$=\$60, and $\frac{250}{250}$=\$15000. Or, if $\frac{2}{5}$%=\$60, $\frac{1}{5}$%=\$30; $\frac{5}{5}$%, or 1%=\$150, and 100%=\$15000.

14. $62\frac{1}{2}$% equals $\frac{5}{8}$=\$50; hence the wife received \$80.

15. $11\frac{1}{9}$%=$\frac{1}{9}$, $\frac{9}{9}$—$\frac{1}{9}$=$\frac{8}{9}$=160, $\frac{1}{9}$=20, $\frac{9}{9}$=180.

Art. 386. WRITTEN EXERCISES.

10. 1694÷1.40=1210. | 11. 468÷.08=585.

14. 42 A. 112 P.÷.$16\frac{2}{3}$=256 A. 32 P.

15. 14 lb. 10 oz. 16 pwt.÷$1.33\frac{1}{3}$=11 lb. 2 oz. 2 pwt.

16. \$600÷.24=\$2500. | 17. 320 A.÷.15=$2133\frac{1}{3}$ A.

18. \$15÷.30=\$50.

19. He saves 100%—24%, or 76% of his salary; \$760÷.76 =\$1000.

20. \$4788.56÷.35=\$13681.60.

21. If he sold 25% to A, there remained 75%, and if he sold $33\frac{1}{3}$% of the remainder, he sold $\frac{1}{3}$ of 75%, or 25% to C, hence 25% of the whole equals 640 bar., and there were 640÷.25=2560 bar.

22. $33\frac{1}{3}$% of $62\frac{1}{2}$%=$20\frac{5}{6}$%; \$4500÷.$20\frac{5}{6}$=\$21600; 100%−$62\frac{1}{2}$%=$37\frac{1}{2}$%; $37\frac{1}{2}$% of \$21600=\$8100.

23. 100%−$33\frac{1}{3}$%=$66\frac{2}{3}$%; then $66\frac{2}{3}$% of 90%, or 60%, equals amount still invested, or \$4500; her money= \$4500÷.60=\$7500.

Art. 387. MENTAL EXERCISES.

6. $\frac{3}{4}$ is 100% of $\frac{3}{4}$, and $\frac{8}{9}$, which is $\frac{32}{27}$ of $\frac{3}{4}$, is $\frac{32}{27}$ of 100%, or $118\frac{14}{27}$%.

7. $\frac{3}{5}$ is 100% of $\frac{3}{5}$, and $\frac{2}{3}$, which is $\frac{10}{9}$ of $\frac{3}{5}$, is $\frac{10}{9}$ of 100%, or $111\frac{1}{9}$%

8. 75% is 100% of 75%, and 25%, which is $\frac{1}{3}$ of 75%, is $\frac{1}{3}$ of 100%, or $33\frac{1}{3}$%.

9. 2.5% is 100% of 2.5%, and 1.5%, which is $\frac{3}{5}$ of 2.5%, is $\frac{3}{5}$ of 100%, or 60%.

10. 12 gallons is $\frac{2}{15}$ of 90 gallons, or $\frac{2}{15}$ of 100%, which is $13\frac{1}{3}$%.

11. He spends \$2000—\$300, or \$1700, which is $\frac{1700}{2000}$ or $\frac{17}{20}$, or 85% of the whole.

13. He gained \$250, which is $\frac{1}{20}$ of \$5000, or 5%.

Art. 387. WRITTEN EXERCISES.

12. 5 lb. 8 oz. ÷ 18 lb. = .30$\frac{5}{9}$.

14. 1 bushel = 32 qt.; 10 ÷ 32 = .31$\frac{1}{4}$.

15. \$1356 ÷ \$1800 = .75$\frac{1}{3}$.

16. 960 − 600 = 360; 360 ÷ 960 = .37$\frac{1}{2}$.

17. \$7289 ÷ \$15760 = .46$\frac{1}{4}$.

18. After losing 20% there remained 80%; he then sold 25% or $\frac{1}{4}$, and there remained $\frac{3}{4}$ of 80%, or 60%.

19. \$780 = 15%, hence his money out of bank was 85% of the whole. He then deposited 25%, or $\frac{1}{4}$, of 85%, or 21$\frac{1}{4}$%, and had then in bank 15% + 21$\frac{1}{4}$% = 36$\frac{1}{4}$%.

20. 25.8 ÷ 258 = .10.

21. 637 = 65% of the regiment, hence the regiment equals 637 ÷ .65 = 980. Now, $\frac{1}{7}$ of 637, or 91, men were killed, and 91 men is 9$\frac{2}{7}$% of 980 men.

PROFIT AND LOSS.

Art. 393. MENTAL EXERCISES.

2. At a gain of 25%, $\frac{1}{4}$ of the cost equals the gain, hence the gain was $\frac{1}{4}$ of 80 cents, or 20 cents.

3. At 16$\frac{2}{3}$%, $\frac{1}{6}$ of the cost equals the gain, hence the gain is $\frac{1}{6}$ of \$150, or \$25.

4. At 12$\frac{1}{2}$%, $\frac{1}{8}$ of the cost equals the gain, hence the selling price was $\frac{9}{8}$ of 8 cents, or 9 cents.

5. At 6$\frac{1}{4}$%, $\frac{1}{16}$ of the cost equals the loss, hence he sold her for $\frac{15}{16}$ of \$48, or \$45.

6. The whole cost was $\frac{11}{10}$ of \$40, or \$44, and he sold it for $\frac{5}{4}$ of \$44, or \$55.

Art. 393. WRITTEN EXERCISES.

6. 10% off leaves 90%; 90% of 90% = 81%; \$7.50 × .81 = \$6.075.

7. 25% off leaves 75%; 20% off leaves 80%; 10% off leaves 90%; 90% of 80% of 75% = 54%. \$15 × .54 = \$8.10.

8. \$6.50 × 1.15 = \$7.47$\frac{1}{2}$; \$7.47$\frac{1}{2}$ ÷ 196 = \$.038+.

9. \$650 × .60 = \$390; \$390 × 1.25 = \$487.50.

10. 6$\frac{1}{4}$¢ × .20 = 1$\frac{1}{4}$¢; 12$\frac{1}{2}$¢ × .20 = 2$\frac{1}{2}$¢; 18$\frac{3}{4}$¢ × .20 = 3$\frac{3}{4}$¢; 25¢ × .20 = 5¢; 40¢ × .20 = 8¢.

11. 10% off=90%; 15% off=85%; 85% of 90%=76½%; 100%−76½%=23½%; 5% off=95%; 10% off=90%; 15% off=85%; 85% of 90% of 95%=72.675%; 100%−72.675=27.325%=27$\frac{13}{40}$%.

12. 105% of 105%=110.25%; 110.25%−110%=.25% or ¼%; 110% of 120%=132%; 90% of 80%=72%; 132%−72%=60%.

13. $.20×84=$16.80; $16.80×.33⅓=$5.60.

14. Henry gained 25% of cost, and hence sold it for 125% of cost. The buyer paid 125% of $850, and since he lost 20%, he sold it for 80% of 125%, or 100% of $850, which is $850.

15. 10¢×1.35=13½¢; since the first letter of the key is *n*, and the third *w*, and the second *o*, the mark will be $nw\frac{n}{o}$.

Art. 394. MENTAL EXERCISES.

3. 65%, or $\frac{13}{20}$ of the cost equals $91, the selling price; hence the cost was $140.

4. Since $15 was ¾ of the cost, the cost was $20, and to gain 30% or $\frac{3}{10}$ of the cost, he should sell them for $\frac{13}{10}$ of $20, or $26.

5. He bought it for 85%, and sold it for 140%, hence he gained 55% of the value of the horse.

6. He gained ⅕, hence ⅚ of cost=$120, and ⅙ of cost, or the gain=$24; he lost ¼ on the second, hence ¾ of cost=$120, and ¼ of the cost, or loss, equals $40; hence he lost $40−$24=$16.

7. He lost ¼ of cost, hence $30=¾ of cost of the first stove, and ⅓, or the loss, equals ⅓ of $30, or $10. He gained ¼ of the cost of the second, hence he gained ¼ of $30=$7½; hence on both he lost $10−$7½, or $2½.

Art. 394. WRITTEN EXERCISES.

2. 17¢÷.85=20¢. | 3. $7.54÷1.16=$6.50.

4. $25÷.12½=$200; $200−$25=$175.

5. Selling price=$2.25×1.15=$2.5875; asking price=$2.5875÷.95=$2.72$\frac{7}{19}$.

6. Capital=$5760÷.18¾=$30720; $30720×.25=$7680.

7. $16872=114% of the cost, the cost=$16872÷1.14, or $14800; now deduct 14% from this, and we have $12728.

7

8. $960÷.16=$6000; $6000×1.16=$6960.
9. Selling price=$1.20×.95=$1.14; asking price=$1.14 ÷.75=$1.52.
10. On the first he gained 16%, or $\frac{4}{25}$, hence $\frac{29}{25}$ of cost equals $6090, from which we find $\frac{4}{25}$ of the cost, or the gain, $840. On the second he lost 16%, or $\frac{4}{25}$, hence $\frac{21}{25}$ of cost equals $6090, and $\frac{4}{25}$=$1160; hence the loss was $1160—$840, or $320.
11. Selling price=8¢×1.25=10¢; 10¢÷.90$\frac{10}{11}$=11¢.
12. *e.bn*=2.50; $2.50÷1.11$\frac{1}{9}$=$2.25.
13. Original price=$85÷.85=$100; price Mr. Hull paid= $85×1.15=$97.75; $100—$97.75=$2.25.

Art. 395. MENTAL EXERCISES.

2. He gains $\frac{2}{5}$ of the cost, or $\frac{2}{5}$ of 100%, which is 40%.
3. I lost $125, which is $\frac{1}{4}$ of $500, the cost, or 25%.
4. The gain is *once* the cost, or 100%. The loss is $\frac{1}{2}$ of the cost, or $\frac{1}{2}$ of 100%, or 50%.
5. He sells them for 200×15¢, or $30 a barrel; hence he gains $10, which is $\frac{1}{2}$ the cost, or 50%.
6. He takes 3$\frac{1}{5}$÷32, or $\frac{1}{10}$, which equals 10%.
7. Goods are bought at 80% of market value, sold at 84%, hence the gain is 4% on 80%, or $\frac{4}{80}$ or $\frac{1}{20}$ of 100%, or 5%.
8. The cost is 95% of current price; gain is 5%+5%, or 10% of current price; hence my gain is $\frac{10}{95}$ or $\frac{2}{19}$ of 100%, or 10$\frac{10}{19}$%.
10. The gain was $\frac{1}{3}$ of $12, or $4; hence the cost was $8; if she had sold for $6, she would have lost $2, which is $\frac{1}{4}$, or 25% of cost.

Art. 395. WRITTEN EXERCISES.

4. $3.50 ÷ 20 = $.17$\frac{1}{2}$; $.25 − $.17$\frac{1}{2}$ = $.7$\frac{1}{2}$; 7$\frac{1}{2}$ ÷ 17$\frac{1}{2}$ = 42$\frac{6}{7}$%.
5. 90% of 80%=72%; 110% of 120%=132%; 132%−72%=60% of list price; 60%÷72%=83$\frac{1}{3}$%, gain on 72%.
6. 90% of 80% of 75%=54%; 105% of 110%=115$\frac{1}{2}$%; 115$\frac{1}{2}$%−54%=61$\frac{1}{2}$%; 61$\frac{1}{2}$%÷54%=113$\frac{8}{9}$%.
7. 115%—85%=30%; 30%÷85%=35$\frac{5}{17}$%.
8. He lost 16$\frac{2}{3}$%, hence there remained 83$\frac{1}{3}$% of it; he then sold 75%, or $\frac{3}{4}$, hence there remained $\frac{1}{4}$ of 83$\frac{1}{3}$%, which is 20$\frac{5}{6}$%.

9. He sold 400 for the cost of 500, hence he gained the cost of 100 on 400, or 25%.

10. He cleared $\frac{1}{5}$ of \$450, hence $\frac{4}{5}$ of \$450, or \$360, is the original price; \$390—\$360=\$30; \$30÷360=.08$\frac{1}{3}$.

11. Selling price=\$120×1.15=\$138; \$138+\$12=\$150; \$12÷\$150=8%.

12. She cleared 20% of \$350, or \$70, hence the cost was \$280; now if she had gained \$70+\$70, or \$140, she would have gained 50%.

13. n. no $\frac{j}{o}$=4.42$\frac{1}{2}$; \$4.42$\frac{1}{2}$—\$3.75=\$.67$\frac{1}{2}$; \$.67$\frac{1}{2}$÷\$3.75=.18.

14. 100%—35%=65%; 65% of 135%=87.75%; 100%—87.75%=12.25%.

COMMISSION.

Art. 402. Case I.

2. Commission=\$7650×.03$\frac{1}{3}$=\$255; amount paid over=\$7650—\$225=\$7395.

3. Whole charge is 3$\frac{1}{2}$%+1$\frac{1}{4}$%=4$\frac{3}{4}$% of \$5472, which is \$259.92, hence he remits \$5472—\$259 92=\$5212.08.

4. He collects \$1536×.95=\$1459.20. His commission is 4$\frac{1}{2}$% of \$1459.20=\$65.664, hence he remits \$1459.20—\$65.664=\$1393.536.

5. 40 horses at \$150 each cost \$150×40=\$6000, and his commission, which was 3$\frac{1}{2}$% of this, \$210, hence the bill was \$6000+\$210+\$25+\$80=\$6315.

6. \$17.12$\frac{1}{2}$×\$450=\$7706.25; 2$\frac{1}{2}$% of \$7706.25=\$192.65$\frac{5}{8}$; storage=5¢ ×450=\$22.50; \$192.65$\frac{5}{8}$+\$22.50=\$215.15$\frac{5}{8}$; net proceeds=\$7706.25—\$215.15$\frac{5}{8}$=\$7491.09$\frac{3}{8}$.

7. 1$\frac{1}{2}$% of \$12500=\$187.50; \$25850—\$12500=\$13350; 2$\frac{1}{2}$% of \$13350=\$333.75; fees=\$187 50+\$333.75=\$521.25.

8. 1$\frac{1}{2}$%+$\frac{3}{8}$%=1$\frac{7}{8}$%; 1$\frac{7}{8}$% of \$75000=1406.25; \$1500—\$1406.25=\$93.75.

Art. 403. Case II.

4. \$9270÷1.03=\$9000, the amount invested, hence the commission was \$9000×.03=\$270.

5. $4558.75—$25=$4533.75; $4533.75 ÷ 1.00$\frac{3}{4}$ = $4500; the com. was $\frac{3}{4}$% of $4500=$33.75.
6. 1$\frac{1}{4}$ % + 2$\frac{1}{2}$ % = 3$\frac{3}{4}$%, hence the amount sold equals $284.25÷.03$\frac{3}{4}$, which equals $7580.
7. $1132.71÷1.03$\frac{1}{2}$=$1094.40 +; $1094.40 ÷ $.24 = 4560 pounds.
8. The commission was $345 minus the sum of $25+$50, which we find to be $270; hence the cost of the horses was $270÷.04$\frac{1}{2}$=$6000. If 40 cost $6000, one cost $\frac{1}{40}$ of $6000=$150.
9. $388 equals 5% minus 3%, or 2% of the amount received, hence 1% of the amount equals $\frac{1}{2}$ of $388=$194, and 5%, my commission, equals $194×5, which equals $970; and 3%, the brokerage, equals $582; and 100%, the whole amount, equals $194×100=$19400, and the sum paid to my employers was $19400—$970=$18430.

Art. 404. Case III.

2. The land was sold for $7742.10+$117.90=$7860, and the rate is $117.90÷$7860=1$\frac{1}{2}$%.
3. 8234\frac{1}{2}$ minus the sum of 54\frac{1}{2}$+$180, which is $8000, is the sum upon which commission is charged, hence the rate equals 180÷8000=2$\frac{1}{4}$%.
4. $112.50÷$2500=4$\frac{1}{2}$%; $37.50÷$2500=1$\frac{1}{2}$%.
5. Since he remitted a note, which he guarantees, it must be for the amount of the sale; hence the note is the base, and the commissions must be paid independently of the note; $127.50÷$8500=1$\frac{1}{2}$%; $191.25÷$8500=2$\frac{1}{4}$%.

STOCKS AND DIVIDENDS.

Art. 414. Case I.

2. 78 shares at $50 each amount to $3900, and 4% of this is $156.
3. 65 shares at $50 each amount to $3250, and 2$\frac{1}{2}$% of this =$81.25.

4. $3\frac{1}{2}\%$ of \$785000=\$27475.

5. \$50×40=\$2000; A's dividend is \$100, and at \$50 each he could buy 100÷50=2 shares.

6. His stock is \$5000, and dividend \$5000×.08=\$400, for which he could buy 4 shares; hence he will then have 50+4=54 shares.

7. 84÷2400=$3\frac{1}{2}$%; \$250000×.$03\frac{1}{2}$=\$8750; \$8750+\$5760=\$14510.

Art. 415. Case II.

3. \$279÷.09=\$3100; \$3100÷50=62 shares.

4. \$72000÷.08=\$900000; $\frac{1}{8}$ of \$900000=\$112500.

5. \$1260÷.07=\$18000; \$18000÷\$50=360.

6. \$7800÷.12=\$65000; \$65000÷\$50=1300, the number of shares; \$7800÷\$50=156 shares; 1300+156=1456.

7. \$350+\$25=\$375, the dividend; \$375÷.06=\$6250, the stock; \$6250÷\$50=125 shares; 125+7=132 shares.

8. 80÷1.25=64 shares.

9. After receiving the first dividend, he had 110% of his original stock; after receiving the second, he had 112% of 110%, or 123.2%; 308÷1.232=250 shares.

10. \$400000×.$04\frac{1}{2}$=\$18000; 25% of gross earnings=\$18000+\$10000=\$28000; \$28000÷.25=112000.

Art. 416. Case III.

2. \$1875÷\$125000=.$01\frac{1}{2}$.

3. Stock=\$28800; \$1944÷\$28800=.$06\frac{3}{4}$.

4. \$70000÷\$2330000=.03 and \$100 surplus.

5. A's stock is \$7000 and his dividend \$402.50; hence the rate is \$402.50÷\$7000=$5\frac{3}{4}$%, and the whole dividend is $5\frac{3}{4}$% of \$4000000=\$230000.

6. 73 shares and \$10 are equal to the value of 73.2 shares; 73.2 shares−61 shares=12.2 shares; 12.2÷61=20%.

7. 42÷350=12%; 350+42=392 shares; \$40=.8 of a share; 58.8÷392=15%.

PAR, PREMIUM, AND DISCOUNT.

Art. 428. Case I.

3. $100\% - \frac{3}{5}\% = 99\frac{2}{5}\%$; $\$20 \times 99\frac{2}{5}\% = \$19.88$.
4. Premium $= \$560 \times .10\frac{1}{2} = \$58.80$; value in currency $=$ $\$560 + \$58.80 = \$618.80$.
5. The par value was \$3500, discount was $\$3500 \times .03\frac{1}{4} =$ \$113.75, premium was $\$3500 \times .01\frac{1}{2} = \$52.50$; the gain was $\$113.75 + \$52.50 = \$166.25$.
6. $\$4800 \times 1.06 = \$5088$; $100\% - 3\frac{1}{4}\% = 96\frac{3}{4}\%$; $\$5000 \times .96\frac{3}{4}\% = \$4837.50$; $\$5088 - \$4837.50 = \$250.50$.
7. The railroad stock was worth \$4311, and the bank stock \$3675; he paid in cash $\$4311 - \$3675 = \$636$.

Art. 429. Case II.

4. Face $= \$2587.50 \div 1.03\frac{1}{2} = \$2500$; premium $= \$2587.50 - \$2500 = \$87.50$.
6. $\$145 \div .03\frac{1}{3} = \$4350$, the value of the stock, and at \$50 a share there were $\$4350 \div \$50 = 87$ shares.
7. $\$54 \div 1.08 = \$50$, hence there was a gain of \$4 on a share, and on 140 shares there was a gain or premium of $140 \times \$4 = \$560$.
8. The par value of 75 shares is $\$50 \times 75 = \$3750$; deduct 3% from this and we find the real value is \$3637.50, and the face of the check for this amount at $\frac{3}{4}\%$ premium is $\$3637.50 \div 1.00\frac{3}{4} = 3610.42+$.
9. $\$180 \div .04\frac{1}{2} = \$4000$, the value of 40 shares, hence one share is worth $\frac{1}{40}$ of $\$4000 = \$100$.
10. The par value of 700 shares at \$100 each is \$70000, and 5% off of this gives \$66500, which plus $\$70 = \$66570$. Dividing this by $\$100 + \$5$, or \$105, gives 634, the number of bonds.
11. $\$200 \div .05 = \$4000$, the par value, hence at \$50 each he bought 80 shares. Now $\frac{3}{4}$ of $\$4000 = \$3000$; hence he gained $\$3000 \times .07 = \$210$ on the sale, plus the \$200 discount, which equals \$410; and on one share he gains $\frac{1}{80}$ of $\$410 = \$5.12\frac{1}{2}$.

Art. 430. Case III.

3. $96 \times \$50 = \$4800$, the discount was $\$4800 - \$4476 = \$324$; the rate equals $\$324 \div \$4800 = .06\frac{3}{4}$.

4. The *discount* was $\$4800 - \$4699.80 = \$100.20$; $\$100.20 \div \$4800 = 2\frac{7}{80}\%$. The gain was $\$4699.80 - \$4476$, which is $\$223.80$; $\$223.80 \div \$4476 = 5\%$.

5. The notes were worth 2% off of \$7500, which is \$7350, and this buys only \$6125 worth of gold, or \$7350 — \$6125, which is \$1225 less than the cost. Hence \$6125 buys \$1225 more than its face, that is, $\frac{1}{5}$ of \$6125, hence the premium is 20%.

6. The stock cost $10 \times \$55\frac{1}{8} = \$551.25$; gain $= \$600 - \$551.25 = \$48.75$; $\$48.75 \div \$551.25 = 8\frac{74}{147}\%$.

BROKERAGE.

Art. 436. Case I.

2. Stock $= \$50 \times 46 = \$2300$; brokerage $= \$2300 \times .00\frac{1}{4} = \$5.75$.

   Or $\$50 \times .00\frac{1}{4} = \$\frac{1}{8}$; $\$\frac{1}{8} \times 46 = \$5.75$.

3. Since the brokerage on 1 share is $\$\frac{1}{8}$, the cost of 1 share will be $\$47\frac{1}{2} + \$\frac{1}{8}$, or $\$47\frac{5}{8}$; $\$47\frac{5}{8} \times 76 = \$3619.50$.

4. Brokerage $= 72 \times \frac{1}{8} = 9$; proceeds $= \$102\frac{3}{4} \times 72 = \$7398$.

5. Cost of 1 share $= 150 + \frac{1}{4} = 150\frac{1}{4}$; proceeds of 1 share $= 161 - \frac{1}{4} = 160\frac{3}{4}$; gain on 1 share $= \$160\frac{3}{4} - \$150\frac{1}{4} = \$10\frac{1}{2}$; whole gain $= \$10\frac{1}{2} \times 25 = \$262.50$; commission $= \frac{1}{4}\% + \frac{1}{4}\% = \frac{1}{2}\%$; $\$\frac{1}{2} \times 25 = \$12.50$.

6. Cost of 1 share $= 53\frac{1}{2} + \frac{1}{8} = 53\frac{5}{8}$; whole cost $= \$53\frac{5}{8} \times 65 = \$3485.62\frac{1}{2}$; dividend $= 65 \times \$50 \times .04 \times 2 = \$260$; $51\frac{1}{4} - \frac{1}{8} = 51\frac{1}{8}$; $\$51\frac{1}{8} \times 65 = \$3323.12\frac{1}{2}$; whole amount received $= \$3323.12\frac{1}{2} + \$260 = \$3583.12\frac{1}{2}$; gain $= \$3583.12\frac{1}{2} - \$3485.62\frac{1}{2} = \$97.50$.

Art. 437. Case II.

2. $\$12.50 \div .00\frac{1}{8} = \$10000$; $\$10000 \div \$100 = 100$ shares.

   Or, $\$12.50 \div \$\frac{1}{8} = 100$ shares.

3. $\$4712.50 \div .94\frac{1}{4} = \$5000$.

4. $\$4953 \div \$95\frac{1}{4} = 52$ shares.

5. Proceeds of $\$1 = \$1.01\frac{1}{4} - \$.00\frac{1}{4} = \$1.01$; proceeds $= \$1.01 \times 3000 = \$3030$; cost of 1 share stock $= \$131\frac{5}{8} + \$\frac{1}{4} = \$131\frac{7}{8}$; $\$3030 \div \$131\frac{7}{8} = 22$ shares and $\$128.75$ surplus.

6. $49\frac{7}{8} + \frac{1}{8} = 50$; $53\frac{1}{4} - \frac{1}{8} = 53\frac{1}{8}$; profit on 1 share $= \$53\frac{1}{8} - \$50 = \$3\frac{1}{8}$; $\$237.50 \div \$3\frac{1}{8} = 76$ shares.

7. Proceeds of 1 share $= 78\frac{5}{8} - \frac{1}{8} = 78\frac{1}{2}$; $\$5000 \div \$78\frac{1}{2} = 63$ shares, and $54.50 over; to make up $5000, it will be necessary to sell another share and we shall have remaining $78.50—$54.50, or $24; hence it requires 64 shares.

8. $156\frac{1}{2} - \frac{1}{4} = 156\frac{1}{4}$; $\$156\frac{1}{4} \times 25 = \$3906.25$; $99 + \frac{1}{8} = 99\frac{1}{8}$, cost of 1 share; $\$3906.25 \div \$99\frac{1}{8} = 39$ shares, $\$40.37\frac{1}{2}$ surplus.

Art. 438. Case III.

2. $\$25 \times 110 = \$2750$; $\$6.875 \div \$2750 = .0025$ or $\frac{1}{4}\%$.

3. $\$5600 \times 1.10 = \$6160$; brokerage $= \$6188 - \$6160 = \$28$; $\$28 \div \$5600 = \frac{1}{2}\%$.

4. $\$21250 - \$25 = \$21225$; $\$21225 \div 1.06 = \$20000$, and $25 over, which is the brokerage; $\$25 \div \$20000 = \frac{1}{8}\%$.

INCOME FROM INVESTMENTS.

Art. 447. Case I.

3. $\$5631.25 \div 1.12\frac{5}{8} = \$5000$; $\$5000 \times .06 = 300$.

4. $\$5280 \div 1.32 = \$4000$; $\$4000 \times .10 = \$400$.

5. $\$8475 \div 1.13 = \$7500$; $\$7500 \times .02\frac{3}{4} = \$206.25$.

6. $\$1500 \times .06 = \$90$.

7. $\$87.25 \times .06 = \$5.235$.

8. $\$2000 \times 1.17\frac{5}{8} = \$2352.50$; $\$5000 - \$2352.50 = \$2647.50$; dividing $2647.50 by $1.10\frac{1}{2}$, we have bonds amounting to $2350 par value, and a surplus of $50.75. As the bonds are not of lower denomination than $50, the par value must be a multiple of 50, and hence, instead of making the quotient as large as possible, we make it the largest multiple of 50 possible, and leave

the excess for the remainder. Interest on 6's of '81 $=\$2000\times.06=\$120$; int. on $4\frac{1}{2}$'s $=\$2350\times.04\frac{1}{2}=\$105.75$; $\$120+\$105.75=\$225.75$.

9. $\$10000\times1.03\frac{3}{4}=\$10375$; income $=\$10000\times.06=\$600$; $\$10375\div1.10\frac{1}{8}=\$9400$ and $\$23.25$ surplus; $\$9400\times.07=\$658$; $\$658-\$600=\$58$.

10. $\$4500\times1.12\frac{1}{2}=\$5062.50$; $\$5062.50\times.06=\$303.75$, rent.

Art. 448. Case II.

3. Value of ground-rent $=\$75\div.06=\$1250$; purchaser pays value exclusive of the ground-rent; hence the whole value $=\$5750+\$1250=\$7000$.

4. The par value of the bonds is $\$600\div.06=\$10000$; they cost me $\$10000\times1.19\frac{3}{4}=\$11975$.

5. $\$786\div.06=\$13100$; $\$13100\times1.03\frac{1}{4}=\$13525.75$.

6. $\$900\div.04\frac{1}{2}=\$20000$; $1.05\frac{1}{4}\times\$20000=\$21050$.

7. $\$8000\times1.17\frac{3}{4}=\$9420$; $\$560\div.07=\$8000$, par value of Georgia 7's; $\$8000\times1.03\frac{1}{4}=\$8260$; $\$9420-\$8260=\$1160$.

8. The interest on a \$100 bond is \$6; since \$6 is to be 7% of the cost of the bond, $\$6\div.07=\$85\frac{5}{7}$, value of \$100 bond; $7\div.06\frac{3}{4}=103\frac{19}{27}$.

Or, if it cost \$100 to give an interest of 6%, to give an interest of 1% it will cost 6 times \$100, or \$600, and to give 7% interest it will cost $\frac{1}{7}$ of \$600, or $\$85\frac{5}{7}$.

9. $\$6\times1.15=\$6.90$; $6.90\div.07=98\frac{4}{7}$; $\$5\times1.10=\$5.50$; $5.50\div.06=91\frac{2}{3}$.

10. $(.05\div.04)\times100=125$; deducting $\frac{1}{4}$% brokerage, the market value is $124\frac{3}{4}$.

11. $\$5.40\div.06=\$90$, value ground-rent per foot; $\$90\times50=\$4500$, value of property.

12. $\$600\div.06=\$10000$; $1.15\frac{3}{4}\times\$10000=\$11575$; 237 shares at $48\frac{7}{8}$ will produce \$11575 and leave a surplus of $\$8.37\frac{1}{2}$.

13. $15000 × $1.00\frac{7}{8}$ = $15131.25 ; $750 ÷ .06 = $12500 ; $12500 × $1.17\frac{3}{4}$ = $14718.75, amount invested ; $15131.25 − $14718.75 = $412.50.

14. Par value of California bonds = $546 ÷ .07 = $7800 ; $7800 × 1.17 = $9126 ; par value of Philadelphia bonds = $546 ÷ .06 = $9100 ; $9100 × 1.05 = $9555 ; amount added = $9555 − $9126 = $429.

Art. 449. Case III.

3. .06 ÷ $1.04\frac{1}{2}$ = 5.7 %.

4. $54 ÷ $850 = $6\frac{6}{17}$%.

5. .05 ÷ $1.13\frac{3}{4}$ = $4\frac{36}{91}$%; $.04\frac{1}{2}$ ÷ $1.10\frac{3}{4}$ = $4\frac{28}{443}$; $4\frac{36}{91}$ is a larger rate than $4\frac{28}{443}$.

6. $450 ÷ $6575 = $6\frac{222}{263}$%.

7. Cost of mortgage = $5000 × $.97\frac{1}{2}$ = $4875; interest = $5000 × .06 = $300 ; $300 ÷ $4875 = $6\frac{2}{13}$%.

8. .06 ÷ 1.02 = $5\frac{15}{17}$% ; .07 ÷ 1.20 = $5\frac{5}{6}$%.

9. .07 ÷ $1.12\frac{1}{2}$ = $.06\frac{2}{9}$% ; .06 ÷ $1.06\frac{1}{4}$ = 5.6 + %.

10. .05 ÷ .75 = $6\frac{2}{3}$%; .06 ÷ .85 = $7\frac{1}{17}$%; .07 ÷ .90 = $7\frac{7}{9}$%.

11. .06 ÷ 1.08 = $5\frac{5}{9}$%; .06 × $1.05\frac{1}{2}$ = .0633 ; .0633 ÷ 1.10 = $5\frac{83}{110}$%.

GENERAL TAXES.

Art. 458. Case I.

2. Whole amount of taxable property = $640876 + $750472 = $1391348 ; tax on property = $1391348 × .007 = $9739.436 ; poll taxes = $1.50 × 250 = $375 ; whole tax = $9739.436 + $375 = $10114.436, whole tax.

4.

Tax on $9000 =	$135.00
" 700 =	10.50
" 50 =	.75
1 poll =	1.00
Whole tax =	$147.25

5. $7895 + $5634 = $13529

Tax on $10000 =	$150.00
" 3000 =	45.00
" 500 =	7.50
" 20 =	.30
" 9 =	.135
Whole tax =	$202.935

6. Tax on \$8000=\$120.00
   " 500= 7.50
   $1\frac{1}{2}$% on 800= 1.20
   1 poll = 1.50
   Whole tax=\$130.20

7. \$75000+\$8670=\$83670
   $\frac{2}{3}$ of \$83670=\$55780
   Tax on \$50000=\$750.00
   " 5000= 75.00
   " 700= 10.50
   " 80= 1.20
   1 poll = 1.00
   $\frac{1}{4}$% on \$1200= 3.00
   \$840,70

8. .25% + 1.025% + .45% = 1.725%; \$3500 × .01725 = \$60.375; \$60.375+\$1.25=\$61.625.

9. $\frac{2}{5}$ of \$50000=\$20000; $\frac{1}{3}$ of \$3600=\$1200; $\frac{3}{5}$ of \$1500=\$900; \$20000 + \$1200 + \$5000 + \$900 = \$27100, abatement; \$27100×.004$\frac{1}{2}$=\$121.95; \$121.95+\$1=\$122.95.

Art. 460. Case II.

3. \$306.25—\$2.25=\$304; \$304÷\$.008=\$38000.

4. Sum on which tax was reckoned is \$33.07$\frac{1}{2}$÷.002$\frac{1}{4}$=\$14700; \$14700—\$12000=\$2700.

5. Since the collector's com. is $2\frac{1}{4}$% of the sum collected, \$7580=97$\frac{3}{4}$% of the tax, and the tax=\$7754.475703+; \$7754.475703÷.003$\frac{1}{2}$=\$2215564.49—.

6. .45% +.3$\frac{1}{2}$%+.48% =1.28%; \$315.88—\$1.00=\$314.88; \$314.88÷.0128=\$24600.

Art. 461. Case III.

3. \$1.50×500=\$750; \$17250—\$750=\$16500; \$850000+\$250000=\$1100000; \$16500÷\$1100000=.015.

4. Whole tax=\$7650÷.97$\frac{1}{2}$=\$7846.1538+; \$7846.1538÷\$804796=.0097+.

5. \$500+\$42.75+\$32.50=\$575.25; \$575.25 — \$125.25 = \$450; rate per day=\$450÷7280=\$.06$\frac{33}{182}$; \$.06$\frac{33}{182}$ × 90 × 4=\$22 25$\frac{25}{91}$.

MENTAL EXERCISES.

Page 270. MISCELLANEOUS PROBLEMS.

1. 8%=$\frac{2}{25}$; $\frac{25}{25}$+$\frac{2}{25}$=$\frac{27}{25}$; $\frac{27}{25}$ of \$50=\$54.

2. At a premium of 10%, gold is worth 110% in currency; since \$220 is *110%*, or $\frac{11}{10}$ of the value in gold, $\frac{10}{10}$ of the value=*\$200.*

3. 10%, or $\frac{1}{10}$, off leaves $\frac{9}{10}$; $\frac{1}{10}$ off $\frac{9}{10}$ leaves $\frac{81}{100}$, or 81%; 100% —81%=19%.

4. $\frac{1}{5}$ off leaves $\frac{4}{5}$; $\frac{4}{5}$ of $\frac{4}{5}$ equals $\frac{16}{25}$; $\frac{25}{25}$—$\frac{16}{25}$ equals $\frac{9}{25}$, or 36%.

5. $\frac{1}{20}$ off leaves $\frac{19}{20}$; $\frac{19}{20}$ of $\frac{19}{20}$ equals $\frac{361}{400}$; $\frac{400}{400}$—$\frac{361}{400}$ equals $\frac{39}{400}$, or $9\frac{3}{4}$% ; 10%—$9\frac{3}{4}$%=$\frac{1}{4}$%. $\frac{1}{10}$ off leaves $\frac{9}{10}$; $\frac{19}{20}$ of $\frac{9}{10}$ equals $\frac{171}{200}$; $\frac{200}{200}$—$\frac{171}{200}$ equals $\frac{29}{200}$, or $14\frac{1}{2}$% ; 15%—$14\frac{1}{2}$%=$\frac{1}{2}$%.

6. 10 and 10% off equals 19% ; 20%—19%=1%. $\frac{1}{20}$ on, gives $\frac{21}{20}$; $\frac{21}{20}$ of $\frac{21}{20}$ = $\frac{441}{400}$; $\frac{441}{400}$—$\frac{400}{400}$=$\frac{41}{400}$, or $10\frac{1}{4}$% ; $10\frac{1}{4}$%—10%=$\frac{1}{4}$%.

7. 10 and 10% on gives $\frac{11}{10}$ of $\frac{11}{10}$=$\frac{121}{100}$; $\frac{121}{100}$—$\frac{100}{100}$=$\frac{21}{100}$, or 21%. 20 and 10% on gives $\frac{11}{10}$ of $\frac{6}{5}$, or $\frac{33}{25}$; $\frac{33}{25}$—$\frac{25}{25}$=$\frac{8}{25}$, or 32%. 20 and 5% on gives $\frac{21}{20}$ of $\frac{6}{5}$, or $\frac{126}{100}$; $\frac{126}{100}$—$\frac{100}{100}$=$\frac{26}{100}$, or 26%. 20 and 20% off leaves $\frac{4}{5}$ of $\frac{4}{5}$, or $\frac{16}{25}$; $\frac{25}{25}$—$\frac{16}{25}$=$\frac{9}{25}$, or 36%. 20 and 20% on gives $\frac{6}{5}$ of $\frac{6}{5}$, or $\frac{36}{25}$; $\frac{36}{25}$—$\frac{25}{25}$=$\frac{11}{25}$, or 44%.

8. $\frac{3}{8}$ of the cost is $\frac{3}{8}$ of 100%, or $37\frac{1}{2}$%.

9. $1\frac{1}{4}$% equals $\frac{1}{80}$; hence since the commission was $\frac{1}{80}$ of the amount paid for the house, the house was sold for 80 times $200, or $16000, and I received $15800.

10. If 1 share cost $$102\frac{1}{8}$, 5 shares cost 5 times $$102\frac{1}{8}$, or $$510\frac{5}{8}$.

11. $100 cost $$108\frac{3}{8}$, and $4000, or 40 times $100, cost 40 times $$108\frac{3}{8}$, or $4335.

12. If 100 cost $3, one cost 3 cents ; he gained 2¢ on 3¢, or $66\frac{2}{3}$%.

13. 25%=$\frac{1}{4}$; hence she sold them for $\frac{3}{4}$ of cost ; since $3.60 is $\frac{3}{4}$ of cost, the cost must have been $4.80.

14. If she bought at 80 and sold at par, she gained 20%, or $\frac{1}{5}$ of the par value; hence the par value was $2500, and there were 50 shares.

15. I receive $6 on $90, or $\frac{6}{90}$, which equals $6\frac{2}{3}$%. $8 on $120 equals $\frac{8}{120}$, which equals $6\frac{2}{3}$%.

SIMPLE INTEREST.

Art. 471. MENTAL EXERCISES.

2. At 5% for 6 years, $\frac{30}{100}$, or $\frac{3}{10}$ of the principal equals the interest $\frac{3}{10}$ of $60 equals $18.

3. $\frac{20}{100}$, or $\frac{1}{5}$ of the principal, equals the interest; $\frac{1}{5}$ of $40 equals $8.

4. $\frac{20}{100}$, or $\frac{1}{5}$ of the principal, equals the interest; $\frac{1}{5}$ of $30 equals $6.

5. At 8% for $2\frac{1}{4}$ years, $\frac{18}{100}$ of the principal equals the interest; $\frac{18}{100}$ of $600 equals $108.

6. 4 yr. 6 mo. equal $4\frac{1}{2}$ yr., and at 6%, $\frac{27}{100}$ of the principal equals the interest, which is $81.

7. 3 yr. 9 mo. equal $3\frac{3}{4}$ yr., and at 8%, $\frac{3}{10}$ of the principal equals the interest, which is $72.

8. 7 yr. 6 mo. equal $7\frac{1}{2}$ yr., and at 4%, the interest equals $\frac{3}{10}$ of $330, or $99.

9. 3 yr. 7 mo. 6 da. equal $3\frac{3}{5}$ yr. and at 5%, the interest equals $\frac{9}{50}$ of $500, or $90.

10. 5 yr. 3 mo. 18 da. equal $5\frac{3}{10}$ yr., and at 10%, the interest equals $\frac{53}{100}$ of $300, or $159.

11. 2 yr. 2 mo. 12 da. equal $2\frac{1}{5}$ yr., and at 5%, the interest equals $\frac{11}{100}$ of $500, or $55.

13. 7 yr. 6 mo. equal $7\frac{1}{2}$ yr., and at 6%, the amount equals $\frac{29}{20}$ of $600, or $870.

14. 8 yr. 10 mo. equal $8\frac{5}{6}$ yr., and at 6%, the amount equals $\frac{153}{100}$ of $300, or $459.

15. 2 yr. 6 mo. 20 da. equal $2\frac{5}{9}$ yr. and at 9%, the amount equals $\frac{123}{100}$ of $100, or $123.

Art. 471. WRITTEN EXERCISES.

2. $\$360 \times .07 = \$25.20$; $\$25.20 \times 3\frac{1}{2} = \$88.20$.

3. $\$940 \times .06 = \$56.40$; $\$56.40 \times 7\frac{2}{3} = \$432.40$.

4. $\$860 \times .05 = \$43$; $\$43 \times 5\frac{3}{4} = \$247.25$.

5. $\$780 \times .07 = \$54.60$; $\$54.60 \times 8\frac{1}{3} = \$455$.

6. $\$590 \times .08 = \$47.20$; $\$47.20 \times 3\frac{5}{6} = \$180.93\frac{1}{3}$.

7. $\$1296 \times .06 = \$77.76$; $\$77.76 \times 5\frac{7}{8} = \$456.84$.

8. $\$4080 \times .05 = \$204$; $\$204 \times 3\frac{11}{40} = \$668.10$.

Art. 472. WRITTEN EXERCISES.

(2)

$.06 \times 3 = 0.18$
$\frac{1}{2} \times 4 = .02$
$\frac{1}{6} \times 12 = .002$
0.202
380
$\$76.760$

(3)

$.06 \times 5 = 0.30$
$\frac{1}{2} \times 6 = .03$
$\frac{1}{6} \times 6 = .001$
0.331
975
$\$322.725$

(4)

$.06 \times 9 = 0.54$
$\frac{1}{2} \times 10 = .05$
$\frac{1}{6} \times 15 = .0025$
0.5925
834
$\$494.1450$

(5)

$.06 \times 8 = 0.48$
$\frac{1}{2} \times 6 = .03$
$\frac{1}{6} \times 24 = .004$
0.514
45.95
$6)\overline{23.61830}$ = Int. at 6%.
3.93638 = Int. at 1%.
$\$27.55468$ = Int. at 7%.

(6)

$.06 \times 7 = 0.42$
$\frac{1}{2} \times 7 = .035$
$\frac{1}{6} \times 21 = .0035$
0.4585
23.75
$6)\overline{10.889375}$ = Int. at 6%.
1.814895 = Int. at 1%.
$\$9.074480$ = Int. at 5%.

(7)

06 × 9 = 0.54
$\frac{1}{2}$ × 5 - .025
$\frac{1}{6}$ × 14 - .002$\frac{1}{3}$
0.567$\frac{1}{3}$
.325
3).184383$\frac{1}{3}$ = Int. at 6%
.061461$\frac{1}{9}$ = Int. at 2%.
\$0.245844$\frac{4}{9}$ = Int. at 8%.

(8)

06 × 4 = 0.24
$\frac{1}{2}$ × 11 - .055
$\frac{1}{6}$ × 13 - .002$\frac{1}{6}$
0.297$\frac{1}{6}$
147.37$\frac{1}{2}$
6)43.7949375 = Int. at 6%.
7.29915625 = Int. at 1%.
\$51.09409375 = Int. at 7%.

(9)

96 × 9 = 0.54
$\frac{1}{2}$ × 9 - .045
$\frac{1}{6}$ × 11 - .001$\frac{5}{6}$
0.586$\frac{5}{6}$
635.62$\frac{1}{2}$
2)373.00593$\frac{3}{4}$ = Int. at 6%.
186.50296$\frac{7}{8}$ = Int. at 3%.
\$559.50890$\frac{5}{8}$ = Int. at 9%.

(10)

06 × 10 = 0.60
$\frac{1}{2}$ × 7 - .035
$\frac{1}{6}$ × 7 - .001$\frac{1}{6}$
0.636$\frac{1}{6}$
387.18$\frac{3}{4}$
6)246.31578$\frac{1}{8}$ = Int. at 6%.
41.05263 = Int. at 1%.
\$410.5263 = Int. at 10%.

(11)

06 × 3 = 0.18
$\frac{1}{2}$ × 5 - .025
$\frac{1}{6}$ × 5 - .000$\frac{5}{6}$
0.205$\frac{5}{6}$
570.05
12)117.33529$\frac{1}{6}$ = Int. at 6%.
9.77794$\frac{7}{72}$ = Int. at $\frac{1}{2}$%.
\$127.11323$\frac{19}{72}$ = Int. at 6$\frac{1}{2}$%.

(12)

.06 × 5 = 0.30
$\frac{1}{2}$ × 9 - .045
$\frac{1}{6}$ × 17 - .002$\frac{5}{6}$
0.347$\frac{5}{6}$
980.81$\frac{1}{3}$
6)341.15957$\frac{1}{9}$ = Int. at 6%.
56.85992$\frac{23}{27}$ = Int. at 1%.
7$\frac{3}{4}$
\$440.66444$\frac{65}{108}$ = Int. at 7$\frac{3}{4}$%.

Art. 473. WRITTEN EXERCISES.

(3.)

\$15|00 = Int. for 2 mo.
30|00 = " " 4 mo.

(4.)

\$ 7|80 = Int. for 2 mo.
39|00 = " " 10 mo.

(5)

```
  $9|60=Int. for 60 da.
    |96= "   "   6 da.
    |48= "   "   3 da.
$11.04= "   "  69 da.
```

(6)

```
$12|60=Int. for 60 da.
  6|30= "   "  30 da.
   |68= "   "   3 da.
$6.93= "   "  33 da.
```

(7)

```
$8|00=Int. for 60 da.
  |40= "   "   3 da.
$8.40= "   "  63 da.
```

(8)

```
$1|50 =Int. for 60 da.
 1|50 = "   "   60 da.
  |37½= "   "   15 da.
$3.37½  "   "  135 da.
```

(9)

```
 $8|40 -  60 da.
  4|20 -  30 da.
  2|80 -  20 da.
   |84 -   6 da.
   |28 -   2 da.
$16.52 - 118 da.
```

(10)

```
  $12|50    - 60 da.
   12|50    - 60 da.
    4|166+  - 20 da.
    1|25    -  6 da.
     |625   -  3 da.
6)$31.041   -149 da.
   5.173
 $36.214
```

(11)

```
 $2|50 - 60 da.
 15|00 - 1 yr.
 10|00 - 8 mo.
  1|25 - 1 mo.
   |50 - 12 da.
6)26.75
   4.46—
 $31.21—
```

(12)

```
   $8|75    - 2 mo.
   52|50    - 1 yr.
   52|50    - 1 yr.
    4|375   - 1 mo.
    2|916+  - 20 da.
     |583+  - 4 da.
3)121.624
   40.541
 $162.166
```

(13)

```
    2|755 - 2 mo.
   16|530 - 1 yr.
   16|530 - 1 yr.
   11|020 - 8 mo.
     |688 - 15 da.
6)44.768
   7.461
 $37.307
```

(14)

```
     3|605  - 2 mo.
    21|630  - 1 yr.
    86|520  - 4 yr.
     7|210  - 4 mo.
      |6008 - 10 da.
      |3004 - 5 da.
      |6008 - 1 da.
6)116.32128
   19.38688
         4½
  $87.24096
```

(16) Time=89 da.

```
 $24|00 - 60 da.
   8|00 - 20 da.
   2|40 -  6 da.
   1|20 -  3 da.
$35.60 - 89 da.
```

(17) Time=161 da.

```
  $7|50  -  60 da.
   7|50  -  60 da.
   3|75  -  30 da.
   1|25  -  10 da.
    |125 -   1 da.
$20.125 - 161 da.
```

(18) Time=147 da.

```
 $4|80 -  60 da.
  4|80 -  60 da.
  1|60 -  20 da.
   |48 -   6 da.
   |08 -   1 da.
 ----------------
6)11.76 - 147 da.
   1.96
 ------
 $13.72
```

(19) Time=78+3=81.

```
$5|70  - 60 da.
 1|90  - 20 da.
  |095 -  1 da.
----------------
$7.695 - 81 da.
```

(20) Time=161+3=164 da.

```
 10|50  -  60 da.
 10|50  -  60 da.
  5|25  -  30 da.
  1|75  -  10 da.
   |525 -   3 da.
   |175 -   1 da.
 ------------------
$28.700 - 164 da.
```

Art. 474. WRITTEN EXERCISES.

(3)

2 yr. 9 mo.=33 mo.

$$\frac{\overset{60}{\cancel{1}.\cancel{2}\cancel{0}}\times33}{\cancel{2}}=\$19.80.$$

(4)

3 yr. 4 mo.=40 mo.

$$\frac{2.35\times\overset{20}{\cancel{4}\cancel{0}}}{\cancel{2}}=\$49.00.$$

(5)

$$\frac{\overset{.680}{\cancel{1}.\cancel{3}\cancel{6}\cancel{0}}\times\overset{25}{\cancel{7}\cancel{5}}}{\cancel{6}}=\$17.00.$$

(6)

$$\frac{2.240\times\overset{12}{\cancel{7}\cancel{2}}}{\cancel{6}}=\$26.880.$$

(7)

$$\frac{\overset{.070}{\cancel{2}.\cancel{5}\cancel{2}\cancel{0}}\times104\times7}{\cancel{6}\times\cancel{6}}=\$50.96.$$

(8)

$$\frac{.12650\times\overset{4}{\cancel{1}\cancel{4}\cancel{4}}\times5}{\cancel{6}\times\cancel{6}}=\$2.53.$$

(9)

$$\frac{5.000\times162\times9}{6\times6\times2}=\$101.25.$$

(10)

$$\frac{3,600\times93\times9}{6\times6\times2}=\$41.85.$$

Art. 475. WRITTEN EXERCISES.

2. From Jan. 5th, 1860, to January 5th, 1862, is 2 years, and from Jan. 5 to July 12 is 188 days.

```
$327.25
    .07
-------
22.9075 =Int. for 1 yr.
      2
-------
$45.8150
```

```
     22.9075
         188
365)4306.6100
    ---------
     11.7989 =Int. for 188 days.
     45.815
     ------
     57.613
```

(3)

Time = 9 yr. 140 da.

$\$480$
$.06$
28.80
$9\frac{28}{73}$
25920
$1104\frac{48}{73}$
$270.24\frac{48}{73}$
480
$\$750.25$

(4)

Time = 5 yr. 108 da.

$\$1200$
$.05\frac{1}{2}$
66.00
$5\frac{108}{365}$
33000
$19528\frac{56}{73}$
$\$349.528\frac{56}{73}$

(5)

Time = 9 yr. 219 da.

$\$1900\frac{3}{4}$
$.05$
$95.03\frac{3}{4}$
$9\frac{3}{5}$
$85533\frac{3}{4}$
$5702\frac{1}{4}$
912.36
1900.75
$\$2813.11$

(6)

Time = 3 yr. 284 da.

$\$670$
$.07$
46.90
$3\frac{284}{365}$
14070
$36492\frac{4}{73}$
$177.192\frac{4}{73}$
670
$\$847.192\frac{4}{73}$

(6)

```
      $670
       .07
     -----
     46.90
         3
    ------
    140.70

     46.90
       284
    --------
360)13319.60
    ---------
   73)36.998+
      ------
       506
     ------
    36.492
    140.70
    670
    -------
   $847.19
```

(7)

Time = 14 yr. 72 da.

$\$875.48$
$.06$
52.5288
$14\frac{72}{365}$
7354032
$103618\frac{166}{365}$
745.7650
875.48
$\$1621.24$

8. Common interest is greater because the interest for one year is divided into 360 parts, instead of 365, and hence each part must be greater. 360 days are $\frac{72}{73}$ of a year, and hence reckoning 360 days as a year, we receive $\frac{1}{73}$ more interest than we should do by exact interest; hence if we deduct $\frac{1}{73}$ from the common interest for a part of a year, we shall have exact interest.

Art. 476. MENTAL EXERCISES.

2. In 8 yr. at 5%, $\frac{40}{100}$ or $\frac{2}{5}$ of the principal equals the interest, which is $60, and $\frac{5}{5}$ of the principal equals $\frac{5}{2}$ of $60, or $150.

3. In 7 yr. at 4%, $\frac{7}{25}$ of the principal equals the interest, which is $70; hence the principal is $250.

4. In 8 yr. at 6%, $\frac{12}{25}$ of the principal equals the interest, which is $12; hence the principal is $25.

5. In 7 yr. 6 mo. at 6%, $\frac{9}{20}$ of the principal equals the interest which is $18; hence the principal is $40.

6. In 2 yr. 3 mo. at 8%, $\frac{9}{50}$ of the principal equals the interest, which is $54; hence the principal is $300.

7. In 8 yr. 10 mo. at 6%, $\frac{53}{100}$ of the principal equals the interest, which is $106; hence the principal is $200.

8. At 6% for 1 year, $\frac{3}{50}$ of the principal equals the interest, which is $180; hence the principal is $3000.

9. In 5 yr. 4 mo. at 6%, $\frac{8}{25}$ of the principal equals the interest, which is $320; hence the principal is $1000.

10. In 4 years at 5%, $\frac{1}{5}$ of A's money equals the interest upon it, which is $200; hence A's money is $1000, and since A's money is $\frac{2}{3}$ of B's, B has $1500.

Art. 476. WRITTEN EXERCISES.

(2)

3 yr. 8 mo. = 44 mo.
44 ÷ 2 = .22
$\frac{\$462}{.22} = \$2100$

(3)

12 yr. 9 mo. = $12\frac{3}{4}$ yr.
$.07 \times 12\frac{3}{4} = .8925$
$\frac{\$64.26}{.8925} = \$72$

(4)

7 yr. 4 mo. = $7\frac{1}{3}$ yr.
$.08 \times 7\frac{1}{3} = .58\frac{2}{3}$
$\$1.00 + \$.58\frac{2}{3} = \$1.58\frac{2}{3}$
$\frac{\$749.70}{1.58\frac{2}{3}} = \$472.50$

(5)

$\$.3425$ = Int. of $1 at 6%.
$\frac{5}{6}$ of $\$.3425 = \$.2854\frac{1}{6}$, Int. at 5%
$\frac{\$575.40}{.2854\frac{1}{6}} = \$2016$, *Ans.*

(6)

$\$.457\frac{1}{6}$ = Int. of $1 at 6%
$\frac{7}{6}$ of $\$.457\frac{1}{6} = \$.533\frac{13}{36}$ = Int. at 7%
$\$1 + .\$538\frac{13}{36} = \$1.583\frac{13}{36}$ = Amt. at 7%
$\frac{\$2400}{1.533\frac{13}{36}} = \$1565.19-$, *Ans.*

(7)

$\$.297\frac{5}{6}$ = Int. of $1 at 6%
$\frac{7}{6}$ of $\$.297\frac{5}{6} = \$.347\frac{17}{36}$, Int. at 7%
$\$1.347\frac{17}{36}$ = Amt. at 7%
$\frac{\$3363.79}{1.347\frac{17}{36}} = \$2496.37$, *Ans.*

(8)

$.27 = Int. of $1 at 6%
$5400 ÷ .27 = $20000
Hence 4 B's = $20000
B's = $5000
A's = $15000

Note.—It is often easier to run the results out into decimals than to use common fractions.

Art. 477. MENTAL EXERCISES.

2. At 4%, $\frac{1}{25}$ of the principal equals the interest for 1 year, which is \$10; hence to gain \$80 will require 8 years.

3. At 6%, $\frac{3}{50}$ of the principal equals the interest for one year, which is \$9; hence to gain \$45 will require 5 years.

4. At 8%, $\frac{2}{25}$ of the principal equals the interest for 1 year, which is \$8; hence to gain \$32 will require 4 years.

5. At 5%, $\frac{1}{20}$ of the principal equals the interest for 1 year, which is \$3; hence to gain \$21 will require 7 years.

6. At 6%, $\frac{3}{50}$ of the principal equals the interest for 1 year, which is \$1.50; hence to gain \$43—\$25, or \$18, will require 12 years.

7. At 9%, $\frac{9}{100}$ of the principal equals the interest for 1 year, which is \$4.50; hence to gain \$86—\$50, or \$36, will require 8 years.

8. At 10%, $\frac{1}{10}$ of the principal equals the interest for 1 year; if it takes 1 year to gain $\frac{1}{10}$ of the principal, to gain 2 times the principal, or $\frac{20}{10}$, will require 20 years; to gain 3 times, 30 years; to gain 4 times, 40 years.

9. At 5%, $\frac{1}{20}$ of the principal equals the interest for 1 year, and to gain $\frac{20}{20}$ will require 20 years; at 6% it will require $\frac{50}{3}$, or $16\frac{2}{3}$ years; at 8%, $\frac{25}{2}$ or $12\frac{1}{2}$ years; at $12\frac{1}{2}$%, 8 years.

10. In trebling itself, the principal gains *twice* itself; at 5% a principal gains $\frac{1}{20}$ of itself in 1 year, and to gain *twice* itself, or $\frac{40}{20}$, will require 40 years; at 10% it will require 20 years; at 20% it will require 10 years; at 25% it will require 8 years.

11. \$280—\$250 equals \$30, the interest at 3%; at 1% it will be $\frac{1}{3}$ of \$30, or \$10; hence the interest at 5% will be \$50, the principal will be \$250—\$50, or \$200; the interest at 5% for 1 year is $\frac{1}{20}$ of \$200, or \$10, hence to gain \$50, it must be on interest 5 years.

Art. 477. WRITTEN EXERCISES.

2. $\$750\times.06=\$45$; $\$105\div\$45=2\frac{1}{3}$ yr.$=$2 yr. 4 mo.

3. $\$720\times.06=\$43.20$; $\$957.60-\$720=\$237.60$; $\$237.60\div\$43.20=5\frac{1}{2}$ yr.

4. $\$960\times.05=\$48$; $\$54.40\div\$48=1\frac{2}{15}$ yr.$=$1 yr. 1 mo. 18 da.

5 $\$1800\times.04\frac{1}{2}=\$81$; $\$3047.40-\$1800=\$1247.40$; $\$1247.40\div\$81=15\frac{2}{5}$ yr.$=$15 yr. 4 mo. 24 da.

6. $\$26.50\times.07\frac{1}{2}=\$1.9875$; $\$17.46\div\$1.9875=8\frac{208}{265}$ yr.$=$ 8 yr. 9 mo. 12 da.+

7. $\$18.20\times.05\frac{3}{4}=\$1.0465$; $\$10.23\div\$1.0465=$9 yr. 9 mo. 9 da.+

8. The *amount* at 5%, subtracted from the *amount* at 12%, gives the *interest* at 7%; then find the Int. at 5%, and subtract the Int. at 5% from Amt at 5%, and we have the principal, $680, and having the principal and interest, we find the time as before to be 4 yr. 6 mo.

9. Subtracting the Int. at 4% from the Amt. at 4%, we have the principal, $960, from which we find the time as before, to be 6 yr. 8 mo.

Art. 478. MENTAL EXERCISES.

2. For 5 years at 1%, $\frac{1}{20}$ of the principal equals the interest; $\frac{1}{20}$ of $40=$2; to gain $20, it will require 20÷2=10 per cent.

3. For 6 years at 1%, $\frac{3}{50}$ of the principal equals the interest; $\frac{3}{50}$ of $50=$3; hence to gain $15, it will require 15÷3 or 5%.

4. For 7 years at 1%, $\frac{7}{100}$ of the principal equals the interest; $\frac{7}{100}$ of $60=$4.20; hence to gain $21, it will require 21÷4.20, or 5%.

5. For 4 years at 1%, $\frac{1}{25}$ of the principal equals the interest; $\frac{1}{25}$ of $10=$.40, hence to gain $12—$10, or $2, it will require $2÷$.40, or 5%.

6. For 5 years at 1%, $\frac{1}{20}$ of the principal equals the interest; $\frac{1}{20}$ of $90=$4.50; hence to gain $117—$90, or $27, it will require $27÷$4.50, or 6%.

7. For 3 yr. 4 mo. at 1%, $\frac{1}{30}$ of the principal equals the interest; $\frac{1}{30}$ of $60=$2; hence to gain $70—$60, or $10, it will require $10÷$2, or 5%.

8. For 30 yr. at 1%, a principal gains $\frac{3}{10}$ of itself, and to gain 2 times or $\frac{20}{10}$ of itself, it will require 20÷3, or 6⅔%; to gain 4 times or $\frac{40}{10}$ of itself, it will require 40÷3, or 13⅓%; to gain 5 times itself, it will require 50÷3, or 16⅔%.

9. To *double* itself it must gain *once* itself. In 10 yr. at 1%, a principal gains $\frac{1}{10}$ of itself, and to gain $\frac{10}{10}$ will require 10%; in 12 yr. at 1%, a principal gains $\frac{3}{25}$ of itself, and to gain $\frac{25}{25}$ requires 25÷3, or 8⅓%; in 20 yr. at 1% it gains $\frac{1}{5}$, and it gains $\frac{5}{5}$ at 5%; in 25 yr. at 1% it gains $\frac{1}{4}$, and gains $\frac{4}{4}$ at 4%.

10. To *treble* itself it must gain *twice* itself. For 20 yr. at 1% a principal will gain $\frac{1}{5}$ of itself, and to gain *twice* itself or $\frac{10}{5}$, it will require 10 times 1% or 10%; in 25 years at 1% a principal gains $\frac{1}{4}$ of itself, and to gain twice itself will require 8%; in 40 yr. it will require 5%; in 80 yr. 2½%.

11. $600—$540, or $60, is the interest for 3 years at the given rate,

hence the interest for 1 year is \$20; and for 7 years is \$140, hence the principal is \$540—\$140, or \$400, and \$20, the interest for 1 year, is $\frac{20}{400}$, or 5% of the principal.

Art. 478. WRITTEN EXERCISES.

2. 5 yr. 4 mo. $=5\frac{1}{3}$ yr.; $\$240\times.01\times5\frac{1}{3}=\$12.80$; $\$64\div\$12.80=5\%$.
3. 7 yr. 8 mo. $=7\frac{2}{3}$ yr.; $\$654\times.07\frac{2}{3}=\$50.14$; $\$350.98\div\$50.14=7\%$.
4. 3 yr. 4 mo. 15 da. $=3\frac{3}{8}$ yr.; $\$72.50\times.03\frac{3}{8}=\$2.4468\frac{3}{4}$; $\$14.681\frac{1}{4}\div\$2.4468\frac{3}{4}=6\%$.
5. 6 yr. 7 mo. 20 da. $=6\frac{23}{36}$ yr.; $\$39.75\times.06\frac{23}{36}=\$263.89\frac{7}{12}$; $\$2375.06\frac{1}{4}\div\$263.89\frac{7}{12}=9\%$.
6. 8 yr. 10 mo. 18 da. $=8\frac{53}{60}$ yr.; $\$13.25\times.08\frac{53}{60}=\$1.17704\frac{1}{6}$; $\$7.06225\div1.17704\frac{1}{6}=6\%$.
7. $\$3312-\$2430=\$882=$ int. for 7 yr.; int. for 1 yr. $=\frac{1}{7}$ of $\$882=\$126$; int. for 5 yr. $=\$126\times5=\$630$; principal $=\$2430-\$630=\$1800$; $\$1800\times.01=\$18$; $\$126\div\$18=7\%$.
8. $\$6929\frac{3}{4}-\$3551=\$3378\frac{3}{4}=$ int. for 15 yr.; int. for 1 yr. $=\frac{1}{15}$ of $\$3378\frac{3}{4}=\$225\frac{1}{4}$; int. for 4 yr. $=\$225\frac{1}{4}\times4=\$901$; principal $=\$3551-\$901=\$2650$; $\$2650\times.01=\$26.50$; $\$225.25\div\$26.50=8\frac{1}{2}\%$.

Pages 281-2. MENTAL EXERCISES.

1. B's fortune is 4 times \$200, or \$800; in 4 years at 5%, $\frac{1}{5}$ of the principal equals the interest, hence A will receive $\frac{1}{5}$ of \$200, or \$40, and B will receive $\frac{1}{5}$ of \$800, or \$160.
2. D's money is $\frac{4}{3}$ of \$300, or \$400; in 5 years at 6%, $\frac{13}{10}$ of the principal equals the amount; hence C's amounted to $\frac{13}{10}$ of \$300, or \$390, and D's to $\frac{13}{10}$ of \$400, or \$520.
3. B's money is $\frac{3}{2}$ of \$400, or \$600; the difference between A's and B's money is $\frac{1}{3}$ of \$600, or \$200; the interest on \$200 is $\frac{2}{5}$ of \$200, or \$80.
4. In 6 years at 10%, the amount will be $\frac{8}{5}$ of the principal; $\frac{8}{5}$ of \$250=\$400, of which C has $\frac{3}{4}$, or \$300, and D $\frac{1}{4}$, or \$100.
5. In 5 years at 6%, $\frac{3}{10}$ of the principal equals the interest, hence the interest of \$1200 is \$360, of which A receives $\frac{1}{3}$ or \$120, B $\frac{1}{2}$, or \$180, and C $\frac{1}{6}$, or \$60.
6. In 4 years at 10%, $\frac{2}{5}$ of the principal equals the interest; $\frac{2}{5}$ of

$2500=$1000; if the parts are as 2 to 3, the first is $\frac{2}{5}$ of $1000 or $400, and the second $\frac{3}{5}$ of $1000, or $600; $400 is $\frac{1}{3}$ of B's, hence B has $1200; $600 is $\frac{1}{2}$ of A's, therefore A also has $1200.

7. $240 is $\frac{3}{10}$ of the sum of $\frac{1}{2}$ of A's and $\frac{1}{3}$ of B's fortunes ; hence $\frac{1}{2}$ of A's + $\frac{1}{3}$ of B's equals $800, and since $\frac{1}{2}$ of A's and $\frac{1}{3}$ of B's are equal, they must each equal $400; hence A's fortune= $800, and B's=$1200.

8. $600 is $\frac{6}{25}$ of their money, hence they both had $2500, which equals 5 times B's, hence B had $500 and A $2000.

9. We find that $\frac{1}{5}$ of the principal equals the interest, and the difference of the interest on the money he owes and on the money due him is $30; hence $30 is $\frac{1}{5}$ of what is due above what he owes, or $\frac{1}{5}$ of $150.

10. $18000 is $\frac{2}{5}$ of the cost, hence the cost was $45000; they all cost 9 times as much as the store, hence the store cost $5000, the house $10000, and the farm $30000.

11. $360 is $\frac{3}{50}$ of the amount invested, hence the amount invested is $6000.

12. $7800 equals $\frac{13}{10}$ of $\frac{2}{3}$ of A's fortune plus $\frac{3}{4}$ of B's, hence $\frac{2}{3}$ of A's plus $\frac{3}{4}$ of B's equal $6000; $\frac{2}{3}$ of A's=$\frac{1}{2}$ of $6000, or $3000, and A's equals $4500; $\frac{3}{4}$ of B's equals $3000, and B's equals $4000.

INTEREST ON PROMISSORY NOTES.

Art. 487. Page 284.

1. Interest on $1 for 62 days = $.010⅓; $225 × 1.010⅓ = $227.325.

(2)

The rate in New Jersey is 6%.

EXACT TIME.	OPERATION.
Nov. 15 da.	7 | 7925 – 60 da.
Dec. 31 da.	| 1298 – 1 da.
Jan. 15 da.	$7.9223
61 da.	779.25
	$787.1723

3. The rate in Missouri is 6%.

Aug.	10 da.
Sept.	30 da.
Oct.	31 da.
Nov.	30 da.
Dec.	31 da.
Jan.	1 da.
	133 da.

6	50	– 60 da.
6	50	– 60 da.
1	083	– 10 da.
	325	– 3 da.
$14.408		
650.00		
$664.408		

4. The rate is 6%; the time is 5 +31+30+31+31+28+25 =181 da.

7	2775	– 60 da.
21	8325	– 180 da.
	1212	– 1 da.
$21.9537		
727.75		
$749.7037		

5. Interest is reckoned only from the time the note is due until it is paid. It is due 90 days after date, or June 30; hence it draws interest from June 30 to Aug. 12, or 43 days, and at 6% the amount Aug. 12 will be $483.44.

6. The time is 17+31+29+14=91 da.; the Int. is $9.10, and amount $609.10.

ANNUAL INTEREST.

Art. 489. Page 286.

(2)

$840 × .06 = $50.40

aggregated times = 8 yr. 44 da.

$50.40 × $4\frac{121}{360}$ = $228.34

$50.40 × .487$\frac{1}{3}$ = 24.5616

$252.9016.

(3)

Since the interest has been regularly paid, there will be due the interest from June 16, 1876, to Jan. 1, 1877, 199 da., which is 38.69\frac{4}{5}$, and the amount due will be $1038.69.

4. From Feb. 10, 1873, the time when the last interest was paid, to the time of settlement, was 2 yr. 121 da.

$1250 × .06 = $75; aggregated times = 1 yr. 242 da.

$75 × $2\frac{121}{360}$ = 175.20\frac{5}{6}$

$75 × .100$\frac{1}{3}$ = 7.525

1250

1432.733\frac{1}{3}$.

PARTIAL PAYMENTS.

Art. 492. UNITED STATES RULE.

We will indicate the solution of these problems as in the Arithmetic. In several of the problems it will be necessary to compute the interest, to ascertain whether it is less than the payment.

2.	Principal or face of note	$4000.00
	Interest to first payment	240.00
	Amount due May 10, 1871	4240.00
	First payment to be deducted . . .	300.00
	Balance due after first payment . . .	3940.00
	Interest on balance to second payment . .	244.28
	Amount due May 22, 1872	4184.28
	Second payment to be deducted . . .	250.00
	Balance due after second payment . .	3934.28
	Interest to May 10, 1875	700.30
	Amount due May 10, 1875	4634.58
	The sum of third and fourth payments . .	245.00
		Ans.=$4389.58.

NOTE.—The third and fourth payments are less than the interest due; hence, according to the rule, we do not deduct them, but find the interest to the final date and then deduct both the payments.

3	Principal, or face of note	$800.00
	Interest to second payment	77.33
	Amount due Oct. 20, 1871	877.33
	Sum of first and second payments . .	85.00
	Balance due after second payment . .	792.33
	Interest from Oct. 20, 1871, to Jan. 14, 1872	11.09
	Amount due Jan. 14, 1872	803.42
	Third payment to be deducted . . .	15.00
	Balance due after third payment . . .	788.42
	Interest from Jan. 14, 1872, to Sept. 1, 1872	29.83
	Amount due Sept. 1, 1872	818.25
	Fourth payment to be deducted . . .	10.00
	Balance due Sept. 1, 1872	$808.25

4. Principal, or face of note $7000.00
Interest to Jan. 1, 1877 . . . . . 2450.00
Amount due Jan. 1, 1877 . . . . . 9450.00
Sum of payments 1540.00
Balance due Jan. 1, 1877 . . . . $7910.00

5. Principal, or face of note $5860.00
Int from Sept. 10, 1874, to May 18, 1876 . 494.84
Amount due May 18, 1876 . . . . 6354.84
Sum of first and second payments . . 500.00
Balance due after second payment . . 5854.84
Int. from May 18, 1876, to Jan. 1, 1879 . . 766.82
Amount due Jan. 1, 1879 . . . . 6621.66
Sum of third and fourth payments. . . 207.00
Balance due Jan. 1, 1879 . . . . $6414 66

6. Principal, or face of note $3500.00
Int. from May 12, 1870, to June 20, 1872 . 442.166
Amount due June 20, 1872 . . . . 3942.166
Sum of 1st, 2d, 3d, and 4th payments . . 800.000
Balance due June 20, 1872 . . . . . 3142.166
Int. from June 20, 1872, to Jan. 1, 1874 . 288.556
Amount due Jan. 1, 1874 . . . . . 3430.722
Sum of 5th and 6th payments 110.000
Balance due Jan. 1, 1874 . . . . . $3320.722

Art. 493. MERCHANTS' RULE.

1. Principal $5480.00
Int. from March 2 to Dec. 3 (276 da.) . . 252.08
Amt. of principal, Dec. 3 . . . . . 5732.08

Amt. of 1st indorsement (263 da.) . . 208.766
Amt. of 2d indorsement (174 da.) . . 308.70
Amt. of 3d indorsement (116 da.) . . 509.666
Amt. of 4th indorsement (63 da.) . . 707.35
Amt. of indorsements 1734.482
Balance due Dec. 3 . . . . . . $3997.597

2.	Principal	$4774 25
	Int. from Nov. 9, 1875, to Oct. 1, 1876 (327 da.)	303.563
	Amt. of principal, Oct. 1, 1876	$5077.813
	Amt. of 1st indorsement (274 da.). . .	$526.639
	Amt. of 2d indorsement (232 da.) . .	627.067
	Amt. of 3d indorsement (167 da.) . .	464.612
	Amt. of 4th indorsement (113 da.) . .	252 938
	Amt. of 5th indorsement (61 da) . .	252.965
	Amt. of indorsements	$2124.221
	Balance due Oct. 1, 1876	$2953.592

3.	Principal	$1250
	Int. for 1 year	62.50
	Amt. of principal, April 20, 1875 . . .	$1312.50
	Amt. of 1st indorsement (345 da.) . .	$209.583
	Amt. of 2d indorsement (277 da.) . .	51.924
	Amt. of 3d indorsement (207 da.) . .	144.025
	Amt. of 4th indorsement (183 da.) . .	153.812
	Amt. of 5th indorsement (129 da.) . .	356.271
		$915.615
	Balance due April 20, 1875 . . .	$396.885

TRUE DISCOUNT AND PRESENT WORTH.

Art. 496. WRITTEN EXERCISES.

2. Amount of $1=$1.34; $1206÷1.34=$900.
3. Amount of $1=$1.292; $6460÷1.292=$5000; $6460−$5000=$1460.
4. Amount of $1=$1.2625; $2178÷1.2625=$1725.14+.
5. Amount of $1=$1.033; $2500÷$1.033=$2420.13+; $2500−$2420.13=$79.87.
6. The present worth of $300=$275.23−; $280−$275.23=$4.77+.
7. Amount of $1=$1.12; $850÷1.12=$758.93−.
8. Present worth of $200 is $188.68−; present worth of $400 for 2 yr. is $357.14+; their sum is $545.82.

9. Present worth of $600 is $576.92+; present worth of $800 is $754.72—; present worth of $1000 is $917.43+; their sum is $2249.07.

BANK DISCOUNT AND BANKING.

Art. 505. Case I.

2. Interest for 60 days at 6% is $2.75, and at 7% is $\frac{7}{6}$ of $2.75=$3.20$\frac{5}{6}$.

3. Interest for 90 days at 6% =$14.475, and at 7% = $16.8875; $965—$16.8875=$948.1125.

4. The interest of $876.50 for 60 days at 6% =$8.765; $876.50—$8.765=$867.735.

5. True discount equals $690÷$1.15=$600; $690—$600= $90; bank discount equals $690×.06×2½=$103.50; $103.50—$90=$13.50.

REMARK.—In discounting a note, banks in Pennsylvania, Delaware, Maryland, Missouri and the District of Columbia, reckon both the day of discount and the day upon which the note becomes due. This, with the *three days of grace*, makes *four* days more than the usual time. From this some have supposed, incorrectly however, that they reckoned *four days of grace*. The reason for reckoning both days is, the note may be discounted in the morning of the day of discount and not paid until the afternoon of the day of payment, by which the person has the use of the money both of the days.

6. The note is due July 16, hence it has 107 days to run, and the discount=$650.25×.017$\frac{5}{6}$=$11.596125.

7. The note is due Nov. 23, hence it has 78 days to run, and the discount=$135.50×.013=$1.7615.

8. The note is due March 16, 1877, and being dated Chicago, the day of discount is not reckoned, hence time to run is 143 days; amount of note=$750×1.0455= $784.125; discount=$784.125×.023$\frac{5}{6}$=$18.6883125.

Art. 506. Case II.

2. The interest of $1 for 60 days is $0.01; the proceeds of $1 are $1—0.01=$0.99; $1000÷.99=$1010.10.

3. The interest of $1 for 90 days is $0.015, the proceeds are $1 — $0.015 = $0.985; and $2000 ÷ .985 = $2030.456.

4. Discount of \$1 for 60 days is \$0.01; hence the proceeds are \$1—\$0.01=\$0.99; \$5000÷.99=\$5050.505+.

5. Discount of \$1 for 60 days is \$0.01; hence the face=\$20÷.01=\$2000.

6. Discount of \$1=\$0.06; proceeds = \$1 − \$0.06 = \$0.94; \$685.20÷.94=\$730.

7. The interest of \$1 for 90 days, or 3 months, is \$0.0375, and the proceeds are \$0.9625; hence the face was \$1000÷.9625=\$1038.96.

8. As the note was presented in Baltimore the day of discount is reckoned, and therefore the time is 34 days; discount of \$1=\$.005$\frac{2}{3}$; proceeds of \$1=\$.994$\frac{1}{3}$; \$954.56×.994$\frac{1}{3}$=\$960.

Art. 507. Case III.

2. Discount=\$2000—\$1970=\$30; \$30÷\$2000=.015; .015 ÷.000$\frac{1}{6}$=90 days.

3. Discount=\$4500—\$4477.50=\$22.50; \$22.50÷\$4500=.005, which is the discount on \$1 for 30 days.

4. Discount=\$6540—\$6472.60=\$67.40; \$67.40÷\$6500=.0103$\frac{18}{327}$; the interest on \$1 for 1 day at 7% is $\frac{7}{36}$ of a mill, hence the time is 53 days +.

5. Discount=\$8500—\$8402.25=\$97.75; \$97.75÷\$8500=.0115; the time was 69 days, but as the discount was at St. Louis the day of discount is reckoned in this time; the note was due July 18th, and deducting 68 days from this date, we find May 11th, the day of discount.

6. Amount of note at maturity=\$765; discount=\$765—\$759.982=\$5.018; \$5.018÷\$765=.006$\frac{428}{765}$; the interest on \$1 for 1 day at 8% is $\frac{2}{9}$ of a mill; hence the time is 30— days. The time of maturity is Oct. 30, and 30 days before that is Sept. 30.

Art. 508. Case IV.

2. \$4040.40—\$4000=\$40.40; discount on \$1=\$40.40÷\$4040.40=.01—; the discount on \$1 for 60 days at 1% is $\frac{1}{6}$ of a cent; the rate= .01÷.00$\frac{1}{6}$=6%.

3. Discount=\$25.278; \$25.278÷\$2500=.0101$\frac{14}{125}$; time=52 days; .0101$\frac{14}{125}$÷.00$\frac{13}{90}$=7+ %.

4. Time=97 days+day of discount=98 days; discount=\$125.22$\frac{2}{9}$; \$125.22$\frac{2}{9}$÷\$5750=.021$\frac{7}{9}$; .021$\frac{7}{9}$÷.00$\frac{98}{360}$=8%.

STOCK INVESTMENTS WITH INTEREST.

Art. 509.

2. .02×1 =.02
   .02×1.015=.0203
   .02×1.03 =.0206
   .02×1.045=.0209
   .0818=8$\frac{9}{50}$%

3. .03×1.03=.0309
   .03×1 =.03
   .0609
   0609÷1.08$\frac{1}{4}$=5$\frac{271}{433}$%

4. \$37$\frac{1}{2}$×(1+1.015+1.03+1.045)=\$153.375, amount of dividends; \$137$\frac{3}{4}$×15=\$2066.25; \$153.375÷\$2066.25=7$\frac{233}{551}$.

5. \$4000×1.05$\frac{3}{4}$=\$4230; \$4230÷1.05$\frac{1}{4}$=\$4000 Kentucky 6's, and \$20 surplus; interest on Illinois 6's=\$60×(1+1.015+1.03+1.045)=\$245.40; interest on Kentucky 6's=\$120×(1+1.03)=\$243.60; \$245.40 — \$243.60=\$1.80.

6. Cost of stock=\$83$\frac{1}{8}$×20=\$1662.50; dividend=\$30(1+1.02+1.04+1.06)=\$123.60; rate=\$123.60÷\$1662.50=7$\frac{289}{665}$.

COMPOUND INTEREST.

Art. 510.

Compound interest should, in practice, be worked with the table. We solve a few problems to show the method without the table. By the first solution we get the interest for each year, and add the principal; by the second we get the amount by multiplying by 1 plus the rate %. Both methods may be used.

2. $568
.06
34.08
568
602.08
.06
36.1248
602.08
638.2048
.06
38.292288
638.2048
676.497088
568.00
$108.497, *Ans.*

3. $90
1.07
96.30
1.07
103.0410
1.07
10.25387
1.07
117.97164
1.07
126.2297
1.07
$135.0657, *Ans.*

4. Find the amount for 4 yr., which is $438.71074, then find the interest of this for 8 mo., which is $17.5484; add this to the amount, subtract the given principal, and the compound interest will be $108.759.

5. This is the same as 5 yr. at 3 per cent., and is thus solved, the comp. int. being $275.265.

6. This is the same as 9 yr. at 2 per cent., and is thus solved, the comp. int. being $286.82.

8. Amt.=$1.9990046 × 780=$1559.223588.

9. Amt.=$2.9521638 × 300=$885.64914.

10. Amt.=$2.19112314 × 950=$2081.566983; comp. int.=$2081.566—$950=$1131.566.

11. The compound amount for 6 yr.=$851.11146; $851.1146 × 1.031=$877.495+; comp. int.=$877.495—$600=$277.495; simple int.=$600 × .391=$234.60; difference=$277.495—$234.60=$42.895.

DOMESTIC EXCHANGE.

Art. 524. Case I.

3. $1.00—¾%=$0.99¼; $0.99¼ × 4750=$4714.37½.

4. Discount for 30 days=.005; $1.00—$.005=$.995, plus 1½%=$1.01; this multiplied by 3500=$3535.

5. Discount for 18 days=.003×$\frac{7}{6}$=.0035; \$1.00—\$.0035 = \$.9965; .9965—.01$\frac{1}{2}$ = .9815; \$.9815 × 7500 = \$7361.25.

6. The discount on \$1 for 60 da. at 6% is \$0.01; \$1—\$.01=\$.99; .99+.0125=1.0025; \$1.0025 × 1500= \$1503.75.

7. 1.0125×\$4500=\$4556.25.

Art. 525. Case II.

2. \$1.00—\$.005=\$.995; \$2587÷.995=\$2600.

3. Int. on \$1 for 45 da.=\$0.0075, which subtracted from \$1 =\$0.9925; .9925+.01$\frac{1}{8}$=1.00375; hence \$602.25÷1.00375=\$600.

4. \$1.00—\$.00$\frac{3}{4}$=\$.99$\frac{1}{4}$; \$40.20÷.99$\frac{1}{4}$=\$40.50+.

5. \$5000×.02$\frac{1}{2}$=\$125; \$5000—\$125=\$4875; \$1.00+\$.01$\frac{1}{4}$ =\$1.01$\frac{1}{4}$; \$4875÷1.01$\frac{1}{4}$=\$4814.81+.

6. \$1500÷1.00$\frac{1}{8}$=\$1498.127+.

7. Int. for 93 days=\$.0155; \$1—\$.0155=\$.9845; \$1498.127 ×.9845=\$1474.906+.

8. Exchange on Boston being at a premium of $\frac{1}{8}$%, \$1 of the draft is worth \$1.00$\frac{1}{8}$ in Savannah; hence the draft is worth \$1498.13×1.00$\frac{1}{8}$=\$1500.

Art. 526. Case III.

2. Int. on \$1 for 30 days at 7%, the rate in Georgia= \$.0058$\frac{1}{3}$; \$1—\$.0058$\frac{1}{3}$=\$.9941$\frac{2}{3}$; \$3500×.9941$\frac{2}{3}$= \$3479.58$\frac{1}{3}$; \$3532.08—\$3479.58=\$52.50; \$52.50÷\$3500=1$\frac{1}{2}$% premium.

3. \$5000×.97$\frac{1}{2}$=\$4875, proceeds to be remitted; \$4875—\$4814.81 = \$60.19 premium; \$60.19 ÷ \$4814.81 = 1$\frac{1}{4}$%+.

4. Int. on \$1 for 3 mo.=\$.015; cost of \$1=\$.985; \$.985 ×750=\$738.75; \$738.75—\$727.50=\$11.25; \$11.25 ÷\$750=1$\frac{1}{2}$% discount.

FOREIGN EXCHANGE.

Art. 533. Page 308.

2. \$4.84×500×1.10$\frac{1}{2}$=\$2674.10.

7. $1000÷$.93¾ and the quotient multiplied by 4, gives 4266.66+ reichsmarks.

10. 8400×20.1¢=$1688.40; 8400×19.3¢=$1621.20; gain of remitting=$67.20. Or, 20.1¢−19.3¢=.8¢; .8¢×8400=$67.20.

11. He settled the account the day the bill was due, hence there was no interest on it; $2000÷5.24¼=$381.497; $381.497×1.01=$385.31197.

ARBITRATION OF EXCHANGE.

Art. 535. Page 310.

(3)

x=$1200
$.40=1 florin
15 fl.=8 roubles
x=1600 roubles

(4)

$x=2400 crowns
5 cr.=7 francs.
54 fr.=£2
£9=$46
x=$636.049+
Direct exchange=
2400×27¢=$648;
$648−$636.049=$11.951−

(5)

$x=5000 marks
1.875 rm.=1 guilder
1 g.=2.5 francs
25.15 fr.=£1
£1=£1.00¼
£1=$4.85
x=1288.83+

(6)

x S. F.=$5200 Phil.
$1 Phil.=$1.00¾ Balt.
$1 Balt.=$1.01½ S. F.
x=$5317.58½
Direct exchange=
$5200×1.02=$5304
$5317.58½−$5304=$13.58½

(7)

x=$1000
$1 Cin.=$1.00¼ N. Y.
$4.855=£1
£1=£.99¾
£1.00¼=£1
£1=11.75 guilders
1.12 g.=2 marks
x=4332.456 marks
Direct exchange=
$1000÷$.24=4166⅔ marks
4332.456−4166.666=165.79 marks.

DUTIES AND CUSTOMS.

Art. 546. Page 313.

2. Breakage=50×.05=2½ dozen; 50−2½=47½; 48×$6=$288.

3. 2800+101.56=2901.56 fr.=$560; 30% of $560=$168.

4. 350×20=7000 lire; 7000+475=7475 lire; commission =2½% of 7475 lire=186.87½ lire; 7475+186.87½=7661.875 lire, cost; 7661.875 lire=$1478.74; duty=20% of $1479= *$295.80.*

5. Net weight=5 cwt. 1 qr. 3 lb.—21 lb.=5 cwt. 10 lb.; 5 cwt. 10 lb. × 25=127 cwt. 26 lb.; duty=$1¼ × 127 =$158.75; 120 × 35=4200 gal.; 4200 × 5¢=$210; duty in gold=$158.75+$210=$368.75; duty in currency =$368.75 × 1.11½=$411.15625.

6. Commission = £756.75 × .02½ = £18.9187½; £756.75+ £18.9187½ = £775.6687½ = $3774.79—; ad valorem duty=35% of $3775=$1321.25; specific duty=1350 × 50¢=$675; whole duty in gold=$1321.25+$675 = $1996.25; cost in gold = $3774.79+$1996.25 = $5771.04.

7. $2063\frac{3}{4} \times 7\frac{1}{8}$d.$=14704\frac{7}{32}$d.: commission=2½% of $14704\frac{7}{32}$d. $=367\frac{155}{256}$d.; $14704\frac{7}{32}$ d.$+367\frac{155}{256}$ d.$=15071\frac{211}{256}$ d.= £62 16 s.—; £62 16 s.+5 s. =£63 1 s. = $306.83; duty=35% of $307=$107.45.

(8)

WA / R 1/75 75 Drums.			
Cwt. qr. lb.			
Gr. 421 3 3		Cwt. qr. lb.	
Tr. 14 3 23		Net 406 3 8@13/3	269 - 10 - 4
		45564 lb. discount 2½%	6 - 14 - 9
			262 - 15 - 7
Liverpool, April, 1874.		Com. 2½%	6 - 11 - 5
McKeon Bros.,			£269 - 7 - 0
Duty,—45,564 lb.@1½¢=$683.46.			or $1310.79

Cost of invoice=$683.46+$1310.79=$1994.25.

(9)

F B	No. 21, *One Case Pallet Knives.*		
	24 doz. 3 in. Plain.	No. 2/8	£3 - 4 - 0
	12 " 4 " "	2/8	1 - 12 - 0
	4 " 5 " "	3/5	13 - 8
			5 - 9 - 8
Duty as Manuf. Steel,		disc't, 2½%	2 - 9
			5 - 6 - 11
$27@45%=$12.15		case	0 - 2 - 0
			5 - 8 - 11
		Com. 2½%	2 - 9
			£5 - 11 - 8
			or $27.17

SECTION IX.

RATIO AND PROPORTION.

The teacher should be careful that the pupil obtains a clear conception of Ratio, and the principles given under it. Those preferring the French Method, so-called, may use it by taking the reciprocal of the results given. In *The Philosophy of Arithmetic*, the subject of Ratio is fully discussed, and the reasons in favor of the "English Method" fully given.

RATIO.

Page 317.

1. Ratio$=12\div3=4$.
2. Ratio$=24\div4=6$.
3. Ratio$=90\div16=5\frac{5}{8}$.
4. Ratio$=488\div61=8$.
5. Ratio$=\$256\div\$856=\frac{32}{107}$.
6. Ratio$=£144\div£256=\frac{9}{16}$.
7. $\frac{3}{4}\times\frac{3}{2}=\frac{9}{8}$; $\frac{9}{10}\times\frac{5}{4}=\frac{9}{8}$.
8. $\frac{25}{16}\times\frac{12}{15}=1\frac{1}{4}$; $\frac{11}{4}\times\frac{5}{11}=1\frac{1}{4}$.
10. $\left\{\begin{matrix}4:3\\6:8\end{matrix}\right\}=\frac{4}{3}\times\frac{6}{8}=1$.
11. $\left\{\begin{matrix}5:2\\8:6\end{matrix}\right\}=\frac{5}{2}\times\frac{8}{6}=3\frac{1}{3}$.
12. Ratio$=24\div8=3$.
13. Ant.$=8\times9=72$.
14. Cons.$=36\div4=9$.
15. Ant.$=\frac{15}{16}\times\frac{18}{25}=\frac{27}{40}$.
16. Cons.$=\frac{15}{16}\div\frac{25}{32}=\frac{15}{16}\times\frac{32}{25}=\frac{6}{5}=1\frac{1}{5}$.
17. There can be no ratio, because the numbers are not of the same kind.
18. Ratio$=5\times6\div10\times14=\frac{3}{14}$.

SIMPLE PROPORTION.

Be certain that the pupil has a clear idea of a proportion. Fix upon his mind that a proportion is an *equation*—an *equality* of ratios. To do this, require him at first to write a proportion, thus: $6\div3=8\div4$. After he has been drilled upon writing and solving a proportion in this form, the ordinary form may be used.

The pupil should be required to illustrate the *Principles* of Proportion. Thus, take Prin. II. In the proportion $6:3::8:4$, we see that the first extreme 6 equals the product of 3 and 8 divided by 4; that is, $6=\frac{3\times 8}{4}$. In the same way the other extreme $4=\frac{3\times 8}{6}$; and the same should be shown for the other principles.

Page 319.

2. 1st term $=\frac{8\times 18}{9}=16$.

3. 4th term $=\frac{72\times 21}{18}=84$.

4. 4th term $=\frac{48\times 15}{16}=45$.

5. 2d term $=\frac{21\times 96}{32}=63$.

6. 3d term $=\frac{6\times 95}{15}=38$.

7. 4th term $=\frac{68\times 35}{17}=140$lb.

8. 1st term $=\frac{2}{3}\frac{8}{5}\times\frac{6}{7}\div\frac{4}{5}=\frac{6}{7}$.

9. 4th term $=\frac{1.3\times 6.8}{.5}=17.68$, *Ans.*

APPLICATIONS OF SIMPLE PROPORTION.

It will be seen that I make the unknown quantity which is to be found, the first term instead of the last term I have not made this change without what I deem a sufficient reason. The philosophy of it is briefly stated in the Arithmetic. In Trigonometry the advantage of this change is especially evident. Pupils often hesitate to know how to commence a proportion so as to get the unknown quantity in the fourth term. Let them commence the proportion with the unknown quantity, and there will be no difficulty.

The rule generally given for the solution of problems in Simple Proportion is, "*Make the term like the answer the third term, and if the answer is to be larger than the third term, take the larger of the two remaining terms for the second term,*" etc. The objection to such a rule is, that it does not involve the idea of proportion, but is merely a working for the answer. A better rule, and no more absurd, is as follows: "*Write down the term like the answer; if the answer is to be larger than this, multiply by the larger of the two remaining terms, and divide by the smaller,*" etc. My own view is that if the pupil cannot state a problem in proportion by *comparing* the terms, he had better solve it by Analysis, and omit Proportion until he is prepared for it.

Art. 565. Page 321.

2. $x : 250 :: 78 : 13$

$$x = \frac{250 \times 78}{13} = 1500.$$

3. $x : 28 :: \$144 : \$112$

$$x = \frac{28 \times 144}{112} = 36.$$

4. $x : \$8250 :: 132 : 110$

$$x = \frac{8250 \times 132}{110} = \$9900.$$

5. $x : 6 :: 250 : 100$

$$x = \frac{6 \times 250}{100} = \$15.$$

6. $x : 26 :: 36 : 16.$

$$x = \frac{26 \times 36}{16} = 58.50.$$

7. $x : 75 :: 16200 : 9000$

$$x = \frac{75 \times 16200}{9000} = 135.$$

8. $x : 1 :: 3360 : 84$

$$x = \frac{3360}{84} = 40, \textit{ Ans.}$$

9. $x : 25 :: 468 : 36$

$$x = \frac{25 \times 468}{36} = 325.$$

10. $x : 79 :: 675 : 395$

$$x = \frac{79 \times 675}{395} = 135.$$

11. $x : \$4\frac{1}{2} :: 34 \text{ lb.} : 8 \text{ lb. } 8 \text{ oz.}$
or, $x : \frac{9}{2} :: 34 \text{ lb.} : 8\frac{1}{2} \text{ lb.}$

$$x = \frac{\frac{9}{2} \times 34}{8\frac{1}{2}} = \frac{9}{2} \times 34 \times \frac{2}{17}$$

$x = \$18$, *Ans.*

In this problem the compound numbers must be reduced to the same unit value. We reduced the 8 lb. 8 oz. to pounds. We could also reduce the 34 lb. to ounces, and the 8 lb. 8 oz. to ounces, but that would have been longer than the other method.

12. $x : 19 :: 19 : 4$

$$x = \frac{19 \times 19}{4} = 90\frac{1}{4}.$$

13. $x : \$40.50 :: 28.75 \text{ cwt.} : 7.50 \text{ cwt.}$

$$x = \frac{\$40.50 \times 28.75}{7.50} = \$155.25.$$

14. $x : 10 \text{ min. } 45 \text{ sec.} :: 68 : 5$

$x : 10\frac{3}{4} \text{ min.} :: 68 : 5$

$$x = \frac{10\frac{3}{4} \times 68}{5} = 146\frac{1}{5} \text{ min.} = 2 \text{ h. } 26\frac{1}{5} \text{ min.}$$

15. In the three spring months there are $31 + 30 + 31 = 92$ days.

$$x : \$230 :: 365 : 92;\ x = \frac{230 \times 365}{92} = \$912.50.$$

17. $x : 28 :: 12 : 8;\ x = \dfrac{28 \times 12}{8} = 42$ men.

18. $x : 6$ ft. 9 in. : : 41 ft. : 13 ft. 8 in.

$x : 6\frac{3}{4}$ ft. : : 41 ft. : $13\frac{2}{3}$ ft.

$x=\frac{27}{4}\times 41\times\frac{3}{41}=20\frac{1}{4}$, *Ans.*

19. $x : \$6.25 : : 16\frac{1}{5} : 13\frac{1}{2}$; $x=\$6.25\times\frac{81}{5}\times\frac{2}{27}=\$7.50$.

20. $x : \frac{12}{25}$E. : : $15\frac{5}{6} : \frac{5}{6}$

$x : \$\frac{24}{5} : : \frac{95}{6} : \frac{5}{6}$

$x=\$\frac{24}{5}\times\frac{95}{6}\times\frac{6}{5}=\$91.20$, *Ans.*

21. $x : 142 : : 9 : 6\frac{3}{4}$; $x=142\times 9\times\frac{4}{27}=189\frac{1}{3}$.

22. $x : 8 : : 168 : 96$; $x=\frac{8\times 168}{96}=14$.

23. $x : \$437 : :$ 16 A. 80 P. : 4 A. 120 P.

$x : \$437 : :$ 2640 P. : 760 P.

$x=\frac{\$437\times 2640}{760}=\$1518$

$\$25\times 16\frac{1}{2}=$ 412.50

$1105.50, *Ans.*

SUG.—At the same rate per acre, we find 16 A. 80 P. will cost $1518; at $25 less an acre it will cost $412.50 less, hence the cost is $1518 minus $412.50, which is $1105.50.

24. $x : 9$ da. : : 17 : 12

$x=\frac{9\times 17}{12}=\frac{51}{4}$ da.

To mow ½ will take ½ of $\frac{51}{4}=\frac{51}{8}=6\frac{3}{8}$, *Ans.*

SUG.—If 5 men refuse to labor, then 12 men labor, and we find it will take $\frac{51}{4}$ da. to do the whole of it; hence to do ½ of it, it will take ½ of $\frac{51}{4}$ or $6\frac{3}{8}$ days.

25. $x : \$1968 : \$0.75 : \$1.00$

$x=1968\times .75$

$=\$1476$, *Ans.*

26. $x : 9 : : 6 : 8$.

$x=\frac{9\times 6}{8}=6\frac{3}{4}$ oz.

27. $x : 10 : : \$560 : \$800$; $x=\frac{\$560\times 10}{\$800}=7$ mo.

28. $x : \$1.25 : : \$6.25 : \$1.12\frac{1}{2}$; hence $x=\$6.94\frac{4}{9}$.

29. SOL.—In one revolution of the larger the smaller gains $28-20=8$ cogs; also to gain 12 revolutions of the smaller is to gain $12\times 20=240$ cogs; then it will require as many revolutions as $240\div 8=30$, *Ans.*

By Proportion, $x : 1 : : 240 : 8$; hence $x=30$, *Ans.*

30. $x : 2400 : : 1\frac{1}{2}$ lb. : 15 oz.

hence, $x=\frac{2400\times 24}{15}=3840$

hence, $3840-2400=1440$

SOL.—We first find how many men can be kept on 15 oz. per day; then the reinforcement will be 3840 men minus 2400 men, or 1440 men.

SOL. 2D.—$x : 2400 : : 9 : 15$; hence $x=1440$.

COMPOUND PROPORTION.

With pupils not very far advanced, the problems in Compound Proportion should be solved by ANALYSIS. We will solve a few of the problems by both methods.

Art. 567. Page 324.

1. $x=\frac{12\times 7\times 9}{18\times 3}=14.$

2. $x=\frac{32\times 15\times 8}{16\times 12}=20.$

3. $x=\frac{12\times 5\times 9\times 14}{7\times 18\times 20}=3.$

4. $x=\frac{26\times 12\times 22\times 7}{21\times 13\times 11}=16.$

5. $x=\frac{4}{5}\times\frac{8}{7}\times\frac{7}{16}\times\frac{25}{36}\times\frac{11}{8}\times\frac{9}{5}\times\frac{4}{3}=\frac{11}{12}.$

APPLICATIONS OF COMPOUND PROPORTION.

Art. 569. Page 325.

2. ANALYSIS.—If 36 men earn \$324, 1 man will earn $\frac{1}{36}$ of \$324, and 42 men will earn 42 times $\frac{1}{36}$ or $\frac{42}{36}$ of \$324. If 42 men earn $\frac{42}{36}$ of \$324 in 18 days, in 1 day they will earn $\frac{1}{18}$ of $\frac{42}{36}$ of \$324, and in 27 days they will earn 27 times $\frac{1}{18}$ of $\frac{42}{36}$ of \$324, which is $\frac{27}{18}\times\frac{42}{36}$ of \$324, which by cancelling and multiplying we find equals \$567.

OPERATION.

$\frac{27}{18}\times\frac{42}{36}\times\$324=\$567$

2. BY PROPORTION.—Here the sum earned is in proportion to the number of men and time they labor, hence the required sum is to \$324 as 42 to 36 and 27 to 18, from which we have the compound proportion as written in the margin, etc.

OPERATION.

$$x:\$324::\left\{\begin{matrix}42:36\\27:18\end{matrix}\right\}$$

$$x=\frac{\$324\times 42\times 27}{36\times 18}=\$567$$

3. No. cows $=58\times\frac{35}{29}\times\frac{25}{14}=125$ cows, *Ans.*

$$x:58::\left\{\begin{matrix}35:29\\25:14\end{matrix}\right.$$

$$x=\frac{58\times 35\times 25}{29\times 14}=125 \text{ cows, } Ans.$$

4. Int. $=\frac{800}{600}$ of $\frac{8}{6}$ of $\frac{6\frac{1}{3}}{4\frac{1}{2}}$ of $\$162=\$405\frac{1}{3}.$

$$x:\$162::\left\{\begin{matrix}800:600\\8:6\\6\frac{1}{3}:4\frac{1}{2}\end{matrix}\right.$$

$$x=\frac{162\times 800\times 8\times 19\times 2}{600\times 6\times 9\times 3}=405\frac{1}{3}.$$

5. No. men$=12\times\frac{35}{40}\times\frac{144}{140}\times\frac{5}{6}=9$ men, *Ans.*

$$x:12::\begin{cases}35:40\\144:140\\5:6\end{cases}$$

$$x=\frac{12\times35\times144\times5}{40\times140\times6}=9, \textit{ Ans.}$$

6. No. days$=45\times\frac{18}{36}\times\frac{12}{10}=27$ days, *Ans.*

$$x:45::\begin{cases}18:36\\12:10\end{cases}$$

$$x=\frac{45\times18\times12}{36\times10}=27, \textit{ Ans.}$$

7. No. of men$=\frac{360}{120}\times\frac{9}{15}\times\frac{10}{12}\times28=42.$

$$x:28::\begin{cases}360:120\\9:15\\10:12\end{cases}$$

$$x=\frac{360\times9\times10\times28}{120\times15\times12}=42, \textit{ Ans.}$$

8. Cost$=\$1.25\times\frac{10}{8}\times\frac{1\frac{1}{8}}{1\frac{1}{4}}=\$1.40\frac{5}{8}$, *Ans.*

$$x:\$1.25::\begin{cases}10:8\\1\frac{1}{8}:1\frac{1}{4}\end{cases}$$

$$x=\frac{1.25\times10\times1\frac{1}{8}}{8\times1\frac{1}{4}}=\$1.40\frac{5}{8}, \textit{ Ans.}$$

9. SUG.—If 35 horses eat it in 36 days, they will eat 3 times as much in $36\times3=108$ days, and they will eat $\frac{3}{4}$ of it in $\frac{3}{4}$ of 108 days or 81 days, and the remainder in 27 days. If 35 horses eat the remainder in 27 days, $35+5$, or 40 horses, will eat it in $\frac{35}{40}$ of 27 days, or $23\frac{5}{8}$ days, which, added to 81 days, equals $104\frac{5}{8}$ days.

10. SUG.—First find how long it will take 32 men to build 40 rods, and then how long it will take 32—8, or 24 men to build 75—40, or 35 rods, and take the sum of these times, and we will have $10+11\frac{2}{3}=21\frac{2}{3}$, *Ans.*

11. Cost$=\$8.10\times\frac{28}{147}\times\frac{7}{6}\times\frac{9}{7}=\$7.93$, *Ans.*

12. Cost$=\$68\times\frac{40}{17}\times\frac{16}{35}\times\frac{25}{14}\times\frac{7}{6}\times\frac{6}{5}=\$182.85^{5}$, *Ans.*

SUG.—Since it is worth $\frac{1}{5}$ more, we take $\frac{6}{5}$ of the value at the same rate.

13. Cows$=\$24\times\frac{14}{11}\times\frac{40}{18}\times\frac{75}{60}\times\frac{12}{9}=240$, Ans.

INSURANCE.

Art. 578. Case I.

4. $\$3000+\$1500+\$750=\$5250$; $\$5250\times.01\frac{1}{4}=\$65.62\frac{1}{2}$; $\$65.62\frac{1}{2}+\$1.25=\$67.87\frac{1}{2}$.

5. From April 18, 1877, to Sept. 30, 1887, equals 5 mo. 12 da.; hence we look in the table opposite 6 mo. under 50 cents, and find 35 cents to be the insurance on \$100. Multiplying \$975 by .35 and removing the decimal point two places to the left, we have \$3.4125 premium.

6. $\$75000\times.00\frac{3}{4}=\$562.50$; $\$25000\times.01\frac{1}{8}=\$281.25$; amt. of premiums $=\$562.50+\$281.25=\$843.75$; $\$75000+\$6250=\$81250$; $\$81250-\$843.75=\$80406.25$,

7. $\$10000+\$15000=\$25000$; $\$24000\times.75=\$18750$; premium $=\$18750\times.00\frac{3}{4}=\$140.62\frac{1}{2}$; loss to insurers, $\$18750-\$140.62\frac{1}{2}=\$18609.37\frac{1}{2}$; loss to owner $=\$6250+\$140.62\frac{1}{2}=\$6390.62\frac{1}{2}$.

8. $\$180.00\times.20=\$36$; $\$36\times2=\$72$; $\$180.00\times.30=\$54$; $\$72-\$54=\$18$.

Art. 579. Case II.

2. $\$58.12\frac{1}{2}\div.02\frac{1}{2}=\$2325$.

3. $\$86.36\frac{1}{4}\div.01\frac{3}{4}=\$4935$; since \$4935 equals $\frac{4}{5}$ of the value of the house, the whole value equals \$6168.75.

4. $\frac{4}{5}$ of $\$15880=\$12704$; $\$1.00-.02=.98$; $\$12704\div.98=\$12963.265+$.

Art. 580. Case III.

2. $\$55\div\$2500=.02\frac{1}{5}$.

3. $\frac{5}{6}$ of $\$89520=\$74600$; $\$2424.50\div\$74600=.03\frac{1}{4}$.

4. $\$79.25-\$3.25=\$76$; $\$76\div\$5700=.01\frac{1}{3}$.

5. $\$2400+\$1200+\$350=\$3950$; $\$49.375\div\$3950=1\frac{1}{4}\%$; but since the rate for 3 years is twice the annual rate, the annual rate $=\frac{1}{2}$ of $1\frac{1}{4}\%=\frac{5}{8}\%$.

Art. 581. Case IV.

2. Premium $=\$5500\times.0025\times10=\$137.50$; 90% of $\$137.50=\$123.75$.

3. $\$2500-\$500=\$2000$; $.0030-.0026=.0004$; $.0004\times\$2000=\$.80$.

Art. 583. Case V.

2. Whole ins. on hotel $=\$800+\$2500=\$3300$; N. Am. loss on hotel $=\frac{8}{33}$ of $\$2200=\$533.33\frac{1}{3}$; whole loss $=\$533.33\frac{1}{3}+\$500=\$1033.33\frac{1}{3}$; Sun's loss on hotel $=\frac{25}{33}$ of $\$2200.00=\$1666.66\frac{2}{3}$.

SIMPLE PARTNERSHIP. Art. 590.

4. $\frac{1}{3}$, $\frac{1}{4}$, $\frac{1}{5}$, are as $\frac{20}{60}$, $\frac{15}{60}$, $\frac{12}{60}$, or as 20, 15, 12; hence if we divide into 20+15+12=47 equal parts, A's=$\frac{20}{47}$ of 60 =25$\frac{25}{47}$; B's=$\frac{15}{47}$ of 60=19$\frac{7}{47}$; C's=$\frac{12}{47}$ of 60=15$\frac{15}{47}$.

5. C received $\frac{1}{2}$ of \$2400=\$1200, which equals what A and B received, and this we divide in proportion to what they put in; hence A receives $\frac{5}{12}$ of \$1200=\$500, and B receives $\frac{7}{12}$ of \$1200=\$700.

6. Each had $\frac{4}{5}$ of his stock remaining after loss by fire; then find $\frac{2}{5}$ of this remainder, and we have A's \$2048, B's \$2304, C's \$1728. If we deduct the loss by fire we would have other results, but this I think is not required by the language of the problem.

7. \$5000 Wife received $\frac{50}{130}$ of \$10400=\$4000
3500 Son received $\frac{35}{130}$ of 10400=\$2800
4500 Daughter received $\frac{45}{130}$ of \$10400=\$3600
\$13000

Or, \$10400=$\frac{4}{5}$ of \$13000, hence each would receive $\frac{4}{5}$ of the sum mentioned in the will. $\frac{4}{5}$ of \$5000=\$4000; etc.

8. \$1650 Since their gain is in proportion to their stock
1500 A's stock=$\frac{1650}{4750}$ of \$9500=\$3300
1600 B's stock=$\frac{1500}{4750}$ of \$9500=\$3000
\$4750 C's stock=$\frac{1600}{4750}$ of \$9500=\$3200

9. \$4200 A's gain=$\frac{65}{118}$ of \$2950=\$1625
1250 B's gain=$\frac{53}{118}$ of \$2950=\$1325
\$2950=A's and B's gain.

A's and B's gain=$\frac{295}{420}$ of the gain, hence their stock is $\frac{295}{420}$ of the stock; the stock is \$16800, and C's stock is \$5000.

10. \$1500—\$660=\$840=A's and B's gain; A receives $\frac{8}{14}$ of \$840, or \$480; B receives $\frac{6}{14}$ of \$840, or \$360; since A and B receive $\frac{84}{150}$ of the gain, they must own $\frac{84}{150}$ of the stock, which equals \$1400, hence the whole stock is \$2500, and C's land is worth \$1100, or \$110 an acre.

COMPOUND PARTNERSHIP.

Art. 592. Case I.

2. $\$500 \times 9 = 4500$ $\quad \frac{45}{193}$ of $\$488.70 = \$113.94$

$800 \times 8 = 6400$ $\quad \frac{64}{193}$ of $\$488.70 = \$162.06$

$1200 \times 7 = 8400$ $\quad \frac{84}{193}$ of $\$488.70 = \$212.70$

19300

3. $3 \times 7 = 21$ $\quad \frac{21}{104}$ of $\$62.40 = \$12.60$

$4 \times 8 = 32$ $\quad \frac{32}{104}$ of $\$62.40 = \$19.20$

$2 \times 13 = 26$ $\quad \frac{26}{104}$ of $\$62.40 = \$15.60$

$5 \times 5 = 25$ $\quad \frac{25}{104}$ of $\$62.40 = \$15.00$

104

4. $9 \times 10 = 90$

$15 \times 6 = 90$

$10 \times 9 = 90$

$18 \times 5 = 90$

Sol.—Since they worked the same number of days their wages will be the same, and each will receive $\frac{1}{4}$ of $120, or $30.

5. $\$10000 \times 12 = 120000$ $\quad \frac{120}{201}$ of $\$4020 = \$2400$

$7000 \times 9 = 63000$ $\quad \frac{63}{201}$ of $\$4020 = \$1260$

$3000 \times 6 = 18000$ $\quad \frac{18}{201}$ of $\$4020 = \$360$

201000

6.

A's	B's	
$\$2500 \times 9 = \$22500$	$\$3000 \times 9 = \$27000$	$48000
$1700 \times 15 = 25500$	$3500 \times 15 = 52500$	79500
$48000	$79500	$127500

$\frac{480}{1275} \times \$3825 = \$1440$, A's share of loss

$\frac{795}{1275} \times \$3825 = \$2385$, B's share of loss.

A's	B's	C's
$60 \times 3 = 180$	$80 \times 3 = 240$	$90 \times 3 = 270$
$40 \times 2 = 80$	$60 \times 2 = 120$	$72 \times 2 = 144$
260	360	414

$\frac{260}{1034} \times \$51.70 = \$13.00$, A pays.

$\frac{360}{1034} \times \$51.70 = \$18.00$, B pays.

$\frac{414}{1034} \times \$51.70 = \$20.70$, C pays.

8. If A's original capital is represented by 5, the remainder will be 4, and if B's original capital was 7, the remainder will be 6. A's capital$=5 \times 6 + 4 \times 6 = 54$; B's capital$=7 \times 6 + 6 \times 6 = 78$; $54 + 78 = 132$; $\frac{54}{132}$ of $\$1430 = \$585$; $\frac{78}{132}$ of $\$1430 = \$845$.

9. Brown's gain for 1 mo. $=\frac{1}{6}$ of $750=$125
Black's " " " $=\frac{1}{8}$ of $1200= 150
White's " " " $=\frac{1}{10}$ of $800= 80
$355

$\frac{125}{355}$ of $19880=$7000; $\frac{150}{355}$ of $19880=$8400
$\frac{80}{355}$ of $19880=$4480.

Art. 593. Case II.

2. Since there is no excess or deficit of either partner's share, A receives $\frac{2}{3}$ of $1500 or $1000, and B, $\frac{1}{3}$ of $1500 or $500. Then A's capital is $4000+$1000, or $5000, and B's capital is $2000+$500, or $2500.

3. There is no excess or deficit.
Int. on $1500 to end of year, $60. Int. on $900, $18.
$2400, Profits,—$78, Int.=net gain, $2322.

A's account.		B's account.	
$\frac{2}{3}$ of $2322, or A's share of gain	$1548	$\frac{1}{3}$ of $2322, or B's share of gain	$774
A's capital+addition	6500	B's capital+addition	3400
A's interest	60	B's interest	18
Value of A's share	$8108	Value of B's share	$4192

4. $8108+$4192=$12300, entire capital.
$\frac{2}{3}$ of $12300=$8200; $8200—$8108=$92, A's deficit.
$\frac{1}{3}$ of $12300=$4100; $4192—$4100=$92, B's excess.
Int. on $92, A's deficit and B's excess, $5.52.
Int. on $1500, A's withdrawal to end of year, is $45.
Int. on $1200, B's withdrawal to end of year, is $24.
$3000+$69=$3069, net profits.

A's account.		B's account.	
$\frac{2}{3}$ of $3069, or A's gain	$2046.00	$\frac{1}{3}$ of $3069, B's gain	$1023.00
A's capital less withdrawal	6608.00	B's capital less withdrawal	2992.00
Total	$8654.00	Int. on B's excess	5.52
		Total	$4020.52
Int. on A's deficit and withdrawal	50.52	Int. on B's withdrawal	24.00
Value of A's share	$8603.48	Value of B's share	$3996.52

5. $\frac{1}{4}$ of \$8603.48=\$2150.87, C's share; \$8603.48—\$2150.87 =\$6452.61, A's share.

\$8603.48+\$3996.52=\$12600, entire capital.

$\frac{1}{2}$ of \$12600=\$6300, A's; $\frac{1}{3}$ of \$12600=\$4200, B's $\frac{1}{6}$ of \$12600=\$2100, C's.

\$6452.61—\$6300=\$152.61, A's excess; Int. of \$152.61 is \$9.156.

\$4200—\$3996.52=\$203.48, B's deficit; Int. of \$203.48 is \$12.208.

\$2150.87—\$2100=\$50.87, C's excess; Int. of \$50.87 is \$3.052.

Int. of \$1800 is \$108, A's; Int. of \$900 is \$45, B's; Int. of \$300 is \$9, C's.

Int. of \$1500 is \$45, A's; Int. of \$1200 is \$24, B's; Int. of \$400 is \$4, C's.

\$108+\$45+\$9=\$162; \$45+\$24+\$4=\$73.

\$162—\$73=\$89; \$4200—\$89=\$4111.

$\frac{1}{2}$ of \$4111=\$2055.50, A's; $\frac{1}{3}$ of \$4111=\$1370.333, B's; $\frac{1}{6}$ of \$4111=\$685.166, C's.

A's acct.	B's acct.	C's acct.
\$6452.61	\$3996.52	\$2150.87
1800.00	900.00	300.00
9.156	45.00	3.052
108.00	1370.333	9.000
2055.50	6311.853	685.166
10425.266	1200.00	3148.088
1500.00	12.208	400.00
45.00	24.00	4.00
1545.00	1236.208	404.00
10425.266	6311.853	3148.088
1545.000	1236.208	404.000
8880.27-	5075.64	2744.09

EQUATION OF PAYMENTS.

Art. 599. Case I.

2 \$2000×3=\$6000
1500×4= 6000
2500×6=15000
6000)27000(4½ mo.

3. \$500×2 =\$1000
600×5 = 3000
400×7½= 3000
1500)7000(4⅔ mo.

4.
$\$300 \times 4 = \$1200$
$400 \times 5 = 2000$
$700 \times 6 = 4200$
$1000 \times 8 = 8000$
$2400 \quad)15400(6\tfrac{5}{12}$ mo.

5.
$\$4200 \times 0 = \$0000$
$2800 \times 4 = 11200$
$1400 \times 6 = 8400$
$8400 \quad)19600(2\tfrac{1}{3}$ mo.
2 mo. 10 da. or June 11.

(6)
$\$\tfrac{1}{2} \times 4 = \$2$
$\tfrac{1}{3} \times 9 = 3$
$\tfrac{1}{6} \times 12 = 2$
$1 \quad)7(7$ mo.

(7)
$\$\tfrac{1}{2} \times 4 = \$2$
$\tfrac{1}{4} \times 6 = 1\tfrac{1}{2}$
$\tfrac{1}{6} \times 12 = 2$
$\tfrac{1}{12} \times 8 = \tfrac{2}{3}$
$1 \quad)6\tfrac{1}{6}(6\tfrac{1}{6}$ mo.

(8)
$\$\tfrac{1}{3} \times 0 = \$0$
$\tfrac{1}{4} \times 4 = 1$
$\tfrac{1}{6} \times 6 = 1$
$\tfrac{1}{4} \times 8 = 2$
$1 \quad)4(4$ mo.
or May 1st.

Art. 600. Case II.

(2)

1st, due	June 12;	credit 00da.	$360 × 00=$00000
2d, "	Sept. 20;	" 100 "	500 × 100= 50000
3d, "	Sept. 18;	" 98 "	340 × 98= 33320
4th, "	Sept. 30;	" 110 "	600 × 110= 66000
			1800)149320(83da.

Hence it is due 83 da. after June 12, or Sept. 3.

(3)

1st, due	Aug. 14;	credit 00da.	$600 × 00=$00000
2d, "	Sept. 16;	" 33 "	600 × 33= 19800
3d, "	Nov. 10;	" 88 "	600 × 88= 52800
4th, "	Dec. 18;	" 126 "	600 × 126= 75600
			2400)148200(62 da.

Hence it is due 62 da. after Aug. 14, or Oct. 15, and the amount should bear interest from that time.

(4)

1st, due	Oct. 16;	credit 00da.	$800 × 00=$00000
2d, "	Jan. 20;	" 96 "	500 × 96= 48000
3d, "	April 12;	" 178 "	350 × 178= 62300
4th, "	May 24;	" 220 "	450 × 220= 99000
5th, "	June 10;	" 237 "	600 × 237=142200
			2700)351500(130 da.

Hence the average term of credit is 130 da. after Oct. 16, or Feb. 23, 1863.

Art. 601. Case III.

(2)

$600 × 4 = $2400
1200 × 3 = 3600
1800 600)6000(10 mo.
2400
600

Sol.—We find the sum of 600 and 1200 and subtract it from 2400, and divide 6000 by 600.

(3)

$800 × 4 = $3200
400 × 3 = 1200
1200 4400

1600 − 1200 = 400
4400 ÷ 400 = 11 mo.

(4)

$400 × 3 = $1200
600 × 5 = 3000
800 × 6 = 4800
1800 9000
1200 × 4 = 4800
600)4200(7 mo.

(5)

$240 × 20 = $4800
560 × 30 = 16800
800 21600

$300 × 16 = $4800
350 × 24 = 8400
650 13200
800 21600
150)8400(56 da.

AVERAGING ACCOUNTS.

Art. 602.

(2)

Due.	Time.	Items.	Products.	Due.	Time.	Items.	Products.
Jan. 8	00	$600	00000	Jan. 27	19	$500	9500
March 5	57	400	22800	April 10	93	400	37200
April 20	103	550	56650	May 16	129	200	25800
		1550	79450			1100	72500
		1100	72500				
		450	6950				

6950 ÷ 450 = 15 days.

Hence the bill is due 15 days after Jan. 8, or Jan. 23d, 1860.

Note.—Since 1872 is a leap year, we reckon 29 days in February.

(3)

Due.	Time.	Items.	Products.	Due.	Time.	Items.	Products.
Aug. 1	16	$375	6000	July 20	4	$300	1200
Aug. 18	33	280	9240	Aug. 10	25	250	6250
Sept. 20	66	700	46200	Aug. 31	46	350	16100
July 16	00	350	00000	Sept. 12	58	600	34800
		1705	61440			1500	58350

1705 61440
1500 58350
205)3090(15 da.

Hence the bill is due 15 days after July 16, or July 31.

(4)

Due.	Time.	Items.	Products.	Due.	Time.	Items.	Products.
June 14	00	$650	00000	July 5	21	$500	10500
Aug. 20	67	550	36850	Sept. 28	106	350	37100
Aug. 16	63	475	29925	Oct. 12	120	450	54000
Sept. 12	90	350	31500	Dec. 4	173	250	43250
		2025	98275			1550	144850

2025   144850
1550   98275
475    $46575 \div 475 = 98$ da.   46575

Hence the bill is due 98 days *before* June 14th, which is March 8th.

(5)

Due.	Time.	Items.	Products.	Due.	Time.	Items.	Products.
Mar. 19	00	$900	00000	Mar. 24	5	$300	1500
Apr. 8	20	800	16000	Apr. 25	37	300	11100
Apr. 20	32	400	12800	July 17	120	200	24000
May 4	46	200	9200	Aug. 6	140	600	84000
		2300	38000			1400	120600

2300   120600
1400   38000
900    $82600 \div 900 = 92$ da.   82600

Hence interest on the note should commence 92 days *before* March 19th, or upon Dec. 18th.

SETTLEMENT OF ACCOUNTS.

Art. 605.

(1)

Due.	Time.	Items.	Amounts.	Due.	Time.	Items.	Amounts.
April 16	91	$450	$456.825	Mar. 12	126	$200	$204.20
May 24	53	350	353.091⅔	Apr. 18	89	300	304.45
July 12	4	300	300.200	July 3	13	400	400.866⅔
			1110.116⅔				909.516⅔

1110.116⅔
909.516⅔
$200.600, *Ans.*

(2)

Due.	Time.	Items.	Items plus or minus int	Due.	Time.	Items.	Items plus or minus int
May 16	84	$650	$659.10	May 28	72	$500	$506.000
June 20	49	750	756.125	July 12	27	800	803.600
Aug. 24	16	375	374.000	July 20	19	200	200.633⅓
Sept. 12	35	575	571.645⅚	Aug. 4	4	700	700.466⅔
			2360.870⅚				2210.700

2360.870⅚
2210.700
$150.170⅚, *Ans.*

NOTE.—The third and fourth items being due after the date of settlement, should be *discounted* for the time; hence we deduct the interest.

ACCOUNT SALES.

Art. 607.

1. Net proceeds = $5025 − $500.56 = $4524.44. The date of the commission and guaranty being given, we have only to average the account.

Due.	Time.	Items.	Products.	Due.	Time.	Items.	Products.
Oct. 25	00	343	00	Nov. 27	33	1400	46200
Nov. 30	36	10	360	" 11	17	3000	51000
Nov. 18	24	113	2712	" 30	36	625	22500
" "	24	35	840				
		501	3912			5025	119700

5025 − 501 = 4524; 119700 − 3912 = 115788

115788 ÷ 4524 = 26 da.
26 da. from Oct. 25 gives Nov. 20.

2. We first average the sales, using Sept. 1, the earliest date of the account, as a focal date; 114937.50 ÷ 5437.50 = 21 days; hence Sept. 1 + 21 da. = Sept. 22, is the date of commission and guaranty.

Due.	Time.	Items.	Products.
Sept. 3	2	1300	2600.00
Oct. 12	41	1050	43050.00
Sept. 18	17	1687.50	28687.50
Sept. 30	29	1400	40600.00
		5437.50	114937.50

We now average the entire account as in previous example.

Due.	Time.	Items.	Products.	Due.	Time.	Items.	Products.
Sept. 1	0	277.50	0	Sept. 22	21	5437.50	114187.50
Sept. 22	21	135.93$\frac{3}{4}$	2854.68$\frac{3}{4}$				
" "	21	23.62$\frac{1}{2}$	496.12$\frac{1}{2}$				
Sept. 30	29	40.00	1160.00				
		477.06$\frac{1}{4}$	4511.81$\frac{1}{4}$			5437.50	114187.50

	Items.	Products.
	5437.50	114187.50
	477.06$\frac{1}{4}$	4511.81$\frac{1}{4}$
Proceeds,	4960.43$\frac{3}{4}$	109675.68$\frac{3}{4}$

109675.68$\frac{3}{4}$ ÷ 4960.43$\frac{3}{4}$ = 22 da.;
Equated date = Sept. 23.

3. We first average the sales to find the date of the commission and guaranty, which is 20 days from Feb. 20, or March 12. We then average the entire account as in previous examples, thus:

Due.	Time.	Items.	Products.
Mar. 1	9	325	2925
" 10	18	200	3600
Apr. 9	48	105	5040
Mar. 31	39	42	1638
		672	13203

13203 ÷ 672 = 20 days —.

Due.	Time.	Items.	Products.	Due.	Time.	Items.	Products.
Feb. 20	00	45.00	00.00	Mar. 1	9	325	2925
Mar. 12	20	16.80	336.00	" 10	18	200	3600
" "	20	2.36$\frac{1}{4}$	47.25	Apr. 9	48	105	5040
" 31	39	10.00	390	Mar. 31	39	42	1638
		74.16$\frac{1}{4}$	773.25			672.00	13203

Items.	Products.
672.00	13203
74.16$\frac{1}{4}$	773.25
597.83$\frac{3}{4}$	12429.75

12429.75 ÷ 597.8375 = 21 da.
Equated date = March 13.

SECTION X.

INVOLUTION AND EVOLUTION.

Art. 614. MENTAL EXERCISES.

8. The square of the square of 2^3 equals the 4th power of 2^3, or the 12th power of 2.

9. The square of a number is the product of that number into itself; hence if the number multiplied by the number equals the number multiplied by 8, the number must equal 8.

10. Since $\frac{1}{2}$ of the square of the number equals the number multiplied by 6, the square of the number equals the number multiplied by 12, and the number equals 12.

11. Since $\frac{4}{5}$ of the square of the number equals the number multiplied by 16, the square of the number equals the number multiplied by 20, and the number equals 20.

12. Since $\frac{3}{4}$ of the square of the fraction equals the fraction multiplied by $\frac{4}{5}$, the square of the fraction equals the fraction multiplied by $\frac{16}{15}$, and the fraction equals $\frac{16}{15}$.

13. Since $\frac{3}{4}$ of the cube of the number equals the number multiplied by 12 and 9, the cube of the number equals $\frac{4}{3}$ of the product of the number into 12 and 9, or the number multiplied by 12 and 12, hence the number is 12.

Art. 631. EVOLUTION BY FACTORING.

(5)	(6)	(7)
2)13824	2)46656	2)592704
2)6912	2)23328	2)296352
*2)3456	*2)11664	*2)148176
2)1728	2)5832	2)74088
2)864	2)2916	2)37044
*2)432	*2)1458	*2)18522
2)216	3)729	3)9261
2)108	3)243	3)3087
*2)54	*3)81	*3)1029
3)27	3)27	7)343
3)9	3)9	7)49
*3	*3	*7
$2\times2\times2\times3=24$	$2\times2\times3\times3=36$	$2\times2\times3\times7=84$

(8)

2)20736
2)10368
2)5184
*2)2592
2)1296
2)648
2)324
*2)162
3)81
3)27
3)9
*3

$2\times2\times3=12$

(9)

2)1679616
2)839808
2)419904
*2)209952
2)104976
2)52488
2)26244
*2)13122
3)6561
3)2187
3)729
*3)243
3)81
3)27
3)9
*3

$2\times2\times3\times3=36$

(10)

2)248832
2)124416
2)62208
2)31104
*2)15552
2)7776
2)3888
2)1944
2)972
*2)486
3)243
3)81
3)27
3)9
*3

$2\times2\times3=12$

(11)

2)5489031744
2)2744515872
2)1372257936
2)686128968
2)343064484
*2)171532242
3)85766121
3)28588707
3)9529569
3)3176523
3)1058841
*3)352947
7)117649
7)16807
7)2401
7)343
7)49
*7

$2\times3\times7=42$

Art. 631. MENTAL EXERCISES.

2. Since ¾ of the square of the number equals 27, the square of the number equals 4 times ⅓ of 27, or 36, and the number is 6.

3. The square root of 64 is 8, and since 8 is twice the number, the number is ½ of 8, or 4.

4. The square root of 100 is 10, which is ⅖ of the number, hence the number is 5 times ½ of 10, or 25.

5. The square of twice a number equals 4 times the square of the number, therefore 4 times the square is 18 more than twice the square, twice the square equals 18, the square equals 9, and the number is 3.

6. The square of half the number equals ¼ the square of the number, and 6 times the square of half the number equals $\frac{6}{4}$, or $\frac{3}{2}$ of the square, therefore twice the square is 8 more than $\frac{3}{2}$ of the square, or ½ of the square equals 8, the square equals 16, and the number is 4.

7. Since 15 is 3 more than $\frac{3}{2}$ of the cube, 15—3, or 12, equals $\frac{3}{2}$ of the cube and the cube equals 2 times ⅓ of 12, or 8; hence the number is the cube root of 8, or 2.

8. The cube of $\frac{2}{3}$ of the number equals $\frac{8}{27}$ of the cube of the number; $\frac{2}{3}$ of the cube is 10 more than $\frac{8}{27}$ of the cube; hence $\frac{10}{27}$ of the cube equals 10, the cube equals 27, and the number is 3.

9. Since the square of a number is the product of the number into itself, the square of a number divided by the number equals the number itself; hence 8 is the number.

10. The square of a number divided by $\frac{1}{2}$ of the number gives twice the number; hence 12 is twice the number and the number is 6.

11. The cube of a number divided by the number gives the square of the number; hence 36 is the square of the number, and the number is the square root of 36, or 6.

12. The 4th power divided by the square gives the square; hence 49 is the square of the number, and the number is the square root of 49, or 7.

13. The square of a number divided by $\frac{2}{3}$ of a number gives $\frac{3}{2}$ of a number; hence 27 is $\frac{3}{2}$ of the number, and the number is 18.

14. Since the number divided by 6 gives double the square root of the number, the number equals 12 times the square root of the number; but the square root multiplied by itself equals the number; hence 12 is the square root, and the number is 144.

15. The square of the number into half the number equals $\frac{1}{2}$ of the cube of the number, which equals 32; hence the cube of the number equals 64, and the number is the cube root of 64, or 4.

16. $\frac{2}{3}$ of $\frac{1}{6}$, or $\frac{1}{9}$ of the square of a number, multiplied by $\frac{1}{4}$ of $\frac{2}{3}$, or $\frac{1}{6}$ of the number, equals $\frac{1}{54}$ of the cube, which equals 4; hence the cube equals 216, and the number is the cube root of 216, or 6.

SQUARE ROOT.

Page 364.

(24)

	43·04.67·21(65.61
6	36
125	704
	625
1306	7967
	7836
13121	13121
	13121

(25)

	5.00·00·00(2.236+
2	4
42	100
	84
443	1600
	1329
4466	27100
	26796
	304

(26)

$\frac{2}{3}=.66\cdot66\cdot66\cdot66\cdot66+(.81649+$

8	64
161	266
	161
1626	10566
	9756
16324	81066
	65296
163289	1577066
	1469601
	107465

(27)

$\frac{16}{111}=.14\cdot41\cdot44\cdot14\cdot41(.37966+$

3	9
67	541
	469
749	7244
	6741
7586	50314
	45516
75926	479841
	455556
	24285

APPLICATIONS OF SQUARE ROOT.

Art. 636.

2. 1440 acres = 1440 × 160 = 230400 sq. rods; and $\sqrt{230400}=480$, *Ans.*

3. The length $=\sqrt{128\times32}=64$ inches.

4. $80^2=6400$; $6400-500=5900$.

5. $9480-71=9409$; $\sqrt{9409}=97$.

6. The side $=\sqrt{160\times160}=160$ rods; four sides, or the distance around, equals $160\times4=640$; the cost is $640\times\$4=\$2560$.

7. $168+132-200=100$; $27175-100=27075$; $27075\div3=9025$; $\sqrt{9025}=95$.

RIGHT-ANGLED TRIANGLES.

Art. 641.

2. $\sqrt{115^2-92^2}=\sqrt{4761}=69$.

3. $\sqrt{4225-625}=\sqrt{3600}=60$, *Ans.*

4. The distance $=\sqrt{1080^2+810^2}=1350$ rods.

5. The distance they are apart at the end of one hour $=\sqrt{3^2+4^2}=5$ miles; and in 48 hours they are $48\times5=240$ miles apart.

6. The height is 80 ft; hence distance$=\sqrt{82^2-80^2}=18$.

7. The hyp.$=\sqrt{52^2+39^2}=65$ ft; hence the length$=52+65=117$ ft.

8. Let the figure in the margin represent the conditions of the problem; then $AB=\sqrt{130^2-78^2}=104$ ft.; $BC=\sqrt{130^2-50^2}=120$; $AC=120+104=224$ ft.

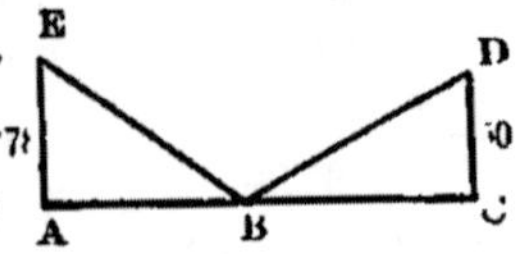

SIMILAR FIGURES.

Art. 643.

2. Area of 2d : Area of 1st : : $30^2 : 5^2$; hence,

$$\text{Area of 2d}=\text{Area of 1st}\times\frac{30^2}{5^2}=\text{Area of 1st}\times 36;$$

hence the first is 36 times as large as the second.

3. Since the area is 4 times as great, the dimensions will be the $\sqrt{4}$ or 2 times as great; hence the length is $20\times 2=40$; and width is $16\times 2=32$.

4. (Diam. of 2d)$^2 : 20^2 : : 78.54 : 314.16$

$$(\text{Diam. of 2d})^2=20^2\times\frac{78.54}{314.16}=20^2\times\tfrac{1}{4}$$

Diam. of 2d.$=\sqrt{400\times\frac{1}{4}}=\sqrt{100}=10$, *Ans.*

5. The area of the first is $80\times 60=4800$ sq. rd.$=30$ acres; hence (Length of 2d)$^2 : 80^2 : : 13\frac{1}{3} : 30$.

$$(\text{Length of 2d})^2=80^2\times\frac{13\frac{1}{3}}{30}=80^2\times\frac{40}{90}=80^2\times\frac{4}{9}$$

Length of 2d $=\sqrt{80^2\times\frac{4}{9}}=80\times\frac{2}{3}=53\frac{1}{3}$; hence, also, width of 2d$=60\times\frac{2}{3}=40$ rods.

6. The relation of the dimensions is the square root of $5\frac{4}{9}$, that is, $\sqrt{\frac{49}{9}}=\frac{7}{3}$; hence the length of rope$=178$li. $\times\frac{7}{3}=415\frac{1}{3}$ li., or 4 ch. $15\frac{1}{3}$ li.

7. The quantity : 45 gal. : : $2^2 : 1\frac{1}{2}^2$; hence,

$$\text{The quantity}=45\times\frac{4}{2\frac{1}{4}}=80\text{ gal.}$$

8. The quantities poured in are as 3^2 to 1.5^2; hence the second$=\left(\frac{3}{1.5}\right)^2=2^2=4$ times the first; hence if the second pours in 4 times as much in an hour, it will require $\frac{1}{4}$ of the time, or $1\frac{1}{4}$ h., to fill the cistern.

9. In the margin we have AB $=\sqrt{48^2+20^2}=52$; AC$=\sqrt{52^2+39^2}=65$, *Ans.* Or, $48^2+20^2=AB^2$, but AC$=\sqrt{AB^2+BC^2}$, or AC$=\sqrt{48^2+20^2+39^2}=65$.

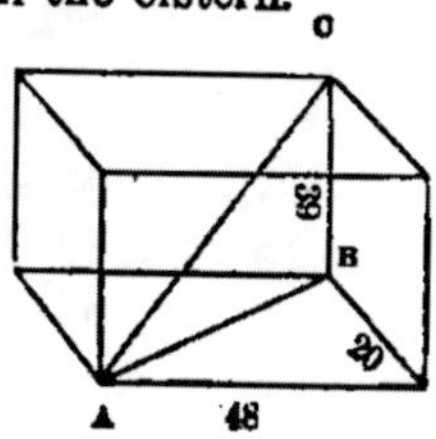

CUBE ROOT.

Page 371.

(14)

$$\begin{array}{r|l}
 & 1{\cdot}124{\cdot}864(104 \\
1^3= & 1 \\
1^2\times300=300 & 124864 \\
10^2\times300=30000 & \\
10\times4\times30=\ \ 1200 & \\
4^2=\ \ 16 & \\
31216 & 124864
\end{array}$$

(15)

$$\begin{array}{r|l}
 & 130{\cdot}323{\cdot}843(507 \\
5^3= & 125 \\
5^2\times300=7500 & 5323843 \\
50^2\times300=750000 & \\
50\times7\times30=\ \ 10500 & \\
7^2=\ \ 49 & \\
760549 & 5323843
\end{array}$$

16. $\frac{1728}{4096}=\frac{27}{64}$; $\sqrt[3]{\frac{27}{64}}=\frac{3}{4}$.

(17)

$$\begin{array}{r|l}
 & 389.017(7.3 \\
7^3= & 343 \\
7^2\times300=14700 & 46017 \\
7\times3\times30=\ \ 630 & \\
3^2=\ \ 9 & \\
15339 & 46017
\end{array}$$

(18)

$$\begin{array}{r|l}
 & 259.694{\cdot}072(6.38 \\
6^3= & 216 \\
6^2\times300=\ \ 10800 & 43694 \\
6\times3\times30=\ \ 540 & \\
3^2=\ \ 9 & \\
11349 & 34047 \\
63^2\times300=1190700 & 9647072 \\
63\times8\times30=\ \ 15120 & \\
8^2=\ \ 64 & \\
1205884 & 9647072
\end{array}$$

(19)

4.000·000·000·000(1.5874+

$1^3=$		1
$1^2\times300=$	300	3000
$1\times5\times30=$	150	
$5^2=$	25	
	475	2375
$15^2\times300=$	67500	625000
$15\times8\times30=$	3600	
$8^2=$	64	
	71164	569312
$158^2\times300=$	7489200	55688000
$158\times7\times30=$	33180	
$7^2=$	49	
	7522429	52657003
$1587^2\times300=$	755570700	3030997000
$1587\times4\times30=$	190440	
$4^2=$	16	
	755761156	3023044624
		7952376

(20)

5.000·000·000·000(1.7099+

$1^3=$		1
$1^2\times300=$	300	4000
$1\times7\times30=$	210	
$7^2=$	49	
	559	3913
$17^2\times300=$	86700	87000000
$170^2\times300=$	8670000	
$170\times9\times30=$	4590	
$9^2=$	81	
	8674671	78073039
$1709^2\times300=$	876204300	8926961000
$1709\times9\times30=$	461430	
$9^2=$	81	
	876665811	7889992299
		1036968701

(21)

		6.000 000·000·000(1.8171+
$1^3=$		1
$1^2\times300=$	300	5000
$1\times8\times30=$	240	
$8^2=$	64	
	604	4832
$18^2\times300=$	97200	168000
$18\times1\times30=$	540	
$1^2=$	1	
	97741	97741
$181^2\times300=$	9828300	70259000
$181\times7\times30=$	38010	
$7^2=$	49	
	9866359	69064513
		1194487000

(22)

		$\frac{2}{3}$=.666·666·666+(.873+
$8^3=$		512
$8^2\times300=$	19200	154666
$8\times7\times30=$	1680	
$7^2=$	49	
	20929	146503
$87^2\times300=$	2270700	8163666
$87\times3\times30=$	7830	
$3^2=$	9	
	2278539	6835617
		1328049

Art. 648. NEW METHOD.

2.	1st col.	2d col.	12·326·391(231
	2	12 . . t. d.	8
	4	189	4326
	63	1389 c. d.	4167
	6	9	159391
	691	1587 . . t. d.	
		691	
		159391 c. d.	159391

3.

1st col.	2d col.	34·965·783(327
3	27 . . t. d.	27
6	184	7965
92	2884 c. d.	5768
4	4	2197783
967	3072 . . t. d.	
	6769	
	313969 c. d.	2197783

4.

1st col.	2d col.	41·063·625(345
3	27 . . t. d.	27
6	376	14063
94	3076 c. d.	12304
8	16	1759625
1025	3468 . . t. d.	
	5125	
	351925	1759625

5.

1st col	2d col.	277·167·808(652
6	108 . . t. d.	216
12	925	61167
185	11725 c. d.	58625
10	25	2542808
1952	12675 . . t. d.	
	3904	
	1271404 c. d.	2542808

6.

1st col.	2d col.	633·839.779(85.9
8	192 . . t. d.	512
16	1225	121839
245	20425 c. d.	102125
10	25	19714779
2559	21675 . . t. d.	
	23031	
	2190531 c. d.	19714779

7.	1st col.	2d col.	4.080·659·192(1.598
	1	3 . . t. d.	1
	2	175	3080
	35	475 c. d.	2375
	10	25	705659
	459	675 . . t. d.	
	18	4131	
	4778	71631 c. d.	644679
		81	60980192
		75843 . . t. d.	
		38224	
		7622524 c. d.	60980192

APPLICATIONS OF CUBE ROOT.

Art. 650.

1. $\sqrt[3]{64000}=40$ ft.
2. The $\sqrt[3]{405224}=74$; and 74 squared equals 5476.
3. The cube root of 91125 is 45: $45^2=2025$ is the area of one face, and the area of the six faces is $2025\times6=$ 12150 sq. ft.
4. $20\frac{1}{2}\times10\frac{3}{8}\times6\frac{3}{4}=1476$ cu. ft.; the cube root of **1476**= 11.4 ft., nearly.
5. $231\times200=46200$; $\sqrt[3]{46200}=35.9$, nearly.
6. 50×2150.42 cu. in.$=107521$ cu. in.; $\sqrt[3]{107521}$ cu. in. $=$ $47.551+$ in. $=3.962+$ft.
7. $231\times31\frac{1}{2}\times100=727650$ cu. in. $=421.09375$ cu. ft.; $\sqrt[3]{421.09375}=7.495$ ft.; $(7.495)^2=56.175$ sq. ft.; $56.175\times5\times\$.06=\$16.8525$.

SIMILAR VOLUMES.

Art. 653.

2. The ratio$=15^3:3^3=\left(\frac{15}{3}\right)^3=5^3=125$.
3. Weight : 9 : : $4^3:3^3$

   Weight$=\frac{9\times64}{27}=21\frac{1}{3}$ lb.

4. Contents : 51.43 : : 6^3 : 4^3

$$\text{Contents}=51.43\times\left(\frac{3}{2}\right)^3=173.57\tfrac{5}{8}\text{ bu.}$$

5. Diameter of 2d : 12 : : $\sqrt[3]{120}$: $\sqrt[3]{15}$

$$\text{Diameter of 2d}=12\times\sqrt[3]{\tfrac{120}{15}}$$

$$=12\times\sqrt[3]{8}=12\times 2=24\text{ ft.}$$

6 Weight : 150 : : 6^3 : 5^3

$$\text{Weight}=150\times\frac{6^3}{5^3}=259\tfrac{1}{5}\text{ lb}$$

7. $\text{Relation}=885680^3:7912^3=\left(\frac{885680}{7912}\right)^3=112^3$, nearly.

8. Their contents are as 3^3 to 4^3, hence we may represent their contents by 27 and 64, and the ball, whose contents equal both, will contain $27+64=91$ cu. units. Hence we have

$(\text{Diam.})^3 : 3^3 : : 91 : 27$

$$\text{Diam.}=\sqrt[3]{\frac{27\times 91}{27}}=\sqrt[3]{91}=4.5\text{, nearly.}$$

EXTRACTION OF HIGHER ROOTS.

Art. 654.

2. The square root of 625 is 25, and the square root of 25 is 5.

3. The square root of 729 is 27, and the cube root of 27 is 3, or extract the cube root and then the square root.

4. The square root of 20736 is 144, and the square root of 144 is 12.

5. The square root of 390625 is 625, and the square root of 625 is 25, and the square root of 25 is 5.

6. The cube root of 262144 is 64, and the cube root of 64 is 4.

7. The square root of 16777216 is 4096, the square root of 4096 is 64, and the cube root of 64 is 4.

SECTION XI.

ARITHMETICAL PROGRESSION.

Art. 661. Case I.

2. 12th$=4+3\times11=37$, *Ans.*
3. 22d$=3+4\times21=87$, *Ans.*
4. 76th$=80-\frac{2}{3}\times75=30$, *Ans.*
5. 50th$=\frac{1}{2}+\frac{1}{2}\times49=25$, *Ans.*
6. 25th$=\$105+\$5\times24=\$225$, *Ans.*

Art. 662. Case II.

2. 1st term$=95-5\times17=10$, *Ans.*
3. 1st term$=25¢-\frac{1}{2}¢\times24=13¢$, *Ans.*
4. 1st term$=32\frac{1}{2}-2\frac{1}{2}+9=10$, *Ans.*

Art. 663. Case III.

2. Com. Diff.$=(76-4)\div24=3$, *Ans.*
3. Com. Diff.$=(\$225-\$105)\div24=\$5$, *Ans.*
4. Com. Diff.$=(46-26)\div10=2$, *Ans.*

Art. 664. Case IV.

2. No. of terms$=(397-5)\div7+1=57$, *Ans.*
3. No. of terms$=(\$344-\$212)\div\$12+1=12$, *Ans.*
4. No. of terms$=(3.75-.75)\div.10+1=31$, *Ans.*

Art. 665. Case V.

2. Sum $=\frac{(3+65)\times20}{2}=680$, *Ans.*
3. Last term$=25+4\times7=53$; sum of terms$=\frac{(25+53)\times8}{2}$ $=312$, *Ans.*
4. Last term$=2+3\times74=224$, then the sum $=\frac{(2+224)\times75}{2}=8475¢=\$84.75$.
5. $\frac{(1+6)\times6}{2}=21$; $\frac{(1+12)\times12}{2}=78$.
6. The first term is 4 and common difference is 4, the last term$=4+4\times99=400$.

   Sum$=\frac{4+400}{2}\times100=20200$ yd.$=11$ mi. 152 rd. 4 yd.

7. The first term is $16\frac{1}{12}$; the com. diff. is $32\frac{1}{6}$; the last term $=16\frac{1}{12}+32\frac{1}{6}\times 59=1913\frac{11}{12}$;

$$\text{Sum}=\frac{16\frac{1}{12}+1913\frac{11}{12}}{2}\times 60=57900\text{ ft.}=10\text{ mi. }309\frac{1}{11}\text{ rd.}$$

GEOMETRICAL PROGRESSION.

Art. 670. Case I.

2. $10\text{th}=3\times(2)^9=1536$, *Ans.*
3. $14\text{th}=64\times(\frac{1}{2})^{13}=\frac{1}{128}$, *Ans.*
4. $12\text{th}=2187\times(\frac{1}{3})^{11}=\frac{1}{81}$, *Ans.*
5. $30\text{th}=1\times(2)^{29}=536870912$, *Ans.*
6. $21\text{st}=1\times(3)^{20}=3486784401$.
7. The series consists of 5 terms; hence 4th term $=5000\times(2)^4=\$80000$.
8. Last cost $=2\times(2)^{19}=\$10485.76$.

Art. 671. Case II.

2. $\text{Sum}=\frac{500\times 5-4}{5-1}=\frac{2500-4}{4}=624.$

3. $\text{Sum}=\frac{64-2\times\frac{1}{2}}{1-\frac{1}{2}}=\frac{64-1}{\frac{1}{2}}=126$, *Ans.*

4. Last term $=243\times(\frac{1}{3})^4=\frac{243}{81}=3.$

$$\text{Sum}=\frac{243-3\times\frac{1}{3}}{1-\frac{1}{3}}=\frac{243-1}{\frac{2}{3}}=363, \textit{ Ans.}$$

5. Last term $=1\times(3)^{11}=177147.$

$$\text{Sum}=\frac{177147\times 3-1}{3-1}=\frac{531440}{2}=\$2657.20, \textit{ Ans.}$$

6. Last term $=1\times(2)^{20}=1048576.$

$$\text{Sum}=\frac{1048576\times 2-1}{2-1}=\$20971.51, \textit{ Ans.}$$

7. Last term $=1\times(3)^{14}=4782969.$

$$\text{Sum}=\frac{4782969\times 3-1}{3-1}=\$71744.53.$$

The cost of 15 yd. at $\$1\frac{1}{2}$ is $15\times 1\frac{1}{2}=\$22.50$.
Hence, $\$71744.53-\$22.50=\$71722.03$, *Ans.*

8. Last$=1\times(2)^{31}=2147483648$.

$$\text{Sum}=\frac{2147483648\times 2-1}{2-1}=\$42949672.95,\ \textit{Ans.}$$

INFINITE SERIES.

Art. 673.

2. $\text{Sum}=\frac{\frac{1}{2}}{1-\frac{1}{2}}=\frac{\frac{1}{2}}{\frac{1}{2}}=1.$

3. $\text{Sum}=\frac{\frac{1}{3}}{1-3}=\frac{1}{3}\div\frac{2}{3}=\frac{1}{2}.$

4. $\text{Sum}=\frac{\frac{1}{4}}{1-\frac{1}{2}}=\frac{1}{4}\div\frac{1}{2}=\frac{1}{2}.$

5. This series may be regarded as 12, 6, 3, etc., or as 8, 4, 2, etc., after the first 8 ft. fall to the floor.

$\text{Sum}=\frac{12}{1-\frac{1}{2}}=24$, *Ans.*; or, by 2d method,

$\text{Sum}=8+\frac{8}{1-\frac{1}{2}}=8+16=24$, *Ans.*

6. The series is 10, 1, $\frac{1}{10}$, etc.; hence we have

$\text{Sum}=\frac{10}{1-\frac{1}{10}}=10\div\frac{9}{10}=11\frac{1}{9}$ rd.

ANNUITIES AT SIMPLE INTEREST.

Art. 681. Case I.

2. Last term$=400+24\times6=544$.

Sum of terms$=\frac{400+544}{2}\times7=3304$.

3. Last term$=600+24\times4=696$.

Sum of terms$=\frac{600+696}{2}\times5=3240$.

4. Last term$=580+29\times7=783$.

Sum of terms$=\frac{580+783}{2}\times8=5452$.

5. Last term=500+30×7=710.

Sum of terms$=\frac{500+710}{2}\times 8=4840.$

Art. 682. Case II.

2. Last term=400+20×5=500.

Sum of terms$=\frac{400+500}{2}\times 6=2700$

Amount of $1 for 6 yr. at 5% is $1.30.
$2700÷$1.30=$2076.92.

3. Last term=800+48×9=1232.

Sum of terms$=\frac{800+1232}{2}\times 10=10160.$

Amount of $1 for 10 yr. at 6% is $1.60,
10160÷1.60=6350, *Ans.*

4. Last term=$750+60×11=1410.

Sum of terms$=\frac{750+1410}{2}\times 12=129.60.$

Amt. of $1 for 12 yr. at 8%=$1.96.
$12960÷1.96=$6612.24+.

5. Last term=80+1.60×3=84.80.

Sum of terms$=\frac{80+84.80}{2}\times 4=329.60$

329.60÷$1.08=$305.185, *Ans.*

NOTE.—In this problem the interest is 2% a quarter, since it is 8% a year. We regard a quarter as a unit of time, and proceed as before.

ANNUITIES AT COMPOUND INTEREST.

Art. 684. Case I.

2. 250÷.05=5000. On page 299 we find the amount of $1 at compound interest to be $1.3400956, hence the compound interest of $1=$0.3400956.
Hence, $0.3400956×5000=$1700.478.

3. 360÷.06=$6000; amount of $1=$1.5036303;
Comp. Int.=$0 5036303×6000=$3021.7818, *Ans.*

4. 40÷.08=500; amount of \$1=\$4.6609571.

Comp. Int.=\$3.6609571×500=\$1830.47855.

5. 120÷.06=\$2000; amt. of \$1 for 12 yr.=\$1.0121965.

Comp. Int. = \$1.0121965 × 2000 = \$2024.393; \$2024.393—\$120=\$1904.393.

NOTE.—These deposits are regarded as an annuity, and since the principal producing the annuity must have been on interest 1 year before a payment is due, \$2000 must be on interest 12 years, to equal the amount of the deposits. We subtract \$120, because no deposit is made on the day she is 21 years old, but the account is then settled.

Art. 685. Case II.

2. \$600÷.06=\$10000.

Int.=\$0.5938481×10000=\$5938.481.

5938.48÷1.593848=\$3725.88, *Ans.*

3. 480÷.08=\$6000.

Int.=\$1.158925×6000=6953.55.

\$6953.55÷\$2.158925=\$3220.84, *Ans.*

4. The rate is 2% for 4 quarters; \$120÷.02=\$6000.

The compound interest of \$1 for 4 periods at 2%, is \$0.08243216. Then, \$0.08243216×6000=\$494.59296; and \$494.59296÷\$1.08243216=\$456.927+.

Hence, the present value of the rent by the second condition is \$456.927; therefore the second method is more profitable by the difference between \$456.927 and \$450, or \$6.927.

5. First, 1200÷.06=\$20000.

Int.=\$0.418519×20000=\$8370.38.

Then, \$8370.38÷\$1.418519=\$5900.789.

Hence, \$6000—\$5900.789=\$99.211.

PARTITIVE PROPORTION

Art. 688. MENTAL EXERCISES.

2. If twice the less, $+7=45$, twice the less $=45-7$, or 38, once the less $=\frac{1}{2}$ of 38, or 19, and the greater $=19+7$, or 26.

3. Twice Joseph's money, +\$5=\$35, twice Joseph's = \$35—\$5, or \$30, once Joseph's = $\frac{1}{2}$ of \$30, or \$15, and James's = \$15+\$5, or \$20.

4. Twice Susan's number, −5 peaches = 15 peaches; twice Susan's number = 15+5, or 20 peaches, once Susan's number = $\frac{1}{2}$ of 20, or 10, and Mary's number = 10—5, or 5 peaches.

Art. 688. WRITTEN EXERCISES.

2. *Twice* the number of cows, $+125=427$; hence *twice* the number of cows $=427-125=302$, the number of cows $=151$, and number of sheep $=276$.

3. *Twice* the less, $+\frac{14}{39}=\frac{112}{117}$; hence *twice* the less $=\frac{112}{117}-\frac{14}{39}=\frac{70}{117}$, *once* the less $=\frac{35}{117}$, and the greater $=\frac{77}{117}$.

4. *Twice* the cost of Charles's house, +\$758=\$8976; hence *twice* the cost of Charles's house=\$8976—\$758=\$8218; Charles's house cost \$4109 and William's cost \$4867.

5. 3 times the third's share, +\$1000+\$1000+\$500=\$10000; 3 times the third's share=\$7500; the third received \$2500, the second \$3500, and the first \$4000.

Art. 689. MENTAL EXERCISES.

2. Six times George's number = 36 apples, hence once George's number = $\frac{1}{6}$ of 36, or 6 apples, and James's number = 5 times 6, or 30 apples.

3. $\frac{6}{5}$ of the fallen part = 60 feet, hence $\frac{1}{5}$ of the fallen part, or the part standing = $\frac{1}{6}$ of 60 feet, or 10 feet, $\frac{5}{5}$ of the fallen part = 5 times 10 feet, or 50 feet.

4. The second is twice the first, and the third 3 times 2 times, or 6 times the first; hence the sum of the numbers = the first + 2 times the first + 6 times the first = 9 times the first = 63, hence the first = $\frac{1}{9}$ of 63, or 7, the second = 2 times 7, or 14, and the third = 3 times 14, or 42.

Art. 689. WRITTEN EXERCISES.

2. By the conditions of the problem, 7 times the cost of the harness plus *once* the cost of the harness equals 8 times the cost of the harness, which equals \$328; the cost of the harness $=\frac{1}{8}$ of \$328 = \$41, and the cost of the horse = \$287.

3. 4 times the cargo + *once* the cargo = 5 times the cargo, which equals \$75800; hence the cargo is insured at \$15160 and the vessel at \$60640.

4. C's + 2 C's + 5 C's = 8 C's = \$11480; *once* what C earns = = \$1435; A earned \$1435 × 2 = \$2870; B earned \$1435 × 5 = \$7175.

5. $\frac{5}{8}$ of the second plus $\frac{8}{8}$ of the second equals $\frac{13}{8}$ of the second, which equals \$30784, from which we find the first is \$11840, and the second, \$18944.

Art. 690. MENTAL EXERCISES.

2. Since 5 times Jane's number = 6 times Mary's, Jane's number $=\frac{6}{5}$ of Mary's, and subtracting Mary's number, we have $\frac{1}{5}$ of Mary's, which equals 10 plums, hence Mary had 50 plums and Jane 60.

3. Since $\frac{2}{3}$ of their money equals \$60, $\frac{1}{3}$ of their money equals $\frac{1}{2}$ of \$60, or \$30, and $\frac{3}{3}$ of their money equals 3 times \$30, or \$90; since 4 times John's = 5 times William's, once John's = $\frac{5}{4}$ of William's, which, added to William's, equals $\frac{9}{4}$ of William's, which equals \$90, hence $\frac{1}{4}$ of William's = \$10, William's = \$40, and John's = \$50.

4. Since 80 feet is $\frac{4}{5}$ of the height of the tree, the height of the tree = 5 times $\frac{1}{4}$ of 80 feet, or 100 feet; 7 times the part below the first fork + once the part = 8 times the part, which equals 100 feet, hence the part below the first fork = $\frac{1}{8}$ of 100 feet, or $12\frac{1}{2}$ feet, and the part above = 7 times $12\frac{1}{2}$ feet, or $87\frac{1}{2}$ feet.

Art. 690. WRITTEN EXERCISES.

2. Since 4 times the share of the first equals 5 times the share of the second, the share of the first equals $\frac{5}{4}$ of the share of the second; hence $\frac{9}{4}$ of the share of the second = \$7560; $\frac{1}{4}$ of the share of the second = \$840; hence the first has \$4200 and the second \$3360.

3. $\frac{7}{6}$ of N's $+\frac{6}{6}$ of N's $=\frac{13}{6}$ of N's, which equals $8450 acres; $\frac{1}{6}$ of N's $=650$ acres, N's $=3900$ acres, and M's $=4550$ acres.

4. $\frac{8}{5}$ of the quantity of oats $+\frac{5}{5}$ of the quantity of oats $=\frac{13}{5}$ of the quantity of oats, which equals 234 bushels; hence $\frac{1}{5}$ of the quantity of oats $=18$ bu., and he therefore shipped 144 bu. of corn, and 90 bu. of oats.

5. The quantity of wheat $=2$ times the quantity of corn, $+$ 250 bushels; hence 3 times the quantity of corn, $+$ 250 bushels $=2500$ bushels; the quantity of corn $=750$ bu.; the quantity of wheat $=1750$ bu.

Art. 691. MENTAL EXERCISES.

2. If $\frac{1}{2}$ of the first equals $\frac{1}{3}$ of the second, $\frac{2}{2}$ of the first equals $\frac{2}{3}$ of the second, which subtracted from the second, equals $\frac{1}{3}$ of the sec ond, which equals 5; hence the second equals 15 and the first equals 10.

3. If $\frac{3}{13}$ of the price of the coat equals $\frac{3}{5}$ of the price of the vest, the price of the coat $=\frac{13}{5}$ of the price of the vest, which added to the price of the vest, equals $\frac{18}{5}$ of the price of the vest, which equals \$36; hence the vest cost \$10, and the coat \$26.

4. If $\frac{2}{3}$ of what one pours in equals $\frac{2}{7}$ of what the other pours in, $\frac{3}{3}$ of the first equals $\frac{3}{7}$ of the second, which added to the second $=\frac{10}{7}$ of the second, which equals 165 gallons; hence the first equals $49\frac{1}{2}$ gallons, and the second equals $115\frac{1}{2}$ gallons.

Art. 691. WRITTEN EXERCISES.

2. $\frac{2}{5}$ of 1st $=\frac{4}{9}$ of 2d; $\frac{1}{5}$ of 1st $=\frac{2}{9}$ of 2d; 1st raised $\frac{10}{9}$ of what the second raised; hence $\frac{10}{9}+\frac{9}{9}=\frac{19}{9}$ of second $=3800$; 1st raised 2000 bushels, second 1800.

3. $\frac{2}{3}$ of 1st $=\frac{3}{4}$ of 2d; $\frac{1}{3}$ of 1st $=\frac{3}{8}$ of 2d; $\frac{3}{3}$ of 1st $=\frac{9}{8}$ of 2d; hence $\frac{8}{8}+\frac{9}{8}$, or $\frac{17}{8}$ of second $=510$; the first had 270, the second 240 votes.

4. $\frac{1}{25}$ of a ton $=\frac{1}{25}$ of 2000 lb. $=80$ lb.; $\frac{8}{9}$ silver $=\frac{11}{12}$ lead; $\frac{1}{9}$ silver $=\frac{11}{96}$ lead; silver $=\frac{33}{32}$ lead; $\frac{33}{32}+\frac{32}{32}=\frac{65}{32}$ of lead $=80$ lb.; silver $=40\frac{8}{13}$ lb.; lead $=39\frac{5}{13}$ lb.

5. $\frac{2}{3}$ of man's salary $=\frac{5}{6}$ of wife's, $+\$200$; $\frac{1}{3}$ of man's $=\frac{5}{12}$ of wife's, $+\$100$; man's $=\frac{5}{4}$ of wife's, $+\$300$; $\frac{4}{4}+\frac{5}{4}$ $+\$300=\frac{9}{4}$ of wife's, $+\$300=\$2100$; wife's $=\$800$; man's $=\$1300$.

Art. 692. MENTAL EXERCISES.

2. If we divide 60 into 7+5, or 12 equal parts, $\frac{7}{12}$ of 60, or 35, will be the number of girls, and $\frac{5}{12}$ of 60, or 25, the number of boys.

3. If 24 is divided into 1+2+3, or 6 parts, the first will receive $\frac{1}{6}$ of 24, or 4, the second $\frac{2}{6}$ of 24, or 8, and the third $\frac{3}{6}$ of 24, or 12.

4. They should receive in the proportion of 3, 4, and 5, hence the first should receive $\frac{3}{12}$ of 1200, or 300, the second $\frac{4}{12}$ of 1200, or 400, and the third $\frac{5}{12}$ of 1200, or 500.

5. Since the numbers are to each other as $\frac{2}{3}$ to $\frac{3}{4}$, or as $\frac{8}{12}$ to $\frac{9}{12}$, or as 8 to 9, if we divide 68 into 8+9, or 17 equal parts, the first number will be $\frac{8}{17}$ of 68, or 32, and the second $\frac{9}{17}$ of 68, or 36.

6. The parts are to each other as $\frac{4}{5}$ to $\frac{5}{6}$, or as $\frac{24}{30}$ to $\frac{25}{30}$, or as 24 to 25; hence if we divide $\frac{7}{8}$ into 24+25, or 49 equal parts, $\frac{24}{49}$ of $\frac{7}{8}$, or $\frac{3}{7}$, will be the first number, and $\frac{25}{49}$ of $\frac{7}{8}$, or $\frac{25}{56}$, the second part.

7. The parts are in the proportion of $\frac{1}{3}$ and $\frac{1}{5}$, or of $\frac{5}{15}$ and $\frac{3}{15}$, or of 5 and 3; hence if we divide $\frac{1}{4}$ into 8 equal parts, $\frac{5}{8}$ of $\frac{1}{4}$, or $\frac{5}{32}$, will be the first part, and $\frac{3}{8}$ of $\frac{1}{4}$, or $\frac{3}{32}$, the second part.

Art. 692. WRITTEN EXERCISES.

2. We divide 32149 into 6+7, or 13 equal parts; $\frac{6}{13}$ of 32149=14838; $\frac{7}{13}$=17311.

3. We divide $64800 into 12+15, or 27 equal parts; the first partner has $\frac{12}{27}$ of $64800=$28800, and the second $\frac{15}{27}$ of $64800=$36000.

4. Since the parts are as $\frac{3}{4}$ to $\frac{5}{6}$, or as $\frac{9}{12}$ to $\frac{10}{12}$, or as 9 to 10, if we divide $26106 into 9+10, or 19 equal parts, the brother has $\frac{9}{19}$ of $26106, or $12366, and the sister $\frac{10}{19}$ of $26106=$13740.

5. Divide into 4+7+9=20 parts; $\frac{4}{20}$ of 75280=15056; $\frac{7}{20}$ of 75280=26348; $\frac{9}{20}$ of 75280=33876.

6. The parts are as $\frac{1}{5}$ to $\frac{1}{6}$, or as $\frac{6}{30}$ to $\frac{5}{30}$, or as 6 to 5; hence we divide into 6+5, or 11 parts, and the quantity of zinc will be 3144 lb. and of copper, 2620 lb.

7. 9+10+12=31 equal parts; the first raised $\frac{9}{31}$ of 15810 =4590 bu.; the second $\frac{10}{31}$ of 15810=5100 bu.; the third $\frac{12}{31}$ of 15810=6120 bu.

8. The parts are as $\frac{3}{4}$ to $\frac{5}{6}$, or as 9 to 10; 9+10=19; $\frac{9}{19}$ of $3800=$1800; $\frac{10}{19}$ of $3800=$2000.

9. The parts are as $\frac{4}{5}$, $\frac{5}{6}$, and $\frac{6}{7}$, or as 168, 175, and 180; $168+175+180=523$; $\frac{168}{523}$ of $\$263069=\$84504$; $\frac{175}{523}$ of $\$263069=\$88025$; $\frac{180}{523}$ of $\$263069=\$90540$.

10. $\frac{5}{6}$ is to $\frac{7}{8}$ as 20 to 21; $20+21=41$; $\frac{20}{41}$ of $\$4059=\$1980$; $\frac{21}{41}$ of $4059=\$2079$; $\$1980=\frac{9}{10}$ of 1st daughter's share, hence her share is $\frac{10}{9}$ of $\$1980=\$2200$; $\$2079=\frac{11}{12}$ of 2d daughter's share, hence her share is $\frac{12}{11}$ of $\$2079=\$2268$.

CONJOINED PROPORTION.

Art. 694. MENTAL EXERCISES.

2. If 2 sheep are worth 10 pigs, 1 sheep is worth $\frac{1}{2}$ of 10 pigs, or 5 pigs, and 12 sheep are worth 12 times 5 pigs, or 60 pigs; if 2 cows are worth 12 sheep or 60 pigs, 1 cow is worth $\frac{1}{2}$ of 60 pigs, or 30 pigs, and 3 cows are worth 3 times 30 pigs, or 90 pigs.

3. If 3 apples are worth 5 cents, 6 apples are worth 2 times 5 cents, or 10 cents; if 4 oranges cost as much as 6 apples, or 10 cents, 1 orange cost $\frac{1}{4}$ of 10 cents, or $2\frac{1}{2}$ cents, and for 25 cents you can buy as many oranges as $2\frac{1}{2}$ is contained times in 25, or 10 oranges.

4. If 12 sheep are worth 3 cows, 1 cow is worth $\frac{1}{3}$ of 12 sheep, or 4 sheep, and 12 cows are worth 12 times 4 sheep, or 48 sheep: if 6 horses are worth 12 cows or 48 sheep, 1 horse is worth 8 sheep, and 24 horses are worth 24 times 8 sheep, or 192 sheep.

5. If 3 hens cost \$6, 1 hen cost $\frac{1}{3}$ of \$6, or \$2, and 4 hens cost 4 times \$2 or \$8; if 4 hens or 2 turkeys cost \$8, 1 turkey costs $\frac{1}{2}$ of \$8 or \$4, and 20 turkeys cost 20 times \$4 or \$80.

6. A can do 2 times 5 times, or 10 times as much as C in 1 day, hence to do 20 times as much as C does in a day will take A 2 days.

Art. 694. WRITTEN EXERCISES.

(2)

10 girls – 7 boys
7 boys – 5 men
28 men – x

$$x=\frac{10\times7\times28}{7\times5}=56 \text{ girls}$$

(3)

27¢ – 4 lb. ginger
10 lb. ginger – 3 lb. white pepper
14 lb. w. pepper – 9 lb. cloves
2 lb. cloves – 5 lb. S. pepper
20 lb. S. pepper – x

$$x=\frac{20\times2\times14\times10\times27}{4\times3\times9\times5}=\$2.80.$$

(4)

$2.40 – 15 lb. Manila
17 lb. Manila – 16 lb. Jamaica
18 lb. Jamaica – 17 lb. Laguayra
7 lb. Laguayra – 6 lb. Java
11 lb. Java – 14 lb. Rio
20 lb. Rio – x

$$x=\frac{2.40\times17\times18\times7\times11\times20}{15\times16\times17\times6\times14}=\$3.30.$$

(5)

9 R. – 3 Penn.
10 Penn. – 4 Norr.
16 Norr. – 11 U. C.
22 U. C. – x

$$x=\frac{9\times10\times16\times22}{3\times4\times11}=240.$$

(6)

$6.20 – 2 10 d.
10 10 d. – 9 8 d.
6 8 d. – 5 4 d.
3 4 d. – 2 2 d.
3 2 d. – x

$$x=\frac{6.20\times10\times6\times3\times3}{2\times9\times5\times2}=\$18.60$$

(7)

$1.98 – 6 lb. almonds
2 lb. almonds – 11 lb. currants
7 lb. currants – 4 lb. raisins
120 lb. raisins – 7 boxes raisins
6 boxes raisins – x

$$x=\frac{1.98\times2\times7\times120\times6}{6\times11\times4\times7}=\$10.80$$

(8)

24 N. Y. – 14 Ch.
28 Ch. – 45 Phila.
15 Phila. – 12 Boston
72 Boston – x

$$x=\frac{24\times28\times15\times72}{14\times45\times12}=96$$

(9)

6 Jos. – 5 Jona.
7 Jona. – 4 John
8 John – 6 James
18 James – x

$$x=\frac{6\times7\times8\times18}{5\times4\times6}=50\tfrac{2}{5}$$

(10)

$52 – 10 bar. E. R. H. Ohio
$37\frac{1}{2}$ bar. E. R. H. O. – 26 bar. Minn. Extra
44 bar. Minn. Extra – 75 bar. rye
11 bar. rye – 900 lb. buckwheat
200 lb. buckwheat – x

$$x=\frac{52\times37\frac{1}{2}\times44\times11\times200}{10\times26\times75\times900}=\$10.75\tfrac{5}{9}$$

MEDIAL PROPORTION.

Art. 697. Case I.

(2)

¢
25 × 50 = 1250
34 × 80 = 2720
41 × 110 = 4510
100)8480(.84$\frac{4}{5}$

(3)

¢
18 × 50 = 900
26 × 80 = 2080
20 × 120 = 2400
6 × 0 = 0
70)5380(.76$\frac{6}{7}$

(4)

$$\begin{array}{r} 8\times 21=168 \\ 12\times 22=264 \\ 18\times 20=360 \\ 28\times 0=0 \\ \hline 66 \quad)792(12 \end{array}$$

(5)

$$\begin{array}{r} 12\times 90\%=1080 \\ 7\times 80\%=560 \\ 10\times 75\%=750 \\ 11\times 70\%=770 \\ \hline 40 \quad)3160(79\% \end{array}$$

(6)

$$\begin{array}{r} 30\times 20=600 \\ 40\times 25=1000 \\ 30\times 28=840 \\ \hline 100 \quad)2440(24.40 \end{array}$$

$\$24.40\times 1.25=\$30.50$

Art. 698. Case II.

(2)

Mean	Rates					*Ans.*
12	7	$\frac{1}{5}$		6		6
	10		$\frac{1}{2}$		4	4
	16		$\frac{1}{4}$		2	2
	18	$\frac{1}{6}$		5		5

(3)

Mean	Rates					*Ans.*
18	10	$\frac{1}{8}$		1		1
	14		$\frac{1}{4}$		1	1
	20		$\frac{1}{2}$		2	2
	22	$\frac{1}{4}$		2		2

(4)

Mean	Rates					*Ans.*
20	16	$\frac{1}{4}$		1		1
	18		$\frac{1}{2}$		1	1
	22	$\frac{1}{2}$	$\frac{1}{2}$	2	1	3

(5)

Mean	Rates					*Ans.*
65	50	$\frac{1}{15}$	$\frac{1}{15}$	17	10	27
	75		$\frac{1}{10}$		15	15
	82	$\frac{1}{17}$		15		15

(6)

Mean	Rates					*Ans.*
60	54	$\frac{1}{6}$	$\frac{1}{6}$	8	1	9
	63		$\frac{1}{3}$		2	2
	76	$\frac{1}{16}$		3		3

(7)

Mean	Rates					*Ans.*
10	3	$\frac{1}{7}$		40		40
	5		$\frac{1}{5}$		15	15
	25		$\frac{1}{15}$		5	5
	50	$\frac{1}{40}$		7		7

NOTE.—In the 5th we reduce all the numbers to 4ths and compare the numerators; in the 6th we reduce to 12ths. In the 2d problem other results could be obtained by comparing the 1st with the 3d, and the 2d with the 4th. Many problems in Alligation will admit of several different results.

Art. 699. Case III.

(2)

Mean	Rates							
12	5	$\frac{1}{7}$		4		4	$\times 4=$	16
	7		$\frac{1}{5}$		4	4		16
	16	$\frac{1}{4}$	$\frac{1}{4}$	7	5	12		48

$48\div 12=4$

(3)

35	10	$\frac{1}{25}$			1			1		36
	15		$\frac{1}{20}$			1		1	$\times 36 =$	36
	30			$\frac{1}{5}$			1	1		36
	40	$\frac{1}{5}$	$\frac{1}{5}$	$\frac{1}{5}$	5	4	1	10		360

$360 \div 10 = 36$

(4)

10	6	$\frac{1}{4}$		5		40	
	8		$\frac{1}{2}$		4		40
	14		$\frac{1}{4}$		2		20
	15	$\frac{1}{5}$		4		32	

SOL.—We find we must take 5 lb. at 6 ct. as often as 4 lb. at 15 ct.; hence when we take 40 lb. at 6 ct., we must take 8 times 4 lb., or 32 lb., at 15 ct. For a similar reason we take 20 lb. at 14 ct.

(5)

90	150	$\frac{1}{70}$		3		15	
	100		$\frac{1}{20}$		1		21
	70		$\frac{1}{10}$		2		42
	50	$\frac{1}{30}$		7		35	

SOL.—Reduce to cents and compare. We must take 3 lb. at 150 cents as often as 7 lb. at 50 cents; hence when we take 15 lb. at 150 cents, we must take 5 times 7, or 35 lb., at 50 cents. For a similar reason we take 42 lb. at 70 cents.

(6)

25	3	$\frac{1}{22}$			25			25		250
	5		$\frac{1}{20}$			5		5	$\times 10 =$	50
	10			$\frac{1}{15}$			5	5		50
	50	$\frac{1}{25}$	$\frac{1}{25}$	$\frac{1}{25}$	22	4	3	29		290

Art. 700. Case IV.

(2)

35	25	$\frac{1}{10}$		2		2		8
	30		$\frac{1}{5}$		9	9	$\times 4 =$	36
	44		$\frac{1}{9}$		5	5		20
	55	$\frac{1}{20}$		1		1		4
						17		

$68 \div 17 = 4$

(3)

8	5	$\frac{1}{3}$		4		4		24
	7		1		3	3	$\times 6 =$	18
	10		$\frac{1}{3}$		1	1		6
	12	$\frac{1}{4}$		3		3		18
						11		

$66 \div 11 = 6$

(4)

4	1	$\frac{1}{3}$		4		4		40
	2		$\frac{1}{2}$		1	1	$\times 10 =$	10
	5		1		2	2		20
	8	$\frac{1}{4}$		3		3		30
						10		

SOL.—The average price is 1 cent. Reduce the numbers to 4ths and then compare the numerators. We find 10 in all and wish 100; hence we take 10 times each

(5)

15								
	8	$\frac{1}{7}$		5		5	×6=	30
	13		$\frac{1}{2}$		3	3		18
	18		$\frac{1}{3}$		2	2		12
	20	$\frac{1}{5}$		7		7		42
	102÷17=6					17		

(6)

10								
	3	$\frac{1}{7}$		40		40	×20=	800
	5		$\frac{1}{5}$		15	15		300
	25		$\frac{1}{15}$		5	5		100
	50	$\frac{1}{40}$		7		7		140
	1340÷67=20					67		

(7)

10										
	1	$\frac{1}{9}$			10			10	×2=	20
	2		$\frac{1}{8}$			5		5		10
	5			$\frac{1}{5}$			2	2		4
	20	$\frac{1}{10}$	$\frac{1}{10}$	$\frac{1}{10}$	9	4	1	14		28
	62÷31=2							31		

(8)

6		(1)	(2)	(3)	(4)	(5)	(6)	(7)	(8)	(9)	(10)	(11)	(12)	(13)	(14)
	21	$\frac{1}{15}$		1		1	5		5	10		10	15		15
	8		$\frac{1}{2}$		3	3		42	42		24	24		6	6
	3	$\frac{1}{3}$	$\frac{1}{3}$	5	2	7	25	28	53	50	16	66	75	4	79
				6	5	11			100			100			100

SOL.—The average is $1. We reduce to 6ths and compare, and we have columns (3) and (4); uniting these we have column (5), the sum of which is 11. Now if 100 was a multiple of 11 we would multiply column (5) by the number of times 11 which equals 100, but this we cannot do. We then see if we cannot combine columns (3) and (4) so as to make 100. Since 5 times 6=30 and 14 times 5=70, and their sum is 100, we add 5 times the (3) and 14 times the (4) columns, which gives us column (8). We then take the sum of 10 times the (3) and 8 times the (4) and have column (11). We then take the sum of 15 times column (3) and 2 times column (4), and have column (14).

INSURANCE.

Art. 701.

1. He lost $\frac{1}{4}$ of the value, plus the premium; $1\frac{1}{4}$% of $\frac{3}{4}$ of the value equals $3\frac{3}{4}$% of $\frac{1}{4}$ of the value; hence $4150=$\frac{1}{4}$ of the value+$3\frac{3}{4}$% of $\frac{1}{4}$ of the value=$103\frac{3}{4}$% of $\frac{1}{4}$ of

the value; then $\frac{1}{4}$ of the value=\$4150÷1.03$\frac{3}{4}$=\$4000; and the value=\$16000.

2. \$25.00×.17=\$4.25; \$25.00×.25=\$6.25; \$25.00×.34= \$8.50; \$25.00×.42=\$10.50; if the annual rate on the house is $\frac{1}{2}$%, according to Art. 694, it will be twice as much for 3 years, hence the premium=\$2500×.01= \$25; \$4.25+\$6.25+\$8.50+\$10.50+\$25=\$54.50.

3. Whole ins. on mill=\$1200+\$1000=\$2200; whole ins. on machinery=\$800+\$500=\$1300; Ætna's loss on mill=$\frac{12}{22}$ of \$80=\$43.63$\frac{7}{11}$; Lancaster's loss on mill= $\frac{10}{22}$ of \$80=\$36.36$\frac{4}{11}$; Ætna's loss on machinery=$\frac{8}{13}$ of \$150=\$92.30$\frac{10}{13}$; Ætna's whole loss=\$43.63$\frac{7}{11}$+ \$92.30$\frac{10}{13}$=\$135.94$\frac{58}{143}$; Lancaster's loss on machinery =$\frac{5}{13}$ of \$150=\$57.69$\frac{3}{13}$; Lancaster's whole loss= \$36.36$\frac{4}{11}$+\$57.69$\frac{3}{13}$=\$94.05$\frac{85}{143}$.

LIFE INSURANCE.

Art. 709. Case I.

2. Annual premium on \$1000 = \$113.70; \$113.70×5 = \$568.50.

3. Annual premium on \$1000 at 40 years, \$68.45; on \$1000 at 45 years=\$70.85; \$70.85−\$68.45=\$2.40; \$2.40× 10×15=\$360.

4. Annual premium on \$1000 at 35 years=\$48.50; \$48.50 ×17.500 = \$848.75; \$848.75×20 = \$16975; annual premium at 40 years=\$1197.875; \$1197.875×15= \$17968.125; \$17968.125−\$16975=\$993.125.

Art. 710. Case II.

2. Annual premium on \$1000=\$26.50; amount of premiums =\$26.50×5×16=\$2120; \$5000−\$2120=\$2880.

3. Annual premium = \$562.40; since the last payment would be made at the beginning of the fifteenth year, and the endowment would not be paid till the end of

the year, the first term of the progression is the payment plus the interest for one year, or \$596.144; then last term $=\$596.144+33.744\times14=\$1068.56$; final value of premiums $=\dfrac{(\$596.144+\$1068.56)\times15}{2}=$ \$12485.28; loss$=\$12485.28-\$8000=\$4485.28$.

4. Annual premium $=\$400.82$; there have been 9 premiums paid, the last being on interest 3 months, hence 1st term $=\$400.82+\$6.0123=\$406.8323$; common difference$=\$24.0492$; last term$=\$406.8323+\$24.0492\times8=\$599.2259$; final value equals $\dfrac{(\$406.8323+\$599.2259)\times9}{2}=\$4527.2619$; gain $=\$7000-\$4527.2619=\$2472.7381$.

5. Annual premium$=\$525.80$; there have been three premiums paid; hence, as in previous example, 1st term $=\$544.203$; common difference$=\$36.806$; last term $=\$544.203+\$36.806\times2=\$617.815$; final value$=\dfrac{(\$544.203+\$617.815)\times3}{2}=\$1743.027$; annual premium on life policy$=\$265.10$; 1st term$=\$274.3785$; com. diff. $=\$18.557$; last term $=\$311.4925$; final value$=\dfrac{(\$274.3785+\$311.4925)\times3}{2}=\$878.8065$; gain on endowment $=\$11000-\$1743.027=\$9256.973$; profit of life policy over endowment$=\$1743.027-\$878.8065=\$864.2205$.

BUILDING ASSOCIATIONS.

Art. 719. Case I.

2. The dues are \$1 a month per share, hence in the first series the dues will be \$8 a month, and in $8\frac{1}{3}$ years, or 100 months, they will amount to \$800; in the second series, the installments$=\$12\times12\times9=\$1296$; in the third series, $\$27\times12\times10\frac{1}{2}=\$3402$; $\$800+\$1296+\$3402=\$5498$.

NOTE.—The solution to problems in Cases II. and III., as given in the *first edition, will be found* in Appendix.

3. Dues = $18 a month; fines = $18×10%×2=$3.60; amount at end of 1st year=$18×12+$3.60=$219.60: amount for second year =($18+$20)×12 = $456; whole amount=$219.60+$456=$675.60.

4. $20×24=$480; the first installment of the third year has 12 fines, the second 11, etc., forming an arithmetical progression, of which the last installment plus 1 fine is the first term, and the amount of 1 fine the common difference; 1 fine=$20×10%=$2; 1st term=$20+$2=$22; last term=$22+$2×11=$44; amount of fines and installments at end of third year $=\frac{(\$22+\$44)\times 12}{2}=\$396$; $480−$396=$84.

Art. 720. Case II.

2. Amount of loan=$200×15=$3000; monthly payment = ($1 + $1 + $.65)×15 = $39.75; $39.75×12×9= $4293.

3. Amount of loan =($200−$50)×16 = $2400; monthly payment=($1+$1)×16=$32; $32×12×8⅔=$3328.

4. Amount of loan=$200×23=$4600; sum of dues for 8½ years=$1×23×12×8½=$2346; time of loan= 8½−2=6½ years; sum of interest and premium for 6½ years = $1.67 × 23 × 12 × 6½ = $2995.98; $2346 + $2995.98=$5341.98.

5. Stated premium for 4th year=$35; premium=$35+$15 =$50; amount of loan=($200−$50)×20=$3000; balance due on house=$3500−$500; sum of dues for 8⅓ years=$1×20×12×8⅓=$2000; int. on $3000 for 1 month=$15; Int. for 5⅓ years=$15×12×5⅓=$960; $2000+$960=$2960.

Art. 721. Case III.

2. $200−$85=$115; int. on $115 for 1 month=$115×.005 =$.57½; monthly payment = ($1 + $.575) × 12 = $18.90; int. on monthly payments $=18.90\times\frac{108\times 109}{4}$ ¢ =$556.227; sum of payments = $18.90×12×9 =

$2041.20; cost of loan = $2041.20 + $556.227 = $2597.427.

3. Monthly payment $= \$2.65 \times 10 = \$26.50$; interest on monthly payments $= 26.50 \times \frac{112 \times 113}{4}¢ = \$838.46$; sum of payments $= \$26.50 \times 12 \times 9\frac{1}{3} = \$2968$; cost of loan $= \$2968 + \$838.46 = \$3806.46$.

4. Int. on Mr. A's rent $= 12 \times \frac{121 \times 120}{4}¢ = \$435.60$; sum of payments $= \$12 \times 120 = \$1440$; cost of house $= \$1200 + \$1440 + \$435.60 = \$3075.60$; amount of Mr. B's loan $= (\$200 - \$50) \times 8 = \$1200$; monthly payment $= \$2 \times 8 = \$16$; int. on monthly payment $= 16 \times \frac{121 \times 120}{4}¢ = \$580.80$; sum of monthly payments $= \$16 \times 120 = \$1920$; int. on tax $= 24 \times \frac{10 \times 11}{2} \times .06 = \$79.20$; $\$24 \times 10 = \$240$; amount of tax $= \$240 + \$79.20 = \$319.20$; cost of B's $= \$1920 + \$580.80 + \$319.20 = \$2820$; difference $= \$3075.60 - \$2820 = \$255.60$.

Art. 722. Case IV.

2. Sum of payments for 8 years $= \$96$; interest $= \$186.90 - \$96 = \$90.90$; equated time $= \frac{96 \times 97}{24}$; $\$90.90 \div \frac{96 \times 97}{24} = 23.43-\%$.

3. Dues on 1 share for 6 months $= \$6$; value of share at cancellation $= \$180.75 - \$6 = \$174.75$; sum of payments $= \$96$; interest $= \$174.75 - \$96 = \$78.75$; equated time $= \frac{96 \times 97}{24}$; rate $= \$78.75 \div \frac{96 \times 97}{24} = 20.29+\%$.

Art. 723. Case V.

2. $\$4600 \div \$200 = 23$ shares; monthly payments $= \$2.56 \times 23 = \$58.88$; sum of payments $= \$58.88 \times 114 = \$6712.32$; int. on monthly payments $= 58.88 \times \frac{115 \times 114}{4}¢ = \$1929.792$; amt. of payments $= \$6712.32$

$+\$1929.792=\$8642.112$; interest on loan $=\$8642.112-\$4600=\$4042.112$; interest for 1 year $=\$4042.112\div 9\frac{1}{2}=\$425.485\frac{9}{19}$; rate $=425.485\frac{9}{19}\div\$4600=9.25-\%$.

3. Am't of 1st loan $=\$2000$; monthly payment $=\$2.60\times 10=\$26$; sum of payments $=\$26\times 100=\$2600$; int. on monthly payments $=26\times\frac{101\times 100}{4}$¢ $=\$656.50$; cost of loan $=\$2600+\$656.50=\$3256.50$; interest on loan $=\$3256.50-\$2000=\$1256.50$; int. for 1 year $=\$1256.50\div 8\frac{1}{3}=\$150.78$; rate % $=\$150.78\div\$2000=7.539\%$; amt. of 2d loan $=(\$200-\$60)\times 10=\$1400$; monthly payment $=\$20$; sum of payments $=\$2000$; interest on monthly payments $=20\times\frac{101\times 100}{4}$¢ $=\$505$; cost of loan $=\$2000+\$505=\$2505$; interest on loan $=\$2505-\$1400=\$1105$; int. for 1 year $=\$1105\div 8\frac{1}{3}=\$132.60$; rate % $=\$132.60\div\$1400=9.47+\%$.

SECTION XIII.

MENSURATION.

THE TRIANGLE.

Art. 743.

1. Area $=\frac{25\times 18}{2}=25\times 9=225$ sq. rd. $=1$ A. 65 P.

2. Area $=\frac{75\times 57}{2}=\frac{4275}{2}=2137\frac{1}{2}$ P. $=13$ A. $57\frac{1}{2}$ P.

3. Area $=\frac{965\times 576}{2}=277920$ P. $=1737$ A.

4.
$$\begin{array}{r l l}
 20 & & \\
 30 & 45-20=25 & \\
 40 & 45-30=15 & \text{Prod.}=45\times 25\times 15\times 5=84375. \\
 2)\overline{90} & 45-40=\ 5 & \sqrt{84375}=290.47 \text{ sq. ch.} \\
 \overline{45} & &
\end{array}$$

Dividing by 10 to reduce sq. ch. to acres we have 29.047 A., which reduced to sq. rd. $=29$ A. 8 P.

THE QUADRILATERAL.

Art. 747.

1. $20\times 18=360$ sq. ft. $=40$ sq. yd.
2. $192\times 65=12480$ sq. ch. $=1248$ A.
3. Area of 1st is $245\times 42=10290$ sq. rd. $=64$ A. 50 P.
   Area of 2d is $85\times 18=1530$ sq. ch. $=153$ A.
   The difference is 153 A. $-$ 64 A. 50 P. $=$ 88 A. 110 P.

THE TRAPEZOID.

Art. 748.

1. Area $=\dfrac{120+96}{2}\times 48=5184$ sq. in. $=36$ sq. ft.
   The shorter method is to reduce all to feet and then multiply.
2. $\dfrac{365+124}{2}\times 86=21027$ sq. in. $=146$ sq. ft. 3 sq. in.
3. $\dfrac{18+12}{2\times 12}\times 12=15$ sq. ft.
4. $\dfrac{95+75}{2}\times 65=5525$ P. $=34$ A. 85 P.

THE TRAPEZIUM.

Art. 749.

1. Area of 1 triangle $=\dfrac{30\times 145}{2}=2175$ sq. in.
   Area of other triangle $=\dfrac{40\times 145}{2}=2900$ sq. in.
   Trapezoid $=2175+2900=5075$ sq. in. $=35$ sq. ft. 35 sq. in.
2. The sides of one triangle are 20, 30, and 40, hence its area as found in Prob. 4, Art. 743, is 29 A. 8 P.$-$
   The sides of the other triangle are 25, 35, and 40, and its area by the Note under Art. 743 is 43 A. 48 P.$+$
   The sum of these two areas is 72 A. 56 P.

THE CIRCLE.

Art. 752.

1. Circumference $=25\times 3.1416=78.54.$ in.

2. Distance $=16\times 3.1416=50.2656$ rd.

3. Distance $=3.1416\times 45=141.372$.

Art. 753.

1. Diameter $=.3183\times 40=12.732$ ft.

2. Diameter $=.3183\times 78.54=24.999282$ ft.; or, divide 78.54 by 3.1416, and we have 25 ft.

Art. 754.

1. Area $=78.54\times \frac{1}{4}$ of $25=490.875$.

2. The area $=3.1416\times 18^2=1017.8784$.

3. The diameter $=180\times .3183=57.294$; the area $=\frac{1}{4}\times 180\times 57.294=2578.23$.

Art. 755.

1. Side $=14\times .707106=9.899484$ in.

2. Side $=.225079\times 200=45.0158$ in.

THE ELLIPSE.

Art. 756.

1. The area $=8\times 10\times 3.1416=251.328$ sq. in.

2. Area $=3\times 2\frac{1}{2}\times 3.1416=23.562$ sq. ft.

MENSURATION OF VOLUMES.

THE PRISM.

Art. 761.

1. Convex surface $=(6+7+8)\times 50=1050$ sq. in.

2. The convex surface by the 1st problem is 1050 sq. in. We find the area of each base by the Note under Art. 743 to be 20.33; hence the two bases $=40.66$, and the whole surface $=40.66+1050=1090.66$.

Art. 762.

1. Contents $=3^2\times 30=270$ cu. ft.

2. We find the base by Note under Art. 743 to be 110.851 sq. in. and multiplying by 20, the altitude, we have 2217.02 cu. in.

THE PYRAMID.

Art. 765.

1. Perimeter$=3\times 4=12$ ft.; convex surface$=\frac{27}{2}\times 12=$ 162 sq. ft.
2. Perimeter$=5\times 5=25$ ft.; $25\times 30=750$ sq. ft.

Art. 766.

1. Area of base$=8\times 8=64$ sq. ft.; $64\times 23=1472$ cu. ft.
2. We find the area of the base by Note under Art. 743, to be 27.712; this multiplied by $23=637.376$.

THE CYLINDER.

Art. 769.

1. Convex surface$=3.1416\times 6\times 12=226.1952$ sq. ft.
2. Convex surface$=3.1416\times 15\times 40=1884.96$ sq. ft.

Art. 770.

1. The area of the base $=3.1416\times 16=50.2656$; and $50.2656\times 60=3015.936$ cu. ft.
2. Area of end$=3.1416\times(3\frac{1}{3})^2=34.90666+$; $34.90666\times 12=418.87992+$ cu. ft.

THE CONE.

Art. 773.

1. Convex surface$=64\times 20=1280$ sq. in.
2. Convex surface$=3.1416\times 6.5\times 4.125=84.23415$ sq. ft. $=9.35935$ sq. yd.

Art. 774.

1. Contents$=3.1416\times 16\times 6=301.5936$ cu. in.
2. Contents$=.07958\times 20^2+2=63:664$ cu ft.

FRUSTUMS.

Art. 777.

1. Perimeter of lower base is 48 ft., of upper base 32; $(48+32)\times 12=960$ sq. ft.
2. Perimeter of lower base$=3.1416\times 12$; per. of upper base$=3.1416\times 8$; $3.1416\times(12+8)\times 10=628.32$ sq. ft.

Art. 778.

2. The lower base is 36×3.1416; the upper base is 9×3.1416; the square root of their product equals $\sqrt{36\times 9\times (3.1416)^2}=6\times 3\times 3.1416=18\times 3.1416$; hence the sum of all is $(36+9+18)\times 3.1416=197.9208$; this multiplied by $\frac{1}{3}$ of $80=5277.888$ cu. ft.

THE SPHERE.

Art. 781.

1. Surface$=12^2\times 4\times 3.1416=1809.5616$.
2. Surface$=48^2\times 4\times 3.1416=28952.9856$; or, since the diameter of the circle in this problem is 4 times the diameter in the previous problem, the area is 4^2 or 16 times as much.

Art. 782.

1. Contents$=6^3\times \frac{1}{6}\times 3.1416=36\times 3.1416=113.0976$cu. in.
2. Surface$=4000^2\times 4\times 3.1416=201062400$ sq. miles; $8000^3\times \frac{1}{6}\times 3.1416=268083200000$ solid miles.

Art. 783.

1. Side$=21^2\times 3=147$; $\sqrt{147}=12.124$ in.

NOTE.—For GAUGING and REVIEW OF MENSURATION, see page 280.

THE METRIC SYSTEM.

REDUCTION TO THE COMMON SYSTEM.

MEASURES OF VALUE.

1. 19.3¢ × 25=$4.825.
2. 19.3¢ × 47.50=$9.1675.
3. $15.50÷$.193=80.31 fr.+
4. $37.75÷$.193=195.595 fr.+

MEASURES OF WEIGHT.

5. 15.432 gr. × 12=185.184 gr.
6. 15.432 gr. × 480.5 = 7415.076 gr.=1 lb. 3 oz. 8 pwt. $23\frac{19}{250}$ gr. Troy.
7. 15.432 gr. × 976.25 = 15065.49 gr.= 2 lb. 2 oz. 190.49 gr. Av.

8. 480 gr.÷15.432=31.104+G.

9. 12×5760÷15.432=4479.004+G.

10. 12×7000÷15.432=5443.234 G.

MEASURES OF LENGTH.

11. 39.37×24.5÷12=80.38 ft.

12. 39.37×136.54÷36=149.3216 yd.

13. 120×36÷39.37=109.729 M.

14. 2 mi. 120 rd.=150480 in.; 150480÷39.37=3822.199 M.

15. 39.37×4000=157480 in.=2 mi. 155 rd. 5 ft. 10 in.

16. 3 mi. 272 rd.=243936 in.; 243936÷39.37=6195.9867.

MEASURES OF SURFACE.

17. 360÷119.6=3.01 A.

18. 142.5×119.6=17043 sq. yd.

19. 0247×505.6=12 A. 78.1312 P.

20. 30÷.0247=1214.574 A.

21. 5 A. 104 P.=5.65 A.; 5.65÷.0247=228.744 A.

MEASURES OF VOLUME.

22. 35.3166×46=1624.5636 cu. ft.

23. 35.3166×214.78=7585.299348 cu. ft.

24. 128÷35.3166=3.624 S.

25. 16 cu. yd. 8 cu. ft.=440 cu. ft.; 440÷35.3166=12.458 S.

MEASURES OF CAPACITY.

26. 2.1135×36.08÷8=9 gal. 2.12754 qt.

27. 2.1135×45.05÷8=11 gal. 3 qt. 1.213175 pt.

28. 24 gal.=192 pt.; 192÷2.1135=90.844 L.

29. 36 gal. 2 qt.=292 pt.; 292÷2.1135=138.159 L.

30. 6 bu 2 pk.=416 pt.; 416÷1.816=229.07 L.

31. 65.25×1.816÷64=1 bu. 3 pk. 3.247 qt.

MISCELLANEOUS PROBLEMS.

1. 1000÷2.5=400.

2. $4.75×11.5=$54.625.

3. $.18¾×87.5=$16.40625.

4. $.18¾×56.25=$10.546875.

5. 2.2046×1000×56½=124559.9 lb.

6. $4.50 × 2500 = $11250; 2500 ares = 25 hectares; $525 × 25 = $13125; $13125 − $11250 = $1875.

7. Cost of 1 stere = $22.50 ÷ 15 = $1.50; $1.50 × 24.5 = $36.75.

8. $100 ÷ $.21$\frac{3}{4}$ = 459.77+ kilos.

9. 68.325 ÷ 15 = 4.555.

10. 70 ÷ $\frac{5}{8}$ = 112.

11. 8.25 × 23$\frac{3}{4}$ = 195.9375 fr.

12. 3 kilares 7 hectares 6 deciares = 37.006 hectares; $275.25 × 37.006 = $10185.90.

13. 100 ÷ $\frac{5}{8}$ = 160 kilometers.

14. $37.25 × 12$\frac{4}{5}$ = $476.80.

15. 3000 ÷ $\frac{5}{8}$ = 4800 kilometers.

16. $2.65 × 25.25 = $66.9125.

17. The distance according to Ex. 13, is 160 kilometers; 160 ÷ 8 = 20 hours.

18. 18 + 18 = 36 kilometers an hour; 432 ÷ 36 = 12 hours.

19. 3.5 × .75 × .8 = 2.1 cu. meters; $12 ÷ 2.1 = $5.71+.

20. Cost = 40 fr. × 7000 = 280000 fr. = $54040; 7000 grams = 7000 × 15.432 ÷ 24 = 4501 pwt.; $15 × 4501 = $67515; $67515 − $54040 = $13475.

PROBLEMS ON IMPORTS.

1. 18 francs = 19.3¢ × 18 = $3.474; cost of 1 meter = $3.474 + $.25 = $3.724; gain on 1 meter = $5.25 − $3.724 = $1.526; entire gain = $1.526 × 428.5 = $653.891.

2. 10.25 fr. = $1.97825; cost in France = $1.97825 × 325.75 = $644.4149375; selling price = $644.4149375 + $6.25 + $150 = $800.6659475; price per gram = $800.6659475 ÷ 325.75 = $2.4579+.

3. 45.25 fr. = $8.73325; cost per liter = $8.73325 + $1.25 = $9 98325; $12.50 − $9.98325 = $2.51675; $2.51675 × 125.75 = $316.4813125.

4. 7.55 fr. = $1.45715; $1.45715 + $.15 = $1.60715; $1.65 − $1.60715 = $.04285; $.04285 × 625.5 = $26.802675.

5. $16.25 \times 200 = 3250$ fr. $=$ \$627.25; 200 meters $= 218\frac{13}{18}$ yd.; \$4.62$\frac{1}{2}$ $-$ \$.12$\frac{1}{2}$ $=$ \$4.50; \$4.50 $\times$ $218\frac{13}{18}$ $=$ \$984.25; \$984.25 $-$ \$627.25 $=$ \$357.

6. $12.25 \times 480 = 5880$ fr. $=$ \$1134.84; 480 grams $= 15.432$ oz. Troy; \$102.75 $-$ \$5.25 $=$ \$97.50; \$97.50 $\times$ 15.432 $=$ \$1504.62; \$15C4.62 $-$ \$1134.84 $=$ \$369.78.

7. Cost in Havre $= (3.2\frac{1}{2}$ fr. $+ .2\frac{1}{2}$ fr.$) \times 180 = 630$ fr. $=$ \$121.59; 180 liters $= 47.55375$ gal.; \$6.75 $-$ \$2.25 $=$ \$4.50; \$4.50 $\times$ 47.55375 $=$ \$213 991875; \$213.991875 $-$ \$121.59 $=$ \$92.401875.

PART III

ANSWERS.

Art. 58.

3. 688.
4. 999.
5. 749.
6. 959.
8. $9.97.
9. $65.48.
10. $97.78.
11. $777.78.
12. $86.98.
13. $77.89.
14. 8965898.
15. $59.77.
16. 7787.
17. 5768.
18. 3677.
19. $7889.
20. $3.97.
21. 198686.
22. $4.98.
23. 39980.

Art. 59.

2. 21517.
3. 18762.
4. 14954.
5. 64101.
6. 19040.
7. 193863.
8. 460446.
9. 2587853.
10. 12603189.
11. 19916178.
12. 3829168.
13. 8402681.
14. 5782418.
15. 87335176.
16. 1010081.
17. 537722.
18. 1252582.
19. 10006600.
20. 2860191.
21. 683112.
22. 164161.
23. 2123220.
24. 2165848.
25. 1953114.
26. 13885986.
27. 1477743.

Page 26.

MENTAL.

2. $35.
3. 27 cents.
4. 26 inches.
5. 24; 25; 28; 33; 44; 49; 54; 64.
6. 32; 35; 42; 54; 52; 52; 71.
7. 111; 115; 123; 130; 140; 147; 163.
8. 141; 211; 215; 216; 241; 334; 700.
9. 36 robins.
10. 60 cents.
11. 43 cents.
13. 63; 63; 73; 112; 115; 121.
14. 75; 66; 122; 176; 131; 165; 168; 378.
19. $54.

Page 27.

WRITTEN.

2. $26303.
3. $1781.
4. 268 pupils.
5. $14165
6. $4116.
7. $32794.
8. $11.95.
9. $19617.
10. $1459.
11. $4.31
12. $4400.
13. $735.85.
14. $68.75
15. 25050 bu.
16. $266620.
17. $4105.50.

18. $5587.25.
19. $73,659.30.
20. $24,055.
21. $3232.25.
22. $9,950,760.99.
23. $6,275,201,174.

Art. 61.

2. 874358.
3. 713627.
4. 688736.
5. $7887.89.
6. $4985.62.

Art. 66.

2. 241.
3. 252.
4. 203.
5. 641.
6. 172.
7. 246.
8. 525.
9. 321.
10. 182.
11. 403.
12. $26.22.
13. $30.21.
14. 3615.
15. 5352.
16. $12.23.
17. $41.53.
18. 1512.
19. 1703.
20. 5235.
21. $44.44.
22. 33344.
23. 40044.
24. 64451.
25. 71123.
26. 41754.
27. 25542.
28. $9753.12.
29. $5241.62.

Art. 68.

2. 229.
3. 287.
4. $3.77.
5. $4.68.
6. 1708.
7. 3528.
8. 5482.
9. 1204.
10. 1208.
11. 1998.
12. 826.
13. 3691.
14. $292.72.
15. $87.14.
16. $184.17.
17. $318.82.
18. 31705.
19. 44708.
20. 38529.
21. 55159.
22. 13279.
23. $77.39.
24. 13748.
25. 32069.
26. 2998816.
27. 1009999.
28. 20540.
29. 68369.
30. $2.35.
31. 9001.
32. 996998.
33. 399556.
34. 69923.
35. 98999996.
36. 5925925998.

Page 35.

MENTAL.

2. 8 eggs.
3. 34 birds.
4. 9; 5; 14; 17; 17; 27.
5. 29; 39; 44; 42; 35; 91; 112.
6. 104; 113; 117; 127; 136; 145; 140.
7. 10 apples.
8. 18 cents.
9. $18.
10. $83.
11. 16; 17; 22; 33; 27; 36; 34; 26.
12. 24; 113; 133; 250; 137; 237.
13. 47 pupils.
14. $215.
15. $50.
16. 9 cents.
17. $7.
23. 17.
24. 25.
25. 24.

Page 37.

WRITTEN.

2. 241 bushels.
3. 547 acres.
4. $525.
5. $2287.
6. $1856.
7. $9865.
8. 5556 acres.
9. 60 years.
10. 69 years.
11. 70 years.
12. 61 years.
13. 124 years.
14. 506 cows.
15. 62 years.
16. 117 pounds.
17. 986 years.
18. 579 years.
19. 399 years.
25. 248 miles.

26. $2155.
27. $2966.
28. 10 years.
29. 5383 votes.
30. $4236.
31. 6647 men.
32. $781.
33. $590.
34. 3832 ; 2990.

Art. 70.

2. 2869.
3. 47382.
4. 32910.
5. 0.
6. 46 bu.
7. 300 acres.
8. 1595 bu.
9. $1.

Page 40.

1. $12000.
2. $3925.
3. $77 05.
4. $21000.
5. $1995.25
6. $11627.75.
7. $1.75.
8. $0.65.

Art. 76.

2. 1701.
3. 2728.
4. 1590.
5. 5747.
6. $24.56.
7. $35.16.
8. $62.90.
9. $225.72.
10. 45664.
11. 22526.
12. 12642.
13. 36323.
14. 48304.
15. 109380.
16. 96561.
17. 352794.
18. 128835.
19. 167748.
20. 661672.
21. 630855.
22. 877932.
23. 7631514.
25. 6720 ft.
26. $1200.
27. 9625.
28. 1155.
29. 770000.
30. 2160000.

Art. 77.

3. 4956.
4. 3510.
5. 5024.
6. 5778.
7. $87.36.
8. $95.91.
9. $58.80.
10. $54.50.
11. 9672.
12. 7946.
13. 11286.
14. 17500.
15. 13872.
16. 11060.
17. 24588.
18. 25536.
19. 31629.
20. 29725.
21. 18791.
22. 72945.
23. 81098.
24. 60466.
25. 333234.
26. 105056.
27. 126498.
28. 172929.
29. 209576.
30. 381951
31. 195548
32. 336777
33. 740070.
34. 801222.
35. 1540080.
36. 3085326.
37. 7481888.
38. 5226412.
39. 6419945.
40. 8074528.
41. 6153606.
42. 6160320.
43. 5133032
44. 14963776.
45. 10452824.
46. 12839890.
47. 216912714.
48. 16149056.
49. 433825428.
50. 18511956.
51. 22445664.
52. 26132060.
53. 32099725
54. 32298112.
55. 64596224.
56. 278484876.
57. 305099406.
58. 135475022.
59. 6953140080.
60. 4223745376.
61. 35471868568.
62. 47102968926.
63. 129652565329.
64. 413424056270.

Page 46.

MENTAL.

2. $96.
3. $7.20.
4. $7.20.
5. 30 days.
6. 126 days
7. 240 trees.

8. 64 melons.
9. $64.
10. $132.
12. 78; 112; 175; 276; 371; 600; 780; 968; 1250.
13. 284; 975; 2315; 2232; 2856; 7404; 16056; 6530; 5588; 4884.
14. 216 miles.
15. $4.48.
16. $1200.
17. $180.
18. 0.
19. 24 cents.
20. $9.

Page 47.

WRITTEN.

2. 10976 bushels.
3. 16225 oranges.
4. $14,375.
5. $17,765.
6. $267.75.
7. $890.
8. $4372.50.
9. 118544 times.
10. $46.08.
11. $4768.
12. $1063.75.
13. $8394.60.
14. $1196.
15. 17446 miles.
16. $56000.
17. $3426.28.
18. $245,680.
19. 2208 panes.
20. 2256 papers.
21. 3,781,512.
22. 7504 miles.
23. $23760.
24. $6191.25.
25. $6375.50.
26. 66356 miles.
27. $2730.
28. 3528 men.
29. 17280 panes.
30. $2107008.
31. 81317520.

Art. 80.

2. 2975.
3. 1568.
4. 5400.
5. 4872.
6. 7749.
7. 13392.
8. 16290.
9. 43757.
10. 125020.
11. 110349.
12. 375354.
13. 2932488.
15. $2.94.
16. $195.
17. $3960.
18. $1134.
19. $273.
20. $53.76
21. $7672.
22. $16384; $20736.

Art. 81.

2. 43500.
3. 74160.
4. 656100.
5. 2054500.
6. 3563000.
7. 44130000.
8. 19530000.
9. 21355000.
10. 56071300.
11. 16250000.
12. 52260000.
13. 445000000.
14. 2005600000.
15. 4598490000.
16. 22425600000.
17. 23403000000.
18. 296916000000.
19. 309960000000.
20. 5511560000000.

Page 52.

1. $13.75.
2. $1975.
3. 21438 men.
4. 125.
5. 83 miles.
6. 42494760000000.
7. $6087.25.
8. $462.
9. $314.75.
10. $227.80.
11. $185.28.
12. $830.85.

Art. 90.

2. 186.
3. 228.
4. 206.
5. 284.
6. 261.
7. 242.
8. 139.
9. 247.
10. 170.
11. 192.
12. 279.
13. 1151.
14. 464.
15. $1026\frac{3}{7}$.
16. $1156\frac{5}{7}$.
17. 1142.
18. 9044.
19. 11459.
20. 2641.
21. 3396.
22. $1410929\frac{1}{7}$.
23. $533594\frac{3}{6}$.
24. $523375\frac{2}{8}$.
25. $9300278\frac{5}{9}$
27. 97 yards.

28. 216 pecks.
29. 52 weeks.
30. 54 boys.
31. 215 sheep.
32. 47563 shillings.
33. 42 sheets.
34. 2423 minutes.

Art. 91.

1. 35.
2. 43.
3. 35.
4. 354.
5. 234.
6. 314.
7. 236.
8. 321.
9. 416.
10. 417.
11. 169.
12. 218.
13. 372.
14. 274.
15. 328.
16. 418.
17. 625.
18. 408.
19. 683.
20. 672.
21. 811.
22. 725.
23. 672.
24. 1621.
25. 1763.
26. 1234.
27. 2821.
28. 6080.
29. 6171.
30. 1876.
31. 2181.
32. 2931.
33. 2851.
34. 2839.
35. 24132.
36. 20302.
37. 10032.
38. 31210.
39. 12135.
40. 17321.
41. 21823.
42. 2521.
43. 1782.
44. 3124.
45. 3142.
46. *Rem.* 272.
47. 2181.
48. 4321.
49. 4671.
50. 4321.
51. 3180.
52. 3615.
53. 4182.
54. 1142.
55. 7328.
56. 2567.
57. 3007.
58. 4106.
59. 1276.
60. *Rem.* 3858.
61. 180071.
62. *Rem.* 25846.
63. 360073.
64. 75204.

Art. 93.

MENTAL.

2. 6 oranges.
3. 12 sheep.
4. 12 melons.
5. 14 oranges.
6. 9 yards.
7. 10 bushels.
8. $7\frac{4}{8}$ barrels.
9. 5 cents.
11. 34; 23; 14; 24; 15; 19; 21; 21; 22.
12. 90; 50; 80; 13; 21; 102; 301; 302; 144.
13. 12 weeks.
14. 20 hours.

Art. 93.

WRITTEN.

2. 245 hhd.
3. 12 horses.
4. 72 hours.
5. 18 years.
6. 136 acres.
7. 300 cows.
8. 188 oxen.
9. 2400 bushels.
10. 200 days
11. 8 min.+
12. 3200 hours
13. 1253 acres.
14. 58 acres.

Art. 94.

MENTAL.

2. 3; 5; 9; 12; 8; 10; 11.
3. 3; 5; 6; 7; 8; 10; 12.
4. 5; 8; 9; 5; 9; 11; 12.
8. 5; 9; 12; 14; 18.
9. 7; 9; 10; 12; 16.
10. 3; 6; 8; 9; 12
11. 8; 12; 14; 15, 16.
13. 30 cents.
14. \$8.
15. 40 cents.
16. 60 cents.

Art. 94.

WRITTEN.

2. 53.
3. 37.
4. 65.

5. 74.
6. 25.
7. 32.
8. 123.
9. 234.
10. 315.
11. 132.
12. 325.
13. 4476.
15. $32.
16. 66 miles.
17. 63 gallons.
18. 231 cu. in.
19. 282 cu. in.
20. 5280 feet.
21. 1119 feet.
22. $2570.
23. 136\frac{360}{365}$.
24. 70 acres.

Art. 96.

2. 38.
3. 41.
4. 33.
5. 124.
6. 321.
7. 365.
8. 225.
9. 314.
10. 317.
11. 439.
12. 537.
13. 379.

Art. 97.

2. *Rem.* 12.
3. *Rem.* 11.
4. *Rem.* 17.
5. *Rem.* 13.
6. *Rem.* 27.
7. *Rem.* 98.
8. *Rem.* 77.
9. *Rem.* 301.
10. *Rem.* 301.
11. *Rem.* 711.

Art. 98.

2. 17; *Rem.* 26.
3. 2; *Rem.* 153.
4. 3; *Rem.* 233.
5. 3; *Rem.* 665.
6. 9; *Rem.* 659
7. 10; *Rem.* 763.
8. 7; *Rem.* 1573.
9. 10; *Rem.* 2075.
10. *Rem.* 11254.
11. *Rem.* 32856.
12. *Rem.* 1037220.
13. *Rem.* 1895700.

Art. 99.

2. 210.
3. 549.
4. 1540.
5. 23.
6. 19.
7. 24032.
8. 16.
9. 158730.
10. 407028.
11. 9.
12. 8064.
13. 912.

Page 68.

1. 735.
2. 5738.
3. 8520.
4. 339720.
5. 347.
6. 899.
7. 679.
8. 246.
9. 5120401.
10. 1621; 42.
11. 29.
12. 9695.
13. 1902 pages.
14. 849 miles.
15. 8950 bushels.
16. $25248.
17. $196.
18. $3380.
19. $8074; $9050.
20. 400.
21. $32.
22. $1210.
23. 3 horses.
24. $9000.
25. $1476; $41.

Art. 108.

2. 1680.
3. 84.
4. 10800.
5. 625.
6. 576; 1728; 4096.
7. 210.
8. 96577.
9. 6; 10; 14; 15; 21; 35; 30; 42; 105; 70; 310.
10. 6; 10; 14; 22; 15; 21, etc.
11. 48.

Art. 115.

2. 2, 2, 7.
3. 2, 2, 3, 7.
4. 5, 5, 5.
5. 5, 5, 13.
6. 2, 3, 5, 7.
7. 2, 3, 19.
8. 2, 2, 2, 2, 3, 3, 3.
9. 2, 3, 71.
10. 2, 2, 2, 2, 3, 3, 13.
11. 2, 2, 3, 7, 7, 13.
12. 2, 2, 2, 2, 2, 37.
13. 2, 2, 3, 5, 19.

Art. 116.

2. 4, 4; 6, 6; 10,

10; 14, 14; 16, 16; 18, 18; 30, 30; 36, 36; 45. 45.
3. 15; 24; 42; 56; 63; 72.
4. 3; 4; 5; 6; 8; 10.
5. 2; 3; 4; 6; 8; 12.
6. 2; 3; 4; 5.

Art. 121.

2. 10.
3. 6.
4. 18.
5. 24.
6. 30.
7. 105.
8. 84.
9. 165.
10. 156.

Art. 122.

2. 45.
3. 24.
4. 28.
5. 42.
6. 56.
7. 72.
8. 72.
9. 192.

Art. 123.

2. 23.
3. 13.
4. 37.
5. 41.
8. 61.
9. 73.
10. 1021.
11. 1117.
6. 13.
7. $6; 113; 151; 191.

12. 48 fields; 41 acres.

Art. 128.

2. 360.
3. 336.
4. 1260.
5. 1008.
6. 1512.
7. 2520.
8. 770.
9. 5940.
10. $1260.

Art. 129.

2. 240.
3. 168.
4. 240.
5. 3000.
6. 2400.
7. 3600.
8. 2240.

Art. 130.

2. 8723.
3. 150629.
4. 463417.
8. 518760.
9. 816359.
10. 55692.
11. 17934671.
6. $560.
7. 5544 rods.
8. 1680 bushels.
12. 180 minutes.
13. A, 140; B, 105; C, 84; D, 72.

Art. 131.

2. 8.
3. 70.
4. $\frac{5}{9}$.
5. 10.
6. $\frac{4}{5}$.

7. $\frac{27}{28}$.
8. $42\frac{2}{8}$.
9. $1\frac{1}{5}$.

Page 87.

2. 50.
3. 91.
4. 240.
5. 14.
6. 7 cents.

Art. 160.

MENTAL.

2. $\frac{31}{4}$; $\frac{22}{4}$; $\frac{37}{4}$; $\frac{51}{4}$.
3. $\frac{33}{5}$; $\frac{37}{5}$; $\frac{41}{5}$; $\frac{54}{5}$.
4. $\frac{26}{6}$; $\frac{51}{6}$; $\frac{66}{6}$; $\frac{71}{6}$.
5. $\frac{58}{7}$; $\frac{65}{7}$; $\frac{61}{7}$; $\frac{90}{7}$.

Art. 160.

WRITTEN.

2. $\frac{17}{8}$.
3. $\frac{68}{5}$.
4. $\frac{94}{5}$.
5. $\frac{104}{9}$.
6. $\frac{221}{8}$.
7. $\frac{311}{8}$.
8. $\frac{481}{12}$.
9. $\frac{819}{18}$; $\frac{670}{18}$.
10. $\frac{1244}{15}$; $\frac{10099}{100}$.
11. $\frac{2499}{50}$; $\frac{15817}{65}$.

Art. 161.

MENTAL.

2. $4\frac{2}{4}$; $5\frac{1}{5}$; $5\frac{5}{6}$
3. $5\frac{2}{8}$; $5\frac{1}{4}$; $4\frac{1}{6}$.
4. $3\frac{3}{9}$; $3\frac{10}{11}$; 3
5. $1\frac{13}{14}$; $2\frac{1}{16}$; $2\frac{12}{25}$

Art. 161.

WRITTEN.

2. 4.
3. $4\frac{1}{8}$.
4. $4\frac{1}{8}$.
5. $8\frac{7}{8}$.

6. $7\frac{10}{11}$.
7. 9.
8. $18\frac{8}{18}$.
9. $65\frac{7}{16}$.
10. $8\frac{24}{148}$.
11. 25.
12. $16\frac{5}{45}$; $13\frac{4}{25}$.
13. $59\frac{27}{123}$; $29\frac{89}{284}$; $7\frac{2848}{7864}$.

Art. 163.

MENTAL.

2. $\frac{15}{20}$; $\frac{16}{20}$; $\frac{10}{15}$; $\frac{9}{15}$.
3. $\frac{18}{30}$; $\frac{25}{30}$; $\frac{12}{16}$; $\frac{14}{16}$.
4. $\frac{56}{70}$; $\frac{50}{70}$; $\frac{15}{18}$; $\frac{14}{18}$.
5. $\frac{63}{72}$; $\frac{64}{72}$; $\frac{108}{120}$; $\frac{110}{120}$.

Art. 163.

WRITTEN.

2. $\frac{9}{12}$, $\frac{8}{12}$, $\frac{10}{12}$.
3. $\frac{15}{20}$, $\frac{16}{20}$, $\frac{18}{20}$.
4. $\frac{8}{16}$, $\frac{12}{16}$, $\frac{10}{16}$.
5. $\frac{24}{30}$, $\frac{25}{30}$, $\frac{21}{30}$.
6. $\frac{36}{48}$, $\frac{32}{48}$, $\frac{34}{48}$.
7. $\frac{96}{120}$, $\frac{105}{120}$, $\frac{108}{120}$, $\frac{110}{120}$.

Art. 165.

MENTAL.

2. $\frac{3}{4}$.
3. $\frac{4}{5}$.
4. $\frac{2}{6}$.
5. $\frac{6}{7}$.
6. $\frac{6}{8}$.
7. $\frac{4}{9}$, $\frac{6}{9}$.

Art. 165.

WRITTEN.

2. $\frac{2}{3}$, $\frac{5}{6}$.
3. $\frac{2}{3}$, $\frac{3}{5}$.
4. $\frac{3}{5}$, $\frac{1}{2}$.
5. $\frac{1}{4}$, $\frac{2}{3}$.
6. $\frac{1}{4}$, $\frac{1}{8}$.
7. $\frac{5}{7}$, $\frac{9}{10}$.

8. $\frac{11}{12}$, $\frac{8}{9}$.
9. $\frac{15}{77}$, $\frac{7}{9}$.
10. $\frac{11}{12}$, $\frac{5}{7}$.
11. $\frac{61}{71}$, $\frac{101}{281}$.

Art. 166.

MENTAL.

2. $\frac{1}{15}$; $\frac{1}{24}$; $\frac{1}{42}$.
3. $\frac{1}{72}$; $\frac{1}{90}$; $\frac{1}{182}$.
4. $\frac{2}{15}$; $\frac{3}{10}$; $\frac{5}{9}$.
5. $\frac{2}{5}$; $\frac{25}{42}$; $\frac{3}{5}$.
6. $\frac{10}{21}$; $\frac{9}{16}$; $\frac{3}{8}$.

Art. 166.

WRITTEN.

2. $\frac{24}{35}$.
3. $\frac{5}{8}$.
4. $\frac{27}{35}$.
5. $\frac{3}{4}$.
6. $\frac{2}{3}$.
7. 1.
8. $\frac{2}{5}$.
9. $\frac{2}{7}$.
10. $\frac{1}{2}$.
11. $\frac{12}{35}$.
12. $\frac{8}{45}$.
13. $\frac{273}{440}$.

Page 98.

MENTAL.

1. $\$\frac{1}{10}$.
2. $\frac{1}{15}$.
3. $\$\frac{3}{8}$.
4. $\frac{1}{2}$ bushel.
5. $160.
6. $\$\frac{5}{8}$.
7. $\$\frac{8}{15}$.
8. $\$4\frac{1}{2}$.
9. $\$6\frac{2}{3}$.

Page 98.

WRITTEN.

2. $\frac{15}{14}$.
3. $\$6\frac{3}{5}$.
4. $\$13\frac{13}{20}$.
5. $\frac{1}{10}$.
6. $\frac{1}{8}$.
7. $\frac{2}{19}$.
8. $1276.
9. $486.

Art. 169.

MENTAL.

2. $\frac{8}{12}$, $\frac{9}{12}$.
3. $\frac{18}{30}$, $\frac{25}{30}$.
4. $\frac{32}{40}$, $\frac{25}{40}$.
5. $\frac{15}{20}$, $\frac{16}{20}$.
6. $\frac{40}{48}$, $\frac{43}{48}$.
7. $\frac{70}{80}$, $\frac{72}{80}$.

Art. 169.

WRITTEN.

2. $\frac{144}{192}$, $\frac{160}{192}$, $\frac{168}{192}$.
3. $\frac{84}{210}$, $\frac{120}{210}$, $\frac{175}{210}$.
4. $\frac{176}{220}$, $\frac{165}{220}$, $\frac{120}{220}$.
5. $\frac{693}{792}$, $\frac{704}{792}$, $\frac{720}{792}$.
6. $\frac{288}{480}$, $\frac{300}{480}$, $\frac{440}{480}$.
7. $\frac{1344}{1536}$, $\frac{1664}{1536}$, $\frac{6336}{1536}$.
8. $\frac{576}{1152}$, $\frac{768}{1152}$, $\frac{864}{1152}$, $\frac{960}{1152}$, $\frac{1008}{1152}$.

Art. 170.

2. $\frac{30}{36}$, $\frac{16}{36}$, $\frac{21}{36}$
3. $\frac{45}{60}$, $\frac{42}{60}$, $\frac{50}{60}$.
4. $\frac{15}{60}$, $\frac{55}{60}$, $\frac{39}{60}$.
5. $\frac{54}{12}$, $\frac{68}{12}$, $\frac{93}{12}$.
6. $\frac{72}{120}$, $\frac{102}{120}$, $\frac{95}{120}$.
7. $\frac{168}{252}$, $\frac{216}{252}$, $\frac{210}{252}$, $\frac{147}{252}$.
8. $\frac{182}{70}$, $\frac{390}{70}$, $\frac{65}{70}$, $\frac{63}{70}$, $\frac{58}{70}$.
9. $\frac{119}{204}$, $\frac{612}{204}$, $\frac{2822}{204}$.
10. $\frac{1260}{2520}$, $\frac{840}{2520}$, $\frac{630}{2520}$, $\frac{564}{2520}$, $\frac{420}{2520}$, $\frac{360}{2520}$, $\frac{315}{2520}$, $\frac{230}{2520}$.

Art. 171.

MENTAL.

2. $\frac{7}{12}$.
3. $\frac{17}{12}$, or $1\frac{5}{12}$.
4. $\frac{31}{20}$, or $1\frac{11}{20}$.
5. $\frac{9}{10}$.
6. $1\frac{1}{2}$.
7. $1\frac{11}{35}$.
8. $1\frac{5}{8}$.
9. $1\frac{17}{24}$.

Art. 171.

WRITTEN.

2. $2\frac{3}{10}$.
3. $2\frac{5}{72}$.
4. $2\frac{17}{36}$.
5. $2\frac{3}{28}$.
6. $8\frac{1}{6}$.
7. $3\frac{3}{8}$.
8. $3\frac{7}{40}$.
9. $3\frac{21}{40}$.
10. $12\frac{19}{60}$.
11. $27\frac{383}{400}$.
12. $83\frac{47}{154}$.
13. $109\frac{433}{440}$.
14. $2\frac{67}{1680}$.
15. $1\frac{2341}{2520}$.

Art. 172.

MENTAL.

2. $\frac{1}{17}$.
3. $\frac{7}{20}$.
4. $\frac{1}{20}$.
5. $\frac{1}{10}$.
6. $\frac{1}{6}$.
7. $\frac{1}{35}$.
8. $\frac{1}{8}$.
9. $\frac{1}{24}$.

Art. 172.

WRITTEN.

2. $\frac{4}{35}$.
3. $\frac{10}{63}$.
4. $\frac{1}{36}$.
5. $\frac{1}{90}$.
6. $\frac{1}{182}$.
7. $\frac{38}{210}$.
8. $\frac{1}{63}$.
9. $\frac{23}{285}$.
10. $\frac{28}{117}$.
11. $\frac{11}{120}$.
12. $\frac{17}{42}$.
13. $\frac{1}{63}$.
14. $\frac{5}{12}$.
15. $\frac{3}{32}$.
17. $3\frac{1}{3}$.
18. $4\frac{1}{2}$.
19. $9\frac{8}{9}$.
20. $11\frac{7}{11}$.
21. $9\frac{5}{6}$.
22. $19\frac{23}{36}$.

Page 103.

1. $\$16\frac{1}{2}$.
2. $27\frac{17}{60}$ bu.
3. $\$3\frac{1}{2}$.
4. $\$2.12\frac{1}{2}$.
5. $\$1.31\frac{1}{4}$.
6. $25\frac{1}{2}$ yd.
7. $7\frac{11}{16}$ tons.
8. $115\frac{23}{50}$ cwt.

Art. 175.

MENTAL.

2. $1\frac{2}{3}$.
3. $2\frac{1}{3}$.
4. $6\frac{2}{3}$.
5. $6\frac{1}{3}$.
6. $17\frac{1}{2}$.
7. $31\frac{1}{2}$.
8. 54.
9. $38\frac{1}{3}$.

Art. 175.

WRITTEN.

2. $5\frac{1}{2}$.
3. $4\frac{2}{3}$.
4. $11\frac{1}{2}$.
5. $9\frac{1}{2}$.
6. $7\frac{1}{2}$.
7. $28\frac{3}{4}$.
8. 15.
9. $19\frac{1}{12}$.
10. $39\frac{1}{2}$.
11. $56\frac{1}{3}$.
12. $143\frac{3}{4}$.
13. 125.
14. $297\frac{1}{2}$.
15. $605\frac{1}{2}$.
16. $2310\frac{1}{3}$.
17. $4709\frac{7}{11}$.

Art. 176.

MENTAL.

2. 12.
3. 20.
4. 30.
5. $21\frac{2}{3}$.
6. $26\frac{1}{4}$.
7. 210.
8. 190
9. 290.
10. 4; 3.

Art. 176.

WRITTEN.

3. 6.
4. 8.
5. 16
6. $19\frac{2}{7}$
7. 100
8. 2844
9. 102
10. $276\frac{1}{9}$.
11. 2032.
12. $4627\frac{1}{2}$.
13. $110\frac{1}{4}$.
14. $370\frac{3}{7}$.

Art. 177.

MENTAL.

2. $\frac{3}{8}$.
3. [illegible]

4. $\frac{1}{8}$.
5. $\frac{7}{80}$.
6. 8.
7. 3.
8. $\frac{5}{9}$.
9. 22.

Art. 177.

WRITTEN.

2. $\frac{5}{21}$.
3. $\frac{1}{8}$.
4. $\frac{7}{24}$.
5. $\frac{15}{32}$.
6. $\frac{10}{63}$.
7. $\frac{7}{18}$.
8. $\frac{161}{348}$.
9. 1.
10. $104\frac{1}{6}$.
11. 290.
12. $595\frac{5}{11}$.
13. 1320.
14. $\frac{2}{25}$.
15. $\frac{28}{87}$.
16. $\frac{221}{2480}$.

Page 107.

MENTAL.

1. 28 cents.
2. 22 apples.
3. $8.
4. $6.
5. $$3\frac{3}{5}$.
6. $3\frac{15}{16}$ rods.
7. $\frac{1}{4}$.
9. $$8\frac{1}{8}$.
10. $$1.84\frac{7}{8}$.
11. $$31\frac{7}{20}$.
12. $66.

Page 107.

WRITTEN.

1. $2.72.
2. $$32.06\frac{1}{4}$.
3. $$24.37\frac{1}{2}$.
4. $$3328\frac{1}{5}$.
5. $$1912\frac{1}{2}$.
6. $43.78
7. $$56\frac{4}{5}$.
8. $$33\frac{15}{32}$.
9. $$2\frac{9}{28}$.
10. $21.
11. $$461\frac{3}{32}$.
12. $$38\frac{2}{15}$.
13. $$71\frac{1}{4}$.
14. $$3.09\frac{3}{8}$.
15. $\frac{32}{289}$.
16. $\frac{1}{334}$.
17. $\frac{243}{12584}$.
18. $\frac{20}{29}$.
19. $3\frac{827}{1870}$.
20. $3\frac{1}{10}$.
21. $23\frac{139}{770}$.
22. $20\frac{415}{1056}$.
23. $$1667\frac{1}{4}$.
24. $$235\frac{317}{600}$.
25. $$4.43\frac{1}{8}$.

Art. 180.

MENTAL.

2. $\frac{7}{24}$.
3. $\frac{8}{15}$.
4. $\frac{4}{27}$.
5. $\frac{12}{91}$.
6. $2\frac{8}{15}$.
7. $2\frac{1}{10}$.
8. $\frac{8}{9}$.
9. $1\frac{9}{10}$.

Art. 180.

WRITTEN.

3. $\frac{3}{10}$.
4. $\frac{4}{15}$.
5. $\frac{1}{50}$.
6. $\frac{1}{8}$.
7. $\frac{4}{75}$.
8. $\frac{1}{28}$.
9. $\frac{46}{63}$.
10. $112\frac{8}{35}$.
11. $23\frac{31}{32}$.
12. $8\frac{1}{10}$.
13. $58\frac{92}{165}$.
14. $49\frac{139}{333}$.
15. $44\frac{46}{51}$.
16. $80\frac{247}{720}$.

Art. 181.

MENTAL.

2. 9.
3. $9\frac{3}{5}$.
4. 8.
5. $14\frac{2}{3}$.
6. 2.
7. 4.
8. 20.
9. 21.
10. 4 ; 3.

Art. 181.

WRITTEN.

2. $8\frac{1}{3}$.
3. $15\frac{2}{3}$.
4. 14.
5. 12.
6. 48.
7. 54.
8. $1\frac{5}{7}$.
9. 80.
10. 232.
11. 63.
12. 33.
13. $32\frac{2}{5}$.

Art. 182.

MENTAL.

2. $\frac{35}{32}$.
3. $\frac{3}{7}$.
4. $\frac{15}{16}$.
5. $\frac{182}{91}$.
6. $2\frac{2}{5}$.
7. 3.
8. 13.
9. $21\frac{3}{5}$

Art. 182.

WRITTEN.

2. $1\frac{1}{6}$.
3. $1\frac{1}{3}$.
4. $\frac{15}{16}$.
5. $\frac{3}{10}$.
6. 2.
7. $1\frac{13}{36}$.
8. $1\frac{1}{2}$.
9. $1\frac{2}{7}$.
10. $\frac{54}{55}$.
11. $\frac{865}{1504}$.
12. $1\frac{439}{496}$.
13. $1\frac{592}{893}$.
14. $1\frac{19}{26}$.
15. $1\frac{998}{1621}$.
16. $2\frac{694}{903}$.
17. $1\frac{17}{48}$.
18. $6\frac{13}{90}$.
19. $1\frac{1}{4}$.

Page 111.

MENTAL.

1. 20 yards.
2. 5 yards.
3. 12 days.
4. 2 barrels.
5. 16 lots.
6. 5 persons.
7. 24 apples.
8. 24 yards.
9. 3 companions.
10. $12\frac{1}{2}$ dozen.

Page 112.

WRITTEN.

1. $3\frac{1}{3}$ pounds.
2. $2\frac{4}{5}$ quarts.
3. \$4.10.
4. $17\frac{4}{13}$ cents.
5. \$0.85.
6. $\$13\frac{7}{8}$.
7. $\$6\frac{1}{2}$.
8. $\frac{48}{125}$.
9. $\frac{17}{108}$.
10. $\frac{30}{77}$.
11. $2\frac{494}{1085}$.
12. $94\frac{109}{6090}$.
13. $2\frac{862}{1617}$.
14. $2\frac{4}{7}$ weeks.
15. 8 persons.
16. $\$83\frac{1}{4}$.
17. \$1600.
18. $16\frac{1}{36}$.
19. 15 companions.
20. 11 persons.
21. \$6.50.
22. 24 days.
23. \$22.40.

Art. 183.

2. $\frac{20}{21}$.
3. $\frac{21}{22}$.
4. $2\frac{4}{9}$.
5. $\frac{16}{17}$.
6. $1\frac{13}{27}$.
7. $1\frac{83}{525}$.
8. $\frac{15}{22}$.
9. $\frac{11}{16}$.
10. $\frac{80}{81}$.
11. $\frac{99}{188}$.
12. $\frac{70}{123}$.
13. $\frac{3}{16}$.

Art. 185.

MENTAL.

1. $1\frac{1}{2}$; $2\frac{1}{2}$; $1\frac{7}{9}$.
2. $\frac{4}{9}$; $\frac{9}{20}$; $\frac{4}{9}$; $\frac{5}{6}$.
3. $\frac{3}{10}$.
4. \$84.
5. $\$97\frac{1}{2}$.
6. $\frac{3}{4}$.

Art. 185.

WRITTEN.

2. $\frac{1}{3}$.
3. $\frac{1}{8}$.
4. $1\frac{1}{6}$.
5. $\frac{13}{18}$.
6. $\frac{7}{15}$.
7. $\frac{5}{7}$.
8. $\frac{5}{4}$.
9. $\frac{9}{13}$.
11. 56 cents.
12. \$685.
13. \$750.
14. \$1.65.
15. $\frac{2}{7}$.

Art. 186.

MENTAL.

1. $\frac{1}{5}$; $\frac{1}{10}$; $\frac{5}{56}$; $\frac{1}{21}$.
2. $\frac{3}{40}$; $\frac{8}{35}$; $\frac{2}{15}$.
3. $\$20\frac{1}{4}$.
4. $\frac{3}{8}$.
5. $\frac{1}{8}$.
6. $17\frac{1}{3}$ cents.

Art. 186.

WRITTEN.

2. $\frac{1}{12}$.
3. $\frac{1}{28}$.
4. $\frac{1}{20}$.
5. $\frac{1}{30}$
6. $\frac{1}{72}$
7. $\frac{1}{33}$.
8. $\frac{4}{57}$.
9. $\frac{3}{80}$.
10. $\frac{3}{5}$.

Art. 187.

MENTAL.

1. 10; 16; 28.
2. 102; 180; 132.
3. 12 yards.
4. $2\frac{2}{5}$.
5. $5\frac{1}{3}$

Art. 187.

WRITTEN.

2. 414.
3. $112\frac{1}{2}$.

4. 2133.
5. 54.
6. 154.
7. 1260.
8. $1\frac{21}{39}$.

Art. 188.

MENTAL.

1. $\frac{8}{15}$; $\frac{9}{10}$; $\frac{7}{16}$; $\frac{25}{24}$.
2. $3\frac{1}{2}$; $\frac{2}{3}$; $\frac{5}{7}$; $\frac{7}{9}$.
3. $\frac{8}{15}$.
4. $\$22\frac{1}{2}$.
5. $\frac{5}{8}$.
6. $\frac{15}{16}$.

Art. 188.

WRITTEN.

2. $\frac{1}{2}$.
3. $\frac{2}{3}$.
4. $\frac{2}{5}$.
5. $\frac{28}{27}$.
6. $\frac{146}{175}$.
7. $\frac{217}{148}$.
8. $\frac{105}{304}$.
9. $\frac{16}{9}$.
10. $\frac{2}{5}$.
11. $\frac{6}{7}$.
12. $\frac{1}{5}$.
13. $6\frac{19}{20}$ ninths.

Art. 190.

MENTAL.

1. 7 cents.
2. $\$3\frac{3}{4}$.
3. 22 minutes.
4. $12.
5. $18.
6. $\$1\frac{2}{3}$.

Art. 190.

WRITTEN.

2. $4.13.
3. $24.
4. $4.18.
5. $36.
6. $7.60.
7. $\$189\frac{1}{2}$.
8. $122.50.
9. 18 pigs.
10. 39 bushels.

Art. 191.

MENTAL.

1. 90 dimes.
2. $126.
3. $15.
4. $10\frac{1}{8}$ cents.
5. $26\frac{2}{3}$ cents.
6. $200.

Art. 191.

WRITTEN.

2. $3720.
3. $\$21.87\frac{1}{2}$.
4. $22.05.
5. $298.80.
6. $308.40.
7. $1200.
8. $337\frac{1}{2}$ pages.
9. $\$45\frac{5}{8}$.
10. $2551.50.
11. $38.40.
12. $17.50.
13. $149.40.
14. $393.75.

Art. 192.

MENTAL.

1. 6 cents.
2. $\$\frac{7}{8}$.
3. $4.
4. $11\frac{1}{5}$ miles.
5. 36 cents.
6. 23 miles.
7. $7.

Art. 192.

WRITTEN.

2. $19.68.
3. $\$2.18\frac{3}{4}$.
4. $\$2\frac{1}{8}$
5. $\$18\frac{9}{14}$.
6. $\$3174\frac{1}{3}$.
7. $\$42\frac{1}{12}$.
8. $\$167\frac{1}{5}$.
9. $\$14\frac{15}{16}$.
10. $\$37\frac{1}{2}$.
11. $\$92\frac{4}{7}$.
12. $15.20.

Art. 193.

MENTAL.

1. 1 cent.
2. $\$7\frac{1}{5}$.
3. $128.
4. $\$1.90\frac{10}{11}$.
5. $\$6\frac{2}{3}$.
6. $\$8\frac{1}{20}$.
7. $1725.
8. $\$12\frac{1}{2}$.
9. 20 apples.
10. $60.

Art. 193.

WRITTEN.

2. $\$238\frac{1}{3}$.
3. $19\frac{1}{5}$ cords.
4. $38\frac{1}{2}$ barrels.
5. $41\frac{1}{3}$ tons.
6. 28 horses.
7. 84 pigs.
8. 9 barrels.
9. $\$1.28\frac{1}{3}$.
10. $\$30\frac{3}{4}$.
11. $163\frac{1}{3}$ tons.
12. $118\frac{2}{3}$ bushels.
13. $6.50.
14. $693.
15. $\$117\frac{6}{7}$.
16. $\$215\frac{1}{30}$.
17. $\$103\frac{1}{2}$
18. $\$48\frac{3}{4}$.
19. $33\frac{1}{3}$ tons.
20. 189 bushels.
21. 32 bushels.

Art. 194.

MENTAL.

1. \$480.
2. \$7200.
3. \$60.
4. \$40.
5. 3000 men.
6. 60.
7. 21 years.
8. 120 cents.
9. \$50.

Art. 194.

WRITTEN.

2. \$24180.
3. 270 cows.
4. 3135 shares.
5. \$46710.
6. W., \$5376; D., \$4032.
7. 240 trees.
8. 129 feet.

Page 125.

MENTAL.

1. 21.
2. \$$1\frac{3}{8}$.
3. \$$31\frac{1}{4}$.
4. \$$27\frac{1}{5}$.
5. \$12.
6. \$4.
7. $\frac{3}{20}$.
8. \$$\frac{7}{8}$.
9. 60.
10. \$$\frac{3}{20}$.
11. $\frac{1}{6}$.
12. 56 cents.
13. 8 dimes.
14. 20 yards.
15. 24 yards.
16. 210 cents.
17. 140 cents.
18. 32 miles.
19. \$92.
20. 96 cents.
21. 25 cts.; 20 cts.
22. 14.
23. 58 cents.
24. $6\frac{2}{5}$ weeks.
25. 30 roses.
26. \$5.
27. 39 marbles.
28. \$32.
29. 16; 12; 12.
30. 40 years; 50 years.
31. $\frac{1}{15}$.
32. 20.
33. 4.
34. $12\frac{1}{2}$ dozen.
35. \$$15\frac{3}{4}$.
36. \$10; \$60.
37. \$40.
38. \$120.
39. $\frac{5}{8}$.

Page 127.

WRITTEN.

1. $\frac{367}{8}$.
2. $\frac{5014}{18}$.
3. $173\frac{1}{6}$.
4. $38\frac{7}{25}$.
5. $\frac{7}{11}$.
6. $\frac{118}{114}$.
7. $\frac{15}{32}$.
8. $\frac{482}{1875}$.
9. $\frac{80}{120}$, $\frac{90}{120}$, $\frac{100}{120}$, $\frac{105}{120}$, $\frac{108}{120}$.
10. $\frac{1344}{1680}$, $\frac{1400}{1680}$, $\frac{1470}{1680}$, $\frac{1540}{1680}$, $\frac{1560}{1680}$, $\frac{1575}{1680}$.
11. $\frac{8}{35}$.
12. $2\frac{49}{80}$.
13. $3\frac{41}{1980}$.
14. $2\frac{4}{7}$.
15. $\frac{16}{21}$.
16. $15\frac{33}{50}$.
17. $\frac{9}{10}$.
18. $1\frac{11}{84}$.
19. $\frac{1}{6}$.
20. $999\frac{999}{1000}$.
21. $1\frac{295}{608}$.
22. $8\frac{2}{21}$.
23. $3\frac{5}{57}$.
24. $41\frac{5}{8}$.
25. \$$5.71\frac{7}{8}$.
26. \$$1162\frac{1}{2}$
27. \$$13.27\frac{7}{32}$.
28. \$$204.79\frac{1}{6}$.
29. \$$6\frac{2}{3}$.
30. \$8.05.
31. \$40.
32. \$6.50.
33. \$693.
34. \$$117\frac{6}{7}$.
35. \$2568.
36. $507\frac{1}{2}$ acres.
40. \$$742\frac{6}{7}$.
41. 80 cents.
42. $20\frac{2}{5}$ pounds.
43. 180 acres.
44. \$$11.58\frac{3}{4}$.
45. $57\frac{3}{5}$ ft.
46. $14\frac{7}{22}$ hours.
47. \$1620.
48. 1.
49. $37\frac{1}{2}$.
50. $43\frac{5}{12}$.
51. $\frac{6}{25}$.
52. $\frac{21}{95}$.

Page 133.

2. .25.
3. .28.
4. .79.
5. .025.
6. .407.
7. .708.
8. 500.025.
9. .3007.
10. .0709.
11. 300.0078.

12. .56007.
13. .04076.
14. .00969.
15. .200003.
16. .056008.
17. 35000.000008.
18. .0009307.
19. .00018001.
20. 2000000.00006009.
21. .7.
22. .93.
23. .076.
24. .0302.
25. 124.07.
26. 967.104.
27. 96.0209.
28. 75.003017.

Art. 205.

2. $\frac{7}{20}$.
3. $\frac{12}{25}$.
4. $\frac{1}{8}$.
5. $\frac{5}{8}$.
6. $3\frac{1}{4}$.
7. $9\frac{3}{4}$.
8. $12\frac{29}{40}$.
9. $16\frac{3}{40}$.
10. $5\frac{3}{125}$.
11. $17\frac{1}{80}$.
13. $\frac{5}{8}$.
14. $\frac{1}{8}$.
15. $\frac{32}{125}$.
16. $\frac{11}{24}$.
17. \$$\frac{1}{8}$.
18. $4\frac{5}{8}$.
19. $12\frac{3}{16}$.
20. $22\frac{1}{80}$.
21. $50\frac{63}{800}$.
22. \$$6\frac{2}{3}$.

Art. 206.

2. .25.
3. .75.
4. 375.
5. .875.
6. .1875.
7. .3125.
8. .733+.
9. .9375.
10. .64.
11. .9412—.
12. .947368+.
13. .44140625.

Art. 207.

MENTAL.

1. .8.
2. .8.
3. .07.
4. .64.
5. 25.5.
6. .15.
7. .186.
8. 6.75.

Art. 207.

WRITTEN.

2. 341.274.
3. 478.555.
4. 1605.50494.
5. 10611.106843.
6. \$253.88$\frac{3}{4}$.
7. 254.507.
8. 2112.0241349.
9. 798.0196063.
10. .3696245.

Art. 208.

MENTAL.

1. $.\frac{5}{10}$.
2. .5.
3. .02.
4. .5.
5. .3.
6. .45.
7. .38.
8. .33.

Art. 208.

WRITTEN.

2. 83.873
3. 91.502.
4. 49.2217.
5. 846.0839.
6. .637235.
7. .29999997.
8. .990999.
9. 2.4974999975.

Art. 209.

MENTAL.

1. $\frac{6}{10}$; 1.2.
2. 1.2; 3.
3. $\frac{35}{100}$; .35.
4. $\frac{32}{100}$; .32.
5. .18; .42.
6. $\frac{40}{100}$; .4.
7. $\frac{36}{1000}$; .036.
8. .09; .0144.

Art. 209.

WRITTEN.

2. 18.1771.
3. 101.6688.
4. .1.51088.
5. 171.311516.
6. 187.12264.
7. 17963.52084.
8. 381.9438688.
9. 3.859243392.
10. .00020596611.
11. .0005094414.
12. 8.3125.
13. .0175.
14. 1.65
15. \$91.8575
16. 164.7432
17. .10001.
18. .01; .1; 1.

Art. 210.

MENTAL.

1. $\frac{2}{10}$; .2.

2. $\frac{4}{100}$; .04.
3. .25; .25.
4. .075; .075.
5. 1.25; .125; .0125.
6. 20; 20; 200.
7. .2; 20; 200.
8. 1.2; 1.2; 12.
9. 12; 1.2; 12.
10. 120; 12; 1.2.

Art. 210.

WRITTEN.

2. 42.8.
3. 73.21.
4. 6.954.
5. .7431.
6. .3678.
7. 57.03.
8. .06857.
9. 600.8.
10. 6.0708.
11. 9.03446+.
12. 2.5.
13. 15.
14. .2.
15. .2.
16. .0016.
17. 8.
18. 34.
19. 2480.
20. .00025.
21. 4000.
22. 1174.245.
23. 194.62.
24. $8.5436\frac{214}{301}$.
25. 32.
26. 124.

Page 141.

1. $\frac{3}{3125}$.
2. $13\frac{19}{45}$.
3. $2\frac{311}{400}$.
4. .03006 cwt.
5. $\frac{53}{110}$ tons.
6. $307\frac{53}{256}$.

7. $2627\frac{7}{9}$; $1.53\frac{515}{781}$.
8. $1\frac{469}{1808}$.
9. £$285\frac{1}{8}$.
10. $\frac{50}{57}$.
11. 5.6.
12. $8\frac{73}{144}$.
13. $11\frac{301}{320}$.
14. $\frac{3}{32}$.
15. .00125.
16. $1\frac{1}{15}$.
17. 20 cwt.
18. $8\frac{7}{286}$.
19. 1.002002+.
20. $1\frac{585}{616}$.
21. 24.
22. $\$97\frac{8}{9}$.
23. 376.22 tons.
24. 394 casks.
25. 4+patterns.
26. 200625 gal.
27. $10.854.
28. 53 bins; 12.75 bags.
29. 1620; 2700.
30. 27.
31. 49.66+acres.
32. $\$172.87\frac{1}{2}$.
33. 954.75 bu.
34. $1582.
35. 45.66 cords.
36. 43.59+.
37. $2843.75.
38. 1656; 2070; 2300.

Art. 219.

2. 2500.
3. 240.
4. 8000.
5. 20000.
6. 65.
7. 1225.
8. 2305.
9. $14.50.

10. $27.
11. $54.25.
12. $4.17.
13. 25 cents.
14. $86\frac{1}{2}$ cents.
15. $13.875.
16. $185.326.
17. $235.025.
18. $150.105.

Art. 220.

1. $\$63.12\frac{1}{2}$.
2. $\$24.74\frac{1}{2}$.
3. $20.828.
4. $0.999; $499.95.
5. $\$7.08\frac{1}{2}$.
6. $506.25.
7. $4133.25.
8. $19.25.
9. $123.25.
10. 600 yards.
11. 327 cords.
12. 96 days.
13. $139\frac{7}{12}$; 80; 125.
14. $91.25.
15. $\$0.37\frac{1}{2}$.
16. $56.70.
17. $3.72.
18. 2400 bar.
19. $124.95.
20. $63.
21. 50 tons.
22. $1.10.
23. 120 bushels.

Art. 226.

2. $24.
3. $200.
4. $\$14.58\frac{1}{3}$.
5. $30.25.

Art. 227.

2. $\$78.12\frac{1}{2}$
3. $26.58

4. $291.44.
5. $414 80.
6. $281.52.
7. $282.24.
8. $76.61½.

Art. 228.

2. $1.12½.
3. $5¼.
4. $1.25.
5. $3.75.

Art. 229.

2. $49.78.
3. $48.47.
4. $41.47.
5. $25.75.
6. $7.25.
7. $187.03.
8. $16.58.

Art. 235.

1. $827.50.
2. $179.39.
3. $38.61.
4. $18.43.
5. $82.47.
6. $57.11.
7. $47.07.
8. $739.82.

Art. 236.

1. $41.04.
2. $19.03.
3. $18.95.
4. $20.65.
5. $1—.
6. $150.
7. $91.40.

Art. 250.

MENTAL.

1. 50 ; 10 ; 75 ; 60; 80 ; 37½ ; 62½.
2. $\frac{1}{10}$; $\frac{1}{8}$; $\frac{1}{5}$; $\frac{1}{4}$; $\frac{1}{6}$; $\frac{1}{3}$; $\frac{3}{8}$; $\frac{1}{2}$; $\frac{5}{8}$; $\frac{3}{4}$; $\frac{5}{6}$.
3. $\frac{3}{100}$; $\frac{2}{3}$.
4. 6 ; 4 ; 8½ ; 2½.

Art. 251.

MENTAL.

1. 24 far.
2. 96 d.
3. 9 s.
4. 500 s.
5. £24.
6. 31248 d.
7. $\frac{3}{4}$; $\frac{5}{88}$.
8. $\frac{1}{2}$; $\frac{5}{7}$.

Art. 251.

WRITTEN.

3. 467 far.
4. 19102 far.
5. 163 s. 8 d. 3 far.
6. £61 4 s. 2 d. 3 far.

Art. 257.

1. $4.9215.
2. 1326.42+fr.
3. $179.626+.
4. 1913— marks.
5. $3.86.

Art. 260.

MENTAL.

1. 144 gr.; 120 gr.
2. 3 pwt.; 6 pwt.
3. 140 pwt. ; 180 pwt.
4. 5 oz. ; 3 oz.
5. 108 oz.; 132 oz.
6. 10 lb. ; 12 lb.
7. $\frac{1}{8}$; $\frac{1}{2}$; $\frac{3}{8}$
8. $\frac{3}{4}$.

Art. 260.

WRITTEN.

1. 183 gr.
2. 2749 gr.
3. 3 lb. 1 oz. 18 pwt.
4. 13 oz. 1 pwt. 11 gr.
5. 115147 gr.
6. 3 lb. 3 oz. 1 pwt. 15 gr.

Art. 261.

MENTAL.

1. 140 gr.; 220 gr.
2. 27 ℈; 48 ℈.
3. 8 ʒ; 32 ʒ.
4. 40 ʒ; 56 ʒ.
5. 11 ℥; 12 ℥.
6. 9 ℔.; 14 ℔.
7. 60.

Art. 261.

WRITTEN.

1. 712 ʒ.
2. 19 ℔. 11 ℥.
3. 5681 ℈.
4. 275999 gr.
5. 16 ℔. 3 ʒ 1 ℈ 15 gr.
6. 55

Art. 262.

MENTAL.

1. 128 oz. ; 192 oz.
2. 7 lb. ; 900 lb.
3. 48 cwt. ; 2000 cwt.
4. 110 T. ; 125 T.
5. 10 cwt. ; 5 cwt.
6. 5000 lb.; 7500 lb.; 8000 lb.

Art. 262.

WRITTEN.

1. 11675 lb.
2. 3 T. 18 cwt. 97 lb.
3. 47583 oz.
4. 193341 oz.
5. 3 T. 13 cwt. 31 lb. 13 oz.
6. Lead.
7. Silver.

Art. 268.

MENTAL.

1. 6 ft.; 42 ft.
2. 12 yd.; 55 yd.
3. 4 rd.; 80 rd.
4. 5 fur.; 56 fur.
5. 40 mi.; 27 mi.
6. 1 yd.; 2 yd.
7. $\frac{2}{5}$; $\frac{1}{80}$.
8. 21.

Art. 268.

WRITTEN.

1. 332 in.
2. 63½ ft.
3. 2 rd. 4 yd. 2 ft. 3 in.
4. 48121 in.
5. 3 mi. 244 rd. 1 yd. 1 ft.
6. 1527½ yd.
7. 1 mi. 34 rd. 5 yd. 1 ft. 3 in.
8. 242557 in.
9. 5280000 steps.

Art. 270.

MENTAL.

1. 792 inches.
2. 66 feet; 6 feet.
3. 36 feet.
4. 720 feet.

Art. 270.

WRITTEN.

1. 32000 li.
2. 62300 li.
3. 8 mi. 816 fath.
4. 124 ch. 70 li. $\frac{3}{5}$ in.

Art. 274.

MENTAL.

1. 432 sq. in.; 720 sq. in
2. 144 sq. ft.; 63 sq. ft.
3. 16 sq. yd.; 151¼ sq. yd.
4. 4 P.; 480 P.
5. 4 R.; 60 R.
6. 21 A.; 1920 A.
7. 6 sq. ft.; 12 sq. in.

Art. 274.

WRITTEN.

1. 61 A. 110 P.
2. 9468¼ sq. yd.
3. 166889¼ sq. ft.
4. 4295268 sq. in.
5. 5 A. 77 P. 211 sq. ft. 108 sq. in.
6. 1 A. 91 P. 252 sq. ft. 51 sq. in.

Art. 275.

MENTAL.

1. 40000 sq. li.
2. 6 sq. ch.
3. 6 A.; 1280 A.
4. 650 sq. ch.; 420 sq. ch.
5. 2 sq. mi.; 72 sq. mi.
6. 2 Tp.; 4 Tp

Art. 275.

WRITTEN.

1. 1350590000 sq. li.
2. 10 A.
3. 595670 sq. ch.
4. 1 sq. mi. 230 A.
5. 6937090000 sq. li.

Art. 279.

MENTAL.

1. 3456 cu. in.; 6912 cu. in.
2. 81 cu. ft.; 80 cu. ft.

3. 3 cu. yd.
4. 768 cu. ft.; 512 cu. ft.
5. 2 cd.; 9 cd.
6. 5 cu. yd.
7. 6 cu. in.; 24 cu. in.

Art. 279.

WRITTEN.

1. 496 cu. ft.
2. 982 cd.
3. 2062 cu. ft.
4. 155 cd. 36 cu. ft.
5. 17252352 cu. in.
6. 26 cd. 72 cu. ft. 1343 cu. in.

Art. 286.

MENTAL.

1. 14 pt.; $11\frac{1}{4}$ pt.
2. 48 qt.; 60 qt.
3. 24 qt.; 56 qt.
4. 28 pt.; 48 pt.
5. 16 pk.; 36 pk.
6. 5 bu.; 10 bu.
7. 2 f℥.
8. 4 O.; 40 O.
9. $\frac{1}{8}$; $\frac{1}{4}$.
10. 30 bushels.

Art. 286.

WRITTEN.

1. 135 pt.
2. 238 gal. 2 qt. 3 gi.
3. 336300 ♏.
4. 11 Cong. 6 O. 5 f℥ 2 fʒ 35♏.
5. 1727 pt.
6. $592\frac{3}{64}$ bu.
7. $1.41.
8. $\$1307.43\frac{3}{4}$.

Art. 291.

1. 1530″.
2. 1° 40′.
3. 494322″.
4. 1 S. 24° 20′.
5. 1026000″
6. 160050″.

Art. 296.

MENTAL.

1. 1800 sec.; 1500 sec.
2. 6 min.; 180 min.
3. 11 h.; 96 h.
4. 3 da.; 28 da.
5. 1095 da.; 1464 da.
6. 2 com. yr.

Art. 296.

WRITTEN.

1. 86400 sec.
2. 604800 sec.
3. 7665 min.
4. 15 h. 46 min. 20 sec.
5. 8760 h.; 525600 min.; 31536000 sec.
6. 164 days.
7. 263 days.
8. 202 days.

Art. 298.

MENTAL.

1. 18.
2. Jan. 1801.
3. 24; 76.
4. 1760; 1776; 1876; 1880; 2000.
5. 345600.

Art. 301.

MENTAL.

1. 6; 30; 72.
2. 20; 3; $3\frac{1}{2}$; 8.
3. 72; 60; 240; 120.
4. 30; 6; 15.
5. 60; 70; 90.
6. 15; 20.
7. 20; 25.
8. $\frac{1}{2}$ as many.

Art. 301.

WRITTEN.

1. 6048.
2. 15 gross, 9 dozen.
3. \$48.60.
4. \$95.46.
5. 3000.
6. 197 reams, 7 quires, $8\frac{16}{19}$ sheets.

Art. 304.

2. 88407 gr.
3. 101618 gr.
4. 2760 ft.
5. 598014 oz.
6. 4381977 6 in.
7. 26000 li.
8. 113908356 sq. in.
9. 230400 sq. ch.
10. 2631516 cu. in.
11. 429870 ♏.
12. 3136 gi.
13. 414040″.
14. 29347944621 sec.
15. 756000 times.
16. 4308480 in.

Art. 305.

2. £10 14 s. 11 d.
3. 13 lb. 4 oz. 5 pwt. 22 gr.
4. £78 19 s. 8 d. 2 far.
5. 10 ℔. 2 ℈ 2 gr.
6. 2 T. 1 cwt. 11 lb. 8 oz.
7. 2 mi. 265 rd. 1 yd. 8 in.
8. 9 mi. 23 ch. 25 li.
9. 3 cd. 46 cu. ft. 710 cu. in.
10. 16 sq. mi. 511 A.
11. Cong. v. O. v. f℥ iij. fʒ iij. ♏ xvj.
12. 201 gal. 2 gi.
13. 37 bu. 2 pk. 1 pt.
14. 1 yr. 183 da. 21 h. 28 min. 16 sec.
15. 12° 1′.
16. 115 firkins 36 lb.
17. 20 bushels.

Page 185.

MENTAL.

1. 15 cents.
2. 50 cents.
3. 32 cents.
4. 2 cents.
5. 6 cents.
6. \$2.40.
7. \$3.
8. \$8.80.
9. 60 cents.
10. \$2.88.
11. 48 ft.
12. 5 ft. 2 in.
13. 60 cents.
14. 80 cents.
15. 72 cents.
16. 16.
17. 32.
18. 5 cents.
19. 48.
20. $26\frac{2}{5}$ rods.
21. 60 cents.
22. \$1.44.
23. \$5.
24. 15 bands.
25. 10 hours.

Page 186.

WRITTEN.

1. \$37.50.
2. 45 G.
3. 15 lb.
4. \$34.50.
5. \$41.16.
6. 13; $5\frac{1}{4}$ yd. over.
7. 93 doses.
8. 48 balls.
9. $17217\frac{9}{28}$.
10. 1st, 792.

11. 44$\frac{4}{5}$ kegs.
12. 12 lots.
13. 312$\frac{1}{2}$ tons.
14. 2 yr. 30$\frac{5}{12}$ da.
15. 38$\frac{2}{17}$ da.
16. 2880 min.
17. 14 ℔. 3 ℥ 6 ʒ 1 ℈ 16 gr.
18. 17$\frac{13}{36}$ da.
19. 96.
20. 65470.3 sec.
21. 635$\frac{1}{4}$.
22. 10 ℥ 1 ʒ 2 ℈.
23. 606 reams 13 quires 8 sheets.
24. 1440 min.
25. 320 pages.
26. $5299.20.
27. 6975 gross.
28. 0.69\frac{1}{21}$.
29. $70.091.
30. 8 bar.; 67¢.

Art. 306.

3. £849 3 s. 5 d.
4. £2641 7 s. 2 d.
5. 89 lb 1 oz. 4 pwt.
6. 141 cd. 81 cu.ft. 1679 cu.in.
7. 195 T. 19 cwt. 54 lb. 10 oz.
8. 127 ℔. 2 ʒ 1 ℈ 9 gr.
9. 298 hhd. 10 gal. 2 qt. 1 pt.
10. 141 ℔. 3 ʒ 7 gr.
11. 63 mi. 273 rd. 1 ft.
12. 2074 sq. rd. 6 sq. ft. 41 sq. in.
13. 113 A. 144 P. 1 sq. yd. 7 sq. ft.
14. 72 hhd. 34 gal. 1$\frac{1}{2}$ qt.
15. 1373 yr. 3 mo. 3 wk. 6 da. 4 h. 29 min.
16. 1591 cu. yd. 23 cu. ft. 1722 cu. in.

Art. 307.

3. £683 17 s. 11 d. 2 far.
4. 2 lb. 10 oz. 19 pwt. 3 gr
5. 28 lb. 11 oz. 3 pwt. 21 gr.
6. 75 cwt. 47 lb. 15 oz.
7. 109 T. 1 cwt. 46 lb. 2 oz.
8. 21 hhd. 59 gal. 2 qt.
9. 92 yr. 11 mo. 6 wk. 2 da. 20 h.
10. 91 sq. yd. 3 sq. ft. 134 sq. in.
11. 55 mi. 283 rd. 2 ft. 5 in.
12. 44 A. 154 P. 28 sq. yd. 1 sq. ft. 65 sq. in.
13. 142 bu. 2 pk. 5 qt.
14. 79 lb. 3 oz. 4 pwt. 8 gr.
15. 20 mi. 48 rd. 3 in.
16. 31.206\frac{5}{8}$.
17. 115 A. 47 P. 16 sq. yd. 6 sq. ft. 136 sq. in.
18. 46 gal. 3 qt.

Art. 308.

2. 94 cwt. 82 lb. 13 oz.
3. 50 lb. 2 oz. 7 pwt. 3 gr.
4. 352 mo. 15 da. 23 h. 34 min. 40 sec.
5. £109 2 s. 4d.
6. 194 hhd. 7 gal. 3 qt. 1 pt.
7. 140 ℔. 3℥.
8. 154 L. 2 mi. 224 rd.
9. 305 ch. 27 bu. 2 pk. 1 qt. 1 pt.
10. 79 cwt. 50 lb.
11. 208 yr. 7 mo. 3 wk. 5 da.
12. 376 mi. 220 rd.
13. 2925 bu. 3 pk.
14. 652 hhd. 7 gal.
15. 515 A. 50 P.
16. 1145 bu. 3 pk.

Art. 311.

2. £15 9 s. 7 d.
3. 12 lb. 9 oz. 15 pwt. 18 gr.
4. 16 T. 2 cwt. 38 lb.
5. 15 cwt. 74 lb. 5$\frac{1}{2}$ oz.

6. 12 hhd. 4 gal. 2 qt. 1 pt. $3\frac{7}{9}$ gi.
7. 10 mi. 319 rd. 2 yd. 1 ft.
8. 22 A. 92 P. 29 sq. yd.
9. 126 bu. 1 pk. 5 qt. $1\frac{2}{3}$ pt.
10. 4 lb. 8 oz. 17 pwt. 5 gr.
11. 17 mi. $41\frac{7}{11}$ rd.
12. 51 gal. 1 qt. $\frac{17}{26}$ pt.

Art. 312.

2. 8.
3. $10\frac{8}{37}$.
4. 7 days.
5. 25.
6. 5 weeks.

Art. 313.

2. 9 yr. 23 da.
3. 66 yr. 10 mo. 29 da.
4. 84 yr. 3 mo. 11 da.
5. 1 yr. 17 da.
6. 7 yr. 9 mo. 1 da.
7. 3 yr. 11 mo. 28 da.
9. 10; 36 yr. 4 da.
10. 1 day.
11. 2 yr. 1 mo. 15 da. 3 h. 39 min. 11 sec.

Art. 314.

2. Thursday.
3. Friday.
4. Friday.
5. Sunday.
6. Friday.
7. Thursday.
8. Monday.
9. No.

Art. 317.

1. 5° 15′ 4″.
2. 33°
3. 17° 47′ 55″.
4. 96° 9′ 5″.
5. 108° 28′ 40″.
6. 76° 23′.

Art. 319.

MENTAL.

1. 24 hours; $\frac{1}{2}$; $\frac{1}{4}$.
2. 360°; 180°; 60°.
3. 15°; 30°; 45°; 60°.
7. 1 P. M.; 11 A. M.; 2 P. M.; 10 A. M.
9. 15°; 22° 30′; 30°; 41° 15′.
10. West 22° 30′.
11. East 33° 45′.

Art. 320.

2. 2 h. 20 min.
3. 25 min. 1 sec.
4. 1 h. 3 min. 48 sec.
5. 9 h. 22 min. $38\frac{4}{15}$ sec. A. M.
6. 3 h. 6 min. $8\frac{1}{8}$ sec. P. M.
7. Set back 5 h. 7 min. 44 sec.
8. Set ahead 5 h. 5 min. 32 sec.
9. 7 h. 27 sec. A. M.

Art. 321.

2. 9° 20′.
3. 13° 15′.
4. About 75°.
5. 10° 23′.
6. 122° 26′ 15″.
7. 71° 7′ 21″.
8. 11 h. 48 min. 20 sec. A. M.

Art. 326.

2. $\frac{2}{5}$.
3. $\frac{1}{8}$.
4. $2\frac{1}{4}$.
5. $\frac{7}{9}$.
6. $\frac{5}{7}$.
7. $4\frac{2}{7}$.
8. $3\frac{1}{18}$.
9. $3\frac{5}{18}$.

Art. 327.

2. 16 pwt. 16 gr.

3. 3 pk. 1 qt. $1\frac{1}{5}$ pt.
4. 213 rd. 1 yd. $2\frac{1}{2}$ ft.
5. 4 yd. 2 ft. $5\frac{1}{4}$ in.
6. 288 rd.
7. 26° 15′.
8. 114 P. 8 yd. 5 ft. $113\frac{1}{7}$ in.

Art. 328.

2. 9 oz. 18 pwt.
3. 3 yd. $2\frac{11}{80}$ ft.
4. 58 P. $7\frac{13}{50}$ sq. yd.
5. 20 gal. 2 qt. $1\frac{3}{50}$ pt.
6. 3 pk. $7\frac{19}{125}$ qt.
7. 6 cwt. 43 lb. 9.6 oz.
8. 2 tuns, 34 gal. 1 qt. 1 pt.+

Art. 329.

2. $\frac{1}{640}$.
3. $\frac{3}{17600}$.
4. $\frac{1}{36}$.
5. $\frac{5}{1386}$.
6. $\frac{7}{16000}$.
7. $\frac{3}{22400}$.
8. $\frac{3}{8}$.

Art. 330.

2. $\frac{137}{480}$.
3. $\frac{9}{16}$.
4. $\frac{5}{8}$.
5. $\frac{13}{84}$.
6. $\frac{1}{16}$.
7. $\frac{167}{6570}$.
8. $\frac{1}{4}$; $\frac{4}{25}$.

Art. 331.

2. .4604166 lb.+
3. .890625 bu.
4. .76875 lb.
5. .894375 mi.
6. .0725.
7. 92408459 mi.+
8. .04590234375 ton.

Page 206.

MENTAL.

1. 1296000″.
2. $6\frac{1}{4}$ pecks.
3. 486000″.
4. 1152 pages.
5. 6 bushels.
6. 64 cents.
7. $12\frac{1}{2}$ fathoms.
8. 70 years.
9. $26.
10. $3.84.
11. $1.80.
12. 36 cents.
13. 8; 64; 216.
14. 600; 850; 1025.
15. 24; 1801.
16. $\frac{1}{4}$; $\frac{1}{8}$; $\frac{1}{2}$; 90°.
17. 24 cents.
18. $6.40.
19. 46.
20. 5400 words.
21. $1\frac{3}{8}$ cents

Page 207.

WRITTEN.

1. £36 19 s.
2. 166 cwt.
3. £16 12 s. $2\frac{2}{3}$ d.
4. $39.37½.
5. 1 s. $11\frac{5}{8}$ d.
6. 18.1808 sq. in.
7. .0923 G.
8. 9616 cu. ft.
9. 3.2 lb.
10. $161.65½.
11. $1263.375.
12. 85 dozen.
13. $204.039.
14. 9 h. 17 min. $33\frac{3}{8}$ sec.
15. $160.265+.
16. 4479 lb. 2 oz.; 66979 lb. 2 oz.
17. 64° 39′ 3″+.
18. $157.
19. $44.14 1/16.
20. £4 18 s. 4 d.+
21. $655.32.

22. 33 h. 20 min.
23. 36 mi. 298 rd. 1 ft. 6 in.
24. 720; 294.
25. 400; 600.
26. $4.48.
27. 22 mo. 1 wk. $3\frac{1}{2}$ da.
28. 2 da. 16 h.
29. 6 barrels; $20\frac{7}{96}$ lb.
30. 2074.8 mi.
31. 1 mi. 195 rd. 2 yd. 2 ft. 9 in.; 1 mi. 204 rd. 3 yd. 1 ft. 3 in.
32. 6 h. 48 min. $21\frac{3}{42}$ sec. A.M.

Art. 337.

2. 12 sq. yd.
3. $2603\frac{5}{8}$ sq. yd.
4. 20 ft.
5. 28 ft. 3 in.
6. $617\frac{1}{2}$.
7. 31 sq. ft. 12 sq. in.
8. $13\frac{1}{2}$ sq. ft.

Art. 340.

2. 90 sq. ft. 27 sq. in.
3. 174 sq. ft.
4. 5 ft.
5. 18 ft.
6. 18 ft.

Art. 343.

2. 24504.48 miles.
3. 159.15 ft.
4. $11733\frac{1}{3}$.
5. 198 sq. ft. 135 sq. in.
6. 89.36+ sq. yd.
7. 24899 536+ miles; 69.16 + miles.
8. 15.5967 sq. ft.

Art. 344.

2. 1812 A. 80 P.
3. 12795.91\frac{7}{8}$.
4. $2589.
5. 193 A. 137 P. $15\frac{3}{4}$ sq. yd.
6. 16 A. 14 P.
7. 752 rd.
8. 48 A.; $\frac{3}{40}$.
9. 3300 rails; $115.50.
10. 48 rods.
11. $480.
12. 9 A. 155 P.

Art. 347.

2. $80.
3. 18.41\frac{2}{3}$.
4. 322.28\frac{1}{3}$.
5. $668.85.
6. $614.992.
7. 356.83\frac{1}{3}$.
8. $109.40.

Art. 348.

2. 62 yd.; 65 yd.
3. $61\frac{3}{4}$ yd.
4. $62.50.
5. $41\frac{1}{4}\frac{3}{8}$ rolls.
6. $111.78.
7. 24 yd.; $66.

Art. 352.

2. 2 cu. yd. 10 cu. ft.
3. 5 ft.
4. 103680.
5. $109\frac{108}{168}$ cu. yd.
6. 30 ft.
7. 928 cu. yd.

Art. 355.

2. 94.248 sq. ft.
3. 70.686 cu. ft.
4. $2.24—.
5. 23.0384 sq. yd.
6. 353.43 cu. ft.

Art. 358.

2. 72 cords.
3. $6\frac{2}{5}$ ft.
4. 4.736 ft.
5. 59.37\frac{1}{2}$.

Art. 360.

2. 24 sq. ft.
3. $26\frac{2}{3}$ sq. ft.
4. 1344 sq. ft.
5. 420 sq. ft.
6. 18 inches.
7. $29\frac{2}{9}$ sq. ft.
8. $16.50.
9. 1.31\frac{1}{4}$.
10. $266.112.
11. 198 posts; $4900\frac{1}{2}$ sq. ft.; $156.357.

Art. 364.

2. 118.90\frac{2}{3}$.
3. $628\frac{26}{33}$ perches.
4. $3380.
5. 57435 bricks.
6. $1027.75.
7. $8.25—.
8. 374.59\frac{1}{11}$.

Art. 369.

2. $1178\frac{2}{11}$ gal.
3. 981.55+ Imp. gal.
4. $378\frac{63}{64}$ cu. ft.
5. 7.11— ft.
6. $46\frac{6}{11}$ bar.
7. 22.66+ hhd.
8. 14.44+ ft.
9. 13500 lb.
10. $6\frac{6}{11}$ gal.
11. 10 72+ hhd.; $5644\frac{17}{32}$ lb.
12. $76.94+.

Art. 371.

2. 224.99 bu.
3. 9.95+ ft.
4. 6.63+ ft.
5. $204\frac{1}{6}$ bu. corn; $163\frac{1}{3}$ bu carrots.
6. $17\frac{23}{25}$ bu.; $22\frac{2}{5}$ bu.
7. $108.
8. $70\frac{26}{49}$ bar.
9. 12.53\frac{4}{7}$.
10. $211.304.
11. $435\frac{15}{16}$ T.
12. $207.36.
13. 18.66\frac{2}{3}$.
14. $564.48.

Art. 372.

1. 18722.34 cu. in.
2. .5399—.
3. 488.765— bu.
4. 9.31—.
5. 302.4 cu. in. less.
6. $12\frac{57}{64}$ cents.

Art. 373.

1. 101 rings; 31 gr.
2. $86.13.
3. Lead.
4. $12\frac{11}{72}$ lb.
5. 1.8229+.
6. $145\frac{5}{8}$ lb.
7. $65.10.

Art. 375.

1. 121.66\frac{1}{4}$.
2. $71.05.
3. £52 12 s. 9 d—.
4. $1226.358.
5. 1059.03 fr.
6. £34 14.03 s.
7. 6937.568 marks.
8. £214 8 s. 3 d.—
9. $17.610\frac{4}{7}$ lb.
10. $3886; 7.08 gr. rem.

Page 227.

1. 5544.
2. 13.1+ bu.
3. $8\frac{3}{4}$ yd.
4. $\$.31\frac{59}{88}$.
5. 6 tons.
6. 12 cwt. $22\frac{49}{99}$ lb.
7. 123904.
8. $19\frac{37}{45}$.
9. $131.25.
10. $6864.
11. $17600.
12. 30 cars.
13. $12\frac{4}{5}$ in.
14. $423\frac{1}{3}$ loads.
15. $\$78.88\frac{8}{9}$.
16. $\$357.86\frac{2}{3}$.
17. $263—.
18. $1258.915.

Art. 385.

MENTAL.

2. 15.
3. 20.
4. 66.
5. 72.
6. 9.
7. 42.
8. 18.
9. 18.
10. 96 dozen.
11. 72 gallons.
12. 23 miles.
13. $50.
14. $7.50.
15. 120; 20; 24.

Art. 385.

WRITTEN.

2. 57.
3. 150.
4. 237.
5. 157.
6. 644.
7. $83.10.
8. $78.18.
9. $8.43\frac{3}{4}$.
10. $2.61.
11. .12 oz.
12. 11 lb. $11\frac{3}{16}$ oz.
13. 2 lb. 10 oz. $5\frac{1}{10}$ pwt.
14. 500 bar.
15. $216.
16. $261\frac{1}{3}$ lb.
17. 240 A.
18. 15 oz.
19. $555\frac{5}{8}$ A.
20. 2 gal. $1.31\frac{1}{3}$ qt.
21. $1300.
22. $1187.50.
23. $\frac{5}{8}$; $6250.

Art. 386.

MENTAL.

2. 64.
3. 114.
4. 81.
5. 3.
6. $66\frac{2}{3}$ lb.
7. 16 bu.
8. 12 A.
9. £10.
10. 24; 20; 15.
11. 80; 120; 0.
12. 60.
13. $15000.
14. $80.
15. 180 pupils.

Art. 386.

WRITTEN.

2. 225.
3. 300.
4. 280 lb.
5. 1520 A.
6. $\frac{5}{4}$.
7. $10\frac{1}{3}$.
8. $1032.
9. $3606.
10. 1210.
11. 585
12. $\frac{5}{6}$.
13. $\frac{5}{4}$.
14. 256 A. 32 P.
15. 11 lb. 2 oz. 2 pwt.
16. $2500.
17. $2133\frac{1}{3}$ A.
18. $50.
19. $1000.
20. $13681.60.
21. 2560 bar.
22. $8100.
23. $7500.

Art. 387.

MENTAL.

2. 20%.
3. 25%
4. $33\frac{1}{3}$%.
5. $31\frac{1}{4}$%.
6. $118\frac{14}{27}$%.
7. $111\frac{1}{9}$%.
8. $33\frac{1}{3}$%.
9. 60%.
10. $13\frac{1}{3}$%.
11. 85%.
12. 90%.
13. 5%.

Art. 387.

WRITTEN.

3. 25%.
4. 20%.
5. 40%.
6. 60%.
7. 90%.
8. 45%
9. $16\frac{2}{3}$%.
10. 75%.

11. $33\frac{1}{3}\%$.
12. $30\frac{5}{9}\%$.
13. $16\frac{2}{3}\%$.
14. $31\frac{1}{4}\%$.
15. $75\frac{1}{3}\%$.
16. $37\frac{1}{2}\%$.
17. $46\frac{1}{4}\%$.
18. 60%.
19. $36\frac{1}{4}\%$.
20. 10%.
21. 980 men; $9\frac{3}{7}\%$.

Art. 393.

MENTAL.

2. 20 cents.
3. $25.
4. 9 cents.
5. $45.
6. $55.

Art. 393.

WRITTEN.

2. $76.80.
3. $3496.
4. 108 lb.
5. $4.50
6. $6.075.
7. $8.10.
8. $.04—.
9. $487.50.
10. $1\frac{1}{4}$¢; $2\frac{1}{2}$¢; $3\frac{3}{4}$¢; 5¢; 8¢.
11. $23\frac{1}{2}\%$; $27\frac{13}{40}\%$.
12. $\frac{1}{4}\%$; 60%.
13. $5.60.
14. $850.
15. $nw\frac{n}{o}$.

Art. 394.

MENTAL.

2. $5.
3. $140.
4. $26.
5. 55% of the value.
6. $16.
7. $$2\frac{1}{2}$.

Art. 394.

WRITTEN.

2. 20¢.
3. $6.50.
4. $175.
5. $$2.72\frac{7}{19}$.
6. $7680.
7. $12728.
8. $6960.
9. $1.52.
10. $320.
11. 11¢.
12. $2.25.
13. $2.25 less.

Art. 395.

MENTAL.

2. 40%.
3. 25%.
4. 50%.
5. 50%.
6. 10%.
7. 5%.
8. $10\frac{10}{19}\%$.
9. $6\frac{1}{4}\%$.
10. 25%.

Art. 395.

WRITTEN.

2. 50%.
3. 25%.
4. $42\frac{6}{7}\%$.
5. $83\frac{1}{3}\%$.
6. $113\frac{3}{9}\%$.
7. $35\frac{5}{17}\%$.
8. $20\frac{5}{8}\%$.
9. 25%.
10. $8\frac{1}{3}\%$.
11. 8%.
12. 50%.
13. 18%.
14. Loss $12\frac{1}{4}\%$.

Art. 402.

2. $7395 paid over.
3. $5212.08.
4. Com. $65.66.
5. $6315.
6. $7491.09.
7. $521.25.
8. $93.75.

Art. 403.

3. $64000.
4. $270.
5. $33.75.
6. $7580.
7. 4560 lb.
8. $150.
9. My com., $970; agent's, $582; sum paid, $18430.

Art. 404.

2. $1\frac{1}{2}\%$.
3. $2\frac{1}{4}\%$.
4. $4\frac{1}{2}\%$; $1\frac{1}{2}\%$.
5. Com., $2\frac{1}{4}\%$; guaranty $1\frac{1}{2}\%$.

Art. 414.

2. $156.
3. $81.25.
4. $27475.
5. 2 shares.
6. 54 shares.
7. $14510.

Art. 415.

2. $16000.
3. 62 shares.
4. $112500.

5. 360 shares.
6. 1456 shares.
7. 132 shares.
8. 64 shares.
9. 250 shares.
10. $112000.

Art. 416.

2. $1\frac{1}{2}\%$.
3. $6\frac{3}{4}\%$.
4. 3%; $100 surplus.
5. $5\frac{3}{4}\%$.
6. 20%.
7. 12% and 15%.

Art. 428.

2. $4462.
3. $19.88.
4. $618.80.
5. $166.25.
6. $250.50.
7. $636.

Art. 429.

2. $6000.
3. $120.90.
4. Face, $2500.
5. $5400.
6. 87 shares.
7. $50; prem. $560.
8. $3610.42+.
9. $100.
10. 634 bonds.
11. $5.12½.

Art. 430.

2. $\frac{3}{4}\%$.
3. $6\frac{3}{4}\%$.
4. $2\frac{7}{80}\%$; 5%.
5. 20%.
6. 20%; $8\frac{124}{147}\%$ gain.

Art. 436.

2. $5.75.

3. $3619.50.
4. Proceeds, $7398.
5. Profit, $262.50.
6. $97.50 gain.

Art. 437.

2. 100 shares.
3. $5000.
4. 52 shares.
5. 22 sh.; $128.75 surplus.
6. 76 shares.
7. 64 shares; $24 surplus
8. 39 sh.; $40.37½ surplus.

Art. 438.

2. $\frac{1}{4}\%$.
3. $\frac{1}{2}\%$.
4. $\frac{1}{8}\%$.

Art. 447.

2. $900.
3. $329.25.
4. $400.
5. $206.25.
6. $90.
7. $5.23½.
8. Sur., $50.75; In., $225.75.
9. Increase, $11.94.
10. $5062.50; rent, $303.75.

Art. 448.

2. $5000.
3. $7000.
4. $11975.
5. $13525.75.
6. $21050.
7. $1160.
8. $85\frac{5}{7}$; $103\frac{19}{27}$.
9. $98\frac{4}{7}$; $91\frac{2}{3}$.

10. $124\frac{3}{4}$.
11. $4500.
12. 237 sh.; $8.37½ surplus.
13. $412.50.
14. $429.

Art. 449.

2. $5\frac{35}{58}\%$.
3. 5.7%.
4. $6\frac{6}{17}\%$.
5. The 5's.
6. $6\frac{222}{263}\%$.
7. $6\frac{2}{13}\%$.
8. Mo. 6's.
9. Mich. 7's.
10. 7's at 90.
11. 5–20's.

Art. 458.

2. $10114.436.

Art. 459.

4. $147.25.
5. $202.935.
6. $130.20.
7. $840.70.
8. $61.62½.
9. $122.95.

Art. 460.

2. $8400.
3. $38000.
4. $2700
5. $2215564.49.
6. $24600.

Art. 461.

2. .0046+.
3. $.015
4. .0097+
5. $22.25.

Page 270.

MENTAL.

1. $54

2. $200.
3. 19%.
4. 36%.
5. ¼%; ½%.
6. 1%; ¼%.
7. 21%; 32%; 14%; 36%; 44%.
8. 37½%.
9. $16000.
10. $510⅝.
11. $4335.
12. 66⅔%.
13. $4.80.
14. 50 shares.
15. 6⅔%.

Art. 471.

MENTAL.

2. $18.
3. $8.
4. $6.
5. $108.
6. $81.
7. $72.
8. $99.
9. $90.
10. $159.
11. $55.
13. $870.
14. $459.
15. $123.

Art. 471.

WRITTEN.

2. $88.20.
3. $432.49.
4. $247.25.
5. $455.
6. $180.93.
7. $456.84.
8. $668.10.

Art. 472.

2. $76.76.
3. $322.72½.
4. $494.14½.
5. $27.55+.
6. $9.07+.
7. $.24½+.
8. $51.094.
9. $559.51—.
10. $410.53—.
11. $127.11+.
12. $440.66+.

Art. 473.

3. $30.
4. $39.
5. $11.04.
6. $6.93.
7. $8.40.
8. $3.37½.
9. $16.52.
10. $36.21+.
11. $31.21—.
12. $162.17—.
13. $37.31—.
14. $87.24+.
16. $35.60.
17. $20.125.
18. $13.72.
19. $7.695.
20. $28.70.

Art. 474.

3. $19.80.
4. $49.00.
5. $17.00.
6. $26.88.
7. $50.96.
8. $2.53.
9. $101.25.
10. $41.85.

Art. 475.

2. $57.613.
3. $750.25—.
4. $349.53—.
5. $2813.11
6. $847.19.
7. $1621 24.

Art. 476.

MENTAL.

2. $150.
3. $250.
4. $25.
5. $40.
6. $300.
7. $200.
8. $3000.
9. $1000.
10. A, $1000; B, $1500.

Art. 476.

WRITTEN

2. $2100.
3. $72.
4. $472.50.
5. $2016.
6. $1565.19.
7. $2496.37+.
8. $15000; $5000.

Art. 477.

MENTAL.

2. 8 years.
3. 5 years.
4. 4 years.
5. 7 years.
6. 12 years.
7. 8 years.
8. 20 yr.; 30 yr.; 40 yr.
9. 20 yr.; 16⅔ yr.; 12½ yr.; 8 yr.
10. 40 yr.; 20 yr.; 10 yr.; 8 yr.
11. $200; 5 years.

Art. 477.

WRITTEN.

2. 2 yr. 4 mo.
3. 5 yr. 6 mo.
4. 1 yr. 1 mo. 18 da.
5. 15 yr. 4 mo. 24 da.
6. 8 yr. 9 mo. 12 da.
7. 9 yr. 9 mo. 9 da.
8. Prin., $680; time, 4 yr. 6 mo.
9. Prin., $960; time, 6 yr. 8 mo.

Art. 478.

MENTAL.

2. 10%.
3. 5%.
4. 5%.
5. 5%.
6. 6%.
7. 5%.
8. $6\frac{2}{3}$%; $13\frac{1}{3}$%; $16\frac{2}{3}$%.
9. 10%; $16\frac{2}{3}$%; 5%; 4%.
10. 10%; 8%; 5%; $2\frac{1}{2}$%.
11. Prin., $400; 5%.

Art. 478.

WRITTEN.

2. 5%.
3. 7%.
4. 6%.
5. 9%.
6. 6%.
7. $1800; 7%.
8. Prin., $2650; Rate, $8\frac{1}{2}$%.

Page 281.

MENTAL.

1. A, $40; B, $160.
2. C, $390; D, $520.
3. $80.
4. C, $300; D, $100.
5. A, $120; B, $180; C, $60.
6. Each $1200.
7. A, $800; B, $1200.
8. A, $2000; B, $500.
9. $150.
10. Store, $5000; house, $10000; farm, $30000.
11. $6000.
12. A, $4500; B, $4000.
13. Farm, $1800; house, $600.
14. Horse, $84; cow, $14.
15. Harness, $36; carriage, $108; horse, $216.

Art. 487.

1. $227.325.
2. $787.17.
3. $664.41.
4. $749.70.
5. $483.44.
6. $609.10.

Art. 489.

2. $252.90.
3. $1038.69.
4. $1432.73.

Art. 492.

2. $4389.58.
3. $808.25.
4. $7910.
5. $6414.66.
6. $3320.72.

Art. 493.

1. $3997.597.
2. $2953.592.
3. $396.89.

Art. 496.

2. $900.
3. $1460.
4. $1725.14+.
5. $79.87−.
6. $4.77+.
7. $758.93−.
8. $545.82.
9. $2249.07.

Art. 505.

2. 3.20\frac{5}{8}$.
3. $948.1125.
4. $867.735.
5. $13.50.
6. Dis., $11.596+.
7. Dis., $1.76.
8. Dis., $18.68+.

Art. 506.

2. $1010.10.
3. $2030.456.
4. $5050.505.
5. $2000.
6. $730.00.
7. $1038.96.
8. $960.

Art. 507.

2. 90 days.
3. 30 days.
4. 53 days.
5. May 11.
6. Sep. 30.

Art. 508.

2. 6%.
3. 7%.
4. 8%.

Art. 509.

2. $8\frac{9}{50}$%.
3. $5\frac{271}{433}$%.
4. $7\frac{233}{251}$%.
5. Dim., $1.80 ; sur., $20.
6. Div., $123.60. rate, $7\frac{289}{665}$%.

Art. 510.

2. $108.50.
3. 135.06\frac{1}{2}$.
4. $108.76.
5. $275.26.
6. $286.82.
8. $1559.22.
9. $885.65.
10. $1131.57.
11. $42.90.

Art. 524.

3. $4714.375.
4. $3535.
5. $7361.25.
6. $1503.75.
7. $4556.25.

Art. 525.

2. $2600.
3. $600.
4. $40.50.
5. $4814.81.
6. $1474.906.
7. $1474.91.
8. $1500.

Art. 526.

2. $1\frac{1}{2}$% premium.
3. $1\frac{1}{4}$% premium.
4. $1\frac{1}{2}$% discount.

Art. 533.

2. $2420.
3. 695.91— taels.
4. $1058.40.
5. 2814 roubles.
6. 6247.50 francs.
7. 4266.66 rm.
8. 1806.33\frac{3}{4}$.
9. 1153.58\frac{1}{8}$.
10. $67.20.
11. $385.31+.

Art. 535.

3. 1600 roubles.
4. $11.95.
5. $1288.83.
6. 13.58\frac{1}{2}$.
7. 4332.45 marks; circular by 165.79 marks.

Art. 546.

2. $288.
3. $168.
4. $295.80.
5. $411.16.
6. $5771.04.
7. $107.45.
8. $1994.25.
9. $12.15.

Art. 555.

1. 4.
2. 6.
3. $5\frac{5}{8}$.
4. 8.
5. $\frac{32}{107}$.
6. $\frac{9}{16}$.
7. $\frac{9}{8}$.
8. $1\frac{1}{4}$.
10. 1.
11. $3\frac{1}{8}$
12. 3
13. 72.
14. 9.
15. $\frac{27}{40}$.
16. $1\frac{1}{5}$.
18. $\frac{3}{14}$.

Art. 563.

1. 2.
2. 16.
3. 84.
4. 45.
5. 63.
6. 38 yd.
7. 140 lb.
8. $\frac{6}{7}$.
9. 17.68.

Art. 565.

2. $1500.
3. 36 yd.
4. $9900.
5. $15.
6. 58.50.
7. 135.
8. 40.
9. 325.
10. 135 men.
11. $18.
12. 90$\frac{1}{4}$ bu.
13. $155.25.
14. 2 h. 26$\frac{1}{5}$ min.
15. $912.50.
16. 4$\frac{4}{5}$ days.
17. 42 men.
18. 20$\frac{1}{4}$ ft.
19. $7.50.
20. $91.20.
21. 189$\frac{1}{3}$ days
22. 14 days.
23. $1105.50.
24. 6$\frac{3}{8}$ days.
25. $1476

26. $6\frac{3}{4}$ oz.
27. 7 mo.
28. $\$6.94\frac{4}{9}$.
29. 30.
30. 1440 men.

Art. 567.

1. 14.
2. 20.
3. 3.
4. 16.
5. $\frac{11}{12}$.

Art. 569.

2. $567.
3. 125 cows.
4. $\$405\frac{1}{3}$.
5. 9 men.
6. 27 days.
7. 42 men.
8. $\$1.40\frac{5}{8}$.
9. $104\frac{5}{8}$ days.
10. $21\frac{2}{3}$ days.
11. $7.93+.
12. $\$182.85\frac{5}{7}$.
13. 240 cows.
14. $5\frac{1}{3}$ days.
15. 180 men.

Art. 578.

2. $97.50.
3. $243.75.
4. $\$66.87\frac{1}{2}$.
5. $3.41.
6. $80406.25.
7. $\$6390.62\frac{1}{2}$; $\$18609.37\frac{1}{2}$.
8. $18.

Art. 579.

2. $2325.
3. $6168.75.
4. $12963.27.
5. $\frac{5}{8}$%.

Art. 580.

2. $2\frac{1}{5}$%.
3. $3\frac{1}{4}$%.
4. $1\frac{1}{3}$%.

Art. 581.

2. $137.50; $123.75.
3. $0.80.

Art. 583.

2. $\$1033.33\frac{1}{3}$; $\$1666.66\frac{2}{3}$.

Art. 590.

2. $204; $216; $180.
3. $900; $600; $300.
4. A, $25\frac{41}{47}$; B, $19\frac{7}{47}$; C, $15\frac{46}{47}$.
5. A, $500; B, $700; C, $1200.
6. A, $2048; B, $2304; C, $1728.
7. Wife, $1400; son, $2800; daughter, $3600.

8. A, $3300; B, $3000; C, $3200.
9. A, $1625; B, $1325; C, $5000.
10. A, $480; B, $360; C, $110 per acre.

Art. 592.

2. A's, $113.94; B's, $162.06; C's, $212.70.
3. $12.60; $19.20; $15 60; $15.
4. $30.
5. $2400; $1260; $360.
6. A's, $1440; B's, $2385.
7. A, $13; B, $18; C, $20.70.
8. A's, $585; B's, $845.
9. $7000; $8400; $4480.

Art. 593.

2. A, $5000; B, $2500.
3. A, $8108; B, $4192.
4. A, $8603.48; B, $3996.52.
5. A, $8880.27; B, $5075.64; C, $2744.09.

Art. 599.

2. $4\frac{1}{2}$ mo.
3. $4\frac{2}{3}$ mo.
4. $6\frac{5}{12}$ mo.
5. June 11.
6. 7 mo.
7. $6\frac{1}{6}$ mo.
8. May 1.

Art. 600.

2. Term of credit, 83 days; equated time, Sept. 3.
3. Oct. 15.
4. Feb. 23.

Art. 601.

2. 10 mo.
3. 11 mo. after due.
4. 7 mo. after borrowing.
5. 36 days.

Art. 602.

2. Bal., $450; Jan. 23.
3. Bal., $205; July 31
4. Face, $475; int. from March 8th.
5. Bal., $900; Dec. 18, 1871.

Art. 605.

1. $200.60.
2. $150.171.

Art. 606.

1. $4524.44; Nov. 20.
2. $4960.44; Sept. 23.
3. $597.8375; March 13

Art. 614.

MENTAL.

1. 3 times.
2. 5 times.
3. 6 times.
4. 5th power.
5. 7th power.
6. 8th power.
7. 9th power.
8. 12th power.
9. 8.
10. 12.
11. 20.
12. $\frac{16}{15}$
13. 12.

Art. 614.

WRITTEN.

2. 225
3. 1024.
4. 5776.
5. 42025
6. 2744.
7. 42875
8. 300763.

9. 970299.
10. 2025.
11. 13824.
12. 2085136.
13. $\frac{144}{169}$.
14. 8^5.
15. 7^9.
16. 12^6.
17. $(\frac{1}{2})^5$.
18. $1953\frac{1}{8}$.
19. 208.5136.
20. 1.953125.
21. 57720.0625.
22. 4^9.
23. $(\frac{3}{4})^7$.
24. $(2.5)^{10}$.
25. $(3.3)^5$.

Art. 616.

2. 784.
3. 1156.
4. 1521.
5. 2116.
6. 3249.
7. 6084.
8. 7921.
9. 9409.
10. 218089.
11. 494209.
12. 4020025.
13. 21418384.

Art. 620.

3. 1728.
4. 4096.
5. 5832.
6. 12167.
7. 39304.
8. 46656.
9. 74088.
10. 274625.
11. 592704.
12. 34965783.

Art. 631.

WRITTEN.

2. 16.
3. 210.
4. 180
5. 24.
6. 36.
7. 84.
8. 12.
9. 36.
10. 12.
11. 42.

Art. 631.

MENTAL.

1. 8.
2. 6.
3. 4.
4. 25.
5. 3.
6. 4.
7. 2.
8. 3.
9. 8.
10 6.
11. 6.
12. 7.
13. 18.
14. 144.
15. 16.
16. 6.

Page 364.

1. 16.
2. 25.
3. 27.
4. 36.
5. 49.
6. 64.
7. 243.
8. 216.
9. 343.
10. 512.
11. 625.

12. 2401.
13. $\frac{11}{12}$.
14. $\frac{14}{15}$.
15. $\frac{27}{32}$.
16. $\frac{37}{47}$.
17. .47.
18. .56.
19. .27.
20. .125.
21. .256.
22. 7.29.
23. 12.96.
24. 65.61.
25. 2 236+.
26. .81649+.
27. .37966+.

Art. 636.

2. 480 rods.
3. 64 in.
4. 5900.
5. 97.
6. $2560.
7. 95.

Art. 641.

2. 69.
3. 60 ft.
4. 1350.
5. 240.
6. 18 ft.
7. 117 ft.
8. 224 ft.

Art. 643.

2. 36 times.
3. 40; 32.
4. 10 ft.
5. $53\frac{1}{3}$ rd.; 40 rd.
6. 4 ch.; $15\frac{1}{3}$ li.
7. 80 gal.
8. $1\frac{1}{4}$ h.
9. 65 ft.

Art. 647.

1. 25.
2. 27.
3. 35.
4. 38.
5. 42.
6. 56.
7. 67.
8. 74.
9. 83.
10. 95.
11. 123.
12. 137.
13. 104.
14. 345.
15. 507.
16. $\frac{12}{16}$.
17. 7.3.
18. 6.38.
19. 1.5873+.
20. 1.7099+.
21. 1.8171+.
22. .873+.

Art. 648.

4. 231.
5. 327.
6. 345.
7. 652.
8. 1234.
9. 85.9.
10. 2438.
11. 2035.
12. 1.598.
13. 25.46.

Art. 650.

1. 40 ft.
2. 5476 sq. ft.
3. 12150 sq. ft.
4. 11.4 ft.—
5. 35.9 in.—
6. 3.962 ft.+
7. $16.85.

Art. 653.

2. 2d is 125 times 1st.
3. $21\frac{1}{8}$ lb.
4. 173.58 bu.
5. 24 ft.
6. $259\frac{1}{5}$ lb.
7. About 112^3.
8. 4.5 in. nearly.

Art. 654.

2. 5.
3. 3.
4. 12.
5. 5.
6. 4.
7. 4.

Art. 661.

2. 37.
3. 87.
4. 30.
5. 25¢.
6. $225.

Art. 662.

2. 10.
3. 13 cents.
4. 10 miles.

Art. 663.

2. 3.
3. $5.
4. 2 years.

Art. 664.

2. 57.
3. 12 years.
4. 31 days.

Art. 665.

2. 680.
3. 312 mi.
4. $84.75.
5. 21; 78.
6. 11 mi. 152 rd. 4 yd.
7. 10 mi. $309\frac{1}{11}$ rd.

Art. 670.

2. 1536.
3. $\frac{1}{128}$.
4. $\frac{1}{81}$.
5. 536870912.
6. 3486784401.
7. $80000.
8. $10485.76.

Art. 671.

2. 624.
3. 126.
4. 363.
5. $2657.20.
6. $20971.51.
7. 2d, $71722.03 more.
8. $42949672.95.

Art. 673.

2. 1.
3. $\frac{1}{2}$.
4. $\frac{1}{2}$.
5. 24 ft.
6. $11\frac{1}{9}$ rods.

Art. 681.

2. $3304.
3. $3240.
4. $5452.
5. $4840.

Art. 682.

2. $2076.92.
3. $6350.
4. $6612.24.
5. $305.19.

Art. 684.

2. $1700.48.

3. \$3021.78 4. \$1830.48.
5. \$1904.39.

Art. 685.

2. \$3725.88. 3. \$3220.84.
4. 2d, \$6.93. 5. 2d, 99.21.

Art. 688.

MENTAL.

2. 19; 26. 3. \$15; \$20.
4. 10; 5.

Art. 688.

WRITTEN.

2. 151; 276. 3. $\frac{35}{117}$; $\frac{77}{117}$.
4. \$4109; \$4867.
5. \$4000; \$3500; \$2500.

Art. 689.

MENTAL.

2. 6; 36. 3. 10 ft.; 50 ft.
4. 7; 14; 42.

Art. 689.

WRITTEN.

2. \$287; \$41.
3. \$15160; \$60640.
4. A, \$2870; B, \$7175; C, \$1435.
5. \$11840; \$18944.

Art. 690.

MENTAL.

2. J., 60; M., 50.
3. J., \$50; W., \$40.
4. $12\frac{1}{2}$ ft.; $87\frac{1}{2}$ ft.

Art. 690.

WRITTEN.

2. \$4200; \$3360.
3. M's, 4550; N's, 3900.
4. 144 bu. corn; 90 bu. oats.
5. 750 bu. corn; 1750 bu. wheat.

Art. 691.

MENTAL.

2. 10; 15.
3. Vest, \$10; coat, \$26.
4. 1st, $49\frac{1}{2}$ gal.; 2d, $115\frac{1}{2}$ gal.

Art. 691.

WRITTEN.

2. 2000 bu.; 1800 bu.
3. 270; 240.
4. $40\frac{8}{13}$ lb. silver; $39\frac{5}{13}$ lb. lead.
5. \$1300; \$800.

Art. 692.

MENTAL.

2. 35 girls; 25 boys.
3. 4; 8; 12.
4. 300; 400; 500.
5. 32; 36.
6. $\frac{4}{7}$; $\frac{25}{36}$.
7. $\frac{5}{12}$; $\frac{1}{12}$.

Art. 692.

WRITTEN.

2. 14838 ft.; 17311 ft.
3. \$28800; \$36000.
4. \$12366; \$13740.
5. \$15056; \$26348; \$33876.
6. 3144 lb.; 2620 lb.
7. 4590; 5100; 6120.
8. \$1800; \$2000.
9. \$84504; \$88025; \$90540.
10. \$1980; \$2079; \$2200; \$2268.

Art. 694.

MENTAL.

2. 90. 4. 192.
3. 10. 5. \$80.
6. 2.

Art. 694.

WRITTEN.

2. 56. 6. \$18.60.
3. \$2.80. 7. \$10.80.
4. \$3.30. 8. 96.
5. 240. 9. $50\frac{3}{4}$ mo.
10. \$10.75$\frac{5}{8}$

Art. 697.

2. $84\frac{4}{5}$¢.
3. $76\frac{6}{7}$¢.
4. 12 car.
5. 79%.
6. $30.50.

Art. 698.

2. 6; 4; 2; 5.
3. 1; 1; 2; 2.
4. 1; 1; 3.
5. 27; 15; 15.
6. 9; 2; 3.
7. 40; 15; 5; 7.

Art. 699.

2. 16 of each.
3. 36 of each.
4. 20 lb. at 14¢; 32 lb. at 15¢.
5. 42 lb. at 70¢; 35 lb. at 50¢.
6. 250 3-cent; 50 5-cent; 50 10-cent.

Art. 700.

2. 8; 36; 20; 4.
3. 24; 18; 6; 18.
4. 40; 10; 20; 30.
5. 30; 18; 12; 42.
6. 800; 300; 100; 140.
7. 20 ones; 10 twos; 4 fives; 28 twenties.
8. Sheep, 5, 10, 15.
   Calves, 42, 24, 6.
   Pigs, 53, 66, 79.

Art. 704.

1. $16000.
2. $54.50.

3. $135.94\frac{58}{143}$.
   $94.05\frac{85}{143}$.

Art. 709.

2. $568.50.
3. $360.
4. $993.12½ less.

Art. 710.

2. $2880.
3. $4485.28 loss.
4. $2472.74.
5. Gain, $9256.97; $864.22.

Art. 719.

2. $5498.
3. $675.60.
4. $84.

Art. 720.

2. $2400; $4293.
3. $2400; $3328.
4. $4600; $5341.-08.
5. $500; $2960.

Art. 721.

2. $2597.427.
3. $3806.46.
4. A's $255.60.

Art. 722.

2. 23.43%.
3. 20.29%.

Art. 723.

2. $58.88; 9.25%.
3. Inst., 7.54%; gross, 9.47%.

Art. 743.

1. 1 A. 65 P.
2. 13 A. 57½ P.
3. 1737 A.
4. 29 A. 8 P.—

Art. 747.

1. 40 sq. yd.
2. 1248 A.
3. 88 A. 110 P.

Art. 748.

1. 36 sq. ft.
2. 146 sq. ft. 3 sq. in.
3. 15 sq. ft.
4. 34 A. 85 P.

Art. 749.

1. 35 sq. ft. 35 sq. in.
2. 72 A. 56 P.—

Art. 752.

1. 78.54 in.
2. 50.2656 rd.
3. 141.372 rd.

Art. 753.

1. 12.732 ft.
2. 25 ft.

Art. 754.

1. 490.875.
2. 1017.8784 sq. in.
3. 2578.23 sq. rd.

Art. 755.

1. 9.899 in.
2. 45.0158 in.

Art. 756.

1. 251.328 sq. in.
2. 23.562 sq. ft.

Art. 761.

1. 1050 sq. in.
2. 1090.66 sq. in.

Art. 762.

1. 270 cu. ft.
2. 2217.02 cu. in.

Art. 765.

1. 162 sq. ft.
2. 750 sq. ft.

Art. 766.

1. 1472 cu. ft.
2. 637.376 cu. ft.

Art. 769.

1. 226.1952 sq. ft.
2. 1884.96 sq. ft.

Art. 770.

1. 3015.936 cu. ft.
2. 418.88 cu. ft.

Art. 773.

1. 1280 sq. in.
2. 9.35935 sq. yd.

Art. 774.

1. 301.5936 cu. in.
2. 63.664 cu. ft.

Art. 777.

1. 960 sq. ft.
2. 628.32 sq. ft.

Art. 778.

1. 95 cu. in.
2. 5277.888 cu. ft.

Art. 781.

1. 1809.5616 sq. in.
2. 28952.9856 sq. in.

Art. 782.

1. 113.0976 cu. in.
2. Surface, 201062400 sq. mi.; contents, 268083200000 solid mi.

Art. 783.

1. 12.124 in.

Art. 800.

1. $4.825.
2. 9.16\frac{3}{4}$.
3. 80.31 fr.
4. 195.595 fr.
5. 185.184 gr.
6. 1 lb. 3 oz. 8 pwt. 23$\frac{19}{250}$ gr.
7. 2 lb. 2 oz. 190.49 gr.
8. 31.104 G.
9. 4479.004 G.
10. 5443 234 G.
11. 80.38 ft.
12. 149.3216 yd.
13. 109.73 M.
14. 3822.199 M.
15. 2 mi. 155 rd. 5 ft. 10 in.
16. 6195.9867 M.
17. 3.01 A.
18. 17043 sq. yd.
19. 12 A. 78.1312 P.
20. 1214.574 A.
21. 228.744 A.
22. 1624.5636 cu. ft.
23. 7585.2993 cu. ft.
24. 3.624 S.
25. 12.458 S.
26. 9 gal. 2 qt.
27. 11 gal. 3 qt. 1 pt.
28. 90.844 L.
29. 138.16 L.
30. 229.07 L.
31. 1 bu. 3 pk. 3 qt.

Page 421.

1. 400.
2. $54.625.
3. 16.40\frac{5}{8}$.
4. $10.546+.
5. 124559.9 lb.
6. $1875.
7. 36.75.
8. 459.77+.
9. 4.555 days.
10. 112.
11. 195.54— fr.
12. $10185.90.
13. 160 kilometers.
14. $476.80.
15. 4800 kilometers.
16. 66.91\frac{1}{4}$.
17. 20 hours.
18. 12 hours.
19. $5.71+.
20. $13475.

Page 422.

1. $653.89.
2. $2.46.
3. $316.48.
4. $26.80.
5. $357.
6. $369.78.
7. $92.40.

NOTE.—For answers to GAUGING and REVIEW of MENSURATION see page 280.

PART IV

ARITHMETICAL ANALYSIS.

MENTAL AND WRITTEN EXERCISES.

Many of these problems are so old, and present such an excellent combination of conditions as to be regarded as classic. No one can claim to be a good arithmetician, who cannot readily solve them. They are named from the first problem in the case, which is the earliest form in which they appeared.

The first and second problems in each case may be solved mentally, the others on the slate or blackboard. These problems will be found to afford a most valuable drill for those who have time for them.

CASE I.

Working Problems.

1. A can do a piece of work in 4 days, and B can do it in 6 days; in what time can both do it?

SOLUTION.—If A can do it in 4 days, in 1 day he can do $\frac{1}{4}$ of it; and if B can do it in 6 days, in 1 day he can do $\frac{1}{6}$ of it, and they together can do $\frac{1}{4}$ plus $\frac{1}{6}$, which is $\frac{5}{12}$ of it, in 1 day; hence they will do $\frac{1}{12}$ of in $\frac{1}{5}$ of a day, and they will do $\frac{12}{12}$ of it in $\frac{12}{5}$, or $2\frac{2}{5}$ days.

2. A can build a boat in 8 days and B in 12 days; in what time can they together build it? *Ans.* $4\frac{4}{5}$ days.

3. A quantity of flour lasts a man and wife 9 days, and the wife alone 27 days; how long would it last the man alone? *Ans.* $13\frac{1}{2}$ days.

4. A, B, and C can mow a field in 8 days, A and B can do it in 12 days, B and C in 15 days; in what time could each alone do it? *Ans.* A, $17\frac{1}{7}$; B, 40; C, 24.

CASE II.

Laboring Problems.

1. A receives $3 a day for his labor, and pays $1 a day for his board, and at the expiration of 50 days has saved $70; how many days was he idle?

SOLUTION.—Had he labored the 50 days he could have saved 50 times $2, or $100, hence he lost by his idleness $100 — $70, or $30. Each day he was idle he lost $3, hence to lose $30 he must have been idle as many days as $3 is contained times in $30, which is 10 days.

2. A agrees to labor for $2.50 on condition that he should forfeit 50 ct. every day he is idle; at the end of 100 days he receives $190; how many days was he idle? *Ans.* 20.

3. A boy agreed to carry 150 oranges to market for $1\frac{1}{2}$ ct. each, on condition that he should forfeit 4 ct. for each one he ate; he received $1.70; how many did he eat? *Ans.* 10.

4. A girl agreed to carry 80 glasses to the depot for $2\frac{1}{2}$ cents each, on condition that she should forfeit $12\frac{1}{2}$ ct. for every one she broke; she received 20 ¢t.; required the number she carried safely. *Ans.* 68.

CASE III.

Sea Water Problems.

1. If 80 lb. of sea water contain 2 lb. of salt, how much fresh water must be added to these 80 lb. so that 10 lb. of the new mixture may contain $\frac{1}{6}$ of a pound of salt?

SOLUTION.—If 10 lb. of the mixture contain $\frac{1}{6}$ lb. of salt, to contain 1 lb. of salt will require 6 times 10 lb. or 60 lb. of the mixture, and to contain 2 lb. of salt it will require 2 times 60 lb., or 120 lb.; hence there must be added 120 lb. — 80 lb., or 40 lb.

2. If 100 lb. of sea water contain 3 lb. of salt, how much water must be added to these 100 lb. so that 20 lb. of the new mixture may contain $\frac{1}{2}$ lb. of salt? *Ans.* 20 lb.

3. In a mixture of silver and copper consisting of 60 oz. there are 4 oz. of copper; how much silver must be added that there may be $\frac{3}{8}$ oz. of copper in 12 oz. of the mixture? *Ans.* 12 oz.

4. In a mixture of gold and silver consisting of 100 oz. there are 6 oz. of silver; how much gold must be added that there may be $\frac{3}{8}$ oz. of silver to 10 oz. of gold? *Ans.* 56 oz.

CASE IV.

Cow Problems.

1. Suppose that for every 4 cows a farmer has he should plow an acre of land, and allow one acre of pasture for every 2 cows; how many cows could he keep on 30 acres?

SOLUTION.—If for 4 cows he plows 1 acre, for 1 cow he plows $\frac{1}{4}$ of an acre; and if for 2 cows he pastures an acre, for 1 cow he pastures $\frac{1}{2}$ of an acre; hence 1 cow requires $\frac{1}{4} + \frac{1}{2}$ or $\frac{3}{4}$ of an acre, and on 30 acres he could keep as many cows as $\frac{3}{4}$ is contained times in 30, or 40 cows.

2. Suppose that for every 5 cows a farmer has he plows 1 acre of land, and allows 1 acre of pasture for every 4 cows; how many cows could he keep on 54 acres? *Ans.* 120 cows.

3. Suppose that for every 6 cows a farmer has he plows 2 acres, and pastures 2 acres for every 10 cows; how many cows could he keep on 64 acres? *Ans.* 120 cows.

4. A farmer has 110 acres; he plows 3 acres for 7 cows and pastures 4 acres for 9 cows; how many cows did he keep, and how many sheep, if $\frac{2}{3}$ of the number of cows equals $\frac{2}{5}$ of the number of sheep? *Ans.* 126 cows; 210 sheep.

CASE V.

Combination Problems.

1. A has $80 in gold and silver, and for every $3 of gold he has $2 of silver; how much gold must be added that for every $4 of gold there may be $2 of silver?

SOLUTION.—Since the gold is to the silver as 3 to 2, we find there are $48 of gold and $32 of silver. After the addition to the gold, there will be twice as much gold as silver, hence there will be 2 times $32, or $64 of gold, and hence there was added $64 — $48, or $16 of gold.

2. A boy has 150 apples and pears, and he has twice as many apples as pears; how many apples must he buy to have three times as many apples as pears? *Ans.* 50.

3. A farmer has 100 ducks and geese; for every 2 ducks he has 3 geese; how many ducks must he buy that he may have 2 ducks to 1 goose? *Ans.* 80.

4. A drover has 280 animals, consisting of horses and cows; and for every 3 horses there are 4 cows; how many cows must he sell that there may be 4 horses to 3 cows?

Ans. 70.

CASE VI.

Fish Problems.

1. The head of a fish is 20 inches long, the tail is as long as the head and $\frac{1}{2}$ of the body, and the body as long as the head and tail both; required the length of the fish.

SOLUTION.—By the conditions, $\frac{1}{2}$ of the length of the body, plus 20 inches, equals the length of the tail, and this, plus 20 inches, the length of the head, equals $\frac{1}{2}$ of the length of the body, plus 40 inches, which equals $\frac{2}{2}$ of the length of the body; then $\frac{2}{2}$ of the length of the body minus $\frac{1}{2}$ of the length of the body, which is $\frac{1}{2}$ of the length of the body, equals 40 inches; the length of the body equals 2 times 40 inches, or 80 inches, and since the body is as long as the head and tail both, the length of the fish equals twice 80 inches or 160 inches.

2. The head of a fish is 24 inches long, the tail is as long as the head plus $\frac{1}{3}$ of the length of the body, and the body is as long as the head and tail both; required the length of the fish. *Ans.* 144 inches.

3. The tail of a fish weighs 12 ounces, the head weighs as much as the tail plus $\frac{1}{4}$ of the body, and the body weighs as much as the head and tail both; required the weight of the fish. *Ans.* 64 oz.

4. The tail of a fish weighs 36 ounces, the head weighs 12 ounces more than the tail plus $\frac{2}{5}$ of the body, and the body weighs as much as the head and tail; required the weight of the fish. *Ans.* $17\frac{1}{2}$ lb.

CASE VII.

Boat Problems.

1. Twelve men hire a boat for sailing, but by taking in 8 more persons the expense of each is diminished by $\$\frac{1}{2}$; what did the boat cost?

SOLUTION.—If the expense of 1 is diminished $\$\frac{1}{2}$, the expense of 12 is diminished 12 times $\$\frac{1}{2}$, which is \$6, which the 8 men pay. If 8 men pay \$6, one man pays $\frac{1}{8}$ of \$6, which is $\$\frac{3}{4}$, and 12 + 8, or 20 men, pay 20 times $\$\frac{3}{4}$, which is \$15. Hence they paid \$15 for the boat.

2. Sixteen men hire a coach for a certain sum, but by taking in 4 more persons the expense of each is diminished $\$\frac{1}{8}$; what did they pay for the coach? *Ans.* \$10.

3. A company of 12 persons agree to buy a manufactory, but 4 of the company withdrawing, the investment of each is increased \$480; what did the manufactory cost?

Ans \$11520.

4. A company of 50 persons engage dinner at a hotel, but before paying the bill 10 of the company withdraw, by which each person's bill was increased 25 ct.; what was the bill?

Ans. \$50.

CASE VIII.

Coach Problems.

1. How far may a person ride in a coach going at the rate of 12 miles an hour, provided he is gone but 10 hours, and walks back at the rate of 8 miles an hour?

SOLUTION.—If he goes 12 miles an hour, he will go 1 mile in $\frac{1}{12}$ of an hour, and if he returns 8 miles an hour, he will return 1 mile in $\frac{1}{8}$ of an hour; hence to go and return a mile, takes $\frac{1}{12}+\frac{1}{8}$, or $\frac{5}{24}$ of a hour. Therefore in 10 hours he can go and return as many miles as $\frac{5}{24}$ is contained times in 10, or 48 miles.

2. How far may a person ride in a carriage, going at the rate of 8 miles an hour, provided he is gone 11 hours and walks back at the rate of 3 miles an hour? *Ans.* 24 mi.

3. How far may I ride in the cars, going at the rate of 24 miles an hour, supposing I am gone 14 hours, and return at the rate of 4 miles an hour? *Ans.* 48 miles.

4. A boat whose rate of sailing is 12 miles an hour sails down a river whose current is 3 miles an hour; how far may it go that it may be gone 16 hours? *Ans.* 90 miles.

CASE IX.

Animal Problems, First Class.

1. A farmer bought a certain number of sheep for $400; had he bought 20 more for $3 less each they would have cost $500; how many did he buy?

SOLUTION.—By the conditions of the problem, the 20 more at $3 less each, cost $500 — $400, or $100, hence one at $3 less each cost $\frac{1}{20}$ of $100, or $5, hence the price of those purchased was $5+$3, or $8; and since all cost $400 he purchased as many as $8 is contained times in $400, which are 50.

2. A farmer bought a certain number of cows for $1000; had he bought 22 more for $5 less each they would have cost $1440; how many did he buy? *Ans.* 40.

3. A drover bought a certain number of horses for $4500; had he bought 10 more at $15 more each they would have cost $6150; how many did he buy? *Ans.* 30.

4. A drover bought a certain number of mules for $18000; had he bought 15 more at $20 less each they would have cost $20700; how many did he buy? *Ans.* 90.

CASE X.

Cup and Cover Problems.

1. A person has 2 silver cups, and only one cover for both. The first cup weighs 12 ounces. If the first cup be covered, it will weigh twice as much as the second, but if the second cup be covered it will weigh 3 times as much as the first; required the weight of the second cup and cover

SOLUTION.—By the last condition of the problem 3 times 12 ounces, or 36 ounces, equals the weight of the second cup and cover, which, added to 12 ounces, the weight of the first cup, equals 48 ounces, the weight of the two cups and the cover. By the second condition of the problem, twice the weight of the second cup equals the weight of the first cup and cover, which, added to the weight of the second cup, equals 3 times the weight of the second cup, which equals the weight of all, or 48 ounces. If 3 times the weight of the second cup equals 48 ounces, etc.

2. A farmer bought a horse, colt, and saddle; if the horse be saddled it will be worth 4 times as much as the colt, and if the colt be saddled it will be worth $\frac{1}{3}$ as much as the horse; what is the value of each, if the colt is worth $60?

Ans. Horse, $225; Saddle, $15.

3. A man bought a house, store, and barn; the barn cost $1200, the house and store cost 5 times as much as the barn, and the store cost $\frac{1}{3}$ as much as the house and barn; required the cost of each. *Ans.* House, $4200; Store, $1800.

4. A lady has two silver cups and only one cover for both; the first cup weighs 20 ounces, and if the first cup be covered it will weigh 3 times as much as the second, but if the second cup be covered it will weigh 4 times as much as the first; required the weight of the second cup and cover.

Ans. Cup, 25 oz.; cover, 55 oz.

CASE XI.

Chess Problems.

1. A, at a game of chess, won $120, and then lost $\frac{1}{4}$ of what he had, and then found he had 3 times as much as at first; how much had he at first?

SOLUTION.—After losing $\frac{1}{4}$ there remained $\frac{3}{4}$ of what he had after winning, which was 3 times what he had at first, and once what he had at first is $\frac{1}{4}$ of what he then had; hence the difference between $\frac{3}{4}$ and $\frac{1}{4}$

of what he had after winning $120, equals what he had increased his money; hence ¾ of what he had after winning equals $120, and ¼ of what he then had, which is what he at first had, is ⅓ of $120, or $40.

2. A lady at a game of chess won $450, and then lost ⅓ of what she had, and then found she had 4 times as much as at first; how much had she at first? *Ans.* $90.

3. A merchant lost $1400 of his stock, and the next year gained ⅘ as much as remained, and then had ¾ as much as at first; how much was his stock at first? *Ans.* $2400.

4. A and B in business lost $2600, and the next year gained ⅔ as much of their stock as remained, and then had ⅘ as much as at first; how much had each at first, their shares being as 2 to 3? *Ans.* A, $2000; B, $3000.

CASE XII.

Animal Problems, Second Class.

1. A man bought a number of sheep for $1200; 20 of them having died, he sold ¾ of the remainder for cost and received $600; how many did he buy?

SOLUTION.—If ¾ of the remainder cost $600, ¼ of the remainder cost $200, and 4/4 of the remainder cost $800. Since all cost $1200, the 20 cost $1200—$800, or $400, hence one cost $20, and for $1200 he bought 60.

2. A farmer bought a number of hens for $37.50; 18 of them having died, he sold ⅔ of the remainder for cost and received $19; how many did he buy? *Ans.* 75.

3. A drover bought a number of cows for $6250; 50 of them having died, he sold ⅗ of the remainder for cost and received $3000; how many did he buy? *Ans.* 250.

4. A bought a number of horses, and having lost 20, he sold ⅔ of the remainder for cost and received $3360, which was $7440 less than all cost; how many did he retain?

Ans. 42.

CASE XIII.

Partnership Problems.

1. Two men, A and B, are in partnership and gain $1600; A owns ¼ of the stock, plus $2400, and gains $1000; required *the whole* stock and share of each.

SOLUTION.—If A had owned $\frac{1}{4}$ of the stock, his gain would have been $\frac{1}{4}$ of \$1600, or \$400, hence the \$2400 must gain the difference between \$1000 and \$400, which is \$600. If \$2400 gains \$600, to gain \$1 requires \$4, and to gain \$1600 will require 1600 times 4, or \$6400, etc.

2. A and B, in partnership, gain \$1650; A owns $\frac{2}{5}$ of the stock, plus \$300, and gains \$750; required the whole stock and share of each. *Ans.* A's, \$2500; B's, \$3000.

3. C and D, in partnership, gain \$800; C owns $\frac{3}{4}$ of the stock, lacking \$18000, and D's gain is \$560; required the entire stock and share of each.

Ans. C's, \$12000; D's, \$28000.

4. A, B, and C, in partnership, gain \$480; A owns $\frac{1}{4}$ of the stock, plus \$500, B's gain is \$120, and C's \$210; required the stock of each.

Ans. A's, \$2500; B's, \$2000; C's, \$3500.

CASE XIV.

Fox and Hound Problems.

1. A fox is 80 leaps before a hound, and takes 4 leaps while the hound takes 2, but 2 of the hound's leaps equal 5 of the fox's; how many leaps will the hound take to catch the fox?

SOLUTION.—For the fox to run as fast as the hound he must take 5 leaps while the hound takes 2, but he only takes 4 while the hound takes 2, hence the hound gains 5 minus 4, or 1 leap of the fox in taking 2 leaps, and to gain 80 of the fox's leaps he must take 160 leaps.

2. A hare is 120 leaps before a hound, and takes 5 leaps while the hound takes 3, but 3 of the hound's leaps equal 7 of the hare's; how many leaps will the hound take to catch the hare? *Ans.* 180.

3. A thief is 240 steps before an officer, and takes 5 steps to the officer's 4, but 2 of the officer's equal 3 of the thief's how many steps will each take before the thief is caught?

Ans. Officer, 960; Thief, 1200.

4. A boy is 95 steps before a man, and takes 3 steps to the man's 2, but 3 of the man's equal 6 of the boy's; how many steps will each take before being together?

Ans. Man, 190; Boy, 285.

CASE XV.

Time Problems, First Class.

1. What is the time of day, provided $\frac{1}{3}$ of the time past midnight equals the time to noon?

SOLUTION.—By the conditions of the problem, $\frac{1}{3}$ of the time past midnight, plus $\frac{3}{3}$ of the time past midnight, which is $\frac{4}{3}$ of the time past midnight, equals the time from midnight to noon, which is 12 hours; then $\frac{1}{3}$ of the time past midnight equals $\frac{1}{4}$ of 12 hours, or 3 hours, and $\frac{3}{3}$ of the time past midnight equals 9 hours; hence it is 9 o'clock in the morning.

2. What is the time of day, if $\frac{1}{5}$ of the time past noon equals the time to midnight? *Ans.* 10 P. M.

3. Required the time of day, supposing that the time past midnight equals $\frac{1}{2}$ of the time to noon. *Ans.* 4 A. M.

4. Required the time of day, provided the time past noon equals $\frac{2}{3}$ of the time to midnight. *Ans.* 48 min. past 4 P. M.

5 Required the time of day if $\frac{3}{5}$ of the time past midnight equals the time to midnight again. *Ans.* 3 P. M.

CASE XVI.

Age Problems, First Class.

1. A is 40 years old and B is 10 years old; in how many years will A be 3 times as old as B?

SOLUTION.—At the required time, 3 times B's age will equal A's age, then 3 times B's age, minus once B's age, which is 2 times B's age, equals the difference between their ages, which is 40—10, or 30 years, and once B's age at that time is $\frac{1}{2}$ of 30 years, which is 15 years. Hence, when B is 15 years old, A's age will be 3 times B's, but B is now 10 yr. old, hence in 15—10, or 5 years, A will be 3 times as old as B.

2. A is 28 years old and B is 4 years old; in how many years will A be 3 times as old as B? *Ans.* 8 yr.

3. M is 24 years old and N is 48 years old; in how many years will M be $\frac{4}{7}$ as old as N? *Ans.* 8 yr.

4. Mary is 18 years old, which is $\frac{3}{5}$ of her aunt's age; how long since the aunt was twice as old as Mary?

Ans. 6 yr.

5. Henry is 20 years old, which is $\frac{4}{7}$ of his uncle's age; how long since the uncle's age was $2\frac{1}{2}$ times Henry's?

Ans. 10 yr

CASE XVII.

Time Problems, Second Class.

1. What time after 2 o'clock are the hour and minute hands of a clock together?

SOLUTION.—The minute-hand gains on the hour-hand 12 − 1, or 11 spaces, in going 12 spaces; hence to gain 1 space it must go $\frac{1}{11}$ of 12 spaces, which is $\frac{12}{11}$, or $1\frac{1}{11}$ spaces, and to gain 2 spaces, the distance they are apart at 2 o'clock, it must go $2\frac{2}{11}$ spaces, which requires $10\frac{10}{11}$ minutes; hence the time is $10\frac{10}{11}$ minutes past 2.

2. At what time between 4 and 5 o'clock are the hour and minute hands of a watch together? *Ans.* $21\frac{9}{11}$ min. past 4.

3. At what time between 7 and 8 o'clock are the hour and minute hands of a watch together? *Ans.* $38\frac{2}{11}$ min. past 7.

4. In how many minutes after 4 o'clock will the hour and minute hands be 5 minute-spaces apart?

Ans. $16\frac{4}{11}$ min.; $27\frac{3}{11}$ min.

5. In how many minutes after 4 o'clock will the hour and minute hands be 5 minutes of time apart?

Ans. $16\frac{9}{11}$ min.; $26\frac{2}{11}$ min.

CASE XVIII.

Age Problems, Second Class.

1. A's age is 4 times B's age, but in 10 years A's age will be 2 times B's age; required the age of each.

SOLUTION.—By the first condition of the problem, 4 times B's age equals A's age, hence the difference of their ages is 3 times B's age, and once B's age equals $\frac{1}{3}$ of the *difference* of their ages; in 10 years, 2 times B's age equals A's age; hence B's age then equals the *difference* of their ages. Therefore, 10 years is the difference between $\frac{1}{3}$ of the *difference* of their ages, and the *difference* of their ages, or $\frac{2}{3}$ of the *difference* of their ages; and $\frac{3}{3}$, or the *difference* of their ages is $\frac{3}{2}$ of 10, or 15 years. If 3 times B's age, which equals the difference of their ages, equals 15 years, B's age is $\frac{1}{3}$ of 15 years, or 5 years, and A's age is 4 times 5, or 20 years.

2. C is 4 times as old as D, but in 12 years C will be 3 times as old as D; how old is each? *Ans.* 24 yr.; 96 yr.

3. R is $\frac{1}{3}$ as old as S, but in 14 years he will be $\frac{1}{2}$ as old; what is the age of each? *Ans.* R's, 14 yr.; S's, 42 yr.

4. Six years ago when I first met Mr. Wilson I was $\frac{1}{4}$ as old as he, but now I am $\frac{1}{3}$ as old; what is the age of each?

Ans. My age, 18 yr.; Mr. W's, 54 yr.

MISCELLANEOUS PROBLEMS.

These problems are designed both to test the pupils' knowledge of the subjects studied, and their powers of reasoning. They afford a good review of the work, and are to be used according to the needs of the pupil and the judgment of the teacher.

1. Find the greatest common divisor of 847, 1331, and 1573. *Ans.* 121.

2. Find the least common multiple of 78, 156, 260, and 520. *Ans.* 1560.

3. What is the value of $\frac{3}{4}+\frac{5}{6}+\frac{7}{8}$ diminished by $\frac{1}{4}+\frac{1}{6}+\frac{3}{10}$? *Ans.* $1\frac{17}{120}$.

4. What is the value of $\frac{7}{10}+\frac{17}{20}-\frac{19}{30}$ divided by $\frac{2}{3}+\frac{4}{5}-\frac{5}{6}$? *Ans.* $1\frac{17}{36}$.

5. Find the value of $\frac{15}{16}\times\frac{17}{21}\times\frac{19}{36}$ divided by $\frac{38}{63}\times\frac{17}{24}\times\frac{45}{68}$. *Ans.* $1\frac{5}{16}$.

6. What part of $3\frac{3}{4}$ is $2\frac{2}{5}$? Of $7\frac{3}{5}$ is $5\frac{1}{15}$? *Ans.* $\frac{16}{25}$; $\frac{2}{3}$.

7. Add $3\frac{1}{2}$ of $\frac{1}{8}$, $\frac{3\frac{1}{2}}{14}$, and $\frac{1}{2}$ of $\frac{16\frac{2}{3}}{26\frac{2}{3}}$. *Ans.* 1.

8. Add $\frac{\frac{3}{7}}{10}$ of $13\frac{2}{3}$, $\frac{6\frac{3}{7}}{15}$ of $2\frac{2}{3}$, and $\frac{14}{15}$ of $3\frac{1}{7}$. *Ans.* $4\frac{19}{42}$.

9. Subtract $\frac{2}{3}$ of $\frac{3}{5}$ of $9\frac{1}{6}$ from $\frac{5\frac{2}{3\frac{1}{3}}}{18}$ of $\frac{6}{7}$ of 56. *Ans.* $11\frac{4}{15}$.

10. Multiply $\frac{8}{9}$ of $\frac{5\frac{1}{2}}{11}$ of $\frac{6\frac{2}{3}}{12}$ by $24\frac{9}{15}$ of $\frac{7\frac{1}{2}}{10}$. *Ans.* $4\frac{5}{9}$.

11. Multiply $\frac{21}{22}$ of $\frac{14\frac{1}{3}}{20}$ by $\frac{5}{8}$ of $\frac{3}{10}$ of $\frac{9\frac{3}{4}}{13}$ of 100. *Ans.* $9\frac{873}{1408}$.

12. $\left(\frac{\frac{1}{3}+\frac{2}{5}}{3\frac{1}{5}}-\frac{8\frac{7}{16}}{115}\right)\div\left(3\times\frac{3}{81\frac{6}{19}}\right)=$ what? *Ans.* $1\frac{719477}{1578200}$.

13. $\left(\frac{2\frac{5}{18}}{6\frac{5}{6}}+\frac{3\frac{1}{9}}{6\frac{5}{6}}-\frac{4\frac{7}{48}}{24\frac{7}{8}}\right)\times 3\frac{2\frac{13}{16}}{\frac{3\frac{1}{2}}{9}}\div\frac{\frac{1}{16}+\frac{9}{27}-\frac{13}{48}}{\frac{39}{56}\times 1\frac{2}{5}\div 2\frac{3}{5}}=$ what? *Ans.* $18\frac{27}{41}$.

14. What number, when multiplied by $\left(50-\frac{100}{3}+\frac{7\frac{1}{3}}{4\frac{1}{2}}\right)$, will give the product $13\frac{13}{189}$? *Ans.* $\frac{5}{7}$.

15. $3\frac{6\frac{2}{3}}{11\frac{3}{7}}+\frac{5\frac{5}{9}}{28\frac{4}{7}}-.83\frac{1}{3}-\frac{7\frac{1}{2}}{37\frac{1}{2}}$ of $\frac{2\frac{1}{2}}{2\frac{2}{5}}+2\frac{19}{36}=$ what?

Ans. $5\frac{19}{72}$.

16. $\frac{40}{5.6\frac{2}{3}}\times\frac{31.16\frac{4}{6}}{15.1\frac{2}{3}}\times\frac{9.8}{16\frac{1}{2}}\times\frac{10\frac{1.25}{1\frac{1}{2}}}{2.3\frac{1}{3}}+9.2\frac{1}{5}-\frac{9\frac{3}{7}}{4.28\frac{4}{7}}=$ what?

Ans. $47\frac{1}{50}$.

17. Divide $(.101+.5\frac{1}{4}-.3\frac{1}{8})\times\frac{.04\frac{1}{6}}{.1\frac{2}{3}}$ by $.8\frac{4\frac{1}{5}}{.6}$.

Ans. .05225.

18. How many miles in 1580 chains? *Ans.* $19\frac{3}{4}$ miles.

19. How many dollars in £24 16 s. 9 d.? *Ans.* $120.87.

20. How many pounds Troy are there in 432 pounds Avoirdupois? *Ans.* 525 lb.

21. In 752 gallons of wine measure how many gallons of the old beer measure? *Ans.* 616 gal.

22. How many days from January 1st, 1860, to January 1st, 1885? *Ans.* 9132.

23. On what day of the week did the 19th century begin?

Ans. Thursday.

24. If a telegram is sent from Philadelphia, 75° 9′ 5″ W. long. to San Francisco, 122° 26′ 15″ W., at 9 h. 30 min. P. M., at what hour will it be received at the office in San Francisco? *Ans.* 6 h. 20 min. $51\frac{1}{3}$ sec. P. M.

25. A turnpike 40 ft. wide was run through a township; how many acres per mile did it occupy? *Ans.* $4\frac{28}{33}$ A.

26. Mr. Jones has a cylindrical cistern 8 ft. 6 in. in diameter, and 5 ft. 9 in. deep; how many hogsheads of water does it contain? *Ans.* 38.74+ hhd.

27. The house to which the above cistern belongs is 40 ft. long and 34 ft. wide, the eaves projecting 6 in. on each side, and all the water falling on the roof is conducted to the cistern; to what depth would it be filled by a shower in which $\frac{7}{8}$ of an inch of rain falls, and how many inches of rain would fill the cistern? *Ans.* 1 ft. $10\frac{1}{8}$+ in.; $2\frac{48}{55}$ in.

28. 295 is $62\frac{1}{2}\%$ of what number? *Ans.* 472.

29. What is $33\frac{1}{3}\%$ of $4\frac{1}{2}$; also $\frac{3}{5}\%$ of $\frac{50}{51}$? *Ans.* $1\frac{1}{2}$; $\frac{1}{170}$.

30. A lady lost $750, which was 25% of what she then had; how much had she at first? *Ans.* $3750.

31. What per cent. of $3\frac{3}{5}$ is $\frac{3}{5}$; and what per cent. of $3\frac{5}{7}$ is $\frac{13}{14}$? *Ans.* $16\frac{2}{3}\%$; 25%.

32. What is the interest on $680 for 5 yr. 10 mo. 12 da., at 7 per cent.? *Ans.* $279.25.

33. What principal will in 5 yr. 10 mo. 15 da., at 6%, give $456.84 interest? *Ans.* $1296.

34. In what time will $4080, at 5 per cent., give $668.10 interest? *Ans.* 3 yr. 3 mo. 9 da.

35. At what per cent. will $9876, in 6 yr. 2 mo. 12 da., give $5510.808 interest? *Ans.* 9%.

36. What are the contents in liquid measure of a tin pan, whose height is 5 inches, upper diameter 17 inches, and lower diameter 9 in.? *Ans.* $2\frac{4}{7}+$ gal.

37. I have a bin 8 ft. 3 in. long, 3 ft. 6 in. wide, and 4 ft. 9 in. deep, filled with corn in the ear; how many bushels are there (Art. 371, note), and how many bushels when shelled, if 2 bushels on the ear make 1 bushel when shelled? *Ans.* $87\frac{39}{50}$ bu.; $43\frac{89}{100}$ bu.

38. What is my annual rate of profit on a ten-acre wood-lot, which cost $100, the yearly growth of wood averaging 1 cord to the acre, and the market price $4.25 a cord, the cutting and hauling costing 75¢ a cord? *Ans.* 35%.

39. I have a yard 100 feet square, which I wish to pave, making a flagged walk 6 ft. wide around the outside at 75¢ a square yard, and paving the rest with bricks at $9 ℘ M., allowing 4 bricks to the square foot; what will be the whole cost? *Ans.* $466.78.

40. Mr. Snyder has a garden containing $1\frac{3}{4}$ acres, whose width is 180 ft.; it is enclosed with a brick wall 8 ft. 6 in. high and 9 in. thick, in which there are 2 doors, each 6 ft. 3 in. by 4 ft., and a gateway 12 ft. wide; what will be the cost of the wall at $10 ℘ M. for the bricks, and $2 ℘ M. for the labor? *Ans.* $1698.746.

41. A sold 20% of his land to B, and 25% of the remainder to C, and then had 120 acres; how much had he at first? *Ans.* 200 acres.

42. A man bought 40 shares of stock, which is 25% of what he already had; now if he sells 80 shares, the remainder is what per cent. of his first number? *Ans.* 75%.

43. The sum of A's and B's money is $2800, and 25% of A's equals $33\frac{1}{3}$% of B's; how much has each? *Ans.* A, $1600; B, $1200.

44. A sold two dwellings for $3600 each; on one he gained 20%, and on the other he lost 20%; what was his gain or loss? *Ans.* Loss, $300.

45. Cynthia's money is 25% more than Florence's money; then Florence's money is how many per cent. less than Cynthia's? *Ans.* 20%.

46. Miss Poole sold her piano for $360, and cleared $\frac{1}{8}$ of this money; what % would she have gained by selling it for 5% more than she received? *Ans.* 26%.

47. A man owns 80 shares of bank stock, at $50 each; the company declares a 5% dividend, payable in stock; how many shares will he then own? *Ans.* 84 shares.

48. Mrs. Clark receives $300, payable in stock, as her share of a 4 per cent. dividend; how many shares, at $50 each, will she then own? *Ans.* 156 shares.

49. Mrs. Davis received 10 shares and $45 in money as her share of a 5% dividend; how many shares, at $50 each, did she then own? *Ans.* 228 shares.

50. Miss Willard sold her house and lot for $5000, receiving $1\frac{2}{3}$ as much for the house as the lot; on the lot she gained 4 per cent. and on the house lost 4 per cent.; what was the gain or loss? *Ans.* No gain or loss.

51. A sold B 40 sheep, which was 50% of what B already had and 25% of what A had remaining; A afterward sold B 40 more; now what per cent. of B's number equals A's number? *Ans.* 75%.

52. William gave 80 words to Mary to spell, which was $66\frac{2}{3}$% of the number Mary gave William; now if she had given 40 less and he 40 more, what per cent. of those he gave would equal what she gave? *Ans.* $66\frac{2}{3}\%$.

53. Mr. B exchanged 56 shares of bank stock ($50), at $2\frac{1}{2}\%$ discount, for 40 shares of gas stock ($100), at $1\frac{1}{2}\%$ premium, paying the balance in cash; how much cash did he pay? *Ans.* $1330.

54. Harold bought 30 shares of stock, $50 each, at 97%; he sold $\frac{1}{3}$ of it at $99\frac{1}{2}\%$, and the remainder at $101\frac{1}{2}\%$; what did he gain? *Ans.* $57.50.

55. A broker bought for me 45 shares of stock ($50), at $48\frac{3}{4}$; what did it cost me, brokerage $\frac{1}{4}\%$? *Ans.* $2199\frac{3}{8}$.

56. My agent bought some horses for me; he paid $250 for keeping, his commission was $375, and entire bill $15625; what was the rate? *Ans.* $2\frac{1}{2}\%$.

57. I sold goods on commission at 6% through a broker who charged me 2%; my commission after paying the brokerage was $468; required the sum paid to my employers. *Ans.* $10998.

58. An agent buys goods on commission at $2\frac{1}{2}\%$, charging $1\frac{1}{2}\%$ for the money; the agent charges his employer $224; what was the amount of goods bought? *Ans.* $5600.

59. An agent receives 4% commission and $2\frac{1}{2}\%$ for guaranteeing payment; he remits to his employer $7480; what does the agent receive? *Ans.* $520.

60. The amount of a certain principal for a certain time at 4% is $819, and at 8% for the same time is $988; required the time and the principal. *Ans.* $6\frac{1}{2}$ yr.; $650.

61. What is the difference between the true discount and the bank discount of $1200 for 2 years, 9 months, 15 days, at 8 per cent.? *Ans.* $49.73.

62. A man owes $1800, $\frac{1}{3}$ of which is due in 1 yr., $\frac{1}{2}$ of the remainder in 2 yr., and the remainder in 3 yr.; required the present value, money worth 6%. *Ans.* $1610.225.

63. Required the difference between the simple interest and compound interest of $800 for 16 years, 8 months, at 6 per cent. *Ans.* $513.57.

64. Required the cost of a 3 mo. draft on Philadelphia,

exchange at $\frac{3}{4}$% discount, which will pay a debt of $950, money worth 6%. *Ans.* $928.63.

65. My agent sold $6000 worth of goods on commission at 3%, and remits to me the proceeds in a draft bought at $\frac{1}{2}$% premium, which I sell at $\frac{3}{4}$% premium; what did the goods bring me in? *Ans.* $5834.47.

66. Wishing to pay a debt of $960 in Boston, I bought a draft in New York for 2 mo., interest at 6%, exchange at a premium of $\frac{1}{8}$%; what was the cost? *Ans.* $951.12.

67. A, B, and C in partnership gained $3600; A's stock was $5000, B's $6000, and C's gain $1400; required C's stock and A's and B's gain.

Ans. C's, $7000; A's, $1000; B's, $1200.

68. A, B, and C enter into partnership with a capital of $240000; A's stock was $65000, B's gain $3400, and C's gain $3600; required A's gain and B's and C's stock.

Ans. A's gain, $2600; B's stock, $85000; C's stock, $90000.

69. A's capital was in trade 10 mo., B's 15 mo., and C's 18 mo.; A's gain was $1250, B's gain was $1500, C's gain $1350, and the whole capital $6000; what was the capital of each? *Ans.* A's, $2500; B's, $2000; C's, $1500.

70. A and B agree to do a piece of work for $310; A sends 20 men for 12 days and B sends 25 boys for 15 days; what shall each receive, if 3 men do as much as 5 boys?

Ans. A, $160; B, $150.

71. A, B, and C entered into partnership and gained $740; A had $1200 in trade 9 mo., B $1400 in trade 8 mo., and C $1500 in trade 10 mo.; what was the gain of each?

Ans. A's, $216; B's, $224; C's, $300.

72. A borrowed $1200 for 6 mo. and $1500 for 8 mo.; at the end of 4 mo. he paid $2000; when, in equity, should the remainder be paid? *Ans.* 1 yr. 4 mo.

73. A has a sum of money consisting of 3-cent, 5-cent, and 25-cent pieces, which he wishes to exchange for 10-cent pieces; how many of each kind must he take?

Ans. 15 3-ct.; 3 5-ct.; 8 25-ct.

74. A man has bank-notes of $2, $5, $20, and $50, which

he wishes to exchange for 54 ten-dollar notes; how many must he exchange of each kind?

Ans. 30 \$2; 12 \$5; 6 \$20: 6 \$50.

75. A boy has 400 apples in a basket, which he takes out and arranges in a row two feet apart, the first apple being 2 ft. from the basket; how far did he travel, stopping at last at his basket? *Ans.* 320800 ft.

76. What is the distance between the opposite corners of a parallelopipedon 20 inches long, 15 inches wide, and 12 inches high? *Ans.* 27.73 in.

77. A has a circular garden whose diameter is 15 rods, and B has a circular garden whose area is $2\frac{7}{9}$ times as great; what is the diameter of B's garden? *Ans.* 25 rods.

78. A and B start from one corner of a field one mile square; A goes by the walk around and B goes straight across to the opposite corner, where they meet; how much farther did A go than B? *Ans.* 187.452 rods.

79. A man has a lot of land 32 rods long, which contains one acre; required its width. *Ans.* 5 rods.

80. A garrison consisting of 960 men was provisioned for 8 months, but at the end of 6 months they dismissed so many men that the provisions lasted 6 months longer; how many men were sent away? *Ans.* 640.

81. How many square inches in the entire surface of a cube whose dimensions are 15 inches? *Ans.* 1350.

82. Divide \$5000 among A, B, and C, so that A shall have $\frac{2}{3}$ as much as B, and C shall have $\frac{2}{3}$ as much as A and B both. *Ans.* A, \$1200; B, \$1800; C, \$2000.

83. A has a circular garden and B a square one; the distance around each is 64 rods; which contains the most land, and how much? *Ans.* A's, 69.939 sq. rd.

84. Two men, A and B, gain $12\frac{1}{2}\%$ on their stock, and then 20% of A's gain equals \$520, and $\frac{2}{3}$ of B's stock equals $\frac{3}{4}$ of A's; what is the stock of each? *Ans.* \$20800; \$23400.

85. A bought stock 25 per cent. below par and sold it 20 per cent. above par; how much did he invest, if he gained \$1920? *Ans.* \$3200.

86. A at a game of chance won a certain sum, then lost $\frac{2}{3}$ as much as he won, and then won $\frac{1}{4}$ as much as he lost, and had $24 more than at first; how much did he win at first?
Ans. $48.

87. A and B lost $1680, and next year gained $\frac{3}{4}$ as much as remained, and then had $\frac{7}{8}$ as much as at first; how much had each at first, if $\frac{3}{4}$ of A's equals $\frac{6}{7}$ of B's?
Ans. A, $1792; B, $1568.

88. Mary has a circular garden, and Sarah has a square one, and they each contain 4 acres; how much farther around is one than the other? *Ans.* 11.514 rods.

89. Thompson asked for flour 20 per cent. more than cost, but sold it for 90 per cent. of the price asked; what did he gain per cent.? *Ans.* 8%.

90. What must I ask for goods which cost 40 cents a yard, that after falling $33\frac{1}{3}$ per cent. I may gain 10% on the value? *Ans.* 66¢.

91. If I retail flour at a gain of 25%, and sell at wholesale for 4% less than at retail, what is my gain per cent. at wholesale? *Ans.* 20%.

92. A and B constructed 428 miles of railroad, and 3 times the number of miles A made, plus 32 miles, is to 4 times the number B made, minus 24 miles, as $\frac{2}{3}$ to $\frac{3}{4}$; how many miles did each build? *Ans.* A, 224; B, 204.

93. B's loss at wholesale was 5 per cent., and his retail price was 20 per cent. more than his wholesale price; what was his gain at retail? *Ans.* 14%.

94. C's retail gain is $12\frac{1}{2}$%, and his retail price is 5% of his wholesale more than his wholesale price; what is his gain at wholesale? *Ans.* $7\frac{1}{7}$%.

95. D lost 20% of a cargo of flour, and sold the remainder at a gain of 40%; did he gain or lose on the investment, and how much per cent.? *Ans.* 12%.

96. A barrel of vinegar leaked away 25%; what per cent. must I gain on the remainder that I may gain 10 per cent. on the cost of the vinegar? *Ans.* $46\frac{2}{3}$%.

97. A farmer bought 20 turkeys for $12, and lost 20% of

them; how must the remainder be sold to gain $12\frac{1}{2}\%$ by the transaction? *Ans.* $84\frac{3}{8}$¢ apiece.

98. Mr. Peters has a granary in the form of a cube, which will contain 4500 bushels of wheat; required the length of the granary. *Ans.* 17.76 ft.

99. If a ball 7 inches in diameter weigh $13\frac{1}{3}$ lb., what is the diameter of a ball which weighs $106\frac{2}{3}$ lb., provided the materials of both are the same? *Ans.* 14 inches.

100. The amount of B's money for 8 yr. at 6 per cent. is $5100 more than the interest of his money for 10 yr. at 8 per cent.; required B's money. *Ans.* $7500.

101. A man owns 342 acres of land, and twice the number of acres of meadow land is to three times the number of acres of forest land, minus 50 acres, as $\frac{4}{5}$ to $\frac{5}{6}$; required the number of each. *Ans.* 150 A., forest; 192 A., meadow.

102. A man having $100 spent a portion of it, and then earned 5 times as much as he spent, and then had twice as much as at first; how much did he spend? *Ans.* $25.

103. $\frac{2}{3}$ of A's fortune, plus $\frac{3}{4}$ of B's, being on interest for 7 yr. at 6%, amounts to $59640; what is the fortune of each, if they are as $\frac{1}{2}$ to $\frac{1}{3}$? *Ans.* A's, $36000; B's, $24000.

104. A, B, and C can do a piece of work in 24 days, A and B in 36 days, and A and C in 48 days; in how many days can each do it? *Ans.* A, 144 da.; B, 48 da.; C, 72 da.

105. A farmer agreed to buy 96 cows, at the rate of $20 each, but some of them proving to be in poor condition, for these he paid only $10 each, and thus paid $1620 for the whole; how many were in poor condition? *Ans.* 30.

106. In a composition of 124 oz. of gold and silver there are 10 oz. of silver; how much silver must be added that there may be 24 oz. of gold to 3 oz. of silver? *Ans.* $4\frac{1}{4}$ oz.

107. A, B, and C can do a piece of work in 24 days; $\frac{2}{3}$ of what A does equals $\frac{3}{4}$ of what B does, and $\frac{2}{3}$ of what B does equals $\frac{3}{4}$ of what C does; in what time, at this rate, can each do it? *Ans.* A, $64\frac{8}{27}$ da.; B, $72\frac{1}{3}$ da.; C, $81\frac{3}{8}$ da.

108. A has 84 acres, and ploughs 3 acres for 9 cows, and *pastures 3 acres* for 5 cows; how many cows did he keep, and how many sheep, if $\frac{2}{3}$ of the number of cows equals $\frac{3}{4}$ of the number of sheep? *Ans.* Cows, 90; sheep, 80.

109. A farmer has 440 geese and turkeys, and $\frac{2}{3}$ of the number of geese equals $\frac{4}{5}$ of the number of turkeys; how many turkeys must he buy, that $\frac{2}{3}$ of the number of turkeys may equal $\frac{4}{5}$ of the number of geese? *Ans.* 88 turkeys.

110. The head of a fish weighs 36 oz., the tail weighs 12 oz. more than the head and $\frac{1}{4}$ of the body, and the body weighs 21 oz. more than the head and tail both; required the weight of the fish. *Ans.* 259 oz.

111. A company consisting of 50 persons engage a supper at a hotel, but before paying the bill 5 persons withdraw, by which the bill of each was increased $12\frac{1}{2}$ cents; what did the supper cost? *Ans.* \$56.25.

112. A steamboat whose rate of sailing was 16 miles an hour sails up a river whose current is 5 miles an hour, and is gone 10 h. 40 min.; how far did the boat go? *Ans.* 77 mi.

113. A, B, and C eat 63 peaches, of which A owned 40, B owned 23, and C contributed 18 cents; how much of the money ought A and B each to receive, if A eats twice as many as B, and B eats twice as many as C?

Ans. A, 8¢; B, 10¢.

114. A man having a son in England and a daughter in France, willed if the daughter returned, and not the son, she should have $\frac{1}{3}$ of the fortune, but if the son returned and not the daughter, the widow should have $\frac{1}{3}$ of the fortune; what was the share of each, if both returned and the fortune was \$64470? *Ans.* S., \$36840; W., \$18420; D., \$9210.

115. A drover has 120 sheep in one field, and $2\frac{1}{2}$ times as many in another; now, if $\frac{1}{3}$ of the number in each field jumps into the other, what part of the number in the second field equals the number in the first? *Ans.* $\frac{3}{4}$.

116. A boy bought some apples at the rate of 3 for 1 cent, and as many more at the rate of 5 for 1 cent, and sold them all at the rate of 12 for 3 cents, and thereby lost \$4; how many of each kind did he buy? *Ans.* 12000 of each.

117. $\frac{1}{3}$ of A's age equals $\frac{1}{4}$ of B's, and 10 years is $\frac{5}{8}$ of the difference of their ages; in how many years will $\frac{1}{4}$ of A's age equal $\frac{1}{5}$ of B's age? *Ans.* 12 years.

118. A man being asked the time of day, replied that $\frac{1}{5}$ of the time past 8 o'clock A. M., equaled $\frac{1}{3}$ of the time to midnight; what was the time? *Ans.* 6 o'clock P. M.

119. A had \$6435, which equaled $\frac{13}{15}$ of B's money, minus $\frac{5}{11}$ of A's, then A and B each paid to C $\frac{3}{8}$ of their money; required to know what part of C's equals the sum of A's and B's, if C at first had \$4786$\frac{7}{8}$. *Ans.* $\frac{383}{400}$.

120. A lady being asked the time of day said, it is between 4 and 5 o'clock, and the hour and minute hands are together; what was the time? *Ans.* 21$\frac{9}{11}$ min. past 4.

121. A and B are 650 of B's steps apart, and approach each other; how many steps will each take before they are together, if 3 of A's equal 6 of B's, and A takes 4 while B takes 5? *Ans.* A, 200; B, 250.

122. Twenty years ago Mary was $\frac{1}{8}$ as old as her grandmother, but 4 years ago she was $\frac{1}{4}$ as old; how old is each at present? *Ans.* Mary, 32; Grandmother, 116.

123. The sum of two numbers is 212, and $\frac{2}{3}$ of the first, minus 24, is to $\frac{3}{4}$ of the second, plus 24, as $\frac{2}{3}$ to $\frac{3}{4}$; what are the numbers, and how much must be subtracted from the first that the second may be to the first as $\frac{2}{3}$ to $\frac{3}{4}$?

Ans. { The numbers are 140 and 72; and 59 must be subtracted from the first.

124. Two men engage to build a house for \$4800; the first labors $\frac{2}{3}$ as many days as the second, plus 10 days, and receives \$2100; how many days does each labor?

Ans. 1st, 70; 2d, 90.

125. A lost $\frac{2}{5}$ of his hens; now if he find 50, and sell $\frac{2}{5}$ of what he then has for cost price, he will receive \$40; but if he loses 50, and sells $\frac{2}{5}$ of the remainder for cost price, he will receive \$20; how many had he at first? *Ans.* 250.

126. What is the length of a tape that will wind spirally around a cylinder that is 52 feet long and 3 feet in circumference, provided it passes around the cylinder once every 4 feet? *Ans.* 65 feet.

127. A gave $\frac{1}{5}$ of his money, plus $24 to B, $\frac{1}{4}$ of the remainder, plus $18 to C, $\frac{1}{3}$ of what now remained, plus $12 to C, and then had $\frac{1}{5}$ as much as at first; how much had he at first? *Ans.* $180.

128. Having a square yard which contains $\frac{2}{5}$ of an acre, I make a gravel walk around it which occupies $\frac{15}{64}$ of the whole yard; what is the width of the walk? *Ans.* 8 ft. 3 in.

129. A gentleman has a block in the form of a parallelopipedon, which is 48 inches long, 36 inches wide, and 24 inches high; what is the entire surface of the block? *Ans.* 52 sq. ft.

130. There are 3 balls whose diameters are respectively 3 in., 4 in., and 5 in.; required the diameter of a ball of the same material, weighing as much as the three. *Ans.* 6 in.

131. A general wishing to draw up his division into a square, found by the first trial he lacked 144 men to complete the square; he then diminished the side of the square by 2 men and had 204 men over; how many men in the division? *Ans.* 7600.

132. A gentleman has a box whose sides are in the proportion of 2, 3, and 4, which contains 3000 cubic inches; what are the dimensions of the box? *Ans.* 10; 15; 20.

133. A man sold a horse and carriage for $420; on the horse he lost 20 per cent., and on the carriage he gained 20 per cent.; did he gain or lose, if $\frac{2}{3}$ of the cost of the horse equaled $\frac{3}{4}$ of the cost of the carriage? *Ans.* Lost $5.

134. A father left his four sons, whose ages were respectively 5, 9, 13, and 17 years, $27500, to be divided in such a manner that the respective shares being placed out at 5 per cent. simple interest, shall amount to equal sums when they become 21 years of age; what were the shares?

Ans. 1st, $5600; 2d, $6300; 3d, $7200; 4th, $8400.

135. If 3 acres of grass, together with what grew on the 3 acres while they were grazing, keep 12 oxen 4 weeks, and in the same manner 5 acres keep 15 oxen 6 weeks; how many oxen can, in the same manner, graze on 6 acres for 8 weeks? *Ans.* 15 oxen.

SOLUTIONS OF ARITHMETICAL ANALYSIS.

Case I.

2. A can build $\frac{1}{8}$ of the boat in a day, and B $\frac{1}{12}$ of it, hence they can build $\frac{1}{8}+\frac{1}{12}=\frac{5}{24}$ in one day; and they will do $\frac{1}{24}$ of it in $\frac{1}{5}$ of a day; hence to do the whole will take them $\frac{24}{5}$, or $4\frac{4}{5}$ days.

3. The wife uses $\frac{1}{27}$ of the flour in one day, and together they use $\frac{1}{9}$ of the flour in one day; hence the man uses $\frac{1}{9}-\frac{1}{27}$, or $\frac{2}{27}$ of the flour in one day; hence he will use it all in $13\frac{1}{2}$ days.

4. A, B, and C can mow $\frac{1}{8}$ of the field in a day, and A and B $\frac{1}{12}$ of it; hence C can mow $\frac{1}{8}-\frac{1}{12}=\frac{1}{24}$ in a day; B and C do $\frac{1}{15}$ in a day; hence B does $\frac{1}{15}-\frac{1}{24}=\frac{1}{40}$ in a day; and A does $\frac{1}{12}-\frac{1}{40}=\frac{7}{120}$; hence C does it in 24 days, B in 40 days, and A in $\frac{120}{7}=17\frac{1}{7}$ days.

Case II.

2. Had he labored 100 days he would have received $250; he received $190; hence he lost $250—$190, or $60; he lost each day he was idle $2.50+$.50=$3; hence he was idle as many days as $3 is contained in $60, or 20 days.

3. Had he eaten none, he would have received $150\times1\frac{1}{2}$¢= $2.25; he received $1.70, hence he forfeited $2.25—$1.70=$.55; he forfeited 4¢+$1\frac{1}{2}$¢=$5\frac{1}{2}$¢ for every one he ate, hence to forfeit 55¢, he must have eaten as many oranges as $5\frac{1}{2}$¢ is contained times in 55¢, or 10.

4. Had she carried all she would have received $80\times2\frac{1}{2}$¢= $2.00. She received 20¢, hence, she lost $2.00—$0.20=$1.80. She lost on each $2\frac{1}{2}+12\frac{1}{2}=15$¢; hence she broke 180÷15=12, and carried 80—12=68.

Case III.

2. *If 20 lb.* of the mixture contain $\frac{1}{2}$ lb. of salt, to contain

1 lb. of salt will require 2 times 20 lb., or 40 lb. of the mixture, and to contain 3 lb. of salt it will require 3 times 40, or 120 lb.; hence there must be added 120 lb. —100 lb.=20 lb. of water.

3. If 12 oz. of the mixture contain $\frac{2}{3}$ oz. of copper, to contain 1 oz. of copper will require $\frac{3}{2}$ of 12 oz., or 18 oz. of the mixture, and to contain 4 oz. of copper will require 4 times 18 oz.=72 oz. of the mixture, hence there must be added 72 oz.−60 oz.=12 oz. of silver.

4. The gold=100 oz.—6 oz.=94 oz.; if there is $\frac{2}{5}$ oz. silver to 10 oz. of gold, to 1 oz. of silver there are 25 oz. of gold, and to 6 oz. of silver there are 150 oz. of gold; hence there were 150 oz.—94 oz.=56 oz. of gold added.

Case IV.

2. If for 5 cows he plows 1 acre, for 1 cow he plows $\frac{1}{5}$ of an acre; and if for 4 cows he pastures an acre, for 1 cow he pastures $\frac{1}{4}$ of an acre; hence 1 cow requires $\frac{1}{5}+\frac{1}{4}$, or $\frac{9}{20}$ of an acre, and on 54 acres he could keep as many cows as $\frac{9}{20}$ is contained times in 54, or 120 cows.

3. If for 6 cows he plows 2 acres, for 1 cow he plows $\frac{1}{3}$ of an acre; and if for 10 cows he pastures 2 acres, for 1 cow he pastures $\frac{1}{5}$ of an acre; hence 1 cow requires $\frac{1}{3}+\frac{1}{5}$, or $\frac{8}{15}$ of an acre, and on 64 acres he could keep as many cows as $\frac{8}{15}$ is contained times in 64, or 120 cows.

4. One cow requires $\frac{3}{7}+\frac{4}{9}=\frac{55}{63}$ of an acre; hence he had 110 $\div\frac{55}{63}$=126 cows; and $\frac{2}{3}$ of 126, or 84=$\frac{2}{5}$ of the number of sheep, hence he had 210 sheep.

Case V.

2. Since he has twice as many apples as pears, he must have 100 apples, and 50 pears; but after adding to the apples there will be three times 50 apples, or 150 apples, hence he bought 150—100=50 apples.

3. Since the ducks are to the geese as 2 to 3, he has 40 ducks and 60 geese; after buying ducks, he will have

2 times 60, or 120 ducks; hence he bought 120—40, or 80 ducks

4. Since the horses are to the cows as 3 to 4, he had at first 120 horses and 160 cows, but after the sale of cows, the number of cows is $\frac{3}{4}$ of the number of horses, or 90; hence he sold 160—90, or 70 cows.

Case VI.

2. The tail=24 in.+$\frac{1}{3}$ of body, and body=24 in.+tail=2 times 24 in.+$\frac{1}{3}$ of body; hence $\frac{2}{3}$ of length of body= 2 times 24 in., length of body=72 in., and length of fish=twice 72 in., or 144 in.

3. Head=12 oz.+$\frac{1}{4}$ of body; body=12 oz.+head=24 oz. +$\frac{1}{4}$ of body; $\frac{3}{4}$ of body=24 oz.; body=32 oz.; fish= 32 oz.×2=64 oz.

4. Head=36 oz.+12 oz.+$\frac{2}{5}$ of body; body=72 oz.+12 oz. +$\frac{2}{5}$ of body; $\frac{3}{5}$ of body=84 oz.; body=140 oz.; fish =280 oz.=17$\frac{1}{2}$ lb.

Case VII.

1. These problems may also be solved thus. If 12 men pay it, one man pays $\frac{1}{12}$ of the price; if 12+8, or 20 pay it, one pays $\frac{1}{20}$; hence $\frac{1}{12}-\frac{1}{20}$, or $\frac{1}{30}$ of the price is \$$\frac{1}{2}$, and the price is \$$\frac{1}{2}$×30=\$15.

2. The expense of 16 men is diminished 16×\$$\frac{1}{8}$=\$2, which is paid by 4 persons; if 4 persons pay \$2, one pays $\frac{1}{4}$ of \$2, or \$$\frac{1}{2}$, and 20 persons pay 20 times \$$\frac{1}{2}$, or \$10.

3. The investment of 8 persons is increased 8×\$480= \$3840, which should have been paid by the 4 who withdrew; if \$3840 is 4 persons' share, one person's share is $\frac{1}{4}$ of \$3840=\$960; and \$960×12=\$11520.

4. The expense of 50—10, or 40 persons, is increased 40× \$$\frac{1}{4}$=\$10; if \$10 should have been paid by 10 persons, each should have paid \$1, and the whole bill was \$50.

Case VIII.

2. If he rides 8 miles an hour, he will ride 1 mile in $\frac{1}{8}$ of

an hour, and if he walks 3 miles an hour, he will walk 1 mile in $\frac{1}{3}$ of an hour; hence to go and return 1 mile will require $\frac{1}{8}+\frac{1}{3}$, or $\frac{11}{24}$ of an hour; therefore in 11 hours he can go and return as many miles as $\frac{11}{24}$ is contained times in 11, or 24 miles.

3. I shall go at the rate of 1 mile in $\frac{1}{24}$ of an hour, and return at the rate of 1 mile in $\frac{1}{4}$ of an hour; hence I shall go and return 1 mile in $\frac{1}{24}+\frac{1}{4}$, or $\frac{7}{24}$ of an hour, and in 14 hours I shall go 48 miles.

4. It goes 12+3, or 15 miles an hour with the current, and 12−3, or 9 miles an hour against the current; then solving it like the first we have 90 hours.

Case IX.

2. 22 more at $5 less each, cost $1440−$1000=$440; hence one at $5 less each cost $\frac{1}{22}$ of $440, or $20, hence the original price was $20+$5, or $25, and since all cost $1000, he purchased 40.

3. 10 more at $15 more would have cost $6150—$4500=$1650; hence one at $15 more cost $\frac{1}{10}$ of $1650, or $165, and the original price was $165—$15, or $150; hence there were 30 horses.

4. 15 more at $20 less each cost $20700—$18000=$2700; hence one at $20 less each cost $\frac{1}{15}$ of $2700, or $180; hence the original price was $180+$20=$200, and he bought $18000÷$200=90.

Case X.

1. Second cup=16 oz.; cover 20 oz.

2. Horse+saddle=4 times the colt=$240; hence, horse+colt+saddle=5 times colt=$300; colt+saddle=$\frac{1}{3}$ of horse; colt+saddle+horse=$\frac{4}{3}$ value of horse, or $300=$\frac{4}{3}$ value of horse; value of horse=$225; value of saddle=$240—$225=$15.

3. House and store=5 times barn=$6000; house+store+barn=$7200; house+barn=3 times store; house+store+barn=4 times store; 4 times store=$7200; value of store=$1800; house=$4200.

4. Second cup+cover=4 times first=80 oz.; both cups+cover=5 times first=100 oz.; first cup+cover=3 times second; 3 times second+second=100 oz.; second cup=25 oz.; cover=55 oz.

Case XI.

2. After losing $\frac{1}{3}$, there remained $\frac{2}{3}$ of what she had after winning, which was 4 times what she had at first, and $\frac{1}{6}$ of what she had after winning, equals what she had at first; hence $\frac{5}{6}$ of what she had after winning $450, equals what she had increased her money; hence $\frac{5}{6}$ of what she had equals $450, and $\frac{1}{6}$ of what she had, or $\frac{1}{5}$ of $450, which is $90, is what she had at first.

3. After gaining $\frac{4}{5}$ of what remained, he had $\frac{9}{5}$ of what remained, which was $\frac{3}{4}$ of what he had at first, and once what he had at first was $\frac{12}{5}$ of what remained; $\frac{12}{5}$ of what remained minus $\frac{5}{5}$ of what remained leaves $\frac{7}{5}$ of what remained, which equals the amount lost, or $1400, hence $\frac{12}{5}$, or what he had at first, equals $2400.

4. $\frac{5}{6}$ of the remainder equal $\frac{2}{5}$ of the first, then the first equals $\frac{25}{12}$ of the remainder; hence, $\frac{25}{12}-\frac{12}{12}=\frac{13}{12}$ of the remainder=$2600, and $\frac{25}{12}$ of the remainder, which is what he had at first, equals $5000; this divided into two parts as 2 to 3, gives A's $2000, and B's $3000.

Case XII.

2. If $\frac{2}{3}$ of the remainder cost $19, the remainder cost $28.50; $37.50−$28.50=$9, cost of the 18 that died; hence, 1 hen cost 50¢, and for $37.50 he bought 75.

3. If $\frac{3}{5}$ of the remainder cost $3000, the remainder cost $5000, and 50 cost $6250−$5000=$1250; hence 1 cow cost $25, and the whole number was 250.

4. All cost $7440+$3360=$10800; then since $\frac{2}{5}$ of the remainder cost $3360, the remainder cost $8400, and 20 cost $10800−$8400=$2400, and one cost $120; hence the whole number was 90; 90−20=70, the remainder; $\frac{3}{5}$ of 70=42.

Case XIII.

1. A's, \$4000; B's, \$2400.

2. If A had owned $\frac{2}{5}$ of the stock, his gain would have been $\frac{2}{5}$ of \$1650, or \$660, hence \$300 must gain the difference between \$750 and \$660, or \$90; if \$300 gains \$90, to gain \$1 requires $\$3\frac{1}{3}$, and to gain \$1650 requires \$5500; A's $=\frac{2}{5}$ of \$5500 + \$300 = \$2500; B's = \$3000.

3. D owns $\frac{1}{4}$ of the stock + \$18000; $\frac{1}{4}$ of \$800 = \$200; \$560 − \$200 = \$360, the gain on \$18000; to gain \$1 requires \$50, hence to gain \$800 requires \$40000; C's $=\frac{3}{4}$ of \$40000 − \$18000 = \$12000; D's = \$40000 − \$12000 = \$28000.

4. B's and C's gain is \$120 + \$210 = \$330; hence A's gain is \$480 − \$330 = \$150. Had A owned $\frac{1}{4}$, his gain would have been $\frac{1}{4}$ of \$480 = \$120; hence, \$500 gains \$150 − \$120, or \$30, and to gain \$150, which is 5 times \$30, requires \$2500; to gain \$120 requires \$2000, and to gain \$210, requires \$3500.

Case XIV.

2. Since 3 of the hound's leaps equal 7 of the hare's, and the hound makes 3 leaps while the hare makes 5, the hound makes 7 of the hare's leaps while the hare makes 5, hence he gains 2 leaps in 7, and to gain 120 he must take 420 of the hare's leaps, which equal 180 of the hound's, hence he takes 180 leaps to catch the hare.

3. Since 2 of the officer's steps equal 3 of the thief's, 4 of the officer's equal 6 of the thief's; hence, for the thief to run as fast as the officer, he should take 6 steps to the officer's 4; but he only takes 5 to the officer's 4, hence the officer gains 1 step while he takes 4 and the thief takes 5, and to gain 240, he will take $240\times 4=960$, and the thief $240\times 5=1200$.

4. Since 3 of the man's steps equal 6 of the boy's, 2 of the

man's equal 4 of the boy's, hence the man gains 1 of the boy's steps every 2 steps he takes, and to gain 95 he will take $95\times2=190$ steps; and the boy $95\times3=285$ steps.

Case XV.

Let the pupil illustrate these with a line, as in the following solutions:

2. Let NM represent the time from noon to midnight, and P the position of the present time; then $\frac{1}{5}$ of NP=PM; hence $\frac{5}{5}$ of NP+$\frac{1}{5}$ of NP, or $\frac{6}{5}$ of NP =NM or 12 hours; NP=10 P. M.

N———P———M

3. $\frac{3}{2}$ of the time to noon equals 12 hours; the time to noon equals 8 hours; 12—8=4 A. M.
4. $\frac{5}{3}$ of the time to midnight equals 12 hours, and $\frac{2}{3}$ of the time to midnight equals $4\frac{4}{5}$ hours, the time past noon.
5. $\frac{8}{5}$ of the time past midnight=24 hours; time past midnight=15 hours=3 P. M.

Case XVI.

2. At the required time, 3 times B's age will equal A's age, then twice B's age will equal the difference in their ages, which is 28—4, or 24 years; if 24 years is twice B's age, B's age will be 12 years; hence in 12—4, or 8 years, A will be 3 times as old as B.
3. At the required time, $\frac{4}{7}$ of N's age will equal M's age, hence $\frac{3}{7}$ of N's age will equal the difference in their ages, or 24 years; since 24 is $\frac{3}{7}$ of N's age, his age will be 56 years, and 56—48, or 8 years, will be the number of years required.
4. 18 yr.=$\frac{3}{5}$ of the aunt's age; her age is 30 yr.; then *twice* Mary's age, minus *once* her age, or *once* Mary's age =30—18=12 yr., but Mary is now 18 yr.; hence it was 18—12, or 6 years ago.
5. 20 yr.=$\frac{4}{7}$ of uncle's age; uncle's age=35 yr.; $2\frac{1}{2}$ times

Henry's minus *once* Henry's=$1\frac{1}{2}$ times Henry's; 35 −20=15 yr.; 15 is $1\frac{1}{2}$ times Henry's age, his age was 10 years; 20−10=10 years ago.

Case XVII.

2. By the conditions of the problem, the minute-hand, to gain 4 spaces, must go 4 times $1\frac{1}{11}$ spaces, or $4\frac{4}{11}$ spaces, which requires $4\frac{4}{11}\times 5$ minutes, or $21\frac{9}{11}$ minutes.

3. By the conditions of the problem, the minute-hand, to gain 7 spaces, must go 7 times $1\frac{1}{11}$ spaces, or $7\frac{7}{11}$ spaces, which requires $7\frac{7}{11}$ times 5 minutes, or $38\frac{2}{11}$ minutes.

4. At 4 o'clock the hour and minute hands are 4 spaces apart, but the minute-hand only needs to gain 3 spaces to be 5 minute-spaces from the hour-hand, and to gain 3 spaces it requires $\frac{180}{11}$, or $16\frac{4}{11}$ minutes. It may also go 5 minute-spaces beyond, which gives $27\frac{3}{11}$ minutes.

5. At 4 o'clock the hour and minute hands are 4 spaces apart; to gain 1 space the minute-hand goes $\frac{12}{11}$ spaces; to gain 4 spaces it must go $\frac{48}{11}$ spaces, which requires $21\frac{9}{11}$ minutes; hence $21\frac{9}{11}$ minutes−5 minutes, or $16\frac{9}{11}$ minutes after 4 o'clock, they will be 5 minutes of time apart, also in $21\frac{9}{11}+5$, or $26\frac{9}{11}$ minutes.

Case XVIII.

2. 4 times D's age=C's age, hence D's age is $\frac{1}{3}$ of the *difference* of their ages, and by second condition, D's age is $\frac{1}{2}$ of the *difference* of their ages; hence 12 years is the difference between $\frac{1}{2}$ of the *difference* of their ages and $\frac{1}{3}$ of the *difference* of their ages, or $\frac{1}{6}$ of the *difference* of their ages; hence the difference of their ages is 72 years; D's age is 24, and C's 96 yr.

3. By the first condition, R's age equals $\frac{1}{3}$ of S's, hence R's age equals $\frac{1}{2}$ of the *difference* of their ages; and by second condition, R's age equals the difference of their

ages; hence 14 years is the difference between the *difference* of their ages and $\frac{1}{2}$ of the *difference* of their ages, or $\frac{1}{2}$ of the *difference* of their ages, and the *difference* of their ages is 28 years; R's age is 14 years, and S's age is 42 years.

4. By the first condition, my age equals $\frac{1}{4}$ of Mr. Wilson's, hence my age is $\frac{1}{3}$ of the *difference*; by the second condition, my age equals $\frac{1}{3}$ of his, hence my age is $\frac{1}{2}$ of the *difference*; hence 6 years equals the difference between $\frac{1}{2}$ of the *difference* and $\frac{1}{3}$ of the *difference*, which is $\frac{1}{6}$ of the *difference*; hence the *difference* is 36 years; my age is 18 yr. and Mr. Wilson's age is 54 years.

SOLUTIONS OF

MISCELLANEOUS PROBLEMS.

3. $\frac{3}{4}+\frac{5}{6}+\frac{7}{8}=2\frac{11}{24}$; $\frac{1}{4}+\frac{1}{6}+\frac{9}{10}=1\frac{19}{60}$; $2\frac{11}{24}-1\frac{19}{60}=1\frac{17}{120}$.

4. $\frac{7}{10}+\frac{17}{20}-\frac{19}{30}=\frac{55}{60}$; $\frac{2}{3}+\frac{4}{5}-\frac{5}{6}=\frac{19}{30}$; $\frac{55}{60}\div\frac{19}{30}=1\frac{17}{38}$.

5. Solve thus: $\frac{15}{16}\times\frac{17}{21}\times\frac{19}{36}\times\frac{63}{38}\times\frac{24}{17}\times\frac{63}{45}$; then cancel, and the answer is $1\frac{5}{16}$.

6. $2\frac{2}{5}\div3\frac{3}{4}=\frac{12}{5}\times\frac{4}{15}=\frac{16}{25}$; $5\frac{1}{15}\div7\frac{3}{5}=\frac{76}{15}\times\frac{5}{38}=\frac{2}{3}$.

7. $3\frac{1}{2}$ of $\frac{1}{8}=\frac{7}{16}$; $\frac{3\frac{1}{2}}{14}=\frac{1}{4}$; $\frac{1}{2}$ of $\frac{16\frac{2}{3}}{26\frac{2}{3}}=\frac{5}{16}$; $\frac{7}{16}+\frac{1}{4}+\frac{5}{16}=1$.

8. $\frac{\frac{3}{7}}{10}$ of $13\frac{2}{9}=\frac{3}{70}$ of $\frac{119}{9}=\frac{17}{30}$; $\frac{6\frac{3}{7}}{15}$ of $2\frac{2}{9}=\frac{3}{7}$ of $\frac{20}{9}=\frac{20}{21}$; $\frac{14}{15}$ of $3\frac{1}{7}=\frac{44}{15}$; $\frac{17}{30}+\frac{20}{21}+\frac{44}{15}=4\frac{19}{42}$.

9. $\frac{2}{3}$ of $\frac{3}{5}$ of $9\frac{1}{6}=3\frac{2}{3}$; $\frac{5\frac{21}{35}}{18}$ of $\frac{6}{7}$ of $56=\frac{28}{5}\times\frac{1}{18}\times\frac{6}{7}\times56=\frac{224}{15}$ $=14\frac{14}{15}$; $14\frac{14}{15}-3\frac{2}{3}=11\frac{4}{15}$.

10. $\frac{8}{9}$ of $\frac{5\frac{1}{2}}{11}$ of $\frac{6\frac{2}{3}}{12}\times24\frac{9}{15}$ of $\frac{7\frac{1}{2}}{10}=\frac{8}{9}\times\frac{1}{2}\times\frac{5}{9}\times\frac{123}{5}\times\frac{3}{4}=4\frac{5}{9}$.

11. $\frac{21}{22}\times\frac{43}{60}\times\frac{5}{8}\times\frac{3}{10}\times\frac{3}{4}\times100=\frac{13545}{1408}=9\frac{873}{1408}$.

12. $\frac{\frac{1}{3}+\frac{2}{5}}{3\frac{1}{8}}=\frac{11}{15}\times\frac{8}{25}=\frac{88}{375}$; $\frac{185}{16}\times\frac{1}{115}=\frac{27}{368}$; $\frac{88}{375}-\frac{27}{368}=$ $\frac{22259}{138000}$ $3\times\frac{8}{81\frac{6}{19}}=\frac{57}{515}$; $\frac{22259}{138000}\times\frac{515}{57}=1\frac{719477}{1573200}$.

13. $\frac{2\frac{5}{18}}{6\frac{5}{6}}+\frac{3\frac{1}{9}}{6\frac{5}{6}}-\frac{4\frac{7}{48}}{24\frac{7}{8}}=\frac{51}{82}$; $3\frac{2\frac{13}{18}}{\frac{3\frac{1}{2}}{9}}=3\frac{\frac{49}{18}}{\frac{7}{18}}=10$; $\frac{\frac{1}{16}+\frac{2}{27}-\frac{13}{48}}{\frac{32}{56}\times1\frac{2}{5}\div2\frac{3}{5}}=$ $\frac{\frac{1}{8}}{\frac{3}{8}}=\frac{1}{3}$; $\frac{51}{82}\times10\div\frac{1}{3}=18\frac{27}{41}$.

14. $50-\frac{100}{3}+\frac{7\frac{1}{3}}{4\frac{1}{2}}=50-\frac{100}{3}+\frac{44}{27}=\frac{494}{27}$; $13\frac{13}{189}\div\frac{494}{27}=\frac{2470}{189}\times\frac{27}{494}=\frac{5}{7}$.

15. $3\frac{6\frac{2}{3}}{11\frac{3}{7}}=3\frac{7}{12}$; $\frac{5\frac{5}{9}}{28\frac{4}{7}}=\frac{7}{36}$; $.83\frac{1}{3}=\frac{5}{6}$; $\frac{7\frac{1}{2}}{37\frac{1}{2}}$ of $\frac{2\frac{1}{2}}{2\frac{2}{5}}=\frac{1}{5}$ of $\frac{25}{24}=\frac{5}{24}$; $3\frac{7}{12}+\frac{7}{36}-\frac{5}{6}-\frac{5}{24}+2\frac{19}{36}=5\frac{19}{72}$.

16. $\frac{40}{5.6\frac{2}{3}}=\frac{120}{17}$; $\frac{31.16\frac{4}{6}}{15.1\frac{2}{3}}=\frac{187}{91}$; $\frac{9.8}{16\frac{1}{2}}=\frac{98}{165}$; $\frac{10\frac{1.25}{1\frac{1}{2}}}{2.3\frac{1}{3}}=\frac{65}{14}$; $\frac{120}{17}\times\frac{187}{91}\times\frac{98}{165}\times\frac{65}{14}=40$; $40+9.2\frac{1}{5}-\frac{9\frac{3}{7}}{4.28\frac{4}{7}}=40+9\frac{11}{50}-2\frac{1}{5}=47\frac{1}{50}$.

17. $.101+.5\frac{1}{4}-.3\frac{1}{8}=.3135$; $\frac{.04\frac{1}{6}}{.1\frac{2}{3}}=.2\frac{1}{2}$; $.8\frac{4\frac{1}{6}}{.6}=1.5$; $.3135\times .25\times\frac{1}{1.5}=.05225$.

18. $1580\div80=19\frac{3}{4}$ miles.

19. £24 16 s. 9 d. = £24.8375; $4.8665 × 24.8375 = $120.87169375.

20. 432 lb. Av. = 432 × 7000 ÷ 5760 = 525 lb. Troy.

21. 752 gal. = 752 × 231 ÷ 282 = 616 beer gal.

22. There are 25 years = 365 × 25 = 9125 days; and 7 leap years, hence there are 9125 + 7 = 9132 days in all.

23. Since the end of the year 1800 completed 1800 years from the Christian era, the 19th century began on Jan. 1, 1801; from example 4, Art. 314, we find that Jan. 18, 1782, was on Friday, hence January 1 of 1782 fell on Tuesday; and as there are 4 leap years the number of days = 365 × 19 + 4 = 6939 days, which divided by 9 gives a remainder of 2 days, hence 1801 began 2 days after Tuesday, or on Thursday.

24. Diff. of longitude = 47° 17′ 10″; diff. of time = 47° 17′ 10″ ÷ 15 = 3 h. 9 min. $8\frac{2}{3}$ sec.; since the message goes west,

the time will be earlier, hence 9 h. 30 min., minus 3 h. 9 min. $8\frac{2}{3}$ sec. $=$ 6 h. 20 min. $51\frac{1}{3}$ sec.

25. 1 mile $=$ 5280 ft., contents of 1 mile of road $= 5280\times 40 =$ 211200 sq. ft. $= 4\frac{28}{33}$ A.

26. 8 ft. 6 in. $=$ 102 in.; 5 ft. 9 in. $=$ 69 in.; contents $= 102^2 \times .785398 \times 69 \div (231\times 63) = 38.742415+$ hhd.

27. The amount of rain caught is the same whether the roof be flat or sloping, hence adding 6 inches at each side, the surface $= 41\times 35 = 1435$ sq. ft.; amount of rain $= 1435\times 144\times \frac{7}{8} = 180810$ cu. in.; depth $= 180810 \div (102^2\times .785398) = 22\frac{1}{8}+$ in. $=$ 1 ft. $10\frac{1}{8}+$ in.; 69 in. $\div$ $22\frac{1}{8}$ in. $= \frac{184}{59}$; $\frac{7}{8}\times\frac{184}{59} = 2\frac{43}{59}$.

28. $295 \div .62\frac{1}{2} = 472$.

29. $4\frac{1}{2}\times .33\frac{1}{3} = 1\frac{1}{2}$; $\frac{50}{51}\times .00\frac{3}{5} = \frac{1}{170}$.

30. If \$750 was 25%, or $\frac{1}{4}$ of what she then had, she must have had 5 times \$750, or \$3750, at first.

31. $\frac{3}{5}\div 3\frac{3}{5} = .16\frac{2}{3}$; $\frac{13}{14}\div 3\frac{5}{7} = .25$.

32. $\$680\times .07 = \$47.60$; 5 yr. 10 mo. 12 da. $= 5\frac{13}{15}$ yr.; $\$47.60 \times 5\frac{13}{15} = \$279.25\frac{1}{3}$.

33. Int. on \$1 for 5 yr. 10 mo. 15 da. $=$ \$.3525; $\$456.84 \div .3525 = \$1296$.

34. Int. on \$4080 at 5% for 1 yr. $=$ \$204; $\$668.10 \div \$204 =$ 3 yr. 3 mo. 9 da.

35. Int. on \$9876 for 6 yr. 2 mo. 12 da. at 1% $=$ \$612.312; $\$5510.808 \div \$612.312 = 9\%$.

36. The tin pan is the frustum of a cone, and the contents by Art. 778 $=$

$$\left((17^2+9^2)\times .785398 + \sqrt{17^2\times 9^2\times .785398^2}\right)$$

$\times\frac{1}{3}$ of $5 = 684.60525+$ cu. in $= 2\frac{74}{77}+$ gal.

37. $8\frac{1}{4}$ ft. $\times\ 3\frac{1}{2}$ ft. $\times\ 4\frac{3}{4}$ ft. $= 137\frac{5}{32}$ cu. ft.; according to note, Art. 371, corn in the ear being measured by heaped measure, $\frac{4}{5}$ of $\frac{4}{5}$ of $137\frac{5}{32} = 87\frac{39}{50}$ bu.; $87\frac{39}{50}\div 2 =$ 43.89 bu.

38. There are 10 cords yearly growth; profit on 1 cord $=$ $\$4.25 - \$.75 = \$3.50$; $\$3.50\times 10 = \$35$; $\$35 \div \$100 =$ .35 or 35%.

39. Length of one side, subtracting corner $=100-6=94$ ft.; whole length $94\times4=376$ ft.; contents of walk $=376\times6=2256$ sq. ft. $=250\frac{2}{3}$ sq. yd.; cost of walk $=\$.75\times250\frac{2}{3}=\$188$; length of remainder $=100-12=88$ ft.; contents of remainder $=88\times88=7744$ sq. ft.; No. of bricks $=7744\times4=30976$; cost of paving $=\$9\times30.976=\$278.784$; whole cost $=\$188+\$278.784=\$466.784$.

40. $1\frac{3}{4}$ A. $=76230$ ft.; length $=76230\div180=423\frac{1}{2}$ ft.; whole length of wall $=(423\frac{1}{2}+180)\times2=1207$ ft.; to find the cost of labor we make no deductions, hence the contents of wall, Art. 364, Rule II. $=1207\times8\frac{1}{2}\times14=143633$ bricks; cost of labor $=\$2\times143.633=\$287.266$; to find the amount of material we deduct corners, doors, and gateway, hence the whole length of wall $=1207$ ft. $-(4\times9$ in. $+12$ ft.$)=1192$ ft.; square feet in wall $=(1192\times8\frac{1}{2})-(2\times6\frac{1}{4}\times4)=10082$; actual number of bricks $=10082\times14=141148$; cost of material $=\$10\times141.148=\$1411.48$; whole cost of wall $=\$287.266+\$1411.48=\$1698.746$.

41. He had 100%−20%, or 80% left, and sold 25% to C, then he had 75% of 80%, or 60% of the whole left, which equaled 120 acres, hence the original quantity was 200 acres.

42. Since 40 shares is 25% of what he had, he had 160, and now has 200 shares; 200−80=120 shares; 120 is 75% of 160.

43. If 25% of A's $=33\frac{1}{3}$ of B's, 75% of A's = B's; hence 175% of A's = \$2800; A's = \$1600 and B's = \$1200.

44. If \$3600 = 120% of the cost, the cost was \$3000, hence he gained \$600 on the first; if he sold the second for 80%, or \$3600, the cost was \$4500, hence he lost \$900 on the second, and he lost on the transaction \$900−\$600, or \$300.

45. C's is $\frac{5}{4}$ of F's, and F's is $\frac{1}{4}$ of F's less than F's; now $\frac{5}{4}$ of F's, which is C's, is 100% of itself, and $\frac{1}{4}$ of F's. what F's is less than C's, is $\frac{1}{5}$ of $\frac{5}{4}$ of F's, and hence is $\frac{1}{5}$ of 100%, or 20% less.

46. Gain$=\frac{1}{6}$ of \$360, or \$60; 5% of \$360=\$18; \$360+\$18 =\$378; original cost=\$360—\$60=\$300; \$378—\$300=\$78; \$78÷\$300=26%.

47. He owns \$50×80=\$4000; hence his dividend is \$4000 ×.05=\$200, and this is worth \$200÷50=4 shares of stock; hence he has 80+4=84 shares.

48. \$300=4% of her stock; hence her stock is \$7500, and she owned 7500÷50=150 shares at first. The \$300 are worth 300÷50=6 shares; 150+6=156 shares.

49. The 10 shares are worth 10×\$50=\$500; hence the entire dividend was \$545, which is 5% of the stock; hence the stock=\$10900, and the number of shares was 10900÷50=218, and 218+10=228, is the number of shares she then had.

50. $\frac{25}{13}$ of the price of the lot=\$5000; hence she received for the lot \$2600, and for the house \$2400. On the lot she gained 4% or $\frac{1}{25}$, hence $\frac{26}{25}$ of cost=\$2600, and $\frac{1}{25}$ of cost, or the gain$=\frac{1}{26}$ of \$2600=\$100; similarly, $\frac{24}{25}$ of the cost of the second=\$2400; hence $\frac{1}{25}$ of the loss=\$100; hence there was neither gain nor loss.

51. 40 is $\frac{1}{2}$ of what B had, and $\frac{1}{4}$ of what remained to A; hence B had 80 at first and A had 160 remaining. B had after the sale 80+40=120, and after the second gift 120+40=160, and A had 160—40=120, and 120 is $\frac{3}{4}$ of 160, or 75%.

52. 80$=\frac{2}{3}$ of what Mary gave William, hence she gave W. 120; if she had given 40 less and he 40 more, he would have given 80+40=120, and she 120—40=80, and 80 equals $\frac{2}{3}$ of 120, or $66\frac{2}{3}$%.

53. The bank stock was worth 56×50×$.97\frac{1}{2}$=\$2730; the gas stock was worth \$100×40×$1.01\frac{1}{2}$=\$4060; the difference is \$1330.

54. 30×\$50×.97=\$1455; 10×\$50×$.99\frac{1}{2}$=\$497.50; 20×\$50×$1.01\frac{1}{2}$=\$1015; \$497.50+\$1015=\$1512.50; \$1512.50—\$1455=\$57.50.

55. Cost of 1 share=\$$48\frac{3}{4}$+\$$\frac{1}{8}$=\$$48\frac{7}{8}$; whole cost=\$$48\frac{7}{8}$×45=\$$2199\frac{3}{8}$.

56. The horses cost $15625 minus the sum of $250 and $375, which is $15000; $375÷$15000=.02½; hence the rate was 2½%.

57. By the conditions of the problem 6%−2%, or 4%=$468; hence 100% of the amount sold=$11700, and 6% of this is $702; hence $11700−$702=$10998.

58. By the conditions we have 2½%+1½%, or 4%=224; hence 100% equals $5600.

59. 100%−6½%=93½%=$7480; hence 100%=$8000, the amount sold. Then 6½% of $8000=$520.

60. The int. at 8%−4%, or 4%=$988−$819=$169; hence the principal was $819−$169=$650; int. for 1 year at 4%=$26; $169÷$26=6½ yr.

61. The present worth=$1200÷1.22⅓=$980.926+; true discount=$1200−$980.926=$219.074; bank discount for 2 yr. 9 mo. 18 da.=$1200×.224=$268.80; $268.80−$219.074=$49.726.

62. Present worth of $600 for 1 year=$600÷1.06=$566.037; present worth of $600 for 2 yr.=$600÷1.12=$535.714; present worth of $600 for 3 yr =$600÷1.18=$508.474; whole amount=$566.037 + $535.714 +$508.474=$1610.225.

63. Simple interest=$800×1.00=$800; compound interest =($2.5403517 × 1.04 − $1)×800=$1313.5726144; $1313.57−$800=$513.57.

64. The time is 90 days; interest on $1 for 90 da.=$0.015; proceeds of $1=$0.985; this minus the discount=$0.9775; $0.9775×950=$928.625, *Ans.*

65. The commission is 3% of $6000=$180; the proceeds=$5820; the face of the draft is $5820÷1.005=$5791.04; he sells this for $5791.04×1.00¾=$5834.47.

66. The time is 63 days; interest on $1 at 6% is $0.0105: cost of $1 is $0.9895, which increased by the premium =.99075, which multiplied by 960=$951.12.

67. A's and B's gain=$3600−$1400=$2200; A's gain=$\frac{5}{11}$ of $2200=$1000; B's gain=$\frac{6}{11}$ of $2200=$1200;

A and B gained 20% of their stock, hence **$1400 is** 20% of C's stock, and his stock is $7000.

68. $240000—$65000=$175000, which divided in the proportion of 3400 to 3600, or as 34 to 36, gives B's stock=$\frac{17}{35}$ of $175000, or $85000, and C's=$\frac{18}{35}$ of $175000, or $90000; we find also that B and C gain 4% of their stock, hence A's gain=$2600.

69. A's gain per month=$1250÷10, or $125; B's gain per month=$1500÷15, or $100; C's gain per month= $1350÷18=$75; whole monthly gain=$125+$100 +$75=$300; A has $\frac{125}{300}$ of $6000, or $2500; B has $\frac{100}{300}$ of $6000, or $2000; C has $\frac{75}{300}$ of $6000, or $1500.

70. If 3 men do as much work as 5 boys, 15 men will do as much as 25 boys; hence A gives 20×12=240 days' work of a man, and B gives 15×15=225 days' work of a man; A should receive $\frac{240}{465}$ of $310=$160, and B, $\frac{225}{465}$ of $310=$150.

71. A should receive $\frac{108}{370}$ of $740=$216; B, $\frac{112}{370}$ of $740= $224; C, $\frac{15}{37}$ of $740=$300.

72. A credit on $1200 for 6 mo. is equivalent to a credit on $1 for 7200 mo.; a credit on $1500 for 8 mo.=a credit on $1 for 12000 mo., which makes the same as a credit on $1 for 19200 mo. On the other side, there is a credit on $1 for 8000 mo; the difference is 11200 mo., which divided by the remainder of the debt ($700), gives 16 mo., or 1 yr. 4 mo.

(73)

10						
	3	$\frac{1}{7}$		15		15
	5		$\frac{1}{5}$		3	3
	25	$\frac{1}{15}$	$\frac{1}{15}$	7	1	8

(74)

10							×6=
	2	$\frac{1}{8}$		5		5	30
	5		$\frac{1}{5}$		2	2	12
	20		$\frac{1}{10}$		1	1	6
	50	$\frac{1}{40}$		1		1	6
						9	

75. This is solved by Arithmetical Progression. The 1st term is 4 ft., the com. diff. is 4, and number of terms 400; the last term=4+4×399=1600, and the sum of the terms$=\frac{(4+1600)\times 400}{2}=320800$ ft.

76. In the figure on page 159, $AB=\sqrt{20^2+15^2}=25$; $AC=\sqrt{25^2+12^2}=27.73$ in.

77. Since the dimensions of similar surfaces are as the square roots of the areas, the diameter of the 2d is to the diameter of the 1st, as $\sqrt{\frac{25}{9}}:1$, or as $\frac{5}{3}:1$, hence diameter of 2d$=\frac{5}{3}$ of $15=25$.

78. One mile equals 320 rods. A goes $320\times2=640$ rods. B goes $\sqrt{320^2+320^2}=\sqrt{204800}=452.548$; the difference is 187.452.

79. 1 acre=160 sq. rd.; $160\div32=5$ rd.

80. At the end of 6 mo. the provision would last 960 men 2 mo.; hence it would last 1920 men 1 mo., or $\frac{1}{6}$ of 1920 men=320 men, 6 mo.; hence $960-320=640$ men were sent away.

81. Entire surface equals 6 times $15^2=1350$.

82. C's$=\frac{2}{3}$ A's$+\frac{2}{3}$ B's; but A's$=\frac{2}{3}$ B's, and $\frac{2}{3}$ A's$=\frac{4}{9}$ B's; hence C's$=\frac{4}{9}$ B's$+\frac{6}{9}$ B's$=\frac{10}{9}$ B's; hence $\frac{9}{9}+\frac{6}{9}+\frac{10}{9}=\frac{25}{9}$ B's=\$5000. B's=\$1800; $\frac{6}{9}$ B's, or A's=\$1200; $\frac{10}{9}$ B's, or C's=\$2000.

83. Each side of the square garden is 16 rods, hence its area is $16^2=256$ sq. rd. The diameter of the circular garden$=64\times.3183$; the area$=\frac{1}{4}$ of $64\times64\times.3183=325.9392$ sq. rd.; $325.9392-256=69.9392$ sq. rd.

84. $\frac{1}{5}$ of A's gain=\$520, A's gain=\$2600; then $\frac{1}{8}$ of A's stock=\$2600; A's stock=\$20800; $\frac{3}{4}$ of \$20800$=\frac{2}{3}$ B's stock, hence B's stock=\$23400.

85. He bought for 75% of par and sold for 120% of par, hence he gained 45% of par on 75% of par, or $\frac{3}{5}$ of the investment equals the gain, which is \$1920; hence he invested \$3200.

86. After losing $\frac{2}{3}$ of the *sum* he had $\frac{1}{3}$ of the sum; he then won $\frac{1}{4}$ of $\frac{2}{3}=\frac{1}{6}$ of the *sum*, and then had $\frac{1}{3}+\frac{1}{6}=\frac{1}{2}$ of the *sum*, which is \$24; the sum was \$48.

87. After gaining $\frac{3}{4}$ as much as remained, they had $\frac{7}{4}$ (*sum*—\$1680)$=\frac{7}{8}$ *sum*; hence $\frac{1}{8}$ *sum*$=\frac{1}{4}$ (*sum*—\$1680), and the sum=2 *sum*—\$3360; hence the *sum*=\$3360.

from which we readily find A's and B's to be $1792 and $1568.

88. 4 acres=640 sq. rd. The side of the square is $\sqrt{640}$, which multiplied by 4=101.192 rods. From Rule I. Art. 754, we have area=circ.$^2\times$.07958; hence the circumference of the circular garden=$\sqrt{640\div.07958}$, which equals 89.678—. The difference is 11.514 rods.

89. He asked 120% and sold for 90% or $\frac{9}{10}$ of 120%, which is 108%; hence he gained 8%.

90. He sells for $\frac{1}{10}$ of 40+40, or 44¢ a yard; and since he fell $\frac{1}{3}$, 44¢ is $\frac{2}{3}$ of the price asked; hence the price is 66¢.

91. The retail price is 125%, and the wholesale price is 96% or $\frac{24}{25}$ of 125%, which is 120%; hence the gain is 20%.

92. 3 A's+32 : 4 B's−24 : : $\frac{2}{3}$: $\frac{3}{4}$; hence $\frac{9}{4}$ A's+24=$\frac{8}{3}$ B's −16; then $\frac{9}{4}$ A's=$\frac{8}{3}$ B's−40; hence A's=$\frac{32}{27}$ B's−$\frac{160}{9}$; hence $\frac{27}{27}+\frac{32}{27}-\frac{160}{9}$, or $\frac{59}{27}$ B's−$\frac{160}{9}$=428; $\frac{59}{27}$ B's=$\frac{4012}{9}$; B's=204; A's=224.

93. The wholesale price was 95% and the retail price is 120% or $\frac{6}{5}$ of 95%=114%; hence the gain is 14%.

94. The retail price is 112½% of cost, which equals 105% of the wholesale price; then 1% wholesale=$\frac{112.5}{105}$% of cost, and 100% of wholesale equals $\frac{11250}{105}$=107$\frac{1}{7}$%; hence the gain at wholesale is 7$\frac{1}{7}$%.

95. He sold 80% at a gain of 40%, or $\frac{2}{5}$; hence he sold it for $\frac{7}{5}$ of 80% of cost, or 112% of cost; hence the gain was 12%.

96. Selling price is 110% of cost; gain on remainder=110% −75%=35% of cost; he gained 35% of cost on 75% of cost, or $\frac{7}{15}$ of cost, which equals 46$\frac{2}{3}$% of 75%.

97. He sells for $12+$\frac{1}{8}$ of $12=$13.50; he had remaining $\frac{4}{5}$ of 20, or 16 turkeys; he sold each turkey for $13.50 ÷16=$.84$\frac{3}{8}$.

98. One bushel$=2150.42$ cu. in., and $4500=2150.42\times4500$ $=9676890$ cu. in.; the cube root of this is 213.09 in., which divided by $12=17.76$ ft.

99. Diam. of 2d : 7 : : $\sqrt[3]{106\frac{2}{3}}$: $\sqrt[3]{13\frac{1}{3}}$; or, as $\sqrt[3]{\frac{320}{3}}$: $\sqrt[3]{\frac{40}{3}}$. Hence, Diam. of $2d=7\times\sqrt[3]{\frac{320}{3}\div\frac{40}{3}}=7\times\sqrt[3]{8}$; Or diam. of $2d=7\times2=14$, *Ans*

100. $\frac{148}{100}-\frac{80}{100}=\frac{68}{100}$, or $\frac{17}{25}=\$5100$; $\frac{1}{25}=\$300$, and $\frac{25}{25}=$ $7500.

101. 2 times the meadow : 3 times the forest-50 : : $\frac{4}{5}$: $\frac{5}{6}$; hence $\frac{5}{3}$ of the meadow$=\frac{12}{5}$ of the forest-40; hence meadow$=\frac{36}{25}-24$; hence $\frac{25}{25}+\frac{36}{25}-24=342$; hence $\frac{61}{25}=366$, $\frac{25}{25}=150$; and $\frac{36}{25}-24=192$.

102. $100+4 times the *sum*=$200 ; hence 4 times the *sum* equals $100, and the sum equals $25.

103. In 7 yr. at 6%, the amount$=\frac{142}{100}=\frac{71}{50}$ of the principal, hence 59640=\frac{71}{50}$ of the amount at interest and $\frac{50}{50}$ =$42000; hence 42000=\frac{2}{3}$ of A's$+\frac{3}{4}$ of B's fortune; but as the fortunes are to each other as $\frac{1}{2}$ to $\frac{1}{3}$, or as 3 to 2, $\frac{2}{3}$ of A's is to $\frac{3}{4}$ of B's as 2 to $\frac{3}{2}$, or as 4 to 3; hence $\frac{2}{3}$ of A's$=\frac{4}{7}$ of $42000, or $24000, and A's fortune=$36000; $\frac{3}{4}$ of B's$=\frac{3}{7}$ of $42000, or $18000, and B's fortune=$24000.

104. A, B, and C do $\frac{1}{24}$ in 1 day, A and B $\frac{1}{36}$, A and C $\frac{1}{48}$; hence B does $\frac{1}{24}-\frac{1}{48}=\frac{1}{48}$ in 1 day, and to do $\frac{48}{48}$ or the whole, he will require 48 days; A does $\frac{1}{36}-\frac{1}{48}=\frac{1}{144}$ in one day, and to do the whole, he will require 144 days; C does $\frac{1}{48}-\frac{1}{144}=\frac{1}{72}$ in one day, and he will do the whole in 72 days.

105. Had he paid $20 each for the whole, they would have cost $20\times96=$1920; but they only cost $1620: hence they cost $1920−$1620=$300 less, and there were $300\div10=30$ cows.

106. 24 to 3 is the same as 8 to 1, hence there will be 8 oz. of gold to one of silver. No. oz. of gold$=124-10$ $=114$; $\frac{1}{8}$ of $114=14\frac{1}{4}$ oz; $14\frac{1}{4}$ oz.-10 oz.$=4\frac{1}{4}$ oz. to be added.

107. A, B, and C do $\frac{1}{24}$ in one day; B does $\frac{9}{8}$ as much as C; A does $\frac{9}{8}$ as much as B, or $\frac{81}{64}$ as much as C; then $\frac{64}{64}+\frac{72}{64}+\frac{81}{64}$, or $\frac{217}{64}$ of what C does equals $\frac{1}{24}$, $\frac{1}{64}$ of what C does $=\frac{1}{24\times 217}$, and $\frac{64}{64}$ of what C does $=\frac{64}{24\times 217}=\frac{8}{3\times 217}=\frac{8}{651}$; hence C will do it in $\frac{651}{8}$ or $81\frac{3}{8}$ days, B in $72\frac{1}{3}$ days, and A in $64\frac{8}{27}$ days.

108. If he plows 3 acres for 9 cows, for 1 cow he plows $\frac{1}{3}$; if he pastures 3 acres for 5 cows, for 1 cow he pastures $\frac{3}{5}$ of an acre; hence 1 cow requires $\frac{1}{3}+\frac{3}{5}=\frac{14}{15}$ of an acre, and the number of cows equals $84\div\frac{14}{15}=90$, and the number of sheep equals 80.

109. The geese equal $\frac{6}{5}$ of the turkeys; hence $\frac{11}{5}$ of the turkeys $=440$; $\frac{5}{5}$ of the turkeys $=200$, and the geese $=240$; $\frac{2}{3}$ of the turkeys are to equal $\frac{4}{5}$ of $240=192$; hence the turkeys will equal 288; hence he must buy $288-200=88$.

110. Tail $=36+12+\frac{1}{4}$ of body; the body $=36+48+\frac{1}{4}$ of body $+21$; hence $\frac{3}{4}$ of the body $=105$ oz., and the body $=140$ oz.; the tail $=\frac{1}{4}$ of $140+48=83$ oz.; whole weight $=36+83+140=259$ oz.

111. If the bill of one is increased $12\frac{1}{2}$¢, the bill of 45 is increased \$5.62½, which was the share of the 5 who withdrew, hence each one's share was $\frac{1}{5}$ of \$5.62½, or \$1.12½, and the whole cost was 50 times \$1.12½, or \$56.25.

112. If the current was 5 miles an hour, the rate of the steamboat up the river will be 16−5, or 11 miles an hour, and down the river the rate will be 16+5, or 21 miles an hour; then to go 1 mile each way will require $\frac{1}{11}+\frac{1}{21}$, or $\frac{32}{231}$ of an hour, and in $10\frac{2}{3}$ h. the boat will go $10\frac{2}{3}\div\frac{32}{231}$, or 77 miles.

113. A eats 4 times as many as C, and B eats 2 times as many as C; hence all eat 7 times as many as C, which is 63; hence C eats 9, A 36, and B 18; hence A furnishes C with 40—36, or 4, and B furnishes C with 23—18, or 5; hence A has $\frac{4}{9}$ of 18¢, or 8¢, and B has $\frac{5}{9}$ of 18¢, or 10¢.

114. By the conditions, the wife has 2 times as much as the daughter, and the son twice as much as the widow, or 4 times as much as the daughter; hence 7 times what the daughter receives equals $64470, once the daughter's share equals $\frac{1}{7}$ of $64470=$9210; the widow receives $18420; and the son, $36840.

115. $2\frac{1}{2}\times 120=300$, in 2d field; number in 1st field after jumping=120—40+100=180; number in 2d field after jumping=300—100+40=240; 180 is $\frac{3}{4}$ of 240.

116. One cost $\frac{1}{3}$ of a cent, and one cost $\frac{1}{5}$, and 2 cost $\frac{8}{15}$; he sold 2 for $\frac{1}{2}$ a cent; hence he lost on two $\frac{8}{15}-\frac{1}{2}=\frac{1}{30}$ of a cent, and to lose 400 cents takes as many times *one* of each as $400\div\frac{1}{30}=12000$.

117. A's=$\frac{3}{4}$ B's; the difference of their ages=$\frac{1}{4}$ of B's; and since 10 yr. is $\frac{5}{6}$ of the difference, the difference=12 yr.; hence $\frac{1}{4}$ B's=12, B's=48, and A's, 36. If $\frac{1}{4}$ A's= $\frac{1}{5}$ B's, A's=$\frac{4}{5}$ B's; hence, at that time, $\frac{1}{5}$ B's=12, B's =60; hence the time is 60 yr.—48 yr.=12 years.

118. $\frac{5}{8}$ of the time past 8 equals $\frac{5}{3}$ of the time to midnight; hence $\frac{5}{3}$ plus $\frac{3}{3}$ or $\frac{8}{3}$ of the time to midnight=16 hours, and the time to midnight is 6 hours; hence it is 6 o'clock P. M.

119. $\frac{5}{11}$ of A's=$\frac{5}{11}$ of $6435, or $2925; $\frac{13}{15}$ of B's money equals $6435+$2925=$9360; hence B's=$10800. The sum of A's and B's=$17235; they give C $\frac{3}{8}$ of $17235=$6463$\frac{1}{8}$, and retain 10771\frac{7}{8}$. C then had 6463\frac{1}{8}$+$4786$\frac{7}{8}$=$11250. Now the part is $\frac{10771\frac{7}{8}}{11250}=\frac{86175}{90000}=\frac{383}{400}$.

120. The minute-hand gains 11 spaces in going 12; hence to gain 1 space it goes $\frac{12}{11}$ of a space, and to gain 4 spaces, the distance they are apart at 4 o'clock, it goes

$\frac{48}{11}$ spaces. To go one space requires 5 minutes, and to go $\frac{48}{11}$ spaces, requires $\frac{48}{11}\times 5=\frac{240}{11}=21\frac{9}{11}$ minutes.

121. A takes 4 while B takes 5; but 1 of A's=2 B's, hence A goes a distance equal to 8 of B's steps while B goes 5 of his steps; hence B goes $\frac{5}{13}$ of 650 steps, or 250 steps, and A goes a distance equal to $\frac{8}{13}$ of 650 of B's steps, or 400 of B's steps, which we find is equal to 200 of A's steps.

122. By the first condition, 8 times Mary's age equaled her grandmother's age, hence the difference of their ages is 7 times Mary's age, and once Mary's age equals $\frac{1}{7}$ of the *difference* of their ages; in 16 years, 4 times Mary's age equaled her grandmother's age, hence Mary's age equaled $\frac{1}{3}$ of the *difference* of their ages; therefore 16 years is the difference between $\frac{1}{3}$ of the *difference* of their ages and $\frac{1}{7}$ of the difference of their ages, or $\frac{4}{21}$ of the difference of their ages; hence the *difference* of their ages is 84 years, and Mary's age 4 years ago equaled $\frac{1}{3}$ of the difference; hence it was 28 years, and at present is 32 years, and her grandmother's age is 32+84, or 116 years.

123. $\frac{2}{3}$ of 1st—24 : $\frac{3}{4}$ of 2d+24 : : $\frac{2}{3}$: $\frac{3}{4}$; hence $\frac{1}{2}$ 1st—18= $\frac{1}{2}$ of 2d+16, and $\frac{1}{2}$ 1st=$\frac{1}{2}$ of 2d+34, or 1st=2d+68; hence twice the second+68=212; the 2d=72, and 1st=140. By the second condition, $\frac{3}{4}$ of 2d=$\frac{2}{3}$ of the 1st, hence $\frac{2}{3}$ of the 1st=$\frac{3}{4}$ of 72=54, and the 1st=81; hence the part subtracted is 140—81=59.

124. The second receives \$4800—\$2100=\$2700. Had the first labored $\frac{2}{3}$ as many days as the second, he would have received $\frac{2}{3}$ of \$2700=\$1800; hence the labor of 10 days amounts to \$2100—\$1800=\$300, and the labor of 1 day equals \$30; hence 1st labors \$2100÷\$30 =70 days, and the 2d labors \$2700÷\$30=90 days.

125. $\frac{2}{5}$ (Rem.+50) cost \$40, hence the Rem.+50 cost \$100; $\frac{2}{5}$ (Rem.—50) cost \$20, hence Rem.—50 cost \$50; therefore the difference, which is 50+50 or 100, cost \$50, 1 cost \$$\frac{1}{2}$, and \$100 will buy 100÷$\frac{1}{2}$=200; hence

the Rem.+50=200, and the Rem.=150, which is $\frac{3}{5}$ of the No. at first, hence he had 250 at first.

126. One revolution of the tape gives a right-angled triangle, the base of which is 4 ft. and altitude 3 ft.; hence the length of the tape to go once around is 5 ft. Since the cylinder is 52 ft., it goes around $52 \div 4 = 13$ times; hence the length is $5 \times 13 = 65$ ft.

127. First Rem. $= \frac{4}{5}$ of his money—\$24.
Second Rem. $= \frac{3}{5}$ " " —\$36.
Third Rem. $= \frac{2}{5}$ " " —\$36 $= \frac{1}{5}$ of his money.
Hence, $\frac{2}{5} - \frac{1}{5}$ or $\frac{1}{5}$ = \$36.
His money = \$180.

NOTE.—If he gave $\frac{1}{5}$ away, there remained $\frac{4}{5}$; since he gave $\frac{1}{5}$+\$24 there remained $\frac{4}{5}$—\$24. If he gave $\frac{1}{4}$ of this away there remained $\frac{3}{4}$ of this; hence there remained $\frac{3}{4}$ of ($\frac{4}{5}$—\$24) which is $\frac{3}{5}$—\$18; but he gave \$18 more than $\frac{1}{4}$; hence there remained $\frac{3}{5}$—\$36. Some authors find what was given away each time and then subtract. This is more difficult and twice as long as the solution given here.

128. The part inclosed by the walk is $\frac{49}{64}$ of the whole; the whole area is $\frac{2}{5}$ of 160 sq. rods, or 64 sq. rods; hence the part enclosed $= \frac{49}{64} \times 64$, or 49 sq. rd., and the square root of this equals 7 rods; the side, including the walk, is $\sqrt{64} = 8$ rods; hence *twice* the width of the walk is $8 - 7 = 1$ rod; once the width is $\frac{1}{2}$ of a rod, or $\frac{1}{2}$ of $16\frac{1}{2}$ ft. = 8 ft. 3 in.

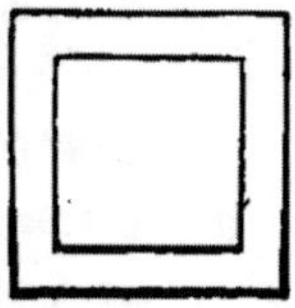

129. Two faces are 4 ft. long and 3 ft. wide; hence the surface of both is twice $4 \times 3 = 24$ sq. ft. Two faces are 4 ft. long and 2 ft. wide; hence their surface is twice $4 \times 2 = 16$ sq. ft. Two faces are 3 ft. long and 2 ft. wide; hence their surface is twice $3 \times 2 = 12$ sq. ft. Hence the whole surface is $24 + 16 + 12 = 52$ sq. ft.

130. Spheres are to each other as the cubes of their diameters, hence weight of 4th ball : weight of 3 other balls :: (diam. of 4th ball)^3 : $3^3 + 4^3 + 5^3$; since weights are equal, Diam. of 4th ball $= \sqrt[3]{3^3 + 4^3 + 5^3} = 6$ in.

131. The difference of men required in the two trials is 144 + 204 = 348, and since there were 2 men on each side more in the first trial than in the second, if we subtract the 4 men that would occupy the corners of the square, we will have 4 times the number of men in the side of the square at the second trial; hence 4 times the number of men in the side=348−4 or 344, and once the number=86; hence $86^2+204=7396+204$ $=7600$.

182. A box whose dimensions are 2, 3, and 4, contains $2\times 3\times 4=24$ cu. in.; hence,

Length of 2d : 4 : : $\sqrt[3]{24}$: : $\sqrt[3]{3000}$.

Length of 2d$=4\times\sqrt{\frac{3000}{24}}=3\times\sqrt[3]{125}$.

In a similar manner we have width of 2d$=3\times 5=15$, and height of 2d$=2\times 5=10$.

183. The horse cost $\frac{9}{8}$ of the cost of the carriage; $\frac{4}{5}$ of the cost of the horse equals what he received for it, and $\frac{6}{5}$ of the cost of the carriage equals what he received for it; but $\frac{4}{5}$ of the cost of the horse$=\frac{4}{5}\times\frac{9}{8}$, or $\frac{9}{10}$ of the cost of the carriage; hence $\frac{9}{10}+\frac{6}{5}$, or $\frac{21}{10}$ of the cost of carriage=$420, and the cost of carriage=$200; the cost of the horse$=\frac{9}{8}$ of $200=$225; both cost $200+ $225=$425; hence the loss was $425−$420=$5.

184. The first was on interest 16 yr., the second 12 yr., the third 8 yr., the fourth 4 yr. At 5% for 16 yr., $\frac{80}{100}$ or $\frac{4}{5}$ of the principal equals the interest; hence $\frac{9}{5}$ of the share of the first equals the *equal amount.* In the same way we find $\frac{8}{5}$ of the share of the 2d equals the *equal amount*, $\frac{7}{5}$ of the share of the 3d equals the *equal amount*, and $\frac{6}{5}$ of the share of the 4th equals the *equal amount.* If $\frac{9}{5}$ of the 1st share=the *equal amount*, the 1st share$=\frac{5}{9}$ of the *equal amount*, and in the same way the 2d share$=\frac{5}{8}$ of the *equal amount*, the 3d share$=\frac{5}{7}$ of the *equal amount*, the 4th share$=\frac{5}{6}$ of the *equal amount*; hence the shares are to each other as $\frac{5}{9}$, $\frac{5}{8}$, $\frac{5}{7}$, $\frac{5}{6}$, or as $\frac{1}{9}$, $\frac{1}{8}$, $\frac{1}{7}$, $\frac{1}{6}$, or as $\frac{56}{504}$, $\frac{63}{504}$, $\frac{72}{504}$, $\frac{84}{504}$, or as 56, 63, 72, 84; hence we divide $27500 into $56+63+72+84=275$ equal parts, and the 1st share$=\frac{56}{275}\times$ $27500=$5600; the 2d share$=\frac{63}{275}\times$

\$27500=\$6300; the 3d share=$\frac{72}{275}\times$\$27500=\$7200; the 4th share=$\frac{84}{275}\times$\$27500=\$8400.

185. If 3 acres+the growth of 3 acres for 4 weeks keep 12 oxen 4 weeks, 1 acre+the growth of 1 acre for 4 weeks will keep 4 oxen 4 weeks, or 4×4 or 16 oxen 1 week. In the same manner 1 acre+the growth of 1 acre for 6 weeks will keep 18 oxen 1 week; subtracting these, and we have the growth of 1 acre for 2 weeks, will keep 2 oxen 1 week, and the growth of 1 acre for 4 weeks keep 4 oxen 1 week; subtracting this from 1 acre+the growth of 1 acre for 4 weeks, we have 1 acre, without the growth, will keep 12 oxen 1 week; hence 6 acres will keep 72 oxen 1 week or $\frac{1}{8}$ of 72, which is 9 oxen, 8 weeks. Again, since the growth of 1 acre for 2 weeks will keep 2 oxen 1 week, the growth of 1 acre 1 week will keep 1 ox 1 week; hence the growth of 6 acres 8 weeks will keep 6 oxen 8 weeks, and adding, we have 6 acres+the growth of 6 acres for 8 weeks will keep 15 oxen 8 weeks.

A. A. W.	O.	W
3+3 for 4	12	4
5+5 for 6	15	6
1+1 for 4	16	1
1+1 for 6	18	1
1 for 2	2	1
1 for 4	4	1
1+0 for 0	12	1
6+0 for 0	9	8
6 for 8	6	8
6+6 for 8	15	8

MANUAL.

THE GREATEST COMMON DIVISOR OF FRACTIONS.

1. The **Greatest Common Divisor** of two or more fractions is the greatest fraction that will exactly divide them.

One fraction exactly divides another when it is contained in it a whole number of times without a remainder.

Prop.—*A divisor of a fraction is a fraction whose numerator is a divisor of the given numerator, and whose denominator is a multiple of the given denominator.*

For, to divide by a fraction we divide by its numerator and multiply by its denominator; hence, to obtain an integral quotient the *numerator* of the divisor must divide the given numerator, and the denominator of the divisor must contain the given denominator.. This may be illustrated by dividing $\frac{6}{7}$ by $\frac{3}{14}$.

1. Find the greatest common divisor of $\frac{6}{7}$, $\frac{9}{14}$, and $\frac{12}{35}$.

SOLUTION.—To be a divisor of each of these fractions the numerator must divide each of the given numerators, and the denominator must contain each of the given denominators; hence, the *greatest* common divisor must be a fraction whose numerator is the *greatest* common divisor of the given numerators, and the denominator the *least* common multiple of the given denominators. The greatest common divisor of the numerators we find is 3, and the least common multiple of the denominators is 70; hence the greatest common divisor of the given fractions is $\frac{3}{70}$.

OPERATION.

$$\frac{6}{7} - \frac{9}{14} - \frac{12}{35}$$

3 = G. C. D. of Numerators.
70 = L. C. M. of Denominators.
$\therefore$ G. C. D. = $\frac{3}{70}$, *Ans.*

Rule.—*Reduce the given fractions to simple ones in their lowest terms, then find the G. C. D. of the numerators and divide it by the L. C. M. of the denominators.*

Find the greatest common divisor of

2. $\frac{4}{5}$, $\frac{5}{6}$, $\frac{7}{8}$. *Ans.* $\frac{1}{120}$.	**6.** $2\frac{5}{8}$, $3\frac{1}{9}$, $2\frac{13}{18}$. *Ans.* $\frac{7}{72}$.
3. $\frac{3}{4}$, $\frac{6}{5}$, $\frac{9}{10}$. *Ans.* $\frac{3}{20}$.	**7.** $\frac{3}{4}$, $\frac{6}{25}$, $\frac{9}{24}$. *Ans.* $\frac{3}{200}$.
4. $2\frac{2}{3}$, 4, $1\frac{7}{9}$. *Ans.* $\frac{4}{9}$.	**8.** $\frac{5}{6}$, $\frac{5}{7}$, $\frac{5}{8}$, $\frac{5}{9}$. *Ans.* $\frac{5}{504}$.
5. 5, $\frac{15}{8}$, $\frac{20}{9}$, $\frac{25}{12}$. *Ans.* $\frac{5}{72}$.	**9.** $\frac{7}{12}$, $\frac{14}{15}$, $\frac{21}{20}$, $\frac{35}{24}$. *Ans.* $\frac{7}{120}$

10. A man has three boards $11\frac{1}{4}$, $16\frac{2}{3}$, and $15\frac{5}{6}$ feet in length respectively; what are the longest equal pieces into which they may be sawed? *Ans.* $\frac{5}{12}$ foot.

11. The sides of a four-sided lot are respectively $36\frac{3}{4}$ feet, $58\frac{4}{5}$ feet, $44\frac{1}{10}$ feet, and $88\frac{1}{5}$ feet; what is the greatest length of boards that can be used in putting a fence around it without cutting the boards? *Ans.* $7\frac{7}{20}$ feet.

THE LEAST COMMON MULTIPLE OF FRACTIONS.

2. The **Least Common Multiple** of two or more fractions is the least number that will exactly contain each of them.

Prop.—*A multiple of a fraction is a fraction whose numerator is a multiple of the given numerator, and whose denominator is a divisor of the given denominator.*

For, to divide by a fraction we divide by its numerator and multiply by its denominator; hence, to give an integral quotient when we divide a multiple by a fraction, the numerator of the multiple must contain the numerator of the fraction, and the denominator of the multiple must divide the denominator of the given fraction. This may be illustrated by examining $\frac{4}{3}$, a multiple of $\frac{2}{3}$.

1. Find the least common multiple of $\frac{8}{5}$, $\frac{16}{15}$, and $\frac{12}{35}$.

OPERATION.

$\frac{8}{5}$ - $\frac{16}{15}$ - $\frac{12}{35}$.

L. C. M. of Num. $= 48$
G. C. D. of Den. $= 5$
$\therefore$ L. C. M. $= \frac{48}{5} = 9\frac{3}{5}$, *Ans*

SOLUTION.—To be a multiple of each of these fractions the numerator must contain each of the given numerators, and the denominator divide each of the given denominators; hence, the *least* common multiple must be a fraction whose numerator is the least common multiple of the given numerators, and whose denominator is the greatest common divisor of the given denominators. The least common multiple of the numerators, we find, is 48, and the greatest common divisor of the denominators is 5, hence $\frac{48}{5}$ is the least common multiple of the given fractions.

Rule.—*Reduce the fractions to simple ones in their lowest terms, then find the L. C. M. of the numerators and divide it by the G. C. D. of the denominators.*

Find the least common multiple of

2. $\frac{2}{5}$, $\frac{3}{10}$, $\frac{4}{15}$. *Ans.* $\frac{12}{5}$.

3. $\frac{5}{6}$, $\frac{10}{27}$, $\frac{25}{27}$. *Ans.* $16\frac{2}{3}$.

4. $\frac{6}{7}$, $\frac{18}{28}$, $\frac{12}{35}$. *Ans.* $5\frac{1}{7}$.

5. $\frac{24}{10}$, $\frac{36}{50}$, $\frac{24}{35}$, $\frac{36}{25}$. *Ans.* $14\frac{2}{5}$

6. $6\frac{2}{3}$, $4\frac{4}{9}$, $\frac{50}{27}$. *Ans.* $66\frac{2}{3}$.

7. $\frac{3}{4}$, $\frac{5}{6}$, $\frac{7}{8}$, $\frac{9}{10}$. *Ans.* $157\frac{1}{2}$.

8. $6\frac{3}{5}$, $7\frac{9}{10}$, $8\frac{14}{15}$, $19\frac{12}{25}$.

9. $7\frac{1}{12}$, 10, $18\frac{5}{6}$, 124

10. What is the least sum of money for which I can buy an integral number of bushels of grain, wheat at $\$1\frac{3}{4}$ a bushel, rye at $\$1\frac{1}{8}$, corn at $\$\frac{7}{8}$, and oats at $\$\frac{3}{8}$ a bushel? *Ans.* $\$15\frac{3}{4}$.

11. What is the least sum of money for which I can buy a number of sheep at $\$5\frac{1}{4}$, a number of hogs at $\$4\frac{3}{8}$, or a number of cows at $\$26\frac{1}{4}$? *Ans.* $\$26\frac{1}{4}$.

12. A, B, and C start at the same place and travel around an island, A making the circuit in $\frac{4}{5}$ of a day, B in $\frac{8}{15}$ of a day, and C in $\frac{12}{25}$ of a day; in how many days will they all be together at the place of starting, and how far will each have traveled? *Ans.* $4\frac{4}{5}$ days; A, 6 times around, etc.

CIRCULATING DECIMALS.

3. A Circulate, or **Circulating Decimal,** is a decimal in which one or more figures are repeated in the same order; thus, .333 etc.; 2.363636 etc.

4. A Repetend is the figure or set of figures which repeat. A Repetend of one figure is expressed by placing a point over the figure

5. A Repetend of more than one figure is expressed by placing a point over the first and last figure; thus .333 etc., is expressed thus, $.\dot{3}$; 2.3636 etc., is expressed thus, $2.\dot{3}\dot{6}$.

6. A Pure Circulate is one which contains no figures but those which repeat; as, $5.\dot{2}6\dot{7}$.

7. A Mixed Circulate is one which contains one or more figures before the repeating part; as $.45\dot{3}0\dot{6}$. The parts are distinguished as the *repeating* and *non-repeating* parts.

8. A Perfect Repetend is one in which the number of decimal places in the repetend is one less than the number of units in the denominator of the common fraction from which it is derived; thus, $\frac{1}{7}=.\dot{1}4285\dot{7}$.

ORIGIN OF CIRCULATES.—In reducing common fractions to decimals, as has been seen, sometimes the division terminates and sometimes it does not. When the division does not terminate, if it be carried sufficiently far, a figure or set of figures in the quotient will begin to repeat in the same order. Circulating decimals have their origin, therefore, in the reduction of common fractions to decimals. The two classes of decimals are sometimes distinguished as *finite* or *terminate*, and *infinite* or *interminate*. For a full treatise see *Brooks's Higher Arithmetic.*

REDUCTION OF CIRCULATES.

CASE I.

9. ***To reduce a common fraction to a circulate.***

1. Reduce $\frac{1}{7}$ to a circulate.

OPERATION.

$$7)\underline{1.000000}$$
$$.\dot{1}4285\dot{7}$$

SOLUTION.—By reducing, as in Art. 206, we find $\frac{1}{7}=.\dot{1}4285\dot{7}$.

Reduce the following to repetends:

2. $\frac{7}{9}$.	*Ans.* $.\dot{7}$.	7. $\frac{13}{15}$.	*Ans.* $.8\dot{6}$.
3. $\frac{5}{11}$.	*Ans.* $.\dot{4}\dot{5}$.	8. $\frac{17}{18}$.	*Ans.* $.9\dot{4}$.
4. $\frac{9}{11}$.	*Ans.* $.\dot{8}\dot{1}$.	9. $\frac{19}{21}$.	*Ans.* $.\dot{9}0476\dot{1}$.
5. $\frac{12}{13}$	*Ans.* $.\dot{9}2307\dot{6}$.	10. $\frac{16}{17}$.	
6. $\frac{11}{14}$.	*Ans.* $.7\dot{8}5714\dot{2}$.		

10. The pupils will now prove by actual division the truth of the following principles:

1. That $\frac{1}{9}=.\dot{1}$.	4. That $\frac{1}{9999}=.\dot{0}00\dot{1}$.
2. That $\frac{1}{99}=.\dot{0}\dot{1}$.	5. That $\frac{1}{99999}=.\dot{0}000\dot{1}$.
3. That $\frac{1}{999}=.\dot{0}0\dot{1}$.	6. That $\frac{1}{999999}=.\dot{0}0000\dot{1}$.

CASE II.

11. ***To reduce a pure circulate to a common fraction.***

1. Reduce $.\dot{3}2\dot{4}$ to a common fraction.

SOLUTION.—Since $.\dot{0}0\dot{1}$ equals $\frac{1}{999}$, as was shown in the previous case, $.\dot{3}2\dot{4}$, which is 324 times $.\dot{0}0\dot{1}$, equals 324 times $\frac{1}{999}$, which is $\frac{324}{999}$, which, reduced to its lowest terms, is $\frac{12}{37}$. Hence the following

OPERATION.

Since $.\dot{0}0\dot{1}=\frac{1}{999}$

$.\dot{3}2\dot{4}=\frac{324}{999}=\frac{12}{37}$

Rule.—*Write the repetend for the numerator of a fraction, with as many 9's as there are places in the repetend for a denominator, and reduce to lowest terms.*

Reduce the following to common fractions:

2. $.\dot{2}0\dot{7}$.	*Ans.* $\frac{23}{111}$.	6. $.\dot{1}78\dot{2}$.	*Ans.* $\frac{18}{101}$.
3. $.\dot{1}3\dot{5}$.	*Ans.* $\frac{5}{37}$.	7. $.\dot{4}15\dot{8}$.	*Ans.* $\frac{42}{101}$.
4. $.\dot{0}2\dot{7}$.	*Ans.* $\frac{1}{37}$.	8. $.\dot{0}720\dot{9}$.	*Ans.* $\frac{801}{11111}$.
5. $.\dot{2}1\dot{6}$.	*Ans.* $\frac{8}{37}$.	9. $.\dot{0}0232\dot{2}$.	*Ans.* $\frac{86}{37037}$.

CASE III.

12. ***To reduce a mixed circulate to a common fraction.***

1. Reduce $.4\dot{3}\dot{6}$ to a common fraction.

	OPERATION.
SOLUTION.—$.4\dot{3}\dot{6}$ equals $\frac{1}{10}$ of $4.\dot{3}\dot{6}$, which equals $\frac{1}{10}$ of $4\frac{36}{99}$, or $\frac{1}{10}$ of $4\frac{4}{11}$, which equals $\frac{48}{110}$, which, reduced to its lowest terms, equals $\frac{24}{55}$. Hence the following	$.4\dot{3}\dot{6} = \frac{4\frac{36}{99}}{10}$ $= \frac{4\frac{4}{11}}{10} = \frac{48}{110} = \frac{24}{55}$

Rule.—I. *Write beneath the repetend as many 9's as there are places in the repetend, and annex this to the finite part.*

II. *Divide this by 1 with as many ciphers annexed as there are places in the finite part, and reduce the result to a simple fraction, in its lowest terms.*

Reduce the following to common fractions:

2. $.2\dot{2}\dot{7}$.	*Ans.* $\frac{5}{22}$.	6. $.47\dot{2}0\dot{7}$.	*Ans.* $\frac{262}{555}$.
3. $.2\dot{5}\dot{4}$.	*Ans.* $\frac{14}{55}$.	7. $.84\dot{2}3\dot{4}$.	*Ans.* $\frac{187}{222}$.
4. $.2\dot{3}\dot{6}$.	*Ans.* $\frac{13}{55}$.	8. $.35\dot{1}3\dot{5}$.	*Ans.* $\frac{13}{37}$.
5. $.5\dot{9}\dot{0}$.	*Ans.* $\frac{13}{22}$.	9. $.9\dot{2}8571\dot{4}$.	*Ans* $\frac{13}{14}$.

ANOTHER METHOD.

1. Reduce $.\dot{3}\dot{6}$ to a common fraction.

SOLUTION.—Let F represent the common fraction, then if we multiply by 100, to make a whole number of the repetend, we will have 100 times the fraction equals 36.3636 etc. Now, subtracting *once* the common fraction from 100 times the common fraction, we have 99 times the common fraction equal to 36, hence once the fraction equals $\frac{1}{99}$ of 36, which is $\frac{36}{99}$, or $\frac{4}{11}$.

OPERATION.

$$F = .363636 \text{ etc.}$$
$$100 \times F = 36.3636$$
$$99 \times F = 36$$
$$F = \tfrac{36}{99} = \tfrac{4}{11}, \textit{ Ans.}$$

NOTE.—1. With a mixed repetend we multiply by 1 with ciphers to make a whole number of the *non-repeating* part, and then by 1 with ciphers to make a whole number of the repeating part, and then subtract the first result from the second, as is illustrated in the margin.

$$F = .3918918 \text{ etc.}$$
$$10\,F = 3.918918 \text{ etc.}$$
$$10000\,F = 3918.918 \text{ etc.}$$
$$9990\,F = 3915$$
$$F = \tfrac{3915}{9990} = \tfrac{29}{74}, \textit{ Ans.}$$

2. Pupils who are sufficiently advanced may apply this method to the problems given above.

PRINCIPLES OF SIMPLE AND CIRCULATING DECIMALS.

1. *A common fraction whose denominator contains no other prime factors than* 2 *and* 5, *can be reduced to a simple decimal.*

Since 2 and 5 are factors of 10, if we annex as many ciphers to the numerator as there are 2's or 5's in the denominator, the numerator will be exactly divisible by the denominator. Therefore, etc.

2. *The number of places in the simple decimal to which a common fraction may be reduced, is equal to the greatest number of* 2's *or* 5's *in the denominator.*

To make the numerator contain the denominator, we must annex a cipher for every 2 or 5 in the denominator, and the number of decimal places equals the number of ciphers added. Therefore, etc.

3. *Every common fraction whose denominator contains other prime factors than* 2 *or* 5, *will reduce to an interminate decimal.*

Since 2 and 5 are the only factors of 10, if the denominator contains other prime factors the numerator with ciphers annexed will not exactly contain the denominator. Therefore, etc.

4. *Every common fraction which does not give a simple decimal gives a circulate.*

In dividing by the denominator there cannot be more different remainders than there are units in the denominator; hence, if the division be continued, a remainder must occur which has been previously used, and this will give a series of remainders and dividends like those already used, hence the quotients will be repeated. Therefore, etc.

5. *When a common fraction contains* 2's *or* 5's, *with other prime factors in the denominator, it will give a mixed circulate, and the number of places in the non-repeating part will equal the greatest number of* 2's *or* 5's *in the denominator.*

This is evident from the above. Let the pupil show it. Give illustrations of each of the above.

PROBLEMS FOR PUPILS WHO THINK THEY HAVE MASTERED THE BOOK.

Reduce the following to common fractions:

1. Reduce $7.0\frac{1}{2}$.
2. Reduce $2.0\dot{6}$.
3. Reduce $5.00\dot{3}$.
4. Reduce $\dot{1}8.\dot{5}$.
5. Reduce $.\dot{5}7.1428$.
6. Reduce $.0\dot{\frac{1}{2}}$; $.\dot{0}\frac{1}{2}0\dot{\frac{1}{3}}$.

CONTRACTIONS IN MULTIPLICATION AND DIVISION.

CONTRACTIONS IN MULTIPLICATION.

13. Contractions in multiplication and division are abbreviated processes for multiplying and dividing. Many of these are very useful in facilitating the mechanical operations.

CASE I.

14. ***When the multiplier is an aliquot part of* 10, 100, 1000, *etc.***

1. To multiply any number by $2\frac{1}{2}$, *we multiply the number by* 10 *and divide by* 4.

SOLUTION.—Suppose we wish to multiply 38 by $2\frac{1}{2}$. Since $2\frac{1}{2}$ equals $\frac{1}{4}$ of 10, $2\frac{1}{2}$ times a number equals $\frac{1}{4}$ of ten times the number; hence $38\times2\frac{1}{2}$ equals 38×10 divided by 4, which equals 95.

OPERATION.

$38\times2\frac{1}{2}=$

$4)\underline{380}$

95, *Ans.*

2. To multiply by $3\frac{1}{3}$, or 5, *we annex a cipher to the multiplicand and divide respectively by* 3 *and* 2.

3. To multiply by $12\frac{1}{2}$, $16\frac{2}{3}$, 25, $33\frac{1}{3}$, 50, *we annex two ciphers and divide respectively by* 8, 6, 4, 3, *and* 2.

4. To multiply by 125, $166\frac{2}{3}$, 250, $333\frac{1}{3}$, *we annex three ciphers and divide respectively by* 8, 6, 4, *and* 3.

The following relations will enable us to multiply by other aliquot parts:

$37\frac{1}{2}=\frac{3}{8}$ of 100.	$375=\frac{3}{8}$ of 1000.
$62\frac{1}{2}=\frac{5}{8}$ of 100.	$625=\frac{5}{8}$ of 1000.
$66\frac{2}{3}=\frac{2}{3}$ of 100.	$666\frac{2}{3}=\frac{2}{3}$ of 1000.
$75=\frac{3}{4}$ of 100.	$750=\frac{3}{4}$ of 1000.
$83\frac{1}{3}=\frac{5}{6}$ of 100.	$833\frac{1}{3}=\frac{5}{6}$ of 1000.
$87\frac{1}{2}=\frac{7}{8}$ of 100.	$875=\frac{7}{8}$ of 1000.

EXAMPLES FOR PRACTICE.

1. Multiply 956 by $12\frac{1}{2}$.

SOLUTION.—Since $12\frac{1}{2}=\frac{1}{8}$ of 100, $12\frac{1}{2}$ times 956 equals $\frac{1}{8}$ of 100 times 956, which equals $\frac{1}{8}$ of $95600=11950$.

OPERATION.

$12\frac{1}{2}=\frac{1}{8}$ of 100

$8)\underline{95600}$

11950

2. 756 by $2\frac{1}{2}$. *Ans.* 1890.

3. 747 by $3\frac{1}{3}$. *Ans.* 2490.

4. 895 by $12\frac{1}{2}$. *Ans.* $11187\frac{1}{2}$.

5. 7854 by $16\frac{2}{3}$. *Ans.* 130900.

6. 18568 by 25. *Ans.* 464200.

7. 7542 by $33\frac{1}{3}$. *Ans.* 251400.

8. 8577 by $66\frac{2}{3}$. *Ans.* 571800.

9. 7659 by 75. *Ans.* 574425.

10. 38567 by $62\frac{1}{2}$. *Ans.* $2410437\frac{1}{2}$.

11. 28564 by 125. *Ans.* 3570500.

12. 68532 by $166\frac{2}{3}$. *Ans.* 11422000.

13. 98765 by 250. *Ans.* 24691250.

14. 73521 by $333\frac{1}{3}$. *Ans.* 24507000.

15. 35420 by 8125. *Ans.* 287787500.

16. 67324 by $1833\frac{1}{3}$. *Ans.* $123427333\frac{1}{3}$.

17. 93864 by $54166\frac{2}{3}$. *Ans.* 5084300000.

18. 13574 by 125250. *Ans.* 1700143500.

19. 35676 by $250333\frac{1}{3}$. *Ans.* 8930892000.

20. Multiply 67328 by $83\frac{1}{3}$; by $87\frac{1}{2}$; by 750; by $833\frac{1}{3}$; by 875; by $75087\frac{1}{2}$; by $625833\frac{1}{3}$.

CASE II.

15. *To multiply when all the digits of the multiplier are* 9.

1. Multiply 856 by 999.

SOLUTION.—999 times 856 equals (1000—1) times 856, which equals 1000 times 856, minus 856, which equals 856000—856=855144. Therefore,

OPERATION.

```
   856
   999
856000
855144, Ans.
```

Rule.—*Annex to the number as many naughts as there are 9's in the multiplier, and subtract the number from the result.*

What is the product of

2. 875 by 99? *Ans.* 86625.

3. 2378 by 999? *Ans.* 2375622

4. 7352 by 9999? *Ans.* 73512648.

5. 43216 by 99.99? *Ans.* 4321167 84.

6. 32457 by 25.999? *Ans.* 843849.543.

CASE III.

16. ***To square a mixed number in which the fractional part is ½.***

The square of a number is the product of the number multiplied by itself. Thus 3×3, or 9, is the square of 3.

METHOD.—*Multiply the whole number by the next larger whole number, and to the product add ¼.*

DEM.—This may be proved by squaring any such mixed number as $7\frac{1}{2}$. $7\frac{1}{2}\times 7\frac{1}{2}=(7+\frac{1}{2})\ (7+\frac{1}{2})$, and multiplying this as in the margin, we have $7\times 7+1\times 7+\frac{1}{4}$, which equals $8\times 7+\frac{1}{4}$ which proves the method.

OPERATION.

$$\begin{array}{r} 7+\frac{1}{2} \\ 7+\frac{1}{2} \\ \hline 7\times\frac{1}{2}+\frac{1}{4} \\ 7\times 7+7\times\frac{1}{2} \quad \\ \hline 7\times 7+1\times 7+\frac{1}{4}=8\times 7+\frac{1}{4}. \end{array}$$

What is the square

1. Of $9\frac{1}{2}$?	*Ans.* $90\frac{1}{4}$.	5. Of $86\frac{1}{2}$?	*Ans.* $7482\frac{1}{4}$.
2. Of $13\frac{1}{2}$?	*Ans.* $182\frac{1}{4}$.	6. Of $124\frac{1}{2}$?	*Ans.* $15500\frac{1}{4}$.
3. Of $19\frac{1}{2}$?	*Ans.* $380\frac{1}{4}$.	7. Of $425\frac{1}{2}$?	*Ans.* $181050\frac{1}{4}$.
4. Of $28\frac{1}{2}$?	*Ans.* $812\frac{1}{4}$.	8. Of $9999\frac{1}{2}$?	*Ans.* $99990000\frac{1}{4}$.

CASE IV.

17. ***To find the product of two mixed numbers whose fractional parts are halves.***

METHOD.—*Take the product of the integers, increase this by ½ of their sum, and by ¼.*

DEM.—This method can be readily obtained by a process similar to the preceding.

What is the product of

1. $4\frac{1}{2}$ by $6\frac{1}{2}$?	*Ans.* $29\frac{1}{4}$.	5. $21\frac{1}{2}$ by $25\frac{1}{2}$?	*Ans.* $548\frac{1}{4}$.
2. $8\frac{1}{2}$ by $12\frac{1}{2}$?	*Ans.* $106\frac{1}{4}$.	6. $57\frac{1}{2}$ by $79\frac{1}{2}$?	*Ans.* $4571\frac{1}{4}$.
3. $14\frac{1}{2}$ by $18\frac{1}{2}$?	*Ans.* $268\frac{1}{4}$.	7. $97\frac{1}{2}$ by $85\frac{1}{2}$?	*Ans.* $8336\frac{1}{4}$.
4. $17\frac{1}{2}$ by $19\frac{1}{2}$?	*Ans.* $341\frac{1}{4}$.	8. $123\frac{1}{2}$ by $208\frac{1}{2}$?	*Ans.* $25749\frac{3}{4}$.

CASE V.

18. ***To square a mixed number whose fractional part is ¼.***

METHOD.—*First, when the integer is* EVEN, *square the integer, add ½ of itself and the square of ¼.*

Secondly, when the integer is ODD, *square the integer, add $\frac{1}{2}$ of the next smaller number, and $\frac{9}{16}$.*

What is the square

1. Of $6\frac{1}{4}$?	*Ans.* $39\frac{1}{16}$.	5. Of $64\frac{1}{4}$?	*Ans.* $4128\frac{1}{16}$.
2. Of $8\frac{1}{4}$?	*Ans.* $68\frac{1}{16}$.	6. Of $96\frac{1}{4}$?	*Ans.* $9264\frac{1}{16}$.
3. Of $12\frac{1}{4}$?	*Ans.* $150\frac{1}{16}$.	7. Of $158\frac{1}{4}$?	*Ans.* $25043\frac{1}{16}$.
4. Of $25\frac{1}{4}$?	*Ans.* $637\frac{9}{16}$.	8. Of $397\frac{1}{4}$	*Ans.* $157807\frac{9}{16}$.

CASE VI.

19. ***To square a mixed number whose fractional part is $\frac{3}{4}$.***

METHOD.—*First, when the integer is* EVEN, *square the integer, increase this by $\frac{3}{2}$ of the integer, and by the square of $\frac{3}{4}$.*

Secondly, when the integer is ODD, *square the integer, add $\frac{3}{2}$ of the next smaller integer, and also $2\frac{1}{16}$.*

What is the square

1. Of $4\frac{3}{4}$?	*Ans.* $22\frac{9}{16}$.	5. Of $9\frac{3}{4}$?	*Ans.* $95\frac{1}{16}$.
2. Of $8\frac{3}{4}$?	*Ans.* $76\frac{9}{16}$.	6. Of $15\frac{3}{4}$?	*Ans.* $248\frac{1}{16}$.
3. Of $12\frac{3}{4}$?	*Ans.* $162\frac{9}{16}$.	7. Of $39\frac{3}{4}$?	*Ans.* $1580\frac{1}{16}$.
4. Of $64\frac{3}{4}$?	*Ans.* $4192\frac{9}{16}$.	8. Of $345\frac{3}{4}$?	*Ans.* $119543\frac{1}{16}$.

CASE VII.

20. ***To square a number whose unit figure is 5.***

METHOD.—*Multiply the part preceding the units by itself increased by a unit, and prefix the result to 25.*

What is the square of

1. 45?	*Ans.* 2025.	5. 345?	*Ans.* 119025.
2. 75?	*Ans.* 5625.	6. 385?	*Ans.* 148225.
3. 95?	*Ans.* 9025.	7. 875?	*Ans.* 765625.
4. 235?	*Ans.* 55225.	8. 9995?	*Ans.* 99900025.

CASE VIII.

21. ***To square a number ending in 25.***

METHOD.—When the part preceding 25 is EVEN, *square it, and add $\frac{1}{2}$ of it to the result, and prefix the sum to 0625.*

When the part preceding 25 is ODD, *square it, add $\frac{1}{2}$ of the next smaller number, and prefix* the result to 5625.

What is the square of

1. 225?	*Ans.* 50625.	5. 825?	*Ans.* 680625.
2. 425?	*Ans.* 180625.	6. 725?	*Ans.* 525625.
3. 1625?	*Ans.* 2640625.	7. 2125?	*Ans.* 4515625.
4. 1825?	*Ans.* 3330625.	8. 3125?	*Ans.* 9765625.

CASE IX.

22. ***To square a number ending in* 75.**

METHOD.—*We regard the* 75 *as* $\frac{3}{4}$, *and then proceed as in the case of squaring a mixed number whose fractional part is* $\frac{3}{4}$.

What is the square of

1. 475?	*Ans.* 225625.	5. 1075?	*Ans.* 1155625.
2. 875?	*Ans.* 765625.	6. 1275?	*Ans.* 1625625.
3. 975?	*Ans.* 950625.	7. 1175? 1375?	
4. 775?	*Ans.* 600625.	8. 1775? 4175? 2075?	

NOTE.—For other cases and methods, see the author's "METHODS OF TEACHING MENTAL ARITHMETIC, etc."

CASE X.

23. ***To find the product of any two numbers whose unit figures are* 5.**

METHOD.—*Take the product of the figures preceding the* 5 *in each number, increase this by* $\frac{1}{2}$ *of their sum, and prefix the result to* 25.

REMARK.—If the *sum* is *odd*, the $\frac{1}{2}$ or 5 tens, which remains when we take one-half, must be added to the 2 of the 25.

Find the product of

1. 25×45.	*Ans.* 1125.	4. 35×85.	*Ans.* 2975.
2. 45×75.	*Ans.* 3375.	5. 95×75.	*Ans.* 7125.
3. 65×85	*Ans.* 5525.	6. 225×105.	

CASE XI.

24. ***To multiply without writing the partial products.***

METHOD.—*The method is indicated by the following problem and its solution.*

1. *Multiply* 5642 by 345.

$$\begin{array}{r} 5642 \\ 345 \\ \hline 1946490 \end{array}$$

EXPLANATION.—1st. 5 times 2 = 10; we write 0 and reserve 1 to "*carry.*"

2d. 5 times 4 = 20 + 4 times 2, or 8 + 1 = 29; write 9 and reserve 2 to carry.

3d. 5 times 6 + 4 times 4 + 3 times 2 + 2 = 54; write 4 and reserve 5 to carry.

4th. 5 times 5 + 4 times 6 + 3 times 4 + 5 = 66; write 6 and reserve 6 to carry.

5th. 4 times 5 + 3 times 6 + 6 = 44; write 4 and reserve 4 to carry.

6th. 3 times 5 + 4 = 19; write this since it is the last product.

NOTE 1.—The above rule is, in practice, performed mentally. A little practice will enable a pupil to multiply rapidly and accurately by a number consisting of several figures. Adepts can multiply by a number of twelve or fifteen figures, writing the result with great readiness. This is an unusual degree of proficiency, but any one can learn to multiply with a number of four or five figures.

2. Let the pupil solve by this method some of the problems on pp. 45 and 46 of the Arithmetic.

CONTRACTIONS IN DIVISIONS.

25. All the methods of multiplying under Case I. may be applied to division, by reversing the operations. Thus, to divide by $2\frac{1}{2}$ we *multiply* by 4 and *divide* by 10, etc.

Divide

1. 25 by $2\frac{1}{2}$. *Ans.* 10.
2. 54 by $3\frac{1}{3}$. *Ans.* $16\frac{1}{5}$.
3. 225 by $12\frac{1}{2}$. *Ans.* 18.
4. 485 by $16\frac{2}{3}$ *Ans.* $29\frac{1}{10}$.
5. 875 by 25. *Ans.* 35.
6. $4366\frac{2}{3}$ by $33\frac{1}{3}$. *Ans.* 131.
7. 8760 by 50. *Ans.* $175\frac{1}{5}$.
8. 8960 by $37\frac{1}{2}$. *Ans.* $238\frac{14}{15}$.
9. 7532 by $62\frac{1}{2}$. *Ans.* $120\frac{64}{125}$.
10. 8535 by 75. *Ans.* $113\frac{4}{5}$.
11. 9650 by $83\frac{1}{3}$. *Ans.* $115\frac{4}{5}$.
12. 3285 by 125. *Ans.* $26\frac{7}{25}$.
13. $8666\frac{2}{3}$ by $333\frac{1}{3}$. *Ans.* 26.
14. $25666\frac{2}{3}$ by $833\frac{1}{3}$. *Ans.* $30\frac{4}{5}$.
15. 1567355 by 750. *Ans.* $2089\frac{121}{150}$.
16. 85673250 by 875. *Ans.* $97912\frac{2}{7}$.

KEY TO MANUAL.

GREATEST COMMON DIVISOR OF FRACTIONS

Art. 1.

4. G. C. D. of numerators$=4$; L. C. M. of denominators $=9$; G. C. D.$=\frac{4}{9}$.

6. $\frac{21}{8}, \frac{28}{9}, \frac{49}{18}$; G. C. D. of num.$=7$; L. C. M. of den.$=72$; G. C. D.$=\frac{7}{72}$.

7. $\frac{3}{4}, \frac{6}{25}, \frac{3}{8}$; G. C. D. of num.$=3$; L. C. M. of den.$=200$; G. C. D.$=\frac{3}{200}$.

9. $\frac{7}{12}, \frac{7}{8}, \frac{21}{20}, \frac{35}{24}$; G. C. D. of num.$=7$; L. C. M. of den.$=120$; G. C. D.$=\frac{7}{120}$.

10. $\frac{45}{4}, \frac{50}{3}, \frac{25}{6}$; G. C. D. of num.$=5$; L. C. M. of den.$=12$; G. C. D.$=\frac{5}{12}$.

11. $\frac{147}{4}, \frac{294}{5}, \frac{441}{10}, \frac{441}{5}$; G. C. D. of num.$=147$; L. C. M. of den.$=20$; G. C. D.$=\frac{147}{20}=7\frac{7}{20}$.

LEAST COMMON MULTIPLE OF FRACTIONS.

Art. 2.

6. $\frac{20}{3}, \frac{40}{9}, \frac{50}{27}$; L. C. M. of num.$=200$; G. C. D. of den.$=3$; L. C. M.$=66\frac{2}{3}$.

8. $\frac{33}{5}, \frac{79}{10}, \frac{134}{15}, \frac{487}{25}$; L. C. M. of num.$=170127606$; G. C. D. of den.$=5$; L. C. M.$=34025521\frac{1}{5}$.

9. $\frac{89}{12}$, 10, $\frac{113}{6}$, 124; L. C. M. of num.$=119120$; G. C. D of den.$=1$; L. C. M.$=1191020$.

10. $\frac{7}{4}, \frac{9}{8}, \frac{7}{8}, \frac{3}{8}$; L. C. M. of num.$=63$; G. C. D. of den $=4$; L. C. M.$=15\frac{3}{4}$.

11. $\frac{21}{4}, \frac{35}{8}, \frac{105}{4}$; L. C. M. of num.$=105$; G. C. D. of den. $=4$; L. C. M.$=\frac{105}{4}=26\frac{1}{4}$.

12. L. C. M. of $\frac{4}{5}, \frac{8}{15}$, and $\frac{12}{25}=\frac{24}{5}=4\frac{4}{5}$; A goes $\frac{24}{5}\div\frac{4}{5}=6$ times around; B goes $\frac{24}{5}\div\frac{8}{15}=9$ times around; C goes $\frac{24}{5}\div\frac{12}{25}=10$ times around.

CIRCULATING DECIMALS.

Art. 9. Case I.

10. $\frac{16}{17}=0.\dot{9}41176470588235\dot{2}$.

Art. 12. Case III.

2. $.2\dot{2}\dot{7}=.2\frac{27}{99}=.2\frac{3}{11}=\frac{2\frac{3}{11}}{10}=\frac{25}{110}=\frac{5}{22}$.

3. $.2\dot{5}\dot{4}=.2\frac{54}{99}=.2\frac{6}{11}=\frac{2\frac{6}{11}}{10}=\frac{28}{110}=\frac{14}{55}$.

4. $.2\dot{3}\dot{6}=.2\frac{36}{99}=.2\frac{4}{11}=\frac{2\frac{4}{11}}{10}=\frac{26}{110}=\frac{13}{55}$.

5. $.5\dot{9}\dot{0}=.5\frac{90}{99}=.5\frac{10}{11}=\frac{5\frac{10}{11}}{10}=\frac{65}{110}=\frac{13}{22}$.

6. $.47\dot{2}0\dot{7}=.47\frac{207}{999}=.47\frac{23}{111}=\frac{47\frac{23}{111}}{100}=\frac{5240}{11100}=\frac{262}{555}$.

7. $.84\dot{2}3\dot{4}=.84\frac{234}{999}=.84\frac{26}{111}=\frac{84\frac{26}{111}}{100}=\frac{9350}{11100}=\frac{187}{222}$.

8. $.35135=.35\frac{135}{999}=.35\frac{5}{37}=\frac{35\frac{5}{37}}{100}=\frac{1300}{3700}=\frac{13}{37}$.

9. $.9\dot{2}8571\dot{4}=.9\frac{285714}{999999}=.9\frac{31746}{111111}$, dividing by $11=.9\frac{2886}{10101}$; dividing by $3=.9\frac{962}{3367}$; dividing by $481=.9\frac{2}{7}=\frac{65}{70}$ $=\frac{13}{14}$.

NOTE.—$\frac{285714}{999999}$ may also be reduced by finding the G. C. D. of both terms, and dividing by it.

Page 271.

1. $0.0\frac{1}{2}=\frac{1}{2}$ of $\frac{1}{10}=\frac{1}{20}$; hence $7.0\frac{1}{2}=7\frac{1}{20}$.
2. $0.0\dot{6}=.0\frac{6}{9}=.0\frac{2}{3}=\frac{2}{3}$ of $\frac{1}{10}=\frac{1}{15}$; hence $2.0\dot{6}=2\frac{1}{15}$.
3. $0.00\dot{3}=.00\frac{1}{3}=\frac{1}{3}$ of $\frac{1}{100}=\frac{1}{300}$; hence $5.00\dot{3}=5\frac{1}{300}$.
4. $\dot{1}8.\dot{5}=18.518518$ etc. $=18.\dot{5}1\dot{8}=18\frac{518}{999}=18\frac{14}{27}$.
5. $5\dot{7}.142\dot{8}=57.\dot{1}4285\dot{7}=57\frac{1}{7}$.
6. These are mere puzzles. The value of $.\dot{0}\frac{1}{2}$ is $\frac{1}{18}$, and of the second $\frac{16}{297}$.

APPENDIX.

GAUGING.

Art. 784. Page 413.

1. 36−28=8 in.; mean diameter=28+$\frac{2}{3}$ of 8=33$\frac{1}{3}$ in.; capacity=$(33\frac{1}{3})^2\times40\times.0034$=151$\frac{1}{9}$ gal.

2. 29−26=3 in.; mean diam.=26+$\frac{3}{5}$ of 3=27$\frac{4}{5}$ in.; capacity=$(27\frac{4}{5})^2\times36\times.0034$=94.595616 gal.

REVIEW OF MENSURATION.

Page 413.

1. 10$\frac{1}{2}$÷42=$\frac{1}{4}$; hence the scale is $\frac{1}{4}$ inch to a mile.

2. $\frac{1}{2}$ the altitude=9 ft.; 34×9=306 sq. ft.

3. Base of the right-angled triangle=$\frac{1}{2}$ of 24, or 12; height=$\sqrt{324-144}$=13.41+ ft.

4. Half sum of sides=(25+35+40)÷2=50; 50−25=25; 50−35=15; 50−40=10; area=$\sqrt{25\times15\times10\times50}$=433.01+ sq. ft.; cost=$5×433.01=$2165.05.

5. Surface of block=6×12=72 sq. in.=$\frac{1}{18}$ sq. yd.; area of street=500×15=7500 sq. yd.; No. of blocks=7500÷$\frac{1}{18}$=135000.

6. Surface of brick=8×4=32 sq. in.=$\frac{2}{9}$ sq. ft.; surface of pavement=7×18×48=518 sq. ft.; No. of bricks=518÷$\frac{2}{9}$=2331 bricks.

7. Area of plot=135×95=12825; surface of sod=15×24=360 sq. in.=2$\frac{1}{2}$ sq. ft.; 12825÷2$\frac{1}{2}$=5130; cost=$1.50×51.30=$76.95.

8. Space occupied by one picket and distance between two pickets=4+3=7 inches; 20 rods=3960 inches; No. of pickets in side of garden=3960÷7=565 and 5 inches remaining; but as we have allowed for a space outside one of the pickets, we have room for another picket; hence, in the length there are 566 pickets, or 1132 in the two sides; 15 rods=2970 inches; No. of pickets in end of garden=2970÷7=424 and 2 inches remaining; 424×2=848 in two ends; 1132+848=1980; cost =$9×1.980=$17.82.

9. The length of rail is the sum of the hypothenuses of the triangles formed by the rail and the steps. Length=$\sqrt{7^2+9\frac{1}{3}^2}\times18$=210 in.=17$\frac{1}{2}$ ft.

10. Surface of stairs on floor $=15\frac{1}{2}\times 8\frac{1}{4}=127\frac{7}{8}$ sq. ft.; whole surface of floor $=(58\times 34-127\frac{7}{8})\times 3=5532\frac{3}{8}$ sq. ft.; cost $=\$33.25\times 5.532\frac{3}{8}=$ $\$183.95+$.

11. Altitude of rhombus $=\sqrt{225-81}=12$; area of tile $=12\times 15=$ 180 sq. in.; $180\times 1000=180000$ sq. in. $=1250$ sq. ft.; cost $=\$.75\times 1250=\$937.50$.

12. Length of rafter $=\sqrt{24^2+10^2}+\frac{1}{2}=26\frac{1}{2}$ ft.; surface to be slated $=$ $26\frac{1}{2}\times 60\times 2=3180$ sq. ft.; cost $=\$14.75\times 31.80=\$469.05$.

13. Area of yard $=1296$ sq. ft.; area of basin $=113.0976$ sq. ft.; length of flower bed $=36\times 3-4\times 2=100$ ft.; area of bed $=100\times 4=400$ sq. ft.; $113.0976+400=513.0976$; area to be paved $=1296-513.0976=782.9024$ sq. ft. $=86.9891\frac{5}{9}$ sq. yd.; cost $=\$2.25\times 86.9891\frac{5}{9}=\$195.7256$.

14. Surface of globe $=4\times 4\times 3.1416=50.2656$ sq. ft. $=7238.2464$ sq. in.; pressure $=15\times 7238.2464=108573.696$.

15. The rope is the hypothenuse and the post the perpendicular of a right-angled triangle of which the base is the distance of the horse's mouth from the post; base $=\sqrt{100-36}=8$; area of circle grazed $=$ $3.1416\times 64=201.0624$ sq. ft.

16. Area of outer circle $=55^2\times 3.1416$; area of inner circle $=(44\frac{1}{2})^2\times 3.1416$; area of course $=(55^2-(44\frac{1}{2})^2)\times 3.1416=3282.1866$; cost $=$ $\$.10\times 3282.1866=\$328.21866$.

17. Area of square floor $=27\frac{1}{2}\times 16\frac{1}{4}=446.575$ sq. ft.; area of bow $=11^2\times 3.1416\div 2=190.0668$ sq. ft.; whole area $=446.875+190.0668=$ 636.9418 sq. ft.

18. Area of ellipse $=10\times 7\frac{1}{2}\times 3.1416=235.62$ sq. ft.; contents $=235.62\times 4=942.48$ cu. ft.; No. hhd. $=942.48\times 1728\div(231\times 63)=111.90\frac{6}{7}$ hhd.

19. Area of plot $=625\times 3.1416$; area of circle bounded by outer edge of walk $=576\times 3.1416$; area of plot outside of walk $=(625-576)\times 3.1416$; area of plot inside of walk $=529\times 3.1416$; whole area to be sodded $=(625-576+529)\times 3.1416=1815.8448$ sq. yd.; cost $=\$0.12\times 1815.8448=\$217.901376$.

20. Circ. of base $=30\times 3.1416=94.248$ sq. ft.; convex surface $=94.248\times 45=4241.16$ sq. ft. $=471.24$ sq. yd.; cost $=\$.25\times 471.24=\$117.81$.

21. Surface of frustum $=(10+1)\times 2=22$ sq. in.; $1\times 5=5$ sq. in.; $22+5=27$ sq. in.

22. The bin is the frustum of a pyramid; slant height $=\sqrt{\frac{25}{4}+\frac{1}{4}}=$ $2.5495+$; surface $=(2\frac{1}{2}+3\frac{1}{2})\times 4\times 2.5495\div 2=30.594$ sq. ft.; surface of bottom $=2\frac{1}{2}\times 2\frac{1}{2}=6\frac{1}{4}$ sq. ft.; surface to be lined $=30.594+6\frac{1}{4}=36.844$ sq. ft.; cost $=\$.20\times 36.844=\$7.3688$; contents of bin $=(\frac{25}{4}+\frac{49}{4}+\frac{35}{4})\times\frac{5}{2}\div 3$ $=\frac{545}{24}$ cu. ft. $=39240$ cu. in.; $39240\div 2150.42=18.24$ bu.

23. Contents of frustum of cone=(81+16+36)×(3.1416÷144)×40 ÷3=38.688$\frac{2}{9}$ cu. ft.

24. Surface=12^2×3.1416=452.3904 sq. in.; contents of sphere=12^3 ×$\frac{1}{6}$×3.1416; contents of inner sphere=10^3×$\frac{1}{6}$×3.1416; contents of solid part=(12^3—10^3)×$\frac{1}{6}$×3.1416=381.1808 cu. in.

25. Contents of water=24$\frac{1}{2}$×13$\frac{1}{3}$×$\frac{1}{4}$=81$\frac{2}{3}$ cu. ft.; weight of water= 1000 oz.×81$\frac{2}{3}$=81666$\frac{2}{3}$ oz.=5104$\frac{1}{6}$ lb.

26. Surface of wall=25×3.1416×14=1099.56 sq. ft.; surface of dome =25^2×3.1416÷2=981.75 sq. ft.; whole surface to be plastered=1099.56 +981.75=2081.31; cost=$.25×2081.31=$520.32$\frac{3}{4}$.

27. Contents of large box=18×12×8=1728 cu. in.; contents of small box=2×2×2=8; No. of small boxes=1728÷8=216=18 doz.

28. 100 sq. ft.=14400 sq. in.; hence thickness=1÷14400=.000069+ in.

29. Contents of ice-house=40×30×20=24000 cu. ft.; No. sq. ft.= 24000÷$\frac{1}{2}$=48000 sq. ft.; weight=56×24000=1344000 lb.

30. 25 miles=44000 yd.; contents of canal=44000×9×$\frac{11}{6}$=726000 cu. yd.; amount done in 1 day=12×500=6000 cu. yd.; No. days= 726000÷6000=121.

31. Amount paid men=$1.50×500×121=$90750; 5% of $90750= $4537.50; proposal=$90750+$4537.50=$95287.50.

32. Cubic feet in room=60×40×12=28800; No. persons=28800÷ 50=576.

33. No. cubic inches=$4116÷$12=343; edge of cube=$\sqrt[3]{343}$=7; surface of cube=49×6=294 sq. in.; cost=$.02×294=$5.88.

34. Area of end of roller=$(11\frac{1}{4})^2$×3.1416; area of end of hollow part=$(10\frac{1}{2})^2$×3.1416; area of solid part of end=$((11\frac{1}{4})^2-(10\frac{1}{2})^2)$× 3.1416=$\frac{261}{16}$×3.1416; contents of solid part of roller=$\frac{261}{16}$×3.1416×40 =2049.894 cu. in.; weight=4$\frac{1}{2}$×2049.894=9224.523 oz.=576.532$\frac{11}{16}$ lb.

35. Contents of ball=216×$\frac{1}{6}$ of 3.1416=36×3.1416; area of base of cone=9×3.1416; altitude of cone=(36×3.1416÷9×3.1416)×3= 12 in.

36. Area of section, which is a trapezoid=(8+12)×4÷2=40 sq. yd. 5 miles=8800 yd.; contents of embankment=8800×40=352000 cu. yd.; cost=$.15×352000=$52800.